D0832727

Dilemmas of Growth

Dilemmas of Growth
The Indian Experience

M.L. DANTWALA

Edited and with an Introduction by
PRAVIN VISARIA
N.A. MUJUMDAR
T.R. SUNDARAM

Sage Publications
New Delhi/Thousand Oaks/London

First published in 1996 by

Sage Publications India Pvt Ltd
M-32, Greater Kailash Market I
New Delhi 110 048

Sage Publications Inc	**Sage Publications Ltd**
2455 Teller Road	6 Bonhill Street
Thousand Oaks, California 91320	London EC2A 4PU

Published by Tejeshwar Singh for Sage Publications India Pvt Ltd, typeset by Par Graphics, New Delhi, and printed at Chaman Enterprises, Delhi.

Library of Congress Cataloging-in-Publication Data available

Dantwala, M.L. (Mohanlal Lalloobhai), 1909–
    Dilemmas of growth: the Indian experience / M.L. Dantwala; edited and with an introduction by Pravin Visaria, N.A. Mujumdar, T.R. Sundaram.
        p.   cm.
    Includes bibliographical references and index.
        1. India—Economic policy—1947– 2. India—Economic conditions—1947– I. Visaria, Pravin M. II. Mujumdar, N.A. III. Sundaram, T.R., 1928– IV. Title.
    HC435.2.D295   338.954—dc20   1996   95—46608

ISBN: 0–8039–9266–1 (US-hb)   81–7036–499–X (India-hb)
         0–8039–9267–X (US-pb)   81–7036–500–7 (India-pb)

Sage Production Editors: Pooja Advani and Omita Goyal

Contents

I. VALUES IN ECONOMIC THOUGHT

II. AGRICULTURAL DEVELOPMENT AND POLICY

III. PLANNING FOR RURAL DEVELOPMENT

List of tables

Preface

Professor M.L. Dantwala, the doyen of Indian agricultural economics, completed 85 years of age on 18 September 1994. During an illustrious academic career spanning more than three decades at the University of Bombay, Professor Dantwala has contributed to the training and development of more than 3,000 students of agricultural economics reading for their M.A. degree. Another 26 students were privileged to work under his guidance for their Ph.D. degree. His impact on the development of the profession of agricultural economists in India has been much more extensive because of his able stewardship of the 'Society' (Indian Society of Agricultural Economics) for a long period. Frequent calls from the central and state governments and from numerous non-governmental organizations for expert advice and guidance on varied issues have led to the recognition of Professor Dantwala as a highly respected policy-maker.

Professor Dantwala embodies in himself a deep concern for equity, elimination of exploitation and poverty, and development of a humane society, combined with an innate understanding of the complex reality, unusual perceptiveness, exemplary tolerance of human weaknesses, and broad perspective. Numerous students and academics working in different parts of the country seek his comments, advice and guidance in resolving diverse difficult problems; and they always elicit a most considerate and prompt, often handwritten response from Professor Dantwala.

The editors of this volume have enjoyed the privilege of working closely with Professor Dantwala for many years. For the selection of papers to be included in this volume, we have received valuable help from five friends, Dr G. Parthasarathy, Dr V.M. Rao, Dr N. Rath, Dr Tara Shukla. and late Dr D.S.

Tyagi. These colleagues have also provided some notes highlighting the specific key contributions of Professor Dantwala on the themes assigned to them.

We have subsequently discussed various aspects of the collection with Professor Dantwala himself and have benefited from his own assessment of the content and the context of different papers. Our grateful thanks are due to the friends named above and to our distinguished mentor, Professor Dantwala himself.

The process of working on this selection and on various drafts of the Introduction to this volume has enriched our perspective on the problems of development of our continental country. We feel confident that the readers of this volume will find our effort useful.

Ms Kalpana Mehta, librarian at the Gujarat Institute of Development Research (GIDR), has been generous with her time and has helped us in locating the details for several articles listed in the Bibliography. Dr Vijaylaxmi Chari, Ms Arti Dave and Ms Sujata Visaria have helped in proof-reading and checking the text and the Bibliography after they were word-processed by Girija Balakrishnan, Sheela Devadas, and Vasanthi V.A. at the GIDR, Ahmedabad.

PRAVIN VISARIA   N.A. MUJUMDAR   T.R. SUNDARAM

Acknowledgements

Thanks are due to the Indian Council of Social Science Research (ICSSR), New Delhi for a generous financial grant for the publication of this volume.

Our grateful thanks are due to the following publishers for permission to reprint the papers of Professor Dantwala first published by them.

1. Centre of Applied Politics, New Delhi, for the paper entitled 'Ethics and Economics of Socialism'.
2. Cooperative Perspective, for the paper entitled 'Innovative Approaches to the Revival of Village Industries'.
3. *Economic and Political Weekly* for the papers listed below.
   a. 'Rural Development: Investment Without Organization'
   b. 'Prices and Cropping Pattern'
   c. 'Rural Employment: Facts and Issues'
   d. 'Some Neglected Issues in Employment Planning'.
4. Indian Association of Social Science Institutions, New Delhi, for the paper entitled 'Trusteeship: An Alternative Ideology'.
5. *Indian Economic Journal* for the paper entitled 'From Stagnation to Growth: Relative Roles of Technology, Economic Policy and Agrarian Institutions'.
6. Indian Institute of Management, Ahmedabad, for the paper entitled 'Reconciling Growth and Social Justice: Agrarian Structure and Poverty'.
7. *Indian Journal of Agricultural Economics*, Bombay for the papers listed below.
   a. 'Agricultural Policy in India Since Independence'
   b. 'Growth and Equity in Agriculture'
   c. 'The Two-Way Planning Process: Scope and Limitations'

    d. 'Incentives and Disincentives in Indian Agriculture'
    e. 'Agricultural Policy: Prices and the Public Distribution System—A Review'
    f. 'Credit and Its Role in Poverty Alleviation'
    g. 'Notes on Some Aspects of Rural Employment'
8. Indian Society of Agricultural Statistics, New Delhi, for the paper entitled 'Principles and Problems of Agricultural Price Determination'.
9. Oxford University Press, New Delhi, for the paper entitled 'Technology, Growth and Equity in Agriculture'.
10. *Pacific Affairs*, for the paper entitled 'Agricultural Credit in India: The Missing Link'.
11. *The Economic Times*, Bombay, for the papers listed below:
    a. 'Agricultural Price Policy—Facts and Issues'
    b. 'Rural Credit: Restructuring the Credit System and Suggested Reforms'.

Introduction

The process of economic growth all over the world has almost always been accompanied by tensions and conflict of interests because of its unsettling effect on established institutions or hierarchies and traditional values. While the enterprising welcome the hope for a better future, others lament the turmoil and the loss of the tranquillity of the old order and even question the legitimacy of change.

The developed countries of the West have coped with the strains of development and growth with their access to the resources of colonies. Some developing countries have resorted to authoritarian rule to contain and/or overcome domestic dissent and disaffection. India has chosen an unusually difficult path for its development with a democratic form of government and a very large population, which has grown at a faster rate than in the developed countries at a comparable stage of development. The limited scope for international migration or the export of labour, the dispersal of nearly three-fourths of the population over nearly 600,000 villages with a poor infrastructure, and the acute scarcity of cultivable land have accentuated India's dilemmas of growth during the five decades of the post-Independence period.

The 22 papers included in this volume inform the readers about the perceptions and reactions of one of India's most eminent economists, Professor M.L. Dantwala, to the problems of growth and development as they have manifested during the past 50 years. The papers presented here have been selected from a total of more than 300 articles authored by Dantwala during his productive academic life. (A Select Bibliography at the end of this book lists 13 books/monographs/lectures and nearly 200 papers.) The volume offers some glimpses of the thoughts and views and the underlying values of a senior scholar, who was actively involved in India's fight for freedom and in the formulation of economic policy throughout the past five decades.

A brief biographical sketch of Dantwala will help the reader to gain a perspective on the evolution of his outlook on various issues. Dantwala was born in Surat on 18 September 1909, in a family that had traditionally dealt in ivory or *haathi-dant*. He received his school education up to Matriculation in Dhulia, where his father was manager of a cotton ginning factory. He earned his B.A. degree in 1928 from the University of Bombay, whose jurisdiction then extended from Sind in the west to Karnataka in the south. He attained the first rank among the students of History and Economics and was awarded the prestigious James Taylor Prize. His studies for the M.A. degree at the Bombay School of Economics and Sociology were interrupted by his participation in the freedom movement. The last chapter of his thesis was written in the Arthur Road prison in Bombay, while he was an under-trial. He was sentenced to rigorous imprisonment for 2 years and 6 months but was given B class in the Nasik Road central jail, where he came into close contact with senior-most leaders of the Indian National Congress and also the young socialist intellectuals. A voracious reader, he read extensively of the socialist literature and was deeply impressed by the egalitarian ideology of Marx. His participation in the freedom movement had been inspired by Gandhiji, but he became a founder member of the Congress Socialist Party and continued his close links with Jayaprakash Narayan (J.P.) throughout the latter's lifetime.

After his release from prison, Dantwala participated in some trade union activity around Dhulia; but in 1936, Professor C.N. Vakil persuaded him to join the H.L. College of Commerce in Ahmedabad. In 1940, when Gandhiji gave a call for individual civil disobedience, Dantwala responded and resigned from the college. After his second innings in jail, he did not rejoin the college and worked as the Honorary Organizing Secretary of the Gujarat Provincial Congress Committee. His attendance at the AICC session in Bombay in August 1942, when the Quit India movement was launched, led to his arrest and detention again in Nasik Road prison for another spell of 20 months.

After his release from prison, he joined the H.L. College of Commerce again in 1944 for a brief period. But he bid farewell to politics, when he was appointed Lecturer in Agricultural Economics at the University of Bombay. Dantwala rose to be the Director of the Department of Economics of the University of Bombay and retired from the post of Professor of Agricultural Economics in 1973 after nearly three decades of illustrious service.

Throughout his academic career and also after his retirement, Dantwala has frequently been called upon to work on several committees/commissions/working groups and panels of the Planning Commission and the Governments of India and the states. These included membership of the Second Pay Commission (1957–59) and the Chairmanship of the Agricultural Prices Commission when it was first set up (1965–66). Despite his close association with the Government, he has retained his uncompromising loyalty to basic values and had resigned from the Central Board of Directors of the Reserve Bank of India when emergency was declared in June 1975.

The 22 papers in this volume are grouped into six sections. They deal with the themes of (*a*) values in economic growth; (*b*) agricultural development and policy; (*c*) planning for rural development; (*d*) agricultural price policy; (*e*) rural credit; and (*f*) agricultural labour and employment. The selected papers demonstrate Dantwala's intuitive feel for the complexities of Indian economic reality ever since the beginning of his academic career. While each paper has a historical context, the thrust and approach retain their relevance as much now as when they were written. Overall, the volume presents a cohesive picture of Dantwala's views on the six themes.

I. VALUES IN ECONOMIC THOUGHT

The first essay on 'Trusteeship: An Alternative Ideology' is of historical importance. It elucidates Gandhiji's views on ownership and management of wealth. The 'Trusteeship Formula' contains, in a succinct and condensed form, the basic ingredients of Gandhiji's views on property. This formula was originally prepared by some of Gandhiji's disciples in Yerwada prison. Dantwala revised this formula and submitted it to Gandhiji. He met Gandhiji at Birla House in Bombay. Gandhiji made a few alterations in the draft and approved it. The formula is now accepted as the authentic version of Gandhiji's concept of Trusteeship. A photostat copy of Dantwala's (handwritten) draft and alterations made by Gandhiji (in his handwriting) is available. The paper bears testimony to Dantwala's interaction with the Mahatma on the seminal issue of property, its ownership and use. Trusteeship may appear as a Utopian dream, but Dantwala views it as an ideal blending of the capitalist and socialist views on property, retaining the creativity of individual enterprise and social sharing of the output. The paper also includes Dantwala's strong rebuttal of the charge that Gandhiji was either unaware of or chose to ignore the exploitation involved in the accumulation of wealth.

The short essay 'Ethics and Economics of Socialism' (1978) was written many years before it was published in the volume commemorating the birth centenary of the veteran socialist, Acharya Narendra Dev. It was first presented at a meeting of the Socialist Forum in New Delhi in the presence of Prime Minister Jawaharlal Nehru. As Dantwala once recalled, Panditji had talked to him after the meeting and conveyed his agreement with Dantwala's views. The paper expounds the view that the establishment of a socialist society cannot become a reality until a majority of the people, particularly the elite, accept the ethical basis of a socialist society. Merely building an economy modelled on the socialist doctrine—public ownership of productive assets— is no guarantee that it will usher in 'an enduring egalitarian society'. While the expressions like 'socialist ethics' or 'value system' are difficult to define, Dantwala considers (*a*) restraint of acquisitiveness, (*b*) limitation of wants, and (*c*) desire to share the gains from development as their basic components.

The third piece outlines Dantwala's approach to eradicating poverty from India. It is extracted from two lectures on 'Poverty in India: Then and Now: 1870–1970' delivered by him in 1971 on the occasion of the award of the Dadabhai Naoroji Memorial Fellowship Prize for 1969. Dantwala reminds the younger generation that more than 120 years ago, Dadabhai Naoroji had attributed India's poverty to 'UN-British Rule'. However, the persistence of poverty even after 45 years of Independence exposes the weakness of India's development strategy. Presenting his assessment of the appropriate agencies for bringing about a 'basic transformation of the social and economic structure', Dantwala suggests a revival and reorientation of non-partisan constructive work through voluntary agencies with the necessary financial, administrative and technical support from the Government, but which does not impair the autonomy of voluntary agencies. He remains sceptical about the extent to which employment on public works or other direct interventions by the Government will by themselves ameliorate poverty. The lectures also reiterate the view that the people's habits of thought or values, which the Marxists consider as superstructure, should be considered as basic to any radical social change. An emphasis on reorientation of values as a precursor to the establishment of an egalitarian society is a distinguishing feature of Dantwala's approach to socio-economic change.

II. AGRICULTURAL DEVELOPMENT AND POLICY

The five papers in this section mainly address two themes: (*a*) the relative contributions of economic policy, technology and agrarian institutions to agricultural development; and (*b*) the issues of reconciling growth with social justice.

The paper on 'From Stagnation to Growth' was Dantwala's Presidential Address at the Annual Conference of the Indian Economic Association in 1970. The address was prepared at a time when some polemicists such as William Paddock had predicted 'pockets of famine throughout the world' in 1980. His book *Famine 1975* projected India as a basket case and expressed doubts whether it would merit assistance according to the triage formula. Dantwala marshalled convincing evidence to demonstrate the phenomenon of 'Green Revolution' in India but also conceded that it was a product of technological innovations such as the development of high-yielding varieties of seeds rather than economic policy. The paper illustrates Dantwala's fairness in giving credit where it is due as well as an exemplary humility about the role of economists in the process of economic growth.

There has been a recurrent allegation over the past three decades that Indian planning has suffered from an urban bias and that agriculture has been neglected since the beginning of the Second Plan. In a paper prepared for the International Conference of Agricultural Economists at Nairobi, Dantwala demonstrated that the allegations were based on a misinterpretation of the reduction in the share of agriculture in the planned outlay and a rise in the share of industry. A proper assessment of the issue requires an estimate of the investment for agriculture and not only of investment in agriculture. Dantwala's balanced views on these issues differ sharply from those of economists who exaggerate and stress only the negative aspects or implications of India's growth and achievements.

The same balanced perspective is maintained in an examination of the implications of the growth of Indian agriculture for equity. Dantwala highlights the fact that the benefits of increased food production in areas with assured water supply also percolate to the entire country because it restrains the rise in prices (which hurts the poor). The decline in the country's dependence on imports of foodgrains is also an important national gain.

The same issues are examined in greater detail in a paper relating to 'technology, growth and equity', where Dantwala scrutinized the evidence relating to a contention of Pranab Bardhan that the 'new strategy' might have counteracted forces such as high growth of output that tend to improve the income of small farmers and wage labourers. Dantwala agreed that the large farmers pre-empt the use of underground water and the rural rich succeed in pressing for higher administered prices of foodgrains. However, the empirical evidence, particularly for Punjab, does not confirm the allegations of (a) the labour-displacing effect of machinery, attributable to the new strategy; (b) eviction of tenants; (c) an adverse effect of increasing dependence on purchased inputs leading small farmers with limited access to resources and credit to give up cultivation; (d) poor maintenance of old irrigation channels being attributable to the upsurge in tubewell irrigation; and (e) the decline in female participation in agricultural workforce as a result of the new strategy. The paper illustrates Dantwala's patient search for all the relevant evidence before accepting some hypotheses and excluding others.

Of course, Dantwala recognized that growth induced by technological change tends to widen inequalities. Therefore, he welcomed the special programmes to alleviate poverty and promote employment (such as the IRDP, NREP, etc.). However, these programmes have had only a limited effect because they were not really integrated with the main development plan. Dantwala's views on these issues differ sharply from the approach of those who attribute the limited success of these programmes to India's failure to alter the iniquitous socio-economic structure. While he would not be against such an alteration, Dantwala has pointed out that waiting for a revolution to alter the structure could prove a trap. The direct intervention programmes should not be condemned as reformist palliatives, for, if the special programmes improve the income and the resource base of the poor, they thereby affect and alter the socio-economic structure.

III. PLANNING FOR RURAL DEVELOPMENT

Dantwala's interest in economics in general and in agricultural economics in particular has largely stemmed from his concern for rural development and for improving the living conditions of the poor. The three articles in this section highlight the distinctiveness of his approach to these issues.

Dantwala, who had chaired the Working Group on Block Level Planning, set up by the Planning Commission in 1977, has for long been a votary of decentralized planning. His papers on the subject sound a strong caveat that we need to evolve effective linkage between planning from the top and planning from below to make decentralized planning a success. He sees it as a means to discover or awaken dormant resources and of identifying the obstacles to growth and its equitable spread in specific areas. Of course, Dantwala has no illusions about the difficulties in the realization of the widely-held high hopes from decentralized planning. He recognizes that in an unequal society, the 'felt needs' of the people need not be the same. Also, the vested interests can be far more coercive in a small area than in a larger area; but Dantwala holds that these problems can be resolved only through a sincere effort at decentralization.

Much of the discussion on planning in India has focused on the quantum of public investment. Dantwala, on the other hand, has stressed the need to improve the organizational and administrative aspects of both development and welfare projects to improve the efficiency of investments. Investment in rural development without organization is the prime cause of ubiquitous cost escalation, paralleled by under-utilization, low returns and low cost recovery.

Dantwala is equally concerned about the viability of cottage and village industries and the diversification of the rural employment structure in India. From the extensive literature sent to him from different parts of the country, he has identified some success stories, which are an outcome of an affordable upgradation of technology, improved designs, better marketing of inputs and output, with the support of a catalyst organization led by an enlightened and dedicated person. These crafts and traditional skills are a national heritage, worthy of preservation, but they also provide employment to workers, mainly women, who would otherwise drop out of the labour force or be classified as unemployable.

IV. AGRICULTURAL PRICE POLICY

Dantwala, who was the first chairman of the Agricultural Prices Commission (APC), set up by the Government of India in 1965–66, has written extensively on various aspects of agricultural price policy. The important issues covered in these papers have been (a) the role of price policy in agricultural growth; (b) the scope and rationale of state intervention; and (c) determination of administered prices for different crops.

In the mid-sixties, Indian agriculture had struck a bad patch. Agricultural production was stagnant and the country had to depend on the import of large quantities of foodgrains, mostly as food aid under concessional terms. India's agricultural price policy was considered primarily responsible for the poor performance of Indian agriculture. After rejecting the convenient excuses— natural calamities and perversity of farmers—Professor T.W. Schultz identified the real culprit: 'policy preference for industrialization, agriculture's contribution to its attainment being cheap food as a source for cheap labour and public revenue'. Professor Edward Mason discerned in the agricultural development of the period declining incentives to farm output because while the prices of inputs rose, the prices of foodgrains and some other farm outputs were held down by Government action.

These critics provoked Dantwala to write the paper 'Incentives and Disincentives in Indian Agriculture' (1967). Dantwala demonstrated that at no time, by any token, were foodgrains prices low, much less kept low by government policy. Dantwala noted that 'round about 1956–67, in terms of the new price index series, there was a severe fall in agricultural prices' and the foodgrains prices had suffered the most. But the balance between prices of agricultural and non-agricultural commodities was soon restored. Further, all the five-year plans had aimed to ensure reasonable prices for farmers and that was why the APC was set up in January 1965.

In a recent paper on 'Agricultural Policy: Prices and Public Distribution System' (1993), Dantwala has reverted to the question, whether the incentives structure for agricultural commodities is proper or not. He does not accept the view of the World Bank and many good economists that the appropriateness of domestic prices of agricultural commodities should be judged exclusively by the Nominal Protection Coefficient (NPC), i.e., the ratio of domestic prices to import/export parity prices. He contends that while international prices cannot and should not be ignored in the context of the liberal trade regime, domestic price policy has to take into consideration 'agro-climatic potential of different regions [for agricultural growth], the technological horizon for growth of different crops, and domestic demand and supply in the context of balance of payments constraints'.

Earlier in 1985–86, the Government of India was concerned about the imbalance in the cropping pattern and wanted to adopt a long-term price policy that would help to raise the output of certain crops. Dantwala pointed out the limited role of a policy of influencing the relative price of one crop because the production of substitutable crop would thereby be affected adversely. A minimum support price for certain commodities can help prevent an unintended change in the crop pattern by safeguarding against the fear of an excessive decline in price. Likewise, a public distribution network can be used to protect the interests of the poor consumers provided that adequate buffer stocks or the foreign exchange to import the requisite supplies are available. Higher prices cannot solve the problems of small and marginal farmers, landless agricultural labourers and the other rural poor, who tend to be net purchasers of food. The best course for the Government is to encourage research to evolve improved technology to lower costs and/or raise yields and to strengthen the infrastructure such as irrigation, power, roads and extension services.

During his tenure as the Chairman of the APC and earlier, Dantwala has often affirmed the need and scope for resolute state action to ensure that in a situation of shortage of an essential commodity such as the foodgrains, the public distribution system fulfils the social and economic objectives of public policy. He had also supported zonal restrictions on the inter-state movement of foodgrains as essential for a rational and equitable distribution of commodities in short supply. He had shown some impatience with concepts of equilibrium prices and a balanced-cum-integrated price structure, which did not conform to his intimate knowledge and experience of the functioning of the commodity markets. The ground realities required the exercise of informed judgement in deciding the level of support and procurement prices, but such judgement was not affected by political pressures that have unfortunately been exerted in recent years to modify the concepts and methodology of cost estimates. The public distribution system and the open market operations of the Food Corporation of India are essential to protect the interests of the poor consumers as well as of the farmers.

V. RURAL CREDIT

Dantwala's interest in the subject of rural credit has its roots in his study of the financing of production and trade in cotton for his M.A. thesis. It has been sharpened by association with the Board of Directors of the Bank of India, the State Bank of India and the Reserve Bank of India. Dantwala has also served as the Chairman of the Committee appointed by the Reserve Bank during 1977–78 to review the working of the Regional Rural Banks. His views on various questions relating to rural credit merit serious consideration, particularly because of the sea-change in the Indian policy about the extent to which commercial banks can contribute to the improvement in the availability of credit to agriculture and the rural non-farm sector.

Dantwala has always stressed the fact that credit alone cannot make a farmer viable. Yet, lack of timely and adequate institutional credit can thwart the best developmental projects and programmes and tends to perpetuate and even widen inequalities. Credit or financial assistance was essential also for the success of the *zamindari* abolition so that the tenants could buy the land. However, he has always made a distinction between the credit required to rehabilitate the small and marginal farmers and the credit needed for production. He does not find the rural credit agencies to be equipped for the former task. The regional rural banks have become non-viable because their mandate required them to take up non-viable business. Dantwala did not, therefore, see any merit in the recommendation of the Agricultural Credit Review Committee, appointed by the Reserve Bank of India, to merge the RRBs with the commercial banks that had sponsored them.

Dantwala candidly asserts that liberal institutional credit will help but will not make intrinsically non-viable subsistence agriculture viable. The latter task is an integral part of the problem of overall economic development. To enable the poor to gain access to credit, their assets and skills and thereby the income-earning capacity will have to be strengthened and enhanced. The credit institutions seeking to serve the rural economy will have to maintain a low profile, low costs and easy accessibility. Given the current pressures in the organized sector of the Indian economy for a uniform and high salary structure for the public sector that would be almost on par with that in the private sector, the perceptive diagnoses of Dantwala merit careful consideration.

VI. AGRICULTURAL LABOUR AND EMPLOYMENT

Dantwala's contributions to the understanding of India's problems of unemployment, particularly rural unemployment, are likely to be regarded as among the most important. The Report of the Committee of Experts on Unemployment Estimates, which he chaired, has vitally influenced both the Indian and the international thinking on the subject. In its essence, the new approach recognizes the differences between the self-employed and the employees with respect to the level and structure of employment and unemployment and their constraints and preferences about their availability for work or for additional work.

The implicit heterogeneity of labour supply was first highlighted by Dantwala in a paper written in 1953. In recent years, he has stressed the need to understand the anatomy of unemployment, as well as of employment (and poverty) as essential for devising appropriate effective policy action. The latter issue has been discussed in the context of relative merits of public works programmes for casual wage labour and a programme to strengthen the assets and skills of the weaker sections. Dantwala has been keen to safeguard the dignity and the independence of the poor as they avail of the opportunities for supplementing their modest incomes. He is also concerned about the generally weak effort to integrate the special employment programmes with the long-term development needs of the rural infrastructure, such that they raise the productivity of the agricultural sector and improve the viability of the small and marginal farmers. He recognizes that the growth of non-agricultural employment will play a critical role in improving the living standard of the disadvantaged groups in rural areas.

Overall, if employment is to alleviate poverty on an enduring basis, it has to be tailored to the characteristics of those who need it the most. Also, employment generation would have an enduring effect, if, in the process, the assets and skills of those who get employment are enhanced. If policy measures do not pay adequate attention to this issue, it is not unlikely that growth in employment may accentuate inequality. The post-'Third Wave' economy is rooted in information, communication and computerization-based high-tech. The few who have the technical and managerial skills to exploit it will take a large portion of the incremental income, while a large section of the Indian workforce consisting of the poor and the illiterate will continue to toil on a low daily wage. The employment generated by the new technology, which, Dantwala feels, cannot be rejected outright, may percolate to one or two deciles of the workforce below the new rich, but those at the lower level will be left out. This is a new challenge for evolving an appropriate employment policy.

The papers included in this volume are stimulating and provocative even for those who might disagree with the views expressed in them. They have been authored by a sensitive observer of the Indian economy and society, with an unusual intuitive understanding of the complex reality of our continental country. The dilemmas of growth faced by India over nearly

50 years of unprecedented change and development continue to persist. Professor Dantwala has analyzed these problems with a certain clearly egalitarian value orientation. The dilemmas are in fact likely to become sharper in the years ahead in the wake of ongoing policy changes. This volume should, therefore, prove stimulating for the younger generation of economists and social scientists.

I

VALUES IN ECONOMIC THOUGHT

CHAPTER 1

Trusteeship: An alternative ideology[1]

Since Vedic times, thoughts on the acquisition of wealth and its use are reflected in the contemplations of scholars and saints. A verse in *Isavasya Upanishad* says: 'All that there is in this world is pervaded by God' or is 'God's abode' and adds '*Tena tyaktena bhunjeethaha, ma gridhha Kasyaswiddhanam*': enjoy by renouncing, do not covet wealth of any one. (According to a variant of the aphorism, a comma is inserted after the word 'covet'; and the question is asked: 'whose indeed is this wealth'.) An irrepressible desire to acquire wealth and power is at the root of all individual, social, economic, and political conflicts.

Proudhon considered all property as theft. Marx favoured collective ownership of all instruments of production as a remedy for the inequity of the capitalist system. Gandhiji, however, believed that restructuring of institutions would be of no avail unless men who operate these institutions accept, of their own volition, the implicit ethics of the new system.

Gandhiji's views on wealth are condensed in what has come to be known as the Trusteeship Formula. The genesis of the formula has an element of a story in it. The larger question of the value system implicit in the Trusteeship principle is dealt with later.

The Trusteeship Formula has not received serious attention from social scientists. Not many have read it in full and with care. The intellectuals did not take Gandhiji's philosophy seriously. He was recognized as the supreme political leader of the freedom movement, for no better reason than the fact that millions— men and women, old and young, the illiterate and some highly

educated—responded to his call for civil disobedience and gladly
courted imprisonment, faced *lathis* and bullets. But this did not
qualify him as a person whose philosophical thoughts merited
attention. In fact, the views expressed by him on most issues
such as industrialization, celibacy, naturopathy and even non-
violence, appeared impracticable, if not utopian or antediluvian.
His *charkha*, the goat and the loin-cloth evoked amusement among
the tolerant and ridicule among the highbrow. As a matter of
fact, such eccentricities disqualified him for recognition by intellectuals
as a serious thinker.

A close scrutiny of the Trusteeship Formula would dispel
such negative assessment. Here, Gandhiji is clear and categorical.
His views on ownership and use of wealth are not only novel
but radically different from those in vogue among the advocates
of capitalism and communism. Gandhiji does not accept the system
of either private or the public (state) ownership of wealth/capital.
The idea of holding wealth as a trust may be visionary or
even utopian. But a thought does not become irrelevant because
of an element of a distant vision in it. Some thoughts which
embody a vision transcend the immediate and are like a beacon
which lights the path leading to the cherished ideal. Truth in
personal life and non-violence in the affairs of nations do not
become irrelevant because they are almost impossible to practise.
Marx does not become irrelevant because he held a vision of
the 'withering away of the state'. The doctrine 'from each according
to his ability, to each according to his need', reflects an idealism
no less than the one implicit in trusteeship. Had Gandhiji been
simply a visionary, he could not have launched doughty campaigns
like Champaran, Bardoli, Dharasana and Quit India in a placid
and dormant India.

The total philosophy of trusteeship cannot be compressed
into a simple 6-Clause formula. But the formula does extract
its quintessence. Our attempt is to record faithfully the Trusteeship
Formula and to narrate the story of its genesis. It helps to
elucidate Gandhiji's thinking on this subject by referring to his
acceptance or rejection of various suggestions made by this author
while placing before him a revised version of an earlier draft
on trusteeship.

Genesis

Doubts have been cast on the authenticity of the Trusteeship Formula because certain clauses in the formula seem to run counter to Gandhiji's views expressed on different occasions. It has also been suggested, somewhat hesitatingly, that Gandhiji gave his approval to the formula rather hastily and not with the degree of deliberation which an issue of such far-reaching consequences warranted.

We shall deal with the latter view first. I do so with a little hesitation because of my personal association with this matter. On the genesis of the Trusteeship Formula, Shri Pyarelal has recorded:

> On our release from prison, we took up the question [of Trusteeship] where we had left it in the Detention Camp. Two senior members of the Ashram, Kishorelal Mashruwala and Narhari Parikh, joined. Professor Dantwala from Bombay had sent a simple, practical Trusteeship Formula which he had prepared. It was placed before Gandhiji, who made a few changes in it (Pyarelal, 1958).

Pyarelal's recording needs a small amendment. I did not prepare a brand new formula of my own. I had with me a draft prepared by Kishorelalbhai and others. From Gandhiji's comments on my draft, it seems that Gandhiji was fully familiar with the earlier draft and had given careful thought to each clause. (Unfortunately, the original text is not available today.) On reading it, I felt that the phraseology at some places was vague and certain ambiguities needed to be removed. In other words, I wanted the formula to be more precise and operationally more effective. I took the original draft as the basis and made a few amendments, omitting certain portions, adding a few and altering certain phrases.

The draft which I placed before Gandhiji was handwritten. It indicated the changes I had made in the original draft. Gandhiji read every clause and sentence with great care, made several amendments and gave his final approval to my revised draft as amended by him.

The interesting part of this event was that I had sought an appointment with Gandhiji through Pyarelalji. The lovable but absent-minded secretary gave me the appointment on a Monday,

Gandhiji's *maunwar*—day of silence. I was completely nonplussed,
but Gandhiji received me with his usual smile. As it happened,
what appeared to be a misadventure turned out to be a blessing.
Gandhiji wrote his queries on slips of paper and I gave written
answers. After each clause was discussed, Gandhiji recorded his
rejection or acceptance of portions or phrases in my draft—
sometimes in Gujarati and sometimes in English—on the very
paper I had placed before him. In the same way, he substituted
or amended my wording and rewrote practically the whole of
Clause 6.

I mention these details not because they are of autobiographical
interest to me, but because in what follows I wish to acquaint
the reader with the changes I had made in the original draft
and my reasons for the changes. More importantly, I would like
the reader to see which changes Gandhiji accepted or rejected
and why? All this is not a matter of conjecture on my part,
thanks to the *maunwar*. The only sad part of the story is that
I made the mistake—as it turned out—of handing over the document
to another very dear (but no less forgetful than Pyarelal) friend,
Jayaprakash Narain (J.P.), for safe custody in an appropriate archive.
Fortunately, I did this after the full story of the Trusteeship
Formula was narrated by Jayaprakashji at the International Seminar
on Social Responsibility of Business held at the India International
Centre at Delhi during 15–21 March 1965. After a few months,
I received a letter from J.P. informing me with profound apology
that the document was lost in transit from Delhi to Patna, along
with other papers which his secretary was carrying with him.
But all was not lost. A photostat copy[2] of the document was
prepared for the International Seminar on Social Responsibility
of Business and is reproduced in the book with the same title,
containing the proceedings of the Conference (Manektalas, 1965).

The formula

Before we scrutinize the Trusteeship Formula by reference to
the (photostat) copy of the text in which Gandhiji had made
changes in his own handwriting, I should report a brief postscript.
According to Pyarelal,

After the Trusteeship formula was placed before, amended and approved by Gandhiji, it was decided to release it to the Press. But on second thought we felt that before publication it might be shown to G.D. Birla who was favourably inclined towards the doctrine of Trusteeship. A copy was therefore sent to him. He welcomed it, but pointed out that in order that the whole effort might not begin and end with the publication of the formula, he should first canvass some fellow capitalists so that the announcement should be made along with the publication of the draft. No further communication from him however followed. Perhaps he met with a discouraging response from those he had approached (Bhartan, 1979).

As would be evident from the text of the Trusteeship Formula, Gandhiji's views on the ownership and use of wealth constitute a radical departure from all the prevalent views, spanning the entire spectrum. No wonder Gandhiji's views on property have not gained acceptance by the established intellectuals or businessmen and industrialists. By and large, they have been ignored or dismissed as too idealistic and therefore of little practical use. But then, all seminal ideas or philosophies such as non-violence, democracy, communism, or, on a more mundane plane, proposals for disarmament and non-alignment have a core of idealism. Even so, few would dismiss them as irrelevant to our civilization. Each one of these ideas has been inspired by a deep understanding of the malaise which afflicts humanity and a vision of a better world.

Let us leave it at that and revert to the authenticity of some of the elements of the Trusteeship Formula on which doubts have been cast. For our present purpose, we shall examine only two elements: one where Gandhiji expressed his disapproval of the capitalist system and the second where he approved resort to legislation to *regulate* the Trusteeship system after it comes into operation.

Rejection of the capitalist order

Regarding the disapproval of the capitalist system, it has been contended that since Gandhiji did not disapprove of the *accumulation* of wealth by the rich, it is difficult to accept that he was opposed to the capitalist system. Some statements of Gandhiji are quoted from time to time to prove the point. For example, Gandhiji said: 'Earn your crores by all means', but hastened

to add, 'Understand that your wealth is not your own; it belongs
to the people' (Hingorani, 1970: 78). Elsewhere he pleaded that:
'They should be allowed to retain the stewardship of their possession
and *use their talents to* increase their wealth' (emphasis added);
'We must not under-rate the business talent and know-how which
the owning class has acquired through generations of experience
and specialization'; and 'Do not kill the goose that lays the
golden egg'.

Reconciliation of Gandhiji's permissive attitude to accumulation
of wealth with strict restriction on the appropriation of the gains
for personal use is a bit difficult. It is conceivable that Gandhiji
believed that if the end use of wealth is rigorously regulated
and if the rich cannot use their wealth for personal enjoyment
there would be little incentive for them to accumulate it, particularly
by unfair means.

Pyarelal also broached the issue during one of his (recorded)
discussions with Gandhiji. Pyarelal asked: 'Why can we not get
the owning class to renounce their vast possessions? You concede
[that] the vast possessions are today largely the result of exploitation.
Why [then] bring in Trusteeship?' Gandhiji's response was again
tangential. He replied:

> Perhaps you have the example of Russia in mind. Wholesale
> expropriation of the owning class, and the distribution of its assets
> among the people there, did create a tremendous amount of revolutionary
> fervour, but I claim ours will be an even bigger revolution (Pyarelal,
> 1958: 90–93).

On another occasion, however, Gandhiji was more categorical
on the issue of accumulation. He observed: 'Accumulation by
private persons was impossible except through violent means,
but accumulation by state in a non-violent society was not only
possible, it was desirable and inevitable' (*Harijan*, 16 February
1947, quoted by Sethi, 1978).

Gandhiji's seemingly permissive attitude towards accumulation
of wealth has further tempted some industrialists and businessmen
to project Gandhiji's ideas as supportive of the functioning of
free enterprise, which is the essence of the capitalist system.
Gandhiji stated: 'We do not want to produce a dead equality
where every person becomes or is rendered incapable of using
his ability to the utmost possible extent. Such a society must

ultimately perish.' Manohar Malgaonkar has skillfully exploited this statement to champion the cause of free enterprise. Malgaonkar said:

> What a hard nugget of Gandhian wisdom this is. *A social order in which every person must have scope to use his abilities to the utmost possible extent* [emphasis in the original]. *Can there be a more forceful argument in support of free enterprise* [emphasis added]—or to show that free enterprise and trusteeship can never be at cross purposes (cited in Sawhny, 1980).

Malgaonkar paid tribute to Gandhiji as a 'practical visionary' who 'is prepared to lower his sights to achievable targets', and concluded:

> So the basic tenets of trusteeship emerge: that it is voluntary, that, in order to make it successful, the *rich* must go on *earning more and more* (honestly of course), so that their fellow beings should go on benefitting more and more from *their largesse* [emphasis added].

What a travesty of Gandhian thought! The word 'largesse' stinks. That such a statement could be made, printed and published as proceedings of a Seminar on Trusteeship is ominous. It is an indicator of how the system may have degenerated.

Bhartan has rightly observed:

> Apart from the indifference of politicians, industrialists, labour and trade unions, the greatest threat to trusteeship has come from those who while accepting the concepts, tend to interpret it merely in broad philosophic terms, thus watering down the *concepts into total ineffectiveness* [emphasis added] (Bhartan, 1979).

Bhartan adds:

> Trusteeship should not be misunderstood or misinterpreted as mere do-goodism in Gandhian garb. It must not be watered down to imply merely moral attitudes, a vague undefined sense of purity in public life, the paternalistic benevolence of the haves. . . . More specifically, it should not be identified with social responsibility of business or enlightened capitalism.

A question may be asked: knowing as we do that there is no possibility in the foreseeable future of putting into practice trusteeship, as conceived by Gandhiji, should an attempt not be made to encourage its *partial* acceptance by the present owners of wealth? Will even such partial acceptance not have a civilizing influence on the acquisitive society and act as a check on the growing trend towards consumerism? As a 'practical visionary' Gandhiji himself often recommended a step-by-step approach towards many of his ideas.

It is difficult to answer these questions with a simple yes or no. All steps taken by the rich and the owning class of their own volition or under state compulsion to 'humanize' the capitalist system, to make it responsive to social obligations and to push it towards greater egalitarianism should be appreciated and welcomed. This should not however be done in the belief that progressive reform of the capitalist system will ultimately culminate into a Trusteeship system. On the contrary, by accepting enlightened capitalism—which, for example, accepts its 'social responsibility'—as a step towards trusteeship, we would be accepting implicitly the value system of capitalism represented by 'free enterprise' and sanctity of market economy. Did not Gandhiji accept this system when he stated 'earn your crores . . . etc.'? I would categorically say no, Gandhiji did not accept the right to private property. The moment you earn your crores, they cease to be yours. You are only their trustee with all the bindings mentioned in the Trusteeship Formula.

State regulation

Reference to state or legislative regulation in the Trusteeship Formula has been exploited to cast reflection on its authenticity.

According to Clause 3 of the Trusteeship Formula, 'It [the Trusteeship system] does not exclude legislative regulation of ownership and use of wealth.' Of course, there is no suggestion in the Trusteeship Formula to institute trusteeship as a system through state legislation. Legislative regulation is contemplated only to ensure that a trustee behaves as a trustee and does not betray the trust. If and when the Trusteeship system comes into operation, it would become necessary to ensure its proper functioning through some legislation.

Clause 4 refers to 'state-regulated trusteeship'. It is contended that Gandhiji never approved the use of legislation for the implementation of his views. It is pointed 'out that

> he [Gandhiji] wants to use trusteeship as a sort of safety valve for the likely abuses of the free enterprise system. But he does not want the state to be in control of that safety valve. He is quite emphatic about it. Has he not said the state represents violence in a concentrated and organized form? The individual has a soul, but the state is a soulless machine (Malgaonkar, cited in Sawhny, 1980).

The length to which a protagonist of free enterprise can go to lift a quotation out of context to serve his purpose has apparently no limit. Gandhiji's statement about violence embodied in the state is a part of the following dialogue.

> QUESTION: If you say that private possession is incompatible with non-violence, why do you put [up] with it?
> ANSWER: That is a concession one has to make to those who earn money, but would not voluntarily use their money for the benefit of . . . mankind.
> QUESTION: Why, then, not have state-ownership in place of private property and thus minimise violence?
> ANSWER: *It* [State ownership] *is better than private ownership* [emphasis added]. But that too is objectionable on the grounds of violence. It is my firm conviction that if the state suppressed capitalism by violence, it will be caught in the evils of violence itself. [Then follows the quotation cited.] Hence, I prefer the doctrine of Trusteeship (*The Modern Review*, October 1933, quoted in Hingorani, 1970: 50–51).

The free enterprise lobby has endeavoured to take maximum advantage of Gandhiji's aversion to state control. But there is ample evidence in his writings to prove that he was not averse to using the authority of the state to check the abuse of money power. A single quotation is enough to establish this fact: 'I would be very happy indeed if the people concerned behaved as trustees; but if they fail, I believe we shall have to deprive them of their possession through the state with the minimum exercise of violence' (quoted in Tendulkar, 1954). Gandhiji preferred 'extension of the sense of trusteeship to concentration of economic power in the hands of the state'. Nonetheless, he categorically stated that 'if it is unavoidable, I would support a minimum of state ownership'.

NOTES

1. *IASSI Quarterly*, Vol. 10, No. 1, July–September 1991: 179–210.
2. See Annexures 1 and 2.

Fundamental principles of trusteeship approved by Gandhiji[1]

Clause 1

Trusteeship provides a means of transforming the present capitalist order of society 'into an egalitarian one'. It 'gives no quarter to capitalism, but'[2] gives the present owning class an opportunity of reforming[3] itself. It is based on the faith that human nature is never beyond redemption.

Clause 2

It does not recognize any right of private ownership of property except in as much as it may be permitted by society.[4]

Clause 3

It does not exclude legislative regulation of ownership and use of wealth.

Clause 4

Deleted.[5]

Clause 5

'Thus under state-regulated[6] trusteeship, an individual will not be free to hold or use his wealth for selfish satisfaction or in disregard of[7] the interest of society.'

Clause 6

Deleted.[8]

Clause 7

'Just as it is proposed to fix a decent minimum living wage, a limit should be fixed for the maximum income that could be allowed to any person in society.'[9] The difference between such minimum and maximum incomes should be reasonable and equitable, so much so that the tendency would be towards obliteration of the difference.[10]

Clause 8

Deleted.[11]

Clause 9

Deleted.[12]

Clause 10

Deleted.[13]

Clause 11

'Under the Gandhian economic order, the character of production will be determined by social necessity and not by "personal whim or greed".'[14]

NOTES

1. A transcript of a photostat copy of a draft on trusteeship prepared by M.L. Dantwala.
2. The words in quotation marks were added by me and were approved by Gandhiji.
3. My phrase was 'a chance of transforming'. Gandhiji substituted the alternative phrase.
4. The original draft read: 'inasmuch it may be necessary for the service' of society. I had raised the question as to who would determine the necessity. For the words 'permitted' and 'society' I had suggested alternatives of 'deemed harmless' and 'social organization', respectively. Gandhiji approved the former words.
5. I had written: I suggest deletion of this clause because 'safeguarding of property rights' will lend itself to mis-representation. Besides, point 3 includes the essence of this point. Gandhiji wrote, 'I do not see any harm in removing

this.'

6. My version had used the word 'legal' in place of 'state-regulated'.

7. The original version had used the phrase 'irrespective of' in place of 'in disregard of'.

8. I had added this clause. It read: 'The owner will be duty bound to manage his property for the service of society. As a trustee, he will be entitled only to a statutory commission for his labours. This cannot be exorbitant.' Gandhiji commented: 'This is unnecessary. Has been included under Clause 2.' The clause was deleted.

9. This sentence was added by me.

10. My question to Gandhiji had been: 'Would Gandhiji consider the ratio of 1:12 suggested by Shri Kishorelal Mashruwala too high.' Gandhiji wrote that 'obliteration of the difference' was the 'ideal aimed at'.

11. I had suggested deletion of this clause and had added: If it is to be retained, I suggest the word 'trustee' in the place of 'present owners of wealth' and the addition of the following clause: 'subject to the overriding necessity of conforming to the principles of social justice mentioned above (or the ethics of the new economic order)'. Gandhiji wrote: 'Acceptance of suggestion to delete will not affect the meaning. If retained, the revision would be unacceptable.'

12. I had written: 'It is needless to say that a trustee, who does not properly discharge his duties, does not accept the schedule of rights, obligations and functions prepared for him, would be compelled to do so, on pain of dismissal, by legal and social sanctions.' Gandhiji noted that the clause 'has been removed from the original'.

13. I had written: 'It is repetition; otherwise, it is all right.' Gandhiji agreed: 'It is so; I have removed it.'

The following discussion on the subject also took place:

a. One point is fundamental. While explaining trusteeship Bapu stated: 'He considers himself a trustee for all the wealth he collects. . . .' However, it is necessary to say that: 'The efforts of the economic order will be towards an equitable adjustment of remuneration for the various economic functions, skilled or unskilled, manual or mental, administrative and managerial, to see that no person, not even a trustee, collects disproportionate wealth.' Gandhiji wrote: 'This is not necessary. On further thought, it would be seen that this is incorporated in the above.'

b. 'This is necessary on the principle that prevention is better than cure. Rather than allow the property to be accumulated and then order its use as trust, would it not be better to regulate reward for each activity in such a way that excessive wealth does not accumulate with any one person' (translated from the original in Gujarati). Gandhiji commented: The question is not of allowing accumulation of property. The question here is of correcting what already exists.'

14 My words had been 'private profit'. Gandhiji substituted the words in quotation marks. He consented to my request to include this clause.

Trusteeship:
Final draft approved by Gandhiji[1]

1. Trusteeship provides a means of transforming the present
capitalist order of society into an equalitarian one. It gives
no quarter to capitalism, but gives the present owning class
a chance of reforming itself. It is based on the faith that
human nature is never beyond redemption.
2. It does not recognize any right of private ownership of
property except so far as it may be permitted by society
for its own welfare.
3. It does not exclude legislative regulation of the ownership
and use of wealth.
4. Thus, under state-regulated trusteeship, an individual will not
be free to hold or use his wealth for selfish satisfaction
or disregard of the interest of society.
5. Just as it is proposed to fix a decent minimum living wage,
even so a limit should be fixed for the maximum income
that could be allowed to any person in society. The difference
between such minimum and maximum incomes should be
reasonable and equitable and variable from time to time
so much so that the tendency would be towards obliteration
of the difference.
6. Under the Gandhian economic order the character of production
will be determined by social necessity and not by personal
whim or greed.

NOTE

1. As portions of the photostat copy have become illegible, this annexure reproduces
the draft approved by Gandhiji, after taking due account of his comments
and corrections on various clauses.

CHAPTER 2

Ethics and economics of socialism[1]

The contention of this paper is that the establishment of a socialist society cannot become a reality until the majority of the people, particularly its elite, accept the ethical basis of a socialist society. Merely building the base of the economy modelled on the socialist doctrine—public ownership of productive assets—is no guarantee that it will usher in an enduring socialist society. The progress towards socialism can be truly judged not by the number or the sweep of 'socialist' measures but by the nature of change in the value system of the society. In effect, this view rejects the orthodox belief that if the structure of the economy is changed, for example, through public ownership of the instruments of production, it will *ipso facto* change the value system, which, in Marxist literature, is considered as merely a superstructure. We could go further and say that if there is a basic change in the value system appropriate to a socialist society, it may not be necessary to enact a succession of cultural revolutions after the overthrow of the capitalist system.

Expressions like 'Socialist Ethics' and 'Value System' are difficult to define and an attempt to bind them in words would perhaps circumscribe their import. Even so, it is not difficult to perceive their quintessence. Hopefully, some of it will be sensed from observations made later. If pressed to be more explicit, I may define them, negatively, as repudiation of acquisitiveness and, positively, as an urge to share the 'surplus', material as well as non-material, which may accrue from birth, wealth or wisdom (skill) or sheer chance. The ethics of it is embodied in the dictum 'from each according to his capacity to each according to his needs'.

It is necessary to remove a likely misunderstanding that the emphasis on ethical values implies relegation of structural change in the material conditions of production and production relations to a secondary position. The latter are not emphasized because it is presumed that there is no difference of opinion on this issue amongst the socialists. Equality in income and status is inconceivable in a milieu of marked inequality in the ownership of assets. But the inequality of income and status emanating from a wide spectrum of disparities in educational and professional attainments is basically a consequence of social valuation.

In a way, the experience gained from India's endeavour to establish a socialist society illustrates this theme. Since Independence several measures have been adopted with the avowed purpose of moving towards the establishment of a socialist society. There has been a marked increase in the share of the public sector both in industrial production and foreign trade. The cooperatives have gained ground in the internal trade in the country. Some years ago, a 10-point programme was adopted to accomplish

1. nationalization of banks,
2. nationalization of general insurance,
3. state trading in imports and exports,
4. state trading of foodgrains,
5. ceiling on urban poverty,
6. regulated removal of monopolies,
7. abolition of privy purses,
8. expansion of cooperatives,
9. provision of minimum needs of the community, and
10. rural works programme.

It was hoped that the implementation of the programme would alter the economic structure of the country and usher in an egalitarian, if not a socialist society. Most of the programmes which could be implemented with legislative action—such as nationalization of banks and insurance, and abolition of privy purses, etc.—have already been implemented. Others like ceiling on urban property are still on the anvil.

The 10-point programme embodied many of the known instruments for the establishment of democratic socialism. Though its implementation has been tardy, the sad fact is that the measures that have been implemented have not made any visible impact on the inequities of the capitalist system. On the contrary, there is every reason to believe that the intensity as well as the spread of poverty and inequality have been accentuated. Where does the flaw lie, in the content of the programme or in the lack of the political will to implement it? Some will argue that the programme itself is inadequate for the purpose of socialist transformation, that nothing short of total public ownership of the instruments of production would be of any avail. While such a point of view has its own merit, we would contend that the instruments failed and even got distorted because the ethics and the morality from which they derived their justification did not receive the recognition and emphasis necessary for their success. Their initiation could never be a substitute for the moral underpinning they needed.

A new cultural ethos

A similar view has been expressed by Dr V.K.R.V. Rao in his inaugural address to the 56th Session of the Indian Economic Conference (1973). Speaking on 'Some Fundamental Aspects of Socialist Change in India' and reviewing the Indian experience in this area since Independence, he concluded that 'the missing element in the Indian strategy has been political, social and cultural mobilization for socialist transformation'. According to him, the most powerful obstacles to the socialist transformation of the Indian economy exist on the non-economic plane. The crux of this theme can be summed up in the following observation of Dr Rao: 'Socialism, therefore, implies a new cultural ethos, a new social ethics, a new educational system and new motivation.' This is not to ignore the importance of socialist institutional framework. 'It is a necessary but certainly not a sufficient condition for socialist transformation' (Rao, 1974: 189, 197, 199).

While the political leadership—past and present—has been professing its allegiance to Socialist and Gandhian ideology, hardly any attempt has been made to influence the social ethics in a direction appropriate to a socialist society. On the contrary, social differentiation has been implicitly or explicitly recognized, if not encouraged. Wealth and its exhibition have not become less respectable. The upper middle class and even the middle class norms of life-style have received, if anything, widespread support.

Whether there is more or less concentration of wealth may be a matter of dispute, but an increased concentration of remunerative knowledge and managerial skills, and the high price tags attached to them is quite evident. While we are lamenting our inability to concede need-based minimum wages, the Company Law Board has shown no qualms in approving a salary of Rs 7,500 per month, plus a commission on net profits not exceeding Rs 45,000 per annum, plus all the perquisites such as free and furnished residential accommodation, car with driver, medical expenses (Rs 5,000 per annum), and paid holiday, over and above the usual provident-fund, gratuity and superannuation benefits, to the managing directors of even medium-size firms. The elite in every walk of life—political, economic or academic—have become more elitist than ever, in spite of our avowed commitment to socialism.

It is now being increasingly recognized that the value system does not automatically respond to the change in ownership of property. One method of inculcating egalitarian values is to de-emphasize functional compartments such as intellectual and manual work. In most societies, particularly ours, status, and along with it income, are associated with occupations or the type of work one does. Functional division and even specialization is a necessity in any modern society. But there is much to be said in favour of the Chinese practice under which 'all professional and managerial personnel in various institutions have to spend a part of every year in a factory or on a farm doing manual labour'. Perhaps Gandhiji was not so anachronistic in his insistence on manual work by the high and low, as he appeared to many a socialist in those days. As reported by Professor Leontief and many other eminent social scientists, in China

> great emphasis is put on manual labour in all school curricula. One day (sometimes one and a half days) of the regular six-day school week is spent in a shop or in other activities referred to as productive. . . . In public parks one often sees groups of youngsters weeding lawns or planting flowers, their lunch boxes waiting on nearby benches. . . . [And] a group of neatly dressed, jiggling school girls engaged in tasks—usual for our school children—of constructing a low brick wall, mix mortar, chip old bricks

clean (Leontief: 2, 6).

Educational practice

Egalitarian ethic is not an automatic result of structural change
in the economy; it has to be independently inculcated through
intense educational percept and practice. Joan Robinson has endorsed
that 'the Chinese system depends upon a high level of morality
(or political consciousness) in every sphere from top to bottom'.
But she hastens to add: 'The Chinese communists are not at
all sentimental; they do not rely on morality alone'. How then
does the system work? Her answer is:

> The success of the Chinese economy in reducing the appeal of
> the money motive is connected with its success in economic
> development. When everyone has enough to eat today and hope
> of improvement tomorrow, when there is complete social security
> at the prevailing level of the standard of life and employment
> for all, then it is possible to appeal to the people to combat
> egoism and eschew privilege. It would not make much sense to
> the workers and the peasants, say in Mexico or Pakistan.

Does it make sense in the Soviet Union? As for that, she
observes in another place, 'Soviet experience shows that power,
privilege, access to education can (still) form the basis of class
distinctions' (Robinson, 1969: 12) in spite of the social base
of state ownership and control of industry. Even Chairman Mao
concedes that

> a mere public ownership of production cannot usher in socialism,
> because such a change does not by itself rid men's minds of
> selfishness, personal concept or the desire to have the better of
> others, nor end workers' alienation arising from division of labour.

The socialist content in any social or political system is
determined by this division of labour, the degree of its rigidity
and perpetuating forces and correspondingly by the social prestige
attached to each class of work and more importantly by the
price tags attached to them. At the root of these differentiations
is the implicit value system of the society. A person who removes
human excreta or sweeps the road is an untouchable in the

Hindu society. On the other hand, a money-lender who has grown rich by charging usurious rates of interest to a helpless labourer is a *mahajan*—a big man. When Gandhiji insisted on referring to the untouchables as Harijans—men of God—he was attacking inegalitarianism at its root. Perhaps his understanding of historical materialism was not perfect, but he almost intuitively sensed the root cause of the offending inegalitarianism. Did he begin at the wrong end? Is the value system merely an outward manifestation of the ownership of means of production? As we have seen, Chairman Mao does not wholly think so. Changes in economic and political structures appear vain, unless they bring about a profound mutation in the consciousness of the individual citizen.

NOTE

1. *Acharya Narendra Dev Commemoration Volume*, Centre of Applied Politics, New Delhi, 1978.

CHAPTER 3

An approach to eradicating poverty[1]

There are two approaches to the problem of eradication of poverty.
One suggests that only through a rapid overall growth of the
economy can a sure and lasting impact be made on the living
standards of the poorer sections of the population. To achieve
this end, the limited investible resources of the economy should
be channelled into the most profitable and productive enterprises,
the profitability being judged by the quantum of surplus generated
in the process for further investment and accelerated growth.
Any deviation from this path, it is argued, will only delay the
realization of the objective of improving the living standards
of the poor. Investments in any but the most profitable enterprises
will only slow down the growth rate of the economy and hence
its capacity to sustain the ameliorative or welfare programme
in the transitional stage. This strategy is based on faith in what
is known as the 'spread effect' of overall growth through the
enlargement of employment opportunities. Past experience, however,
belies such faith. As David Morse has observed, 'Until recently,
economists tended to regard unemployment in less developed countries
as a symptom of under-development which would disappear as
development proceeds' (Morse, 1970). But experience shows this
is not so. Several instances can be cited which show an increase
in unemployment in spite of rapid economic growth. In Venezuela,
for example, a World Bank study indicated that, notwithstanding
a growth rate of eight per cent between 1950 and 1960, there
was more unemployment at the end of the decade than at the
beginning.[2]

Growth in India has no doubt been slow, but there is enough

evidence to show that certain regions and sections of the population, specially the most vulnerable, have not benefitted even from this slow growth. Maybe a different growth path, particularly one which would have contributed to restraining the rise in prices of wage goods, would have made a difference.

The other school emphasizes a more direct approach to the problem of poverty and suggests a set of policies and programmes specifically directed towards improving the living standards of the poor. Our planning strategy accepts this approach and several programmes have been developed over the years for the purpose. The Second Five-Year Plan had stated that 'the benefits of economic development must accrue more and more to the relatively less privileged classes of society' (Government of India, 1956: 22). This sentiment is expressed repeatedly in all announcements of public policy on the objectives of economic development.

The Government has a major role in bringing about a basic transformation of the social and the economic structure, and of the appropriate agencies which can perform this task effectively. It must be accepted that the Government has a major role in the task; for in the absence of an appropriate policy framework for growth with equity, no such transformation . can take place. But even assuming that such a policy framework exists, the political and administrative machinery of the Government—authoritarian or democratic—has grave limitations when it comes to bringing about a basic transformation insofar as it concerns the thoughts, attitudes and the behaviour of the people at large. Secondly, it has limitations in reaching the nooks and corners of the country where the majority of the weaker sections of the population live.

Dedicated political party cadres can perhaps help in the process of transformation. But under an authoritarian set-up, they generate fear rather than spontaneous cooperation of the people; and under a democratic set-up, they generate inter-party feuds. Occasionally, when either of them succeeds in generating mass enthusiasm, it is often frenzied and therefore short-lived; and when the frenzy abates, it leaves behind a sediment of undissolved discontent. Even so, under a democratic set-up, there is at least a viable alternative worth considering, viz. non-partisan constructive work through voluntary agencies. Its revival holds hope of bringing about upliftment where it is needed most and provides a countervailing force against the power-seeking radicalism of the professional politician.

In a different context, Gandhiji did succeed in combining constructive work with revolutionary mass movements. As he put it: 'It should be clear the Civil Disobedience without the cooperation of millions by way of constructive effort is mere bravado and worse than useless.' In his characteristic way, he concluded his booklet on constructive programme by stating: 'Civil Disobedience without the constructive programme will be like a paralyzed hand attempting to lift a spoon' (Gandhi, 1948: 29, 30). The relevance of Gandhiji's constructive programme lay not so much in its content, as in the psychological and educational role it played in inculcating some basic values—concern for the poor (the *daridra-narayan* and the *harijan*), humility, austerity, restraint in words and deeds—without which revolutionary movements either peter out or leave an ugly backwash.

Today, any talk of constructive work by political workers or any other group, like students or trade unions, would be a subject of ridicule as an escape from revolutionary commitment. But reading a recent article on the Cultural Revolution in China, I am tempted to believe that behind its much advertised bizarre appearance lay Chairman Mao Tse-tung's idea of inculcating some basic values like identity with the masses, reducing the gap between the elite and the common man through participation of the former in farm and factory work, in learning by doing, etc. As an ex Red Guard observed: 'To be intellectually right is not enough' (Michael, 1971). Like Chauri Chaura in the midst of civil disobedience, there were excesses in the Cultural Revolution, more crude and more frequent than ours. The latter can be attributed to a missing point in Mao's thought, namely the emphasis on the civil aspect of disobedience or revolt.[3]

In the original script of these lectures, I had with some bitterness suggested: 'Let the politician concentrate on the glamorous task of 'take-overs' and leave the anti-poverty programme—which by the way has very little glamour—to voluntary agencies and constructive workers.' In retrospect, I realize that such a dichotomy would be unworkable. What I wish to emphasize is the revival of the Constructive Programme. While its value orientation will be the same as in the pre-Independence days, its content will be different. Besides, it need not be a single, centrally ordained and organized programme. Within a broad framework, there should be enough latitude for regional adjustments and experimentation. What is needed for its revival is inspiring leadership, not necessarily of a single charismatic national leader but of many smaller men who have the necessary conviction and urge to devote time to such constructive work.

As it is, there are many voluntary agencies which, in spite of many odds against them, are persevering in the rather lonely task of constructive work. Similarly, there are, to my knowledge, thousands of lesser known—and unknown—social workers, who, though somewhat dispirited and frustrated, are doing some quiet work in a lonely corner. True, the efforts of these agencies and men also haven't had much visible impact on poverty and unemployment. But their efforts need to be recognized and encouraged, because, by and large, they have the necessary qualities of sincerity and commitment.

Earlier, I mentioned power politics—the desire to gain and retain political influence—as a formidable block to the effective implementation of the programme for aiding the weaker sections of the population. Being outside the arena of power politics can be both an advantage and a disadvantage for the constructive worker. Without political and government backing, he may find it impossible to get anything done. Even constructive work, if it goes beyond the charitable and the ameliorative and involves a development programme, would need sympathetic cooperation and active assistance of government departments and agencies in various matters. A case in point is the Sarva Seva Sangh's Koraput experiment which had all the elements of success, not the least a dedicated and inspiring leadership. But it had to be virtually abandoned because of official apathy and, according to its sponsors, proven hostility for reasons not difficult to guess. Reviewing the Koraput experiment, A.W. Sahasrabudhe wrote:

> From June 1957, we had to face for the first time open opposition from Government. It was obvious from their actions that they had decided to put every possible impediment to the growth of our movement. Government officials and their henchmen started encouraging donors of land to take back their gifts and withdraw from the Gramdan community. Applications began to be sent to Revenue Offices stating that the applicant did not intend to give his land in Gramdan and did not want the land to be transferred

to common ownership. Few hundred of such applications were considered by revenue authorities. In some places, Bhoodan workers were summoned to give evidence. Criminal cases were launched. It began to be whispered that most of the Gramdans were bogus. They said signatures were obtained by dangling false promises to the poor, ignorant people. There was no doubt that an all out offensive was set in action against the movement (Sahasrabudhe, 1966: 9).

Generally, neither the politician nor the bureaucracy takes kindly to non-official constructive work, especially if it threatens to be effective. Success of constructive work is likely to be interpreted as failure of the political party in power and that of the official agencies. I do not know how this dilemma can be resolved. I am not suggesting that the official agencies should withdraw from the implementation of programmes for the benefit of the weaker sections of the population. But I do suggest they should adopt a deliberate policy of handing over as much of their implementation as possible to voluntary agencies and of actively assisting these agencies. Even a veteran *sarvodaya* worker like Annasaheb Sahasrabudhe writing about Koraput had to concede that 'the initiative and responsibilities of development work in such a backward area must be taken by the Government'. The policy of democratic decentralization (*panchayati raj*) was expected to serve precisely this purpose. Unfortunately, the organs of decentralized functioning, the *panchayats* and the cooperatives, could not remain immune from power politics in which the poor are not high stakes.

The alternative is to try the voluntary agencies with a renewed faith. Perhaps, the suggestion of voluntary self-denial on the part of organized political agencies—be they the Congress Party or the *panchayats*—is naive, as can be inferred from the fate of the suggestion made by no less a person than the Father of the Nation, on the eve of Independence, to convert the National Congress into a Lok Sevak Sangh. But our suggestion is much more modest. What is suggested is not abandonment of political action, but a deliberate tolerance of a countervailing force, not merely at a political level (parliamentary opposition) or a semi-political level (trade unions, cooperatives, etc.), but also at the level of the people in the form of voluntary organizations. On their part, the voluntary agencies will have to reorient themselves to the new tasks, adopt better management practices, and show willingness to seek technical assistance where needed. In brief, their isolation from the mainstream of the developing economy should end. The political leaders and the official agencies, I would urge, should actively assist this process by recognizing and adopting the voluntary agencies in the interest of more meaningful democracy and social progress.

The state effort at the national level and constructive work at the grassroots will have to be integrated. Diffused and isolated constructive work cannot be a substitute for State action for economic development and social change. If the two have contrary purposes and work in hostility, nothing can be accomplished. But our country is so vast and its problems so complex that the State by itself will not be able to cope with the requirements of the situation. The State, with its authority can eliminate obstacles to growth—be they monopoly capitalism or privy purses—but when it comes to building up from below, its effectiveness remains to be demonstrated. This is true not only of India but of all countries, both capitalist as well as communist. This is probably vaguely realized by the political leadership.

The 13-point Constructive Programme of Gandhiji indicates his concern for the poor. It continues to be relevant in the post-Independence context. The 13 points are as follows:

1. communal unity,
2. removal of untouchability,
3. prohibition,
4. *khadi,*
5. *gramodyoga,*
6. village sanitation,
7. basic education,
8. adult education,
9. education in health and hygiene,
10. propagation of *rashtra bhasha*—national language,
11. uplift of women,
12. love for one's own language, and
13. working for economic equality.

The four pillars of this programme appear to be: education, health, sanitation and employment. These components surely are more relevant for the poor.

It may be necessary to give a development orientation to the earlier constructive programme, but if socialism implies social justice and concern for the poor, the relevance of the 13 points remains undiminished. Gandhiji's elaboration of 'economic equality' provides a glimpse of his concept of socialism, which he equated with a non-violent society. To use his words:

> Working for economic equality means levelling down of the few rich in whose hands is concentrated the bulk of the Nation's wealth on the one hand, and the levelling up of the semi-starved naked millions on the other. A non-violent system of government is clearly an impossibility so long as the wide gulf between the rich and the hungry millions persists; the contrast between the palaces of New Delhi and the miserable hovels of the poor labouring class remains. It cannot last one day in free India, the poor will enjoy the same power as the rich in the land (Gandhi, 1948: 21).

My contention is that in the overall economic policy of the Government even with its *garibi hatao* (remove poverty) orientation, there is a preoccupation with the levelling down aspect of the problem, and an apparent neglect—perhaps lack of will or even understanding—of the levelling up aspect of the problem. Or, if this is denied, the obvious lack of success in this regard will have to be attributed to failure to devise suitable instruments for implementing the policy for elimination of poverty. It is in this context that I am suggesting the formulation of an agreed policy of revival and reorientation of constructive work, entrusting it to voluntary agencies and giving them the financial, administrative and technical support they may need, without impairing their autonomy.

Finally, I should like to emphasize the importance of generating a psychological climate for the acceptance of some basic values implicit in the building up of an egalitarian society. The manner in which this should be attempted has to be basically different from the one adopted, say, in an election campaign. The current emphasis is on demonstrating our socialistic stance through spectacular measures like legislation for bank nationalization; takeover of general insurance, export and import trade; abolition of privy purses; imposition of ceiling on urban poverty; amendment of the Constitution with respect to Fundamental Rights. I will not go into the question of the essentiality of these measures in the interest of socialism, or the priorities attached to them. What I would like to point out is that something more, if not something different, is needed to influence the outlook, the behaviour and the values of the people in general, which alone can provide a solid base for the superstructure of socialist institutions. In this connection, I should like to refer to the distinction made in Marxist literature between the base and the superstructure, and the relative importance of the two. Joan Robinson states it as follows:

> Marxist analysis distinguishes between the *base* of a social system and the *superstructure*. The base is a system of economic foundation. The base of capitalism is personal property in the means of production, which yields *rentier* income and gives private enterprise control over economic development. Similarly, the base of socialism is State ownership and control of industry. A superstructure is the pattern of institutions, organizations, chain of authority, traditions and habits of thought which grow up in society. Inequality in consumption, the love of rank, status and power, untrammelled individualism and a social hierarchy based on wealth, belong to the bourgeois superstructure of capitalism; the superstructure of proletarian socialism requires acquisitiveness to be replaced by a spirit of service (Robinson, 1969: 11, 12).

I will pass over this rather simplistic differentiation between the capitalist and socialist characteristics of the base and the superstructure. Whatever may be the Marxist theoretical analysis, facts as observed in socialist countries do not conform to the description particularly of the superstructure. But this is not the point which I want to discuss for my present purpose. In fact, it is the lack of confidence in the attitudes, behaviour and values of the masses which necessitates incorporating institutions like State ownership and State control of economic enterprise at the base of the socialist system. As Joan Robinson herself admits: 'Soviet experience shows that power, privilege and access to education can form the basis of class distinctions' in spite of the socialist *base* of 'State ownership and control of industry'. And if one is to believe her, the Cultural Revolution in China was justified and encouraged by Chairman Mao precisely because he apprehended the emergence of a socialist elite divorced from the masses in Communist China. As she says: 'Class is defined by the state of mind and the state of mind is revealed in conduct.' She also talks of 'a government of the people by the people *for officials*', and 'the price of freedom from Party bosses is eternal vigilance'. Such vigilance culminated in the 'Cultural Revolution' twenty years after the foundation of Communist China. Stalin needed many more draconian measures to preserve communism. Such upheavals become inevitable because of the inverted relationship between base and superstructure in Marxist thought. This is precisely what Gandhiji meant by saying that '*Swaraj* must come from within'. In other words, value reorientation should be the forerunner of the establishment of socialist society of *Purna Swaraj*, as Gandhiji would have liked to call it, in which 'the poorest shall feel that it is their country, in whose making they have an effective voice, in which there will be no high class or low class of people'.

NOTES

1. *Poverty in India: Then and Now: 1870–1970*, Dadabhai Naoroji Memorial Fellowship Lectures, Macmillan India, Delhi, 1973: 32–67.
2. This seems to be a world-wide phenomenon. The Secretary General of the United Nations, in his foreword to the budget estimates for the financial year 1972 wrote as follows: 'The 1970 Report on the World Social Situation has shown dramatically that although per capita incomes rose in all regions during the United Nations Development decade, social conditions have generally deteriorated and social policies have frequently failed to bring about improvements in mass levels of living or to meet new social problems.'
3. The following paragraph in point 6 of the Sixteen-Point Guidelines of the Cultural Revolution is worth noting:

   The method to be used in debates is to present facts, reason things out, and persuade through reasoning. Any method of forcing a minority holding different views to submit is impermissible. The minority should be protected because sometimes the truth is with the minority. Even if the minority is wrong, they should still be allowed to argue their case and reserve their views (Robinson, 1969: 90).

II
AGRICULTURAL DEVELOPMENT
AND POLICY

CHAPTER 4

From stagnation to growth[1]

The post-war era has been very rewarding for agricultural economics. The tardy growth of agricultural production in most of the developing economies, right upto 1965, provided fertile soil for a rich crop of literature. The inspiration and the raw material for this address have been derived from this literature.

In the literature on the economics of development of less developed countries, agriculture was assigned a critical developmental role. But in the post-war period, agriculture, more often than not, proved a drag on economic development. This considerably perplexed the economists; and while searching for the culprit, they held the policy-makers in the developing countries responsible for the failure of agriculture to play its assigned role. This pursuit yielded ample literature—often impatient and angry—on post-war agriculture in developing countries. As one critic observed:

> The less-developed world is clearly losing the capacity to feed itself; stated otherwise, a growing share of the increase in population is being sustained by food shipments from the developed regions, largely from the United States, under the Food for Peace Programme (Brown, 1965: vi).

It appeared that the 'White Man's Burden' would not ease even after he shed the political deadweight of colonial rule! In fact, the new burden seemed to be getting so heavy that, according to the celebrated authors of *Famine-1975!*, it would become necessary 'to apply the classical medical triage method' to the starving world of less developed countries. 'Like doctors on the battlefield trying to make the best out of the limited resources, the affluent countries will have to decide which starving countries to save and which to sacrifice!' (Paddock, 1968)

Fortunately, the countries branded for sacrifice managed to survive. As a matter of fact, the scene changed so dramatically that the critics began to chant the song of the Green Miracle. Paul Paddock graciously extended the reprieve to 1980.[2]

At this stage, I must state that my main theme today is not the Green Revolution *per se*: what I am interested in is the literature on the subject, analyzing the reactions of the economists who have keenly watched the drama of agriculture's 'failures' and 'successes', and attempting to draw some meaningful general conclusion regarding the factors which account for stagnation and/ or growth of agriculture in the context of the situations confronting many of the developing economies.

It may be necessary for this purpose to examine the nature and magnitude of the alleged 'failure' as well as 'success' in agriculture; but only to the extent that this may be relevant to the identification of causal factors. Though my interest is in the larger problem of agricultural stagnation and growth, much of the empirical data pertains to India.

Beginning with the period 1950–65, with which the 'failure' of agriculture is associated, I should like to submit that it should be assessed by reference to the state of affairs prior to 1950, say from 1901 to 1950. A study by S.R. Sen shows that during the first 24 years of this century, foodgrains production in India increased at the meagre annual rate of 0.3 per cent. During the next 24 years, foodgrains production actually declined at an average annual rate of 0.02 per cent. Thus, for 'undivided India', the estimated production in 1947–48 (66 million tonnes) was slightly less than that in 1900–01 (67 million tonnes). Estimates of foodgrains production in the Indian Union from 1936–37 onwards have a firmer basis. For the first 15 years of the 30-year period— 1936–37 to 1965–66—foodgrains production declined at the rate of 0.68 per cent per annum, but in the next 15 years, it increased at the rate of 2.75 per cent per annum (Sen, 1967). Thus, the most striking fact which emerges is that for nearly 50 years, since the turn of the century, foodgrains production was almost stagnant.

George Blyn's study of agricultural output, availability and productivity in India from 1891 to 1947 confirms Sen's results (Blyn, 1966: 96, 337). To ensure comparability of data, Blyn has confined his study to British India and its constituent regions. His study reveals that during the reference period[3] (56 years), aggregate foodgrains production increased at a meagre average rate of 0.11 per cent per year. Rice production, which then accounted for half of foodgrain output, showed a declining trend. The best performance was that of wheat whose production increased at the average annual rate of 0.84 per cent. Rice output in this latter period was declining at the annual rate of 0.12 per cent. The performance of non-foodgrain crops was no better. Population during the entire reference period increased at the annual rate of 0.67 per cent, and during the last four 'reference decades' by 1.12 per cent. As a result, the per capita all-crop output declined sharply, and the index number, with 1891 as the base year, dropped to 84.2 in 1946. Inter-regional differences were considerable, and the decline in per capita availability was the largest in 'Greater Bengal' where the index dropped to 54.1.

I would also submit that in judging .the performance of agriculture in the developing countries in the period following their independence from colonial rule or domination, it would be relevant to derive some idea regarding the time required to bring about a yield breakthrough, from the early experience of the developed countries. In the United Kingdom, 'from the time national yield data first became available in 1884 until the advent of Second World War, the average rate of increase (in grain yields) was only 0.2 per cent per year'. For the United States, the annual compound rate of increase in the grain yields per acre was 0.3 per cent between 1866–70 and 1901–05, nil between 1901–05 and 1936–40, 1.5 per cent between 1936–40 and 1951–53, and a breakthrough of 4.8 per cent only in the post-war period of 1951–53 to 1961–63. Only in Japan was the growth rate consistently above 1 per cent per annum during the corresponding first two periods (Brown, 1965: 15).

It is in the light of this record of early performances of the successful developed countries that India's 'stagnation' in agricultural production and productivity during the corresponding stage of her economic development should be viewed. In India, between 1949–50 and 1964–65, the compound rate of growth (1949–50 to 1951–52 = 100) of production was 2.98 per cent for foodgrains and 3.19 per cent for all crops. Productivity growth rates were 1.60 per cent for both.[4] If, however, the base for the calculation of percentage increase is shifted to 1952–53/1954–55, the compound rate for foodgrains production drops to 2.50 per cent, and for productivity to 1.51. This was certainly not stagnation, but in view of the annual growth of population at 2.2 per cent, the balance between food and population became precarious. The two successive disastrous droughts which brought down foodgrains production from 89 million tonnes in 1964–65 to 72 million tonnes in 1965–66 and 74.2 million tonnes in 1966–67 added the last straw. It was then that Paddock's *Famine-1975!* became a bestseller.

With this background review of the nature and magnitude of the 'stagnation' period in agriculture, we may now examine what the economists thought were the causes of the stagnation. The literature on this question is so voluminous that we will have to pick and choose from the lengthy array of explanations. These could perhaps be divided into three major groups:

1. *Institutional and Organizational*: Land Tenure, Credit, Marketing, Extension, Education.
2. *Economic*: Incentives-disincentives, Prices, Taxes, Subsidies.
3. *Technological*: Seeds, Fertilizers, Irrigation.

Obviously, these are not mutually exclusive categories and their interactions should not be ignored. The classification has been suggested merely for the convenience of discussion. Further, we shall confine ourselves only to a few items under each category. Before proceeding with this discussion, it would be helpful to indicate the line of reasoning that will be adopted.

The contention is that if one or more of the above factors 'explained' the stagnation, it would be reasonable to expect their full or partial removal to be able to explain the success of the post-1965 period. More specifically, it should be possible to identify the inhibiting factors which were present during the stagnation period but were absent during the success period. Usually, in the discussion of this issue, several explanatory factors— institutional, economic, technological—are bundled together to explain 'stagnation' or 'growth'. At that level of generalization, no one can disagree with such propositions, but, at the same time, little can be said about the critical factor which makes all the difference between stagnation and growth. The ideal procedure of course would be some sort of regression analysis, but factors like land reforms do not lend themselves to the kind of quantification needed for the purpose. Under the circumstance, the sort of 'yes-yes', 'no-no' analysis suggested earlier would be more appropriate, as we have both the stagnation and growth situation spanned between a period of 20 years.

Another profitable line of enquiry would be a cross-country analysis. Rates of growth between countries have varied a great deal. For example, growth rates of agricultural production in Taiwan and North Korea in South-East Asia have been markedly higher than those in India and Burma; or in Mexico, compared to several other countries in Latin America. We could perhaps identify the factor(s) which may explain such glaring differences. Such analysis has indeed been made and much has been made of its findings. But, as we shall see, their scientific validity becomes doubtful on closer scrutiny. Quite often, a single factor like land reform or fertilizer-product price ratio is picked up as an explanatory factor. Such partial analysis is not only questionable but it breaks down when extended beyond the restricted sample. But a more important point is the distinction between reproducible and non-reproducible factors like soil, climate and, to some extent, even the natural advantage in the creation of irrigation facilities. If the analysis is to benefit from the experience of the more successful, the transferability of such experience is critical.

One observation, however, could be made on the cross-country analysis. Speaking about South-East Asia, the phenomenon of the low rate of growth in agricultural production was pervasive till 1964—exceptions like Taiwan were non-typical. And after 1965, when the breakthrough began to occur, it was shared by most countries. In both the periods, these countries were pursuing diverse economic and political policies, and yet, in all these countries, they produced almost identical results: stagnation before 1964, and breakthrough thereafter. If economic policies mattered much, the near identical outcome of diverse policies would be difficult to explain. Further, as we shall see, in none of these countries is there clear evidence of deliberate reversal of policies which could explain the rather sudden emergence of success after a long spell of failure. It is obvious that the only thing which happened was the discovery of the high-yielding varieties and their commercial application, in which economists and economic policies played a marginal role, if at all. As a matter of fact, when the curtain rose, many economists were caught rehearsing their gloomy roles. That they are reappearing with another set of gloomy roles—'Seeds of Disaster',[5] etc.—is a different story.

Let us now quickly review the Indian scene and try to identify the factor(s) which would explain the sudden change in the agricultural situation. We shall see a little later whether what has happened deserves the name of 'Green Revolution' and whether a confident full stop, a sarcastic question mark or a hesitant 'can't say' sigh of explanation would be more appropriate after the phrase.

This task should prove pretty simple: for in regard to most of the explanatory factors mentioned above, nothing really noteworthy happened either in policy or in fact. Some observers, mainly from abroad, have no doubt suggested that the disastrous droughts of 1965 and 1966 taught a lesson to Indians who belatedly realized the sheer folly of 'neglecting' agriculture. It is difficult to see where they found the evidence of this purging. The 'neglect' story was perhaps no more than a professional racket which yielded a crop of bestselling scientific fictions and rewarding international travel. My position, which I have repeatedly stated, is that I can see evidence neither of deliberate neglect in the past,[6] nor of any sudden later awakening.

Take land reform to begin with. The one remarkable piece of land reforms—the abolition of intermediary tenures—was enacted during the early fifties and even the critics concede that it was almost fully implemented. The erstwhile predominantly *zamindari* states like Uttar Pradesh, Bihar and West Bengal did not reveal any impact of this reform on their agricultural production during the fifties. Tenancy laws and laws imposing ceiling on holdings were also enacted during the fifties in most states but were so indifferently implemented that it is difficult to assess to what extent they benefitted or hindered agricultural growth. But the relevant point is that nothing new happened in this sphere immediately preceding 1965 which could explain the sudden emergence of the Green Revolution. If anything, there was a distinct sign of waning interest in land reform and a frozen cynicism about it. Of course, no one said anything openly against land reforms;

prudence suggested 'the less said the better'. It is only after the Green Revolution—which is alleged to have made the 'rich richer and the poor poorer'— that there is a rekindling of interest in land reforms. With stagnant agriculture, there was not much attraction in land grabbing by the rich or the poor. Thus land reform, far from being a catalytic agent of change, assumed relevance only as an aftermath of growth. Incidentally, it is in states like Punjab, Andhra Pradesh and Tamil Nadu—states not particularly known for their zest for land reforms—that the Green Revolution appears to be taking hold.

Much the same story can be told regarding community development, farmers' education, the rest of the institutional and organizational factors, and even the credit policy. The Reserve Bank and the Planning Commission stuck to their slogan 'Cooperation has failed, Cooperation must succeed'. They must have been taken by surprise when one of the major grounds of imposition of social control on commercial banks—and their subsequent nationalization—was stated to be the latter's neglect of agricultural finance. The multi-agency idea was mooted by the Ministry of Food and Agriculture when it was convinced of the utter incapability of the Cooperatives to cope with the credit requirements of the new technology. The reluctant Reserve Bank acquiesced, but it has now adopted an ingenious strategy of 'where Cooperatives have failed, commercial banks should rush in, revive the Cooperatives and retire'. Under the new policy orientation, in some selected districts where cooperative Central Banks are weak, commercial banks will now finance the primary societies directly as a transitional measure. In these districts the commercial banks will be precluded from financing farmers who are not members of the cooperative societies, a blatant example of compulsory 'cooperativization'.

The Intensive Agricultural District Programme (IADP) should, however, be mentioned as a major pre-1965 policy decision. Though even the IADP has been criticized for accentuating regional disparities, it was a step in the right direction. It was a pioneering effort in the direction of intensive agricultural development and by the time the High-Yielding Varieties (HYV) arrived, the IADP districts had built up an impressive organizational infrastructure. While I do not want to say anything which would detract from its achievements, I should like to mention that the programme was launched in the early 1960s, but the phrase Green Revolution

was not heard till the HYV arrived in 1965. As the Fourth
Report of the Expert Committee on Assessment and Evaluation
states, the IADP has played the role of the 'path-finder' rather
than that of a 'pace-setter' (Government of India, 1969: 4, 10).
It could not still be the Famine 1975! chorus. HYV, however,
has driven the boys back to the greenroom.

The gravamen of the charge against India's agricultural policy
was its 'urban bias' which deliberately led to the low foodgrain
prices in the interest of urban consumers.[7] I have dealt with
this issue at length elsewhere (Dantwala, 1967) and would content
myself with highlighting only a few points for fuller consideration.
Presumably, the PL-480 imports were the instrument with which
foodgrain prices were kept low. Wheat was by far the major
component of these imports, yet wheat is the one foodgrain in
which the Green Revolution is most evident. Prices of commercial
crops like cotton and oilseeds—in spite of marginal imports of
PL-480 cotton and soyabean—have remained consistently high;
the price ratios between foodgrain and non-foodgrain crops were
highly favourable to the latter, and yet, there is no sign of
a breakthrough in their production and the productivity index
of groundnuts has been declining. None of this needs to be
interpreted as representing the view that farmers in India or
elsewhere are insensitive to price incentives or that prices do
not matter for production. The fault, if any, lay with the analysis
of the economists, and not with the response of the farmers.

First, the analysis of price response of individual or substitutable
crops to relative prices was erroneously applied to aggregate
production of the agricultural sector. Inadequate note was taken
of the prevailing situation in the input markets and the production
and supply bottlenecks: a situation in which high product prices
would have resulted in higher input prices rather than higher
production. And in the highly inflationary situation, with domestic
prices soaring high above international prices—evident also in
the 1966 devaluation—higher prices were no remedy for boosting
aggregate agricultural or even foodgrain production. In the context
of a traditional agriculture, the potential for increasing production
through price policy is extremely limited. It can, however, play
a more positive role by maintaining the profitability of technological
transformation.[8]

Even less tenable is the cross-country comparisons of fertilizer-farm product price ratios. Michael Lipton (quoting Edward Mason, 1966: 102) laments: 'Fertilizer prices relative to farm prices have been higher in India than in Pakistan' (Lipton, 1969: 102). So what? Pakistan has belatedly realized that the policy of heavily subsidizing fertilizer prices was not very productive. Fertilizer prices have been much higher in Taiwan than in Pakistan and yet all through the fifties and the early sixties agricultural growth rates in Taiwan surpassed those in Pakistan.

Those who talk of urban or consumer bias in India's agricultural policy—low food prices and high fertilizer prices—would do well to take a look at the soaring Consumer Price Indices, as well as Commodity Price Indices—with their peaks cut off by the forward shifting of base periods—and the consequent recurring hikes in wage and salary awards.

For several years, domestic prices for almost all agricultural commodities have been ruling far above international prices. Be it as it may, when Lipton tries to establish a link between the 'big farmer' and the 'urban bias' of the planners, he badly strains his own intellect and the readers' indulgence (Lipton, 1969: 104). I would concede the 'big farmer' bias in India's agricultural policy; but by the same token, it cannot be pro-consumer or even pro-urban. Lipton suggests that the true class struggle between the 'food buyer' and the 'food grower' may be, but this should not be equated with rural-urban, because as pointed out later, rural households have to buy 30–50 per cent of their food requirements.[9]

Incidentally, is 'high price' advocacy by India's well-wishers not a syndrome of 'big farmer' bias? As John Mellor explains, for a low income cultivator who sells only 10 per cent of what he produces, a 10 per cent relative increase in agricultural price increases his real income by only 1 per cent. For a (big) cultivator who sells 70 per cent of what he produces, real income rises by 7 per cent with a 10 per cent relative rise in prices. Conversely,

for a low income consumer (rural or urban) who spends 70 per cent of his income on food, a 10 per cent increase in food prices will represent a 7 per cent decline in real income. For a high income urban consumer, spending only 20 per cent of his income on food, a 10 per cent rise in food prices provides only 2 per cent decline in income (Mellor, 1968: 25, 26).

Of course, a high income consumer spends a larger rupee sum on food than does a low income consumer.

All said and done, the coincidence of (relatively) higher foodgrain prices and production breakthrough need not be ignored. That the high prices of foodgrains considerably improved the profitability of HYV cannot be denied. Equally helpful was the policy decision to establish the Agricultural Prices Commission which recommended statutory minimum support prices for foodgrains, at which the Government accepted the responsibility to buy the entire available supplies. In fact, the Government offered to buy all market supplies at procurement prices which were much higher than support prices. Further, the Chief Ministers of the states and the Government of India, yielding to pressure from the states, accepted higher prices than those recommended by the Agricultural Prices Commission. The foreign experts—and critics of urban bias—can now at least have the satisfaction that the policy-makers in India are more inclined to accept their advice on incentive prices rather than that of their own experts and of the Commission expressly established to study the situation and make recommendations. It is a different matter that the cost to the Central Exchequer of the unwillingness to contain prices amounts to Rs 106 crore per year from 1970 onwards. With the State Government employees waiting in the lobby, the cost to the Government may well amount to Rs 200 crore per year, which would imply either more deficit financing or a cut in development expenditure. The fact, however, is that it is the policy which is trying to keep pace with prices and not the other way round. Therefore, the only credit the price policy can take is that it is doing nothing effective to check its rise and, in fact, is making millions of urban *and rural* poor poorer. Except perhaps for wheat, the prevailing prices owe nothing to policy as such. But if this is what is meant by learning a lesson from the disastrous droughts, the lesson can be said to have been learned.

There is, however, one snag. Why are commercial crops not responding to relatively higher prices than those of foodgrains? The key question to ask is: what makes for the sustained profitability of cultivation? Is it the high prices which, in the second round, reduce profitability as a result of higher costs of cultivation, or some technological innovation, which without altering input-product price ratios, improves the input-output ratios in physical terms and hence the profitability of enterprise? And is there anything like an upper limit to incentive prices, beyond which they become a disincentive to investment and exports? Does the positive response of production to prices mean that the key to higher production is just higher prices? To the protest of *who says so* all one can say is that none of the critics of low price policy has cared to indicate the limitations of their incentive-price prescriptions.

The foregoing review indicates that during the years immediately preceding the Green Revolution, there was no significant change in agricultural policies which could explain its sudden emergence. If the earlier policies were in any way responsible for the 'failure' of agriculture, they at least did not come in the way of its subsequent success. As a matter of fact, in the eyes of some critics, some of the policies in operation in the later period, like compulsory procurement below market prices and zonal restriction on movement of foodgrains constituted a severe disincentive, yet they apparently did not prove an obstacle to the breakthrough. It can, of course, be argued that in their absence, the success would have been greater.

As everyone knows, the key factor behind the Green Revolution was the new technology with the High-Yielding Varieties at its core. Once again, it may be noted that several countries in Asia and Latin America, each following diverse economic policies, almost simultaneously experienced the breakthrough.

All this casts serious doubts on the relevance of the economic analysis of the time and its ability to explain the process of stagnation or growth. It would surely be silly to deduce from this that economic policies after all do not matter, but it may be appropriate to say that the policies which appeared to matter, perhaps do not matter. One may put it another way and suggest that in the absence of a technological breakthrough, many otherwise highly relevant policies—land reforms, economic incentives and institutional changes—jointly and severally could not have lifted agriculture above its stagnation threshold. Land reforms and other institutional changes were necessary and highly desirable. There are many reasons why they were not successfully carried out, but there is a possibility that perhaps the very stagnation of agriculture inhibited their success. When yields were miserably low, it was difficult to get enthusiastic about lowering the ceiling on holdings or drastically reducing the rents.

Speaking about India, extremes apart, if there is the injustice of exploitation, it is, by and large, of the poor by the less poor. Sure enough, even after the abolition of the intermediary tenures from over 170 million acres of land, there are several pockets of absentee landlordism. Yet, the bulk of the Indian agricultural sector is poor and depressed even by India's urban standards. Ninety-eight per cent of Household Operational Units have their holdings in the size group of less than 30 acres, irrespective of quality of land. A Reserve Bank Survey in 1961 indicated that out of the 12 districts studied, the value of the gross product of the 'big' (top 10 per cent) cultivators exceeded Rs 4000 in only 2 districts (Jalandhar—Rs 4052 and Akola—Rs 6450). It was below Rs 2000 in 7 out of 12 districts (Dantwala, 1961: 1159). Under such circumstances, how much scope was there for divesting or expropriation of the 'rich'? Now that the possibilities of making a fortune in agriculture have opened up, land reforms can play a vigilant corrective role.

As for agricultural prices, when yields were in the neighbourhood of 1 tonne per hectare, it was a mockery to talk of incentives through higher prices. But if new technology is to be adopted, it is essential to assure the innovating farmers that their efforts to adopt it will not be allowed to be frustrated by unremunerative prices.

It may be argued that the discovery of HYV was not a gift from heaven; and but for appropriate policies, they would not have seen the light of the day. Whose policies? Probably they were the policies of the Rockefeller and Ford Foundations whose generous grants made it possible for scientists in Mexico and Philippines to evolve the High-Yielding Varieties. The Revolution was the reward of scientific research and not of the wisdom of economists; few even dreamt of it and many even do not believe it. It is our professional privilege and duty to question its occurrence or its consequences—Palace Revolt, Pandora's Box, Seeds of Disaster, dualism—but let us not get into a stance that nothing good can ever happen in this country. As for the policy-makers, it was indeed fortunate that around 1965, India had a Minister for Agriculture who in spite of his many detractors, pinned his faith on the new strategy and the scientists behind it.[10] Mercifully, his successors have as yet done nothing to harm it by their irrelevant radicalism, except by their inefficiency and red-tape, but let us keep our fingers crossed.

We have assumed throughout that a revolutionary change has occurred—or rather is occurring in agriculture—not only in India but simultaneously in several developing countries. If this assumption itself is wrong, much of the earlier thesis regarding the role of agricultural policy must fall through. Though it is not possible to present a full case justifying the assumption, a few points may be submitted for consideration.

It is but legitimate to judge the occurrence by reference to growth in production. It is generally conceded that so far as wheat is concerned, both in India and Pakistan, and Mexico what has happened is truly revolutionary. (Wheat production in India has gone up from 12 million tonnes in 1964–65 to about 20 million tonnes in 1969–70.) Success in maize, *bajra* and *jowar*, though not as spectacular and widespread, is also encouraging. But production of rice in India (39.8 million tonnes in 1968-69[11] as against 39.3 million in 1964–65) presents an unrelieved spectacle of stagnation. It should be noted in this context that in West Pakistan, there has been an increase of 75 per cent in rice production between 1960–64 and 1968, as against 15 per cent in East Pakistan, 11 per cent in India, and 13 per cent. in Asia as a whole. Once again, policies have nothing to do with such glaringly disparate performance. The Annual Report (1969) of the Department of Agricultural Economics of the International Rice Research Institute examines this problem in depth and observes that the difference results mainly from environmental conditions under which the two crops, wheat and rice, are grown, and not from cultivation problems. Under favourable conditions, such as for rice in West Pakistan, the potential of the new rice varieties equals or exceeds that of HYV of wheat. The authors contend that 'the major obstacle to the spread of the new rice varieties has not been poor farm management, lack of farmers' knowledge, nor inadequate extension' (International Rice Research Institute, 1969), nor, one may add, low prices, unsatisfactory land tenure or inadequate institutional credit. The latter group of factors could not have affected one cereal (wheat) favourably and another (rice) in a contrary direction, or the same commodity (rice) favourably in West Pakistan and the other way in East Pakistan. Analysis of rice-crop area and production in South and South-East Asia indicates the critical relevance of physical environmental conditions. The double-cropped irrigated area which constitutes 10 per cent of the total rice area, produces 25 per cent of the total crop. Fifty per cent of the rice area is rainfed and another 20 per cent 'upland'; these together account for only 52 per cent of rice production. For the new varieties of rice to succeed, adequate water supply *and* good water control are essential. Wheat cultivation in India and Pakistan and rice in the latter meet these requirements.

It is true that an explanation does not undo the fact of the disappointing performance of rice. New varieties suited to monsoon conditions are being evolved, but if even these fail, rice cultivation will have to shift to the *rabi* season, or to drier regions, with adequate irrigation. Thus, it may as well be conceded that judging by the production performance alone, the Green Revolution cannot yet be said to have spread to rice cultivation, at any rate in India. Which other test, equally relevant and convincing, can we suggest to establish the pervasiveness of its occurrence?

A notable feature of the Indian agricultural scene since 1965 is the marked spurt in use of modern inputs. The spread in the adoption of HYV has surpassed earlier international records. The Pearson Report calls it 'one of the authentic marvels of our time' (Pearson, 1969: 259). The area planted to high-yielding cereals in Asia in the 1964–65 crop year was estimated at 200 acres; by 1968–69, 34 million acres were covered. In the entire history of agricultural progress anywhere in the world, no innovation has been adopted with such speed. Farmers in the societies which are planting these new seeds are achieving in a matter of years progress that took decades in other countries (Brown, Lester, 1970: 41). The agricultural transformation taking place in India has been described as 'one of the most amazing agricultural stories of all time' (Streeter, 1969: 132). One may wisely discount such hyperboles. But there is no reason to question the testimony of the International Rice Research Institute which says: 'The initial thrust of the new technology has been far more rapid than any previous historical experience. In many areas, the level of adoption has exceeded even the most optimistic predictions' (International Rice Research Institute, 1968: 336). In Japan, it took almost two decades for the new dwarf varieties to catch on nationally. In India, from a modest beginning in 1965, more than 9 million hectares have been sown to High-Yielding Varieties in 1968–69. These days, the mention of plan targets may evoke amusement. Even so, it may be mentioned that the 10 million hectare target of land under HYV of rice by 1973–74 would constitute 15 per cent of the entire rice crop area of South and South-East Asia. Even the 2.6 million hectares covered in India in 1968–69 constituted 56 per cent of the area planted to High-Yielding Varieties in South and South-East Asia in that year.

The spurt in fertilizer consumption has been equally remarkable. 'The jump in fertilizer usage in India in recent years has been one of the biggest and fastest-known anywhere in the world' (Streeter, 1969: 14). Let us, however, simply record the facts. The average annual increase in fertilizer (NPK) consumption between 1965–66 and 1969–70 was 3,00,000 tonnes. Whether this can be interpreted as a sign of agricultural transformation or just a big farmer boom may be left to the dialecticians. But what is happening since 1965 is certainly more than ordinary acceleration. Note should be taken of the liberalization of the fertilizer policy in 1965 under which fertilizer plants were permitted to be set up in the private sector, and fertilizer price and distribution constraints were relaxed. This was a welcome departure, but its impact on domestic production has been limited. In 1968–69, domestic production of nitrogenous fertilizers accounted for only 45 per cent of total consumption, as against 40 per cent in 1965–66.

The same story can be told about the post-1965 pick-up in the spread of farm mechanization. There has been a remarkable upsurge in minor irrigation. Between 1966 and 1969, 1,75,000 tubewells are reported to have been dug. Their total number at the end of the Third Five-Year Plan was only 80,000. The data on energization of pumpsets/tubewells can easily be checked and is, therefore, quite reliable. Between 1961 and 1965, the number of energized pumpsets/tubewells increased from 1,92,814 to 5,12,925, with an average annual increase of 64,000. By 31 March 1970, the number of energized pumpsets had gone up to 13,48,842; and the annual increase since 1966 went up threefold to more than 2 lakhs. Currently, more than 2,50,000 pumpsets are being energized each year. And, as one associated with the

Agricultural Finance Corporation, I may add that the farmers' demand is far in excess of the material and financial resources of the State Electricity Boards   needed to meet it.

The question whether this remarkable upsurge in the use of modern inputs can be characterized as transformation of traditional agriculture or merely an emergence of dualism should be lifted above a mere semantic debate. K.N. Raj has very ably discussed this issue in a scholarly article in the first issue of the *Journal of Development Planning* (Raj, 1969). After a meticulous scrutiny of production performance in Mexico, Taiwan and India, he observes that 'the result is that the availability of modern technology leads very often to dualism in the agricultural sector (as in Mexico) rather than to transformation of traditional agriculture' (Raj, 1969). More importantly, Raj contests the view that

> the institutional framework of agrarian economies is not a serious obstacle to growth and that what is needed is concentration on specific questions relating to the mechanics of the technological change required in each case and the supply of the necessary inputs (Raj, 1969: 15, 37).

Raj has tried to show that what has happened in Mexico is just an 'enclave' development, and in Taiwan it is a continuation of the trends established in an earlier period of its history— in fact under Japanese colonial rule. Regarding India alone, Raj would contest the transformation thesis. Thus, his contribution would appear to counter the entire theme of this address, and, therefore, merits respectful attention. Before discussing some of the basic issues, one or two preliminary points may be dispensed with.

Raj's empirical data pertain to a period which begins with 1950 (post-war) and even earlier for Taiwan—and ends for Mexico at 1959, for Taiwan at 1963 and for India at 1964–65. We are more concerned with the phenomenon which has emerged as a result of the adoption of the newly discovered HYVs in the mid sixties. Though the HYV of wheat were commercially applied in Mexico somewhat earlier, the HYV of wheat and rice came to India and South-East Asia only by 1965. Our submission is that the technological revolution in the tropics and sub-tropics really commenced with the discovery and application of the dwarf varieties with their high-yielding, quick maturing, photo-non-sensitive characteristics.

Coming to the basic issues, we shall first discuss the transformation versus dualism hypothesis, and then the relative roles of institutions and technology in accelerating growth in agriculture. It is quite true that the agricultural growth which has taken place in Mexico and India in the post-war period and even after the discovery of the HYVs is confined to a few regions and is not a national phenomenon.[12] My contention is that the transformation of traditional agriculture is a qualitative technical phenomenon and its authenticity is not conditional upon a given geographical coverage. That it has not permeated the entire country cannot detract from the fact of its occurrence, as testified by the qualitative change in the input-mix in agricultural production leading to the shift in the production function. Even so, it has occurred not on a few experimental farms, but literally over millions of farms covering large regions such as North and Pacific North in Mexico, and Punjab and Tamil Nadu in India. And within the regions where it has occurred, it is not confined to privileged pockets. As the PEO sample survey has shown, in the rabi season of 1968–69, HYV wheat covered 92.3 per cent of cropped area in the package districts and 66.5 per cent in all areas (Mukherjee, 1970: A.17). These regions are bigger than several independent nation states. Had Punjab or Tamil Nadu and Andhra Pradesh been independent nation states, the phenomenon would have been indisputably considered as agricultural transformation, but simply because they are constituent units of a continental country, their more rapid growth compared to other states, is seen as leading to dualism. Even so, if the phenomenon is inherently incapable of spreading to wider areas, its characterization as transformation will perhaps need qualification. No innovation, however benevolent, can all at once become universally applicable. The right question to ask is whether it is inherently incapable of spreading. The discovery of life-saving drugs can rightly be regarded as a revolutionary accomplishment, but currently it is perhaps guilty of generating 'dualism' inasmuch as it saves the lives of those who can afford the treatment and mockingly bypasses the millions of poor. If this appears as caricaturing, read what a reputed British scholar, Michael Lipton, alluding to urban bias in Indian planning, has to say, 'What of the big rise in spending on animal husbandry in the Fourth Five Year Plan? Meat and dairy products are likelier consumed by townspeople

than by villagers, and by rich people, than poor' (Lipton, 1969:
108).

The spread of HYV is certainly constrained by environmental
factors. Research hereafter may succeed in evolving varieties congenial
to all major environmental situations but, at present, their application
will necessarily be confined to areas of assured water supply
and even here, if water control is poor, results will be below
par. This is an inherent limitation but not as big as is generally
believed. Here it becomes necessary to distinguish between cultivated
area and cultivating households. The area under irrigation is 20
per cent of the net cultivated area, but as B. Sen, drawing
on the NSS data, has pointed out, '22.7 million farms, consisting
of 45 per cent of the total, have irrigation facilities' (Sen, 1970:
A.34). More importantly, out of these, as many as 10.5 million
farms are in the size group of 1 to 5 acres, and another 3.5
million in the size group of 0 to 1 acre. As much as 63 per
cent of the farm area of the former and 89 per cent of the
latter is irrigated. These two groups constitute 61 per cent of
all farm households with irrigation facilities. As Sen puts it:
'Credit for this goes to the inherited pattern of the distribution
of irrigated acreage among farms.'

There are, no doubt, other limitations to the spread of HYV
technology. For example, doubt has been expressed about the
capacity of small farmers and tenants to benefit from the rather
expensive HYV cultivation. I shall discuss this issue a little
later, but assuming that this class of cultivators is likely to
be inhibited by institutional factors such as non-availability of
credit or insecurity of tenure, one should agree with Raj when
he states: 'This is where the need to make institutional changes
in agriculture comes in' (Raj, 1969: 38).

To sum up, I do contend that what has happened in Sinaloa
and Sonora in Mexico, and is happening in Punjab and West
Pakistan is, in every sense, a transformation of backward agriculture.
Our effort now should be to extend it to as wide an area as
is inherently capable of utilizing it. Even then vast tracts of
agricultural land in India and elsewhere will not come within
the reach of HYV transformation. If, as a result, disparities are
widened, it will at least be as a consequence of a forward
thrust; *and* those who will be pushed ahead will not necessarily
be a privileged few: there would be millions of big as well

as medium and small farmers and even tenants who, but for HYV, would have remained poor for a long time. If this is to be viewed as dualism, it is at least partially benevolent and must be preferred to a more egalitarian stagnation. The new technology has reduced the threshold of non-viability to something like three irrigated acres. This itself is a great contribution to the softening of dualism. Besides, in the Indian context, one of the most rewarding egalitarian devices is cheaper food; and only through the new technology can food prices be reduced without reducing farmers' incomes.

As to the role of institutional reform—land tenure, etc.— at the outset, I should like to avoid a possible misunderstanding. As an ardent believer in egalitarianism, I advocate and support all institutional changes which have the potential for improving the social and economic conditions of the underprivileged. The point I wish to make is: first, the technological barrier had for long rendered the much-needed institutional changes practically sterile and ineffective,[13] and second, where growth has occurred, institutional reform as a factor had a very low pay-off and technology a very high one.[14] Taiwan is the oft-cited illustration of the contribution of land reforms to agricultural growth. But as Raj himself has shown, the growth rate in Taiwan's agriculture under the 'highly oppressive' land tenure system was slightly higher than that achieved in the post-land-reform period: 'If 1952 is regarded as the year ending the postwar reconstruction period, the growth rate for the postwar period then became 3.22 per cent, which is slightly *lower* than the prewar rate of 3.32 per cent of 1906–39[15] (Raj, 1969: 23). But Raj's other quotation regarding the use of police force under Japanese rule to extract higher yields is so telling that I will not press the point. In fact, the contribution of HYV technology is well brought out by comparing growth rates for 1951–55 to 1956–60, 1956–60 to 1961–65, both the periods covered by land reforms, but only the latter, to some extent, by HYV technology. The growth rate in the yield of brown rice in the earlier period was 2.96 per cent as against 3.26 for the latter.[16] Growth rates for other crops— sugarcane, sweet potatoes and peanuts—not touched by HYV technology, however, show a sharp decline in the latter period.

Regarding the relative roles of technology and institutional factors, Barker and Mangahas, using linear probability functions for adoption of HYV on specified farm type in Central Luzon (Philippines), find that

> the effect of owner-operatorship is generally positive, but rather small. From the viewpoint of land reform, it appears that transfer from share tenancy to owner-operatorship *per se* is of lesser importance than such other aspects of the reform programme as irrigation and extension system to the tenant. Farm size was found to have a very small effect, supporting the contention that no minimum farm size is necessary for the new varieties to be economically acceptable (Barker and Mangahas, 1970).

Incidentally, when compared to dry regions, all independent variables showed higher values under favourable environmental factors such as irrigation and water control.

Nearer home, the evidence regarding the inhibitory influence of tenancy and small size of holding—factors wholly or partially amenable to land reforms—is mixed. Some field investigations have revealed that technology has bypassed the small farmer. Chowdhury's meticulous study, however, shows that

> the participation by small farms in the programme is less than that by the large farms, but the *effective participation* of the former in terms of the proportion of the cultivated area put under HYV crops is no less satisfactory than that of the large farm holders (Chowdhury, 1970: A-91).

Chowdhury also finds that the efficiency in cultivation of HYV, as judged by net return per additional rupee spent, does not improve with increase in farm size. In fact in one of the two districts studied (though not in the other), the net return per rupee spent was highest on relatively small farms with 2.51–5.00 acres of land. In terms of total gains, however, it is obvious that larger farms will gain more, unless there is a marked decrease in the efficiency of resource use with increase in size. Mukherjee also found that for wheat in Punjab, all size groups of farmers participated in the HYV programme; though in Tamil Nadu, for paddy, there was a positive relationship between the size of holding and the proportion of participants. Nonetheless, for the lowest size group—below 2.5 acres—the proportion of participants was as high as 70.3 per cent (Mukherjee, 1970: A-15). It should also be noted, as pointed out by B. Sen, that

> without reference to the size group, the statement that inequality
> is bound to increase between the irrigated farmer and the non-
> irrigated farmer is somewhat misleading. Surely, a small farmer
> with 2 or 3 acres of irrigated land has now got the prospect
> of raising income to the level of a farmer with perhaps 10 to
> 15 acres of dry land (Sen, 1970: A-35).

More relevant to the issue of land reforms is the probable
disadvantage of tenancy for the adoption of HYV technology.
Here again, the evidence is not conclusive either way. The enquiry
conducted by the Department of Economics of the University
of Bombay into tenancy reform in Maharashtra and Gujarat indicates
that tenants-cum-cultivators were distinctly better adopters of improved
practices compared to owner-operators. We were, however, unable
to separate the performance of the former group on owned and
leased-in holdings. The findings of the PEO are, however, more
conclusive and striking. Both in Tamil Nadu for paddy and in
Punjab for wheat, judging by the percentage of area under HYV,
the performance of tenant cultivators has been consistently better
than that of owner-cultivators and tenants were able to obtain
even better per acre yields than owners. Mukherjee concludes:
'What little evidence has been produced does show that no significant
difference in the rate of adoption has been observed between
the owners and the tenants and also among the different size
of holding groups' (Mukherjee, 1970: A-22).

The findings of Sen and Mukherjee must not, however, generate
a feeling of complacency regarding the desirability of institutional
changes. One may not share Martin Abel's gloomy forebodings—
perhaps a Paddock contamination that the Green Revolution may
after all turn out to be 'merely a small palace revolt' and that
'India could easily end up as an importer of 10 million tonnes
of cereal grains by 1980' (Abel, 1970: A.5, A.8)—but one should
not lightly brush aside Wolf Ladejinsky's warning that

> the share-croppers are, if anything, worse off now than before
> because as ownership of improved land is prized very highly there
> is mounting determination among owners not to permit the tenants
> to share in the rights of the land they cultivate. Their preference
> is to be rid of them (Ladejinsky, 1969: A.147).

One's ideas about relevant radicalism in land reforms and other spheres may differ from the views of those who have to win elections, but there is undoubtedly a lot of exploitation still in the agrarian structure and now that the Green Revolution has vastly improved the profit potential of Indian agriculture, the economic feasibility of transfer of gains to the disadvantaged groups in agriculture has improved *pari passu*. It has also augmented the temptation for the big farmer to get more securely entrenched and for the wealthy and the influential to enter the field. This must not be allowed to happen at the cost of the vulnerable sections in agriculture. Preventive land reform is, therefore, even more urgent than a positive one. What is needed is selective action rather than a generalized, largely ineffective legislation. Keeping in view the limited and none-too-efficient administrative-cum-organizational resources of the state governments, the former approach would have a better pay-off.

It would be prudent to recognize that even if all the desirable land reforms and other institutional changes are fully implemented, their impact on traditional agriculture would be rather limited. It is difficult to see how the small farms in dry regions, for example, can be made economically viable through land redistribution. Because of low productivity, the ceiling on holdings in these regions cannot be drastically reduced. It is common knowledge that the tenancy problem in these regions is not acute.

It is because of this recognition of the limited potential of institutional changes that academicians known for their progressive views have, for practical reasons, suggested solutions which appear *politically* non-revolutionary. Minhas, for example, has suggested an Integrated Programme of Compulsory Consolidation of Land Holdings and Compulsory Public Works. After examining the impact of an 'imagined but radical' land redistribution policy, he is constrained to observe that, by itself,

> it would not be able to solve the problem of abject poverty in 1970. The size of the cake is small and the claimants are far too many. One may, however, envisage an even more drastic land redistribution policy for solving the problem of rural poverty. Nonetheless, this kind of arithmetic of redistribution needs to be tempered with a sense of realism. Realistic radicalism and political demagogy must be separated from each other (Minhas, 1970).

It may be emphasized that this structural reorganization of the agrarian economy will at best remove 'the inabilities besetting the small farmers and enhance their absorptive capacity for modern inputs and technology'.

Having discussed the subject at such length, I am not going to end with a non-committal statement such as: 'Institutional reform may be regarded as a real condition of development in agriculture, but it is not a sufficient condition in itself'; nor a wisely innocuous one which would say: 'Both improved technology and institutional reform are essential for transformation of traditional agriculture'. Of course they are; that is not the point. My contention, to sum up, is that the chances of effective implementation of institutional reform in the absence of marked technological breakthrough are meagre. One must seriously challenge Dandekar's assertion that 'there is no doubt that the Communist strategy (of reorganization of the agrarian structure) can break through the vicious circle of poverty and reduce an overpopulated agricultural country from the conditions of overpopulation' (Dandekar, 1970: 1233). All that it can achieve is to cover up poverty and exploitation of the peasantry under a facade of institutions which can be called socialistic simply because they are so labelled. The only abiding solution to poverty in poor underdeveloped economies is to improve the profitability of human endeavour and ensure that its gains are evenly distributed.

Even in a stagnant agriculture, one finds a tiny privileged sector which can extract affluence from general poverty. This is economically and ethically indefensible and must be eliminated through agrarian reforms. At the other extreme, there is a highly vulnerable class of socially and economically disadvantaged persons which needs protection, relief, and rehabilitation. The immediate concern of agrarian reform should be with these two extremes. In a stagnant agriculture, by itself, agrarian reform, Communist or Maoist, cannot solve either the problem of poverty or of overpopulation (unemployment). However, once some such innovation as a Miracle Seed shatters the technological barrier to rewarding human endeavour, economic and institutional policies acquire the grave responsibility of ensuring that the gains of technology are not monopolized by the privileged and the powerful.

If an impression has been created that the Green Revolution has solved the basic problems of Indian agriculture, or will soon

enough do so, it needs to be effaced. The Green Revolution
will, at best, solve the food problem, bring higher incomes to
many farmers and through its forward and backward linkages
give a fillip to general economic development. Apart from the
unresolved problem of dry regions, agronomic research has as
yet not evolved corresponding high-yielding varieties for India's
major commercial crops like cotton, oilseeds and jute. Though
the area devoted to these crops is relatively small compared
to foodgrains, a breakthrough in their productivity is crucial to
the stability and growth of the industrial and export sector.

Even during the bleakest period of the two consecutive droughts
of 1966 and 1967, I had not despaired of India's capacity to
feed her growing population—which of course does not mean
that I approve of the high rate of increase in our population.
In fact, when everybody was talking about food self-sufficiency
as the most important problem in Indian agriculture, I had respectfully
drawn attention to the massive additions to the labour force
in agriculture as the most explosive and perhaps the most intractable
problem of Indian agriculture in the seventies. I crave your indulgence
to let me quote a somewhat lengthy passage from an article
published in 1968:

> The consequences of a massive addition of 60 to 87 million persons
> to the agricultural work-force within the short span of 15 to 20
> years can indeed be very serious. The dark spot of the future
> (however) is not food, but the farmer himself. In 1961, 132 million
> workers—or about 70 per cent of the total workforce—were engaged
> in agriculture. Based on the population projections currently in
> use, and assuming that the ratio of agricultural workforce to the
> total as well as the participation rates remain unchanged, the workforce
> in agriculture will grow to 192 to 219 million by 1976 and 1981
> respectively. The assumption of constant ratio of agricultural to
> non-agricultural workforce may appear unreasonable, because with
> rapid economic development, the ratio is generally expected to
> decline. It did not, however, so decline between 1951 and 1961.
> As it is, there is a lot of unemployment in the non-agricultural
> sector of the economy and even on the assumption of constant
> ratio, the non-agricultural sector will have to absorb an additional
> 26 million people in the years between 1961 and 1976 and 38
> million between 1961 and 1985. If the growth of employment
> in this sector over the last 16 years since 1951 is any indication,
> fulfilment of the above requirements of additional employment

will itself be a formidable task (Dantwala, 1968: 241–42).

The Green Revolution has given us breathing space. Its greatest contribution is that it may help to relieve the tension and distraction caused by chronic food shortages, and bring back economists and planners to the more abiding issues of Indian Planning.

NOTES

1. *Indian Economic Journal*, Vol. XIX, No. 2, October–December 1970: 165–92. Text of Presidential Address to 53rd Annual Conference of Indian Economic Association, Gauhati, December 1970.
2. QUESTION: Dr Paddock, do you still predict that there would be pockets of famine throughout the world?
   William Paddock: I would say that very definitely . . . maybe in 1980 . . . I think it is unavoidable ('Is famine Inevitable?' *War on Hunger*, January 1970, United States Agency for International Development, Washington, D.C.).
3. The time span has been divided into ten equally spaced overlapping 'reference decades'. Five of the reference decades span the census years, 1891–1941, and the other five are centered on the census years, 1896–1946.
4. Growth Rates in Agriculture 1949–50 to 1964–65, Economic and Statistical Adviser, Ministry of Food and Agriculture, Government of India, 1966.
5. A review of Lester Brown's book (1970) *Seeds of Change* in *The Times of India* was captioned 'Seeds of Disaster'.
6. Pearson Report is amongst the few neglected authorities which support this view. 'Agriculture was not neglected during the first three plan periods.' See *Partners in Development*, Praeger Paperback, 1969: 288.
7. Apart from a few exceptions, most foreign economists have blamed India's policy preference for low farm product prices and cheap food for the failure of Indian agriculture; see, amongst others, T.W. Schultz, *Economic Crises in World Agriculture*, Ann Arbor: University of Michigan Press, 1964 ('U.S. Malinvestment is Food for the World') and Edward Mason, *Economic Development in India and Pakistan*, Harvard University, Centre for International Affairs, 1966.
8. For a brief but excellent discussion of supply response to price, see John Mellor, *The Economics of Agricultural Development*, Bombay: Vora, 1969: 196-204; and *Indian Journal of Agricultural Economics*, Vol. XXIII, No. 1, January–March 1968.
9. For conclusion of a similar nature in Lipton's discussion of the Intensive Agricultural Area Programme, see the review of his book *Crisis in Indian Planning*, by T.N. Srinivasan in *Journal of Economic Literature*, Vol. VIII, No. 2, June 1970.
10. Dr Norman E. Borlaug, the US agronomist who pioneered research in HYV and was awarded the Nobel Peace Prize has recently observed that C. Subrahmaniam 'was the first high official to recognise the significance of the new wheat strains and willing to take the risk involved in importing 18,000 tonnes of dwarf Mexican varieties. This act initiated the beginning

of a green revolution in Asia'.

11. 'During 1968–69, weather conditions were less favourable than those in the preceding year.' Annual Report of the Ministry of Food and Agriculture, 1969-70. In spite of this, rice production improved by 2.2 million tonnes, when that of other *kharif* cereals declined by 3.8 million tonnes. As a matter of fact, as the Economic Survey of Asia and the Far East for 1968 points out, 'Unprecedented drought conditions affected the regions as a whole after the middle of the 1960s' (p. 128).

12. Raj concedes that 'Taiwan is clearly a more genuine case of transformation of traditional agriculture than Mexico' ('Some Questions Concerning Growth': 22).

13. One of the best-known students on land reform, Doreen Warriner, writes: 'In India, the question of the relation of reform to development is highly problematical, because, although it seems wrong and unwise that so much legislation should have been enacted without being implemented, yet in the present political situation, the ceiling legislation cannot be implemented, and in the present economic situation it is difficult to believe that the tenancy conditions can be improved.' She adds: 'Agrarian reforms really do liberate. . . . But no conclusion emerges that agrarian reform is necessary to development. It is unfortunately customary to prove that reform is a condition of development by using Humpty-Dumpty definitions' (p. 374). 'It can only be regarded as such if all other things needed for growth will (can) not be undertaken without it' (D. Warriner, *Land Reform in Principle and Practice*, London: Clarendon Press, 1969: 374, 379, 382).

14. In several countries the vehicle for raising productivity is the application of modern technology, rather than institutional and organizational changes and public investments in irrigation. The organizational tasks are centred on the supply and intensive application of the modern inputs. Existing institutional patterns are not, apparently, expected to impede the adoption of the new technology and institutional change is, therefore, not accepted as a pre-requisite for its dissemination. This view derives support from the spectacular success of the new methods in raising agricultural productivity on relatively small holdings in Japan, China (Taiwan) and the Republic of Korea. In addition, it rests on the view that 'farmers in the developing countries can be trusted to make the economically best use of given resources would not by itself raise productivity' (United Nations, Economic Survey of Asia and the Far East, 1968: 127).

15. Ho, Yhi-Min, *Agricultural Development in Taiwan, 1903-1960*, Nashville, Tennessee: Vanderbilt University Press, 1966, quoted by Raj in 'Some Questions Concerning Growth'.

16. Raj has observed that 'the rate of growth of output of rice has been much lower than that of these other agricultural commodities, in fact, only about 3 per cent per annum'. Though true for output, the following table for yield (land productivity) may be kept in mind:

Quinquennial average growth rates of yield of specified
crops in Taiwan, 1951–55 to 1961–65

Crop	1951–55 to 1956–60	1956–60 to 1961–65	1951–55 to 1961–65*
Brown rice	2.96	3.26	3.11
Sugarcane	3.33	0.24	1.79
Sweet potatoes	5.24	0.61	3.91
Peanuts	3.45	2.94	4.15

*For 1951–55 to 1961–65, compound annual averages.

Source: Compiled by R.H. Myers from Taiwan Provincial Food Bureau, Joint
Commission on Rural Reconstruction and Department of Agriculture and Forestry. In Shand, R.T. (ed.), *Agricultural Development in Asia*, University of California Press, Berkeley, 1961: 34, 48.

CHAPTER 5

Agricultural policy in India since Independence[1]

This paper deals with agricultural policies adopted in India since Independence. A fair appraisal of a policy can be made only when it is viewed in the context of the nature of conflicts and the choices confronting the policy-makers at a given point of time. For example, during the latter half of the 1960s, when the food situation was critical and the High-Yielding Varieties (HYVs) of cereals became available, the policy-makers in India faced a conflict: adoption of HYVs would augment food production but it was likely to aggravate inter-class and inter-regional disparities. Given the situation, were they right in the decision they took? If not, what were the available alternatives? Such are the issues discussed in this paper.

India's agricultural policy, and perhaps that of most less developed countries (LDCs), has often been criticized for its 'neglect' of agriculture. This criticism acquires legitimacy because of what is generally characterized as the 'failure' of agriculture. The alleged failure may have a reference to either the growth of agricultural production or the promotion of social justice, or both. It is, therefore, necessary to get a more precise idea of the performance of Indian agriculture in both these fields and identify policies related to this performance.

A reference to agriculture's performance in the pre-Independence period (1901–50) may not be considered quite relevant, but legacies do matter and the state of agriculture as inherited from the colonial days—whether it be India or Taiwan—is not quite irrelevant for the assessment of the post-Independence performance. George Blyn's study has revealed that between 1891 and 1947, aggregate grain output in British India increased at an average rate of 0.11 per cent per year. In fact, in the latter half of the period, the growth rate was a negligible 0.03 per cent. Rice output, constituting half of the total output, actually declined over the 56-year period at an average annual rate of 0.09 per cent (Blyn, 1966: 96, 337). During this period population increased at a mercifully low rate of 0.67 per cent per annum in British India. Even so, between 1911 and 1941, per capita availability of foodgrains—taking into account international trade flows—declined by as much as 26 per cent.

This was from where agriculture in independent India took off. Its subsequent performance, though not a shining example of success, is not as dismal as is sometimes depicted. Between 1951 and 1971, foodgrains production increased from 55.0 million tonnes to 108.4 million tonnes or at the annual rate of 2.7 per cent, slightly ahead of the growth rate of population. The growth was however not smooth and there were quite a few years—particularly 1966, 1967, 1973—when the country experienced a severe food crisis. Throughout the period—with the exception of the year 1972—foodgrains had to be imported, the maximum being 10 million tonnes in 1966. After 1971, foodgrains production started declining again, dropped to 97 million tonnes in 1973 and rose to about 104 million tonnes in the next two years. In 1975–76, foodgrains production staged a remarkable recovery and is currently estimated at 118 million tonnes. As the Economic Review for 1974–75 by the Reserve Bank of India observed: 'Notwithstanding the expansion of irrigation since 1951, the degree of vulnerability of the agricultural sector to vagaries of climate does not seem to have diminished significantly' (RBI, 1974–75).

Equally germane to the assessment of agriculture's production performance is the fact that in these two decades (1951–71), India's population has increased by 187 million, and by 1976 another 60 million have been added. It is worth noting that in spite of this tremendous increase, this backward agriculture has been able to provide a per capita availability of foodgrains—with marginal imports—at about 450 grams per day.

The above should not be interpreted as reflecting a sense of complacency about India's agricultural production performance.

Indeed, in years to come, India will have to do much better
than its best performance in the past. According to a 'medium'
projection, by the end of the century, India's population will
be about 1,000 million. Making a few balanced assumptions regarding
the growth of population, the growth rate of national income
and its more equitable distribution, V.M. Rao has estimated that
by the year 2001, India's requirements of foodgrains (assuming
low population growth) would be 2.5 times its consumption in
1964–65; requirements of 'other foods' would be as high as
4.35 times (Rao, V.M., 1975: 34). We can ignore, only at our
peril, the warning sounded by David Hopper. Presumably reflecting
world opinion and employing the 'whom to save, whom to abandon'
life-boat analogy, he has warned: 'India, along with some of
its neighbours in South Asia, is seldom considered a candidate
for salvation' (Hopper, 1976: 191).

Let us revert to the post-Independence period, and briefly
review agricultural policies germane to the performance of agriculture.
We shall confine our review of agricultural policy in India to
a few specific issues which have figured prominently in the
literature on the subject. These are listed below:

1. Inadequacy of plan investment for agricultural development.
2. Price policy and terms of trade.
3. Urban bias.
4. 'Green Revolution' and inegalitarian growth.
5. Land tenure and institutional reforms.

Plan expenditure on agriculture

The 'neglect' of agriculture for which the Indian policy-makers
have often been criticized is generally identified with the failure
to allocate an adequate share of public expenditure to agriculture.
Everyone was happy that agriculture was given pride of place
in India's First Five-Year Plan (1951–56). The share of agriculture
and community development in the public sector outlay[2] in the
First Five-Year Plan was 15.1 per cent, as against 6.3 per cent
for industries and minerals. The Second Five-Year Plan reversed
the ranking by allocating 14.4 per cent to 'industries' and 11.8
per cent to 'agriculture'. Apart from this, the major sin of the
Second Plan was alleged to be its preference for 'rapid industrialization

with particular emphasis on basic and heavy industries'. We shall not discuss here whether for a country of India's size and geo-political situation it would have been prudent to ignore the establishment of basic industries. Apart from that, the accent on rapid industrialization does not *ipso facto* prove neglect of agriculture. The modernization of agriculture is incompatible with retarded industrialization. In any case, the importance attached to a sector should not be judged by its share in the public sector outlay. The absolute quantum of public expenditure on agriculture in the Second Plan was raised to Rs 568 crore from Rs 357 crore in the First Plan. Besides, it may as well be argued that the first plan 'neglected' industrial development, as the planners were not yet ready with a plan of industrial development and allocated to it a meagre share of 6 per cent. Had the First Plan provided for a steel mill or better still a few power generation units and fertilizer factories, the allocation to 'industries' in the First Plan would have been larger and the appearance of reversal of priorities would have been avoided. Besides, industry-agriculture linkages make it inappropriate to talk in terms of 'shares' of sectors in public expenditure. What is relevant is investment for agriculture, rather than investment in agriculture.

Our contention is not that public investment in agricultural development has been adequate. Our submission is that the charge of inadequacy needs more substantial proof. There is no sector of the Indian economy which has not—perhaps justifiably—complained about inadequacy of public investment, be it power, transport, family planning, education, social services, and even coal, cement and steel. Scarcity of investible resources is chronic to all developing countries and no sector of the economy should put the blame for its poor performance on inadequacy of funds. In fact, it should look inward and examine whether it has used the resources made available to it efficiently. This imposes an unpalatable self-scrutiny and needs more rigorous analysis than a populist demand for more funds.

Agricultural prices

One of the most persistent criticisms of agricultural policy in India and other poor countries is that they have been deliberately 'forcing producers' prices down'. In 1964, T.W. Schultz asked:

'Why are so many poor countries (including India) placing a low economic value on their farm outputs?' (Schultz, 1968). Edward Mason wrote that the prices of foodgrains and some other farm outputs were held down by Government action (Mason, 1966: 8). Michael Lipton (1975) asserted that 'farm prices have been systematically kept down since 1960 in India'. He reiterates the charge in his most recent article and quoting S.R. Levis avers that in Pakistan, in the early 1960s producers' prices for foodgrains were forced down by as much as two-thirds of their real value (Lipton, 1975: 702). An exactly opposite view is expressed by Walter Falcon:

> With the new wheat-fertilizer technology and government-guaranteed price in West Pakistan almost double the world market price at official exchange rate, what was extremely profitable. . . . The Government tied up more than $ 75 million in supporting the prices of wheat. These funds delayed, perhaps even precluded, other expenditures that were more productive (Falcon, 1970).

Writing about the same time as Lipton, Keith Griffin complains that 'in many cases the cost of innovation has been heavily subsidized by the Government. The innovating farmers have not only high prices for their products but also low prices for their inputs'. And more specifically, 'At the moment, however, the governments of several countries, e.g., Pakistan and India, are supporting domestic grain prices at levels which exceed world prices by a considerable margin' (Griffin, 1974: 210). Whom should one believe? In any case, it seems that those who allege high prices and those who allege low prices are all agreed that the LDCs are following a wrong price policy.

In India the terms of trade, as judged by (*a*) Relative Prices of Manufacturers and Agricultural Commodities, and (*b*) Relative Prices of Agricultural and Non-Agricultural Commodities, have been, by and large, favourable to agriculture.

A more sophisticated exercise by Thamarajakshi (1968) pertaining to inter-sectoral terms of trade (all agricultural products purchased by non-agriculture: non-agricultural products purchased by agriculture) also clearly indicates favourable terms for agriculture. Thamarajakshi has also calculated the index of income terms of trade (by correcting the indices of net barter terms of trade with the value at constant (1960–61) prices of the actual marketed surplus) of the agricultural sector to the domestic non-agricultural sector for all uses. The index of income terms of trade has risen at the rate of 4.53 per cent per annum between 1951–52 and 1974–75 (see Table 5.1).

Information regarding farmers' terms of trade, i.e., the ratio of prices paid and prices received is fragmentary. However, we find that while the weighted index of paddy input prices increased by 18.2 per cent between 1971–72 and 1973–74, the increase in the wholesale price index of rice was as much as 60 per cent between July 1972 and July 1974. The increase in the price of diesel oil in March 1974 and in the prices of fertilizers in June 1974 would have led to a rise of 9.5 in the input index (Government of India, 1974). However, in 1975, the prices of fertilizers were reduced in two successive instalments. A further substantial reduction was made in March 1976.[3]

The impression that the Government of India has been deliberately keeping the prices of agricultural commodities low is perhaps due to the fact that in some years foodgrains procurement prices fixed by the Government were below the prevailing market prices, though in quite a few years of good harvest, the Government has also prevented foodgrain prices from falling below the same procurement price as was fixed in deficit years. (For all practical purposes, the distinction between procurement price and the minimum support price has been obliterated.) Thus, when both good and bad years are considered together, the accruals to the farmers from levy and non-levy sales would not be generally less than under free market conditions. Further, it should be noted that the Government does not procure the entire marketable surplus of foodgrains. Even in the best of years, foodgrains procurement has not exceeded 8.8 million tonnes or 10 per cent of the net foodgrains production.[4] Till 1964, it did not exceed 2 per cent, and varied between 5 to 8 per cent between 1965 and 1970. For particular crops and regions, the incidence would however be higher.

It is our contention that the rise in the post-levy free market price, consequent upon the withdrawal of a part of stocks from the market through procurement, more than compensates the farmer for the 'loss' suffered by him from selling the levy portion of the marketed surplus to the Government at below the market price. In other words, the weighted average price of levy and

TABLE 5.1

Composite price indices and inter-sectoral terms of trade: 1951–52 to 1974–75

Years (1)	Agricultural products purchased by non-agriculture for intermediate consumption (2)	Agricultural products purchased by non-agriculture for final consumption (3)	All agricultural products purchased by non-agriculture (4)	Non-agricultural products purchased by agriculture for intermediate consumption (5)	Non-agricultural products purchased by agriculture for final consumption (6)	All non-agricultural products purchased by agriculture (7)	Net barter terms of trade of all products Col. (4) over Col. (7) (8)
1951–52	99.13	93.23	95.44	81.65	96.50	94.76	100.72
1955–56	70.92	75.57	73.83	82.86	77.24	77.90	94.78
1960–61	100.00	100.00	100.00	100.00	100.00	100.00	100.00
1965–66	132.42	141.64	138.18	125.42	120.08	120.71	114.47
1970–71	195.34	200.53	198.58	159.89	155.45	155.97	127.32
1971–72	189.40	202.92	197.85	165.85	164.63	164.77	120.08
1972–73	200.72	222.96	214.61	179.99	180.57	180.50	118.90
1973–74	289.61	275.25	280.64	209.21	204.30	204.87	136.98
1974–75	324.86	355.16	343.79	268.25	255.17	256.71	133.92
Compound rate of growth	5.89	5.96	5.94	4.53	4.43	4.45	1.43

Notes:

1. These composite price indices have been prepared by combining the relevant indices of wholesale prices (Government of India Economic Adviser's Index Numbers) of the individual items identified as being purchased from or sold to the non-agricultural sector by the agricultural sector for different uses, and using as weights the estimated value in 1960–61 of the actual purchases or sales as the case may be.

2. Composite indices using the estimated value of the actual purchases or sales in 1968-69 as weights are being separately prepared by me.

Source: See Thamarajakshi (1968) and (1977).

non-levy sales is likely to be higher and certainly not less than the price the farmer would have received in the absence of levy. The magnitude of the difference between the two would depend on

1. the price flexibility coefficient,
2. the proportion of the marketable surplus procured by the Government, and
3. the relative level of the open market prices before the procurement operations commence and the levy price.[5]

It is however contended that because of the zonal restrictions on the inter-state movement of foodgrains on private trade account (wheat and rice), even the non-levy prices in surplus states would be lower than the prices which would have prevailed in the absence of such restrictions. The position would be exactly the reverse in deficit States. The economic balance sheet of such disincentives in surplus states and incentives in deficit states is anybody's guess. To the best of our knowledge there are no empirical studies on the subject. In any case given the imperative need to maintain a system of public distribution to protect the consumers, half of whom live below the poverty line, from excessive price rise, there is no escape from procurement of a portion (say 50 per cent) of marketable surplus at reasonable prices; and for such procurement to succeed, zonal restrictions are unavoidable.

Imports of foodgrains under concessional terms have also been criticized as constituting a disincentive to food production. Referring to PL-480 Agreements, David Hopper in his Coromandel Lecture has stated: 'This mutual desire to move grain halfway round the world had calamitous long-term consequences: it held farm prices down for the Indian cultivator to a level that sapped incentives to produce. . . . The price effect of the import was notable in wheat.' (Hopper, 1976: 183–84). Prices of wheat relative to all foodgrains did decline slightly—by 3 to 8 per cent—in different years from 1961–62 to 1967–68. But this was probably due to the higher growth rate of wheat production. Foodgrain imports were at their peak between 1965 and 1967—averaging about 9 million tonnes on the eve of the Green Revolution. Yet, wheat production increased steadily from 12.3 million tonnes in 1964–65 to 26.4 million tonnes in 1971–72. Judging by the stupendous private investment in wheat cultivation, it is not at all clear that imports of wheat have sapped the wheat growers' incentive.

While considering the question of price policy it is necessary to carefully examine the price effect on

1. production, and
2. income distribution.

While it is true that a change in the relative prices of two substitutable crops is likely to have a favourable effect on the production of the crop in whose favour the price is changed, it will simultaneously have an adverse effect on the production of the competing crop. In other words, the aggregate supply elasticity for the agricultural sector as a whole is considerably lower than that for individual commodities. Thus, in the situation prevailing in India—where almost all agricultural commodities and critical inputs, including land, are in short supply—price is not an appropriate instrument for augmenting agricultural output. Mahar Mangahas and his colleagues also confirm that 'there is little evidence to indicate that price changes are an effective device for influencing aggregate agricultural output' (Mangahas et al., 1966: 702). This is particularly so in the context of traditional technology.[6] As John Mellor (1974) points out, 'Even if increase in production takes place (as a result of higher prices), it would be a movement along the production function, hence at increasing real cost in resources.'

More important is the income distribution effect of the increase in foodgrains prices. Mellor has shown that an increase in foodgrains prices actually reduces the income of small farmers belonging to the lowest three deciles of expenditure classes, as they are net purchasers of foodgrains. (Many Western writers probably do not know that the majority of rural households are net purchasers of food, otherwise they would not have confused consumer bias with urban bias.) Income transfers resulting from increased prices of foodgrains cause the largest declines in the income of low income consumers and the largest increase in the income of high income producers. 'A ten per cent increase in foodgrains prices compels the bottom two deciles to reduce their real expenditure on foodgrain by 5.9 per cent and consumption of milk products by 18 per cent' (Mellor, 1974). Mellor concludes: 'An increase in foodgrains prices has a substantial income effect in reducing consumption of high nutritive value.'

To sum up, the facts are that far from 'forcing down producers' food prices, the policy-makers in India have kept food prices high and displayed a big farmer and anti-urban and anti-poor bias. Those vicariously concerned with the 'wretched on earth' of the LDCs would do well to advise policy-makers against the folly of keeping food prices high. The (big) farmers in India have enough incentives from the negligible agricultural taxation and heavily subsidized critical inputs like irrigation water and electricity for the pumpsets. To the extent that any bias can be deduced from price policy, one can as well discern an anti-industry bias on the part of Indian policy-makers. For several years, the controlled prices of cement and steel were kept so low that the manufacturers were unable to plough back adequate funds for replacement and modernization of their units.

Urban bias

Before commenting on urban bias in India's (and all LDCs') agricultural policy, let us admit that such bias does exist in several fields of Indian policy, particularly in health, education, and organized labour. In regard to agricultural policy, however, the allegation of urban bias seems to be based on misinformation. As regards the alleged deliberate under-pricing of foodgrains we have adduced enough evidence to dispel the impression of urban bias. We shall deal here with only one more misleading example of urban bias, namely, 'encouraging farmers to devote more resources—especially land—to rich men's food'. Specific instances mentioned are shift from millets to rice, maize to wheat and to milk production. Apart from the facts, which we shall presently cite, it may be mentioned that the most potent factor influencing changes in the cropping pattern in recent years has been the availability of cost-reducing technology. In India, the highest increase in agricultural productivity has taken place in wheat and *bajra* (bulrush millet)—the latter being the most important millet. The rate of increase in the production of *bajra* has been markedly and consistently higher than that in rice. So much for the shift from 'millets to rice'. As for maize, the rate of increase in its acreage has

been next only to ˉwheat. True, hybrid *jowar* (sorghum) has not
been a success, and in pulses there is complete stagnation. The
failures in these crops are mainly attributable to the non-availability
of suitable high-yielding varieties. According to our information,
however, neither funds nor scientific efforts have been lacking
for evolving suitable varieties.

Milk no doubt is rich man's food at present, but in areas
where milk production has increased, consumption of milk in
poor households has increased in both rural and urban areas.
In cities like Bombay, perhaps for the first time in recent history,
cheaper milk has become available to the low-income households,
though not yet to the very poor. More importantly, many scholars
and policy-makers consider production of milk, poultry and vegetables
as the most promising source of additional income for the smaller
farmers and the landless (Government of India, 1971). Several
field investigations indicate that about 70 to 75 per cent of
households owning cattle belong to the category of small farmers
and agricultural labourers (Shrivastava, 1970 and Government of
India, 1971). A study by V.S. Vyas and his colleagues (Vyas
et al., 1969) reveals that in Nadiad *taluka* (Kaira district, Gujarat),
the share of income from dairying in total farm income was
as high as 78 per cent in farms below 5 acres. In dry land
agriculture, animal husbandry provides substantial additional
employment to agricultural labour households, particularly to women,
in the form of self-employment (Patel, 1974). In a recent study
of milk production and marketing, it was found that in the 'dairy'
villages, the landless labourers and small farmers accounted for
57 per cent of milk producers, 48 per cent of total milk production,
and more than 50 per cent of the marketed surplus of milk
and milk products. This however did not deprive them of the
requisite home consumption of milk of more than 200 millilitres
per capita per day (Patel et al., 1975).

Milk consumption is not a mere urban luxury; it is an
important source of income and employment to the poor households
in rural India and a valuable source of animal protein in the
near future, if the discernible trend in lowering the cost of production
and distribution of milk is maintained. There would be little
hope for the small farmers if they are restricted to growing
poor man's food. With state-sponsored irrigation, extension and
marketing facilities, they would be encouraged to grow what

is most profitable for labour-incentive small-scale farming. In India cattle are fed with fodder and oilcakes (and seldom with inferior cereals) and the encouragement of milk production does not involve any significant diversion of land capable of yielding more calories (or nutrition) per acre of land.

It may also be pertinent to mention that in Kerala, whereas the per capita availability of rice from internal production has remained almost stationary, the production of tapioca (poor man's potato) has increased from 1.6 million tonnes in 1961–62 to 5.4 million tonnes in 1971–72. An authentic report from Kerala states (Centre for Development Studies, 1977):

> The drop in the availability of cereals (mainly rice) would have produced under-nourishment among the low income families, say, even the middle class families, who could not afford to buy sufficient quantities of rice at the going price. The sharp increase in the output of tapioca has not only averted a deterioration of the situation, but even improved the average level of calorie intake in the State.

It adds: 'It may be presumed that, by and large, the increase in the production of tapioca, has made a greater impact on the diet of the lower income households' (Centre for Development Studies, 1977: 28).

While Lipton criticizes the policy which encourages shifts towards 'inappropriate foods' such as meat and dairy products, Carl Gotsch is unhappy over the fact that 'relative prices skewed in the direction of cereals through Government support mechanisms have discouraged diversification and further expansion of acreage under vegetables, fodder for dairying, pulses, etc.' (Gotsch, 1973). Since cereals require relatively low labour inputs, such policies reduce aggregate demand for labour significantly. As pointed out earlier, a shift towards dairying, within reasonable limits, is likely to promote both nutrition and employment.

Before concluding this section, it should be mentioned that there is a legitimate criticism that the public distribution of foodgrains through rationing and fair price shops is predominantly in urban areas and there is a clear case for extending it to rural areas, particularly to those which are vulnerable to droughts and where poverty is most acute. But this would necessitate a substantial increase in internal procurement—variously estimated at 12 to 25 million tonnes. Statutory rationing of foodgrains in big cities is however essential for preventing the pre-emption of marketed surplus by metropolitan areas with their higher purchasing power and the consequent shortages and high prices in rural areas.

The Green Revolution:
A bimodal development

The two successive severe droughts in 1965–66 and 1966–67 gave rise to international apprehensions about India's capacity to feed her huge and growing population. The harshest critic (Paddock, 1968) recommended the application of the 'triage' formula to countries like India which were considered beyond redemption. Fortunately for the country, at this very time the HYVs of cereals became commercially available. India's policy-makers jumped for it with alacrity. Dr Norman Borlaug complimented the then Minister for Agriculture as 'the first high officer to recognise the significance of the new wheat strains and willing to take the risk involved in importing 18,000 tonnes of dwarf Mexican varieties'. The Pearson Report characterized the speedy adoption of HYV as 'one of the authentic marvels of our time' (Pearson, 1969: 289). Others described the process of agricultural transformation as 'one of the most amazing stories of our time'. While this was the general observation, the economists, who had neither anticipated the Green Revolution nor played any part in its adoption by way of even policy advice, did not take kindly to it. Their reaction varied from skepticism ('Cornucopia or Pandora's Box') to downright condemnation on the ground that it was leading towards the emergence of dualism. Let us accept that technological changes ushered through the application of HYVs

as such have contributed to the widening of the income disparities between
1. different regions,
2. small and large farms, and
3. landowners on the one hand and tenants and agricultural labourers on the other.

But the question is: situated as the country was in the mid-sixties, when its capacity to feed its people was seriously being questioned, and some critics were advocating the application of 'triage' and 'life-boats' formula to food aid, what was the choice before the policy-makers? The highest priority had to be assigned to augmenting food production and the HYVs offered an excellent means of doing so. The possibility of its inegalitarian effects—assuming that these could be clearly perceived at that time—had to be weighed against the obvious inegalitarian effects of food shortages and high prices, under which the poor suffer the most.

Did the adoption of HYV technology increase food production? It is contended that 'the so-called Green Revolution has failed to raise the overall rate of growth of agricultural output in the country above the level achieved in the 15 years prior to 1965' (Rao, C.H.H., 1975). It is also asserted that 'despite technological changes, the growth of agricultural output in India slowed down in the 1960s as compared to the 1950s'. Such statements are, at best, half truths based on selective time spans. Let us accept the suggestion that 'the comparison of output between successive peaks (in production) would give an idea of output growth adjusted for weather'. According to the data provided by the critic himself, the annual percentage difference between the three pairs of pre-Green Revolution peaks (1953–54 to 1958–59, 1958–59 to 1961–62 and 1961–62 to 1964–65) was 1.8, 1.7 and 2.7, respectively. As against this, the two post-Green Revolution pairs (1964–65 to 1967–68 and 1967–68 to 1970–71) gave the annual percentage change of 2.1 and 4.5 or an average of 3.4 (Rao, C.H.H., 1975, Table 1.2: 7).

Let us look at the statistics differently. Before the Green Revolution, the year 1964–65 was the best year for food production. Even so, the annual (linear) rate of growth of foodgrains production during the five-years ending 1964–65 was just 1.8 per cent. The next two years, 1965–66 and 1966–67, were years of disastrous crop failures. Foodgrains production declined from 89 million tonnes in 1964–65 to 72 million in 1965–66. It was only in 1970–71 that foodgrains production revealed the impact of the Green Revolution. Between 1964–65 and 1970–71, foodgrains production registered a growth rate of 3.4 per cent per year (Minhas, 1976: 10). Mellor commenting on the same phenomenon observes:

> The most realistic analysis of the trend (in foodgrain production) is made by comparing years of similar weather, such as 1964–65 and 1970–71. In the six intervening years (after the Green Revolution) foodgrain production increased by 19.1 million tonnes, a compound

annual growth rate of 3.3 per cent. This rate was 18 per cent higher than the growth rate shown by the same measures between the similar crop years 1949–50 to 1960–61. The weather in 1964–65 was slightly better than in 1970–71, lending a slightly downward bias to estimates of growth rates for the intervening years (Mellor, 1976: 48–49).

As mentioned earlier, foodgrains production declined once again in subsequent years, but the lowest figure of this period (1972–73) at 97 million tonnes was substantially higher than the lower figure of 1966 (72 million). The increase in wheat production was more spectacular. Between 1964–65 and 1970–71, wheat production increased by 90 per cent and the yield per hectare by 43 per cent.

Whether such an achievement can be characterized as Green Revolution is a matter of semantics. In an atmosphere of gloom, a solitary hyperbole may be excused if it helps to prop up a sagging morale, unmindful of the economist's raised eyebrow. The one claim which can however be made with some confidence is that the technology associated with HYVs opened up a process of modernization of Indian agriculture and significantly raised its production capacity. This is all the more important since Indian agriculture had nearly exhausted its capacity to achieve increases in production through additional conventional inputs. Even irrigation, the most beneficent input, was constrained because of the absence of fertilizer-responsive high-yielding varieties of seeds.

Hanumantha Rao maintains, 'There are reasons to believe that even without the Green Revolution the growth rate would have been maintained at 2–2.5 per cent per annum.' The reasons he adduces are:

> The growth of population at about 2.2 per cent per annum has been exerting an upward pressure on prices of agricultural commodities. This would have provided incentives to the farmers for expanding output and would have induced the Government to invest in irrigation, fertilizers, etc. (Rao, C.H.H., 1975: 7-8).

Apart from the fact that under static technology, high prices have little impact on aggregate production, it is surprising that one so deeply concerned with poverty of the Indian masses should wish to rely on the high food price path for growth of production instead of welcoming the cost-reducing technology for achieving increased production! Besides, his argument that 'some of these inputs including fertilizers which were known before the onset of the Green Revolution would have been used at a certain rate even in its absence' is equally questionable. As is well-known, application of higher doses of fertilizers to the traditional seeds was unremunerative, since it resulted mainly in vegetative growth and subsequent lodging and did not increase output. Thirdly, there is clear evidence to indicate that the growth in cropped area was slowing down, from 2.1 per cent per annum during the period from 1949–50 to 1960–61 to 0.6 per cent during the period from 1960–61 to 1970–71. Under the circumstances, adoption of the HYVs was the only solution to the food problem of the country.

Many studies of the distribution of gains of technological change are vitiated by the fallacy of single factor analysis. There are at least two components which determine the additional gains of different classes of producers over time:

1. change in production, and
2. change in prices.

There could be a third namely, changes in the shares of different classes of growers in the total area cultivated. The second and the third have nothing to do with the technological change per se. They reflect the effects of (imperfect) market structure or market behaviour of different classes of growers and the land market.

There is substantial evidence indicating that the big farmers obtain much higher prices than the small farmers for their produce either because of their better bargaining power or the capacity to withhold stocks in a situation of rising prices. But even if the same price is obtained by all classes of producers, the gain from the price rise—which was substantial in the post-Green Revolution period and had nothing to do with it—would be much larger for the big farmers because of the higher percentage of their marketable surplus.

Geoffrey Swenson has analyzed the production and price effect in the distribution of benefits in a situation of technological change (Swenson, 1976: 4). Analyzing the sources of change in the total value of paddy production between 1965–66 and 1970–71 for a sample of farm operators in survey villages, by farm size, Swenson found that the small farmers (2.5 to 5.0 acres) and the very large farmers (20 acres+) had gained almost equally (21.7 and 22.3 per cent) from changes in production. The main difference in the gains emanated from price changes. While the value of the production of small farmers increased by only 17.9 per cent due to the price effect, very large farmers gained by as much as 47.6 per cent. Swenson sums up the position by observing: 'Looking at the Gini ratios, it is evident that the change in the distribution of paddy income would have been in the direction of greater equality *with equal paddy price for all operations in 1970-71*' (emphasis added). The fact that there are 'considerable inter-personal variations in the price received' is also corroborated by K. Subbarao (1973). Subbarao found that 'the average price per quintal rises generally with the increase in the quantity offered for sale'. His investigation showed that the price per quintal of paddy, net of marketing expenses (incurred by the farmer), varied from Rs 50.72 to Rs 58.57 for those selling less than 30 quintals and those selling more than 180 quintals.

The contribution of HYV technology should not be judged exclusively in terms of the increase in output which is often distorted by the vagaries of weather. Its impact on the behavioural response of farmers judged by a sharp step-up in investments in irrigation and increased purchase of modern inputs is an equally relevant criterion for judging its contribution. The number of private tubewells increased from 0.1 million in 1965 to 0.47 million in 1971 and the number of pumpsets—diesel and electric—from 0.88 million to 3.24 million during the same period. The net area irrigated by wells (mostly private) which had increased prior to the advent of HYV technology from 6.5 million hectares in 1951–52 to 8.6 million hectares in 1965–66, sharply increased in the next four years to 11.1 million hectares, and its share in the total net irrigated area increased from 32.8 per cent to 36.7 per cent. Similarly, the consumption of chemical fertilizers per cropped acre increased from 4 kg to 16 kg or by 400 per cent. It is estimated that expenditure by agriculture on modern inputs in real terms (1960–61 prices) increased from Rs 297 million to Rs 734 million during the first decade ending 1960–61. In the second decade ending 1970–71, it went up to Rs 4,355 million and has further gone up to Rs 6,181 million in 1972–73. The percentage of expenditure on modern inputs to the total spent on all inputs for agriculture (Thamarajakshi, 1977) has increased sharply from 6.19 to 21, at constant (1960–61) prices.

Reverting to the issue of the inegalitarian effects of the Green Revolution, let us accept that there has been some aggravation of inter-class and inter-regional disparities. In regard to the former, it can be said that such aggravation could have been arrested by appropriate policy measures, especially in view of the fact that the application of high-yielding varieties is technologically neutral to scale and has lowered the technical threshold of non-viability. In a later section, we shall discuss the policy measures adopted to equalize the inter-class gains of the new technology and their impact, if any.

As for the widening of inter-regional disparities, it is obvious that whatever may be the strategy of agricultural development, regions poorly endowed with soil-climate conditions cannot gain in the same proportion as the better endowed regions, and it would be irrational to blame a particular innovation or the policy which promoted it for such a consequence. Such regions would need a different type of innovation and research to improve their productivity and income. It would be a legitimate criticism if it can be shown that efforts in this direction have been inadequate or that sufficient research funds have not been allocated for this purpose—for example, for dry farming. The establishment of the International Crops Institute for the Semi-Arid Tropics (ICRISAT) should correct the imbalance, if any. For the growth of such regions emphasis should however shift from crop cultivation to development of grasslands, animal husbandry and more importantly, provision of non-farm employment opportunities.

A recent study by Sudhin Mukhopadhyay (1976) suggests that a very large proportion of variation in output in 72 wheat growing districts in India is explained by what he calls 'the region effect'.[7] The implication of this finding is that a mere reallocation of known inputs—land, irrigation, fertilizers, tractors, education, and labour—will not be very effective in reducing regional disparities in productivity. Mukhopadhyay contends that 'the bulk of the disparity' is due to the region effects and it seems to originate from 'sources not yet identified and measures the peculiarities of the specific regions that are stable over time' (Mukhopadhyay, 1976: 64).

Public investment in irrigation, including the exploitation of ground water potential, is suggested as having the largest prospect for equalizing opportunities of growth. Hanumantha Rao has pointed out that 'the inter-State disparities in the ultimate irrigation potential' are significantly lower than the actual position in 1969–70 (Rao, 1975: 199). The prospect of equalization will however depend upon the cost and benefit of different irrigation projects.

Land tenure and institutional reforms

Reviewing the changes in the agrarian structure over the past two decades, the discussants at the recent Conference of Agricultural Economists have concluded (Rao, 1976: 21–22):

> The inequality in the distribution of land owned as well as operated in rural India as a whole has shown some decline, particularly during the fifties. . . . However, the decline in equality in the distribution of area operated is less marked than in the case of owned land. . . . Several factors are responsible for the observed changes in the structural distribution of land. Sub-division of land as a result of population growth, increase in the benami holdings with a view to evade ceiling legislation, market sale and purchase of land, land reforms and sheer reporting biases are important in explaining the observed changes. . . . As a result of these changes, the proportion of small and marginal farmers as well as the proportion of area held by them has increased significantly in the recent period [whereas the importance of large farms has declined both in terms of their number as well as area held].

The failure of the reform measures per se to make the agrarian structure more equitable, and thereby more productive, cannot be condoned. The only relieving feature of the agrarian scene is the abolition of the intermediary (*zamindari*) tenures from 170 million acres of land in the early fifties. The landed interests have probably already queered the pitch for further reform measures; yet, since land reforms continue to hold the interest of agricultural economists, it may be worthwhile to state a few facts about land ownership and tenancy which might help to indicate the scope for further action.

According to the 26th Round of the National Sample survey (Government of India, 1976c), out of 100 million households in the country, an estimated 19.6 million do not own any land and 17.2 million neither own nor operate any land. Another 35.6 million households own less than one acre, and about 15 million own more than one acre but less than 2.5 acres (1 hectare). If all these were to be provided with a minimum holding of one hectare each, an additional 58 million hectares of land would be required. At the other end of the spectrum, 1.76 million households own more than 25 acres each (10.13 hectares) with a total ownership of 29 million hectares, a large portion of which is situated in regions characterized by semi-arid climatic conditions.[8] If a ceiling on ownership is placed at 25 acres— irrespective of soil and climatic conditions—about 11 million hectares of surplus land will become available for redistribution. Under the revised and scaled-down ceiling laws to-date, about 2.5 lakh hectares have been declared surplus, of which about 1.6 lakh hectares have been acquired and only 43 thousand hectares distributed (Government of India, 1976b).[9]

This was the position in 1971–72. Since then there has been an addition of approximately 12 to 13 million households, and by 1981, another 13 million would be added. The efflux of time and division of land holdings due to inheritance and perhaps more importantly, large-scale fictitious partitions have blunted the edge of reform measures. Short of wholesale collectivization of land with all its attendant problems—which the countries that have experimented with it have not been able to sort out— redistribution of land can reduce the inequity in land ownership, but cannot eliminate it. Under the circumstances, the best that land redistribution can, and should, do is to provide a house site with some spare land for a cattle shed, poultry or vegetable growing to the weaker section of the rural population. We are not here discussing other measures like progressive land tax, or graded levy on produce, particularly on foodgrains.

Next to land, irrigation is probably the most crucial factor determining production and income from land ownership. The proportion of irrigated land is larger on smaller holdings. But the recent boom in the tapping of underground water is likely to sharply alter the situation. The number of pumpsets and tubewells energized has increased from 21,000 in 1951 to 2,441,000 in 1974. About 46.7 per cent of area irrigated by tubewells is in holdings of 4 hectares and above. Irrigation through tubewells and pumpsets is a costly business, and unless urgent steps are taken to regulate the use of ground water, most of the available resources are likely to be pre-empted by large farmers. For example, in the Kosi region of Bihar, the number of tubewells (masonry and bamboo) increased from a mere 300 in 1965–66 to 23,000 in 1972–73, but more than half the investment in this expansion was made by farmers with holdings of 20 acres and above; the share of farmers holding less than 5 acres was negligible (Clay, 1975: 77–78). Several years back, the Central Government had circulated a Model Bill to the states for the regulation of utilization of ground water, but no firm action has been taken. Will it be unreasonable to suggest that hereafter underground water should be allowed to be tapped and utilized exclusively for the benefit of small farmers?

As for tenancy, out of 130 million hectares under operational holdings, 89.4 per cent is owner-operated and 10.6 per cent is leased in. The magnitude of tenancy thus does not appear to be alarming, but once again there is perhaps under-reporting of tenancy and reduction in tenancy is largely attributed to unlawful evictions of erstwhile tenants.[10] As against this, it also needs to be noted that many large farmers lease in land and many small farmers lease it out. It is therefore difficult to be certain as to who is the exploited and who is the exploiter. Even so, in many states share-cropping and other forms of exploitative tenancy are widely prevalent. Here is an area of land reforms which does not suffer from any physical constraints to hinder land redistribution; it is only the lack of political will which can explain the persistence of exploitative tenancy relationships.

Apart from the economic and social benefits of land reforms, one of their major objectives is to loosen the land-based power structure in rural India. If accomplished, it would remove a major obstacle in the implementation of several programmes undertaken specifically for the benefit of the weaker sections. While it is true that the big landowners provide the base of political leadership, by now the latter has so entrenched itself by dispersing its stakes in diverse areas of influence and patronage that a slight erosion of its land base is not likely to impair its dominance. Besides, a new class of political leadership is emerging which uses its political influence, acquired through the show of appropriate allegiances, to acquire wealth rather than vice versa. Even so, measures to eliminate excessive land ownership, with the excess judged on the basis of the potential income from its land holdings, will certainly have a wholesome effect.

The dominant interests in the rural economy also utilize other agrarian institutions, such as credit, marketing and input supply to strengthen and perpetuate their dominance. Policy instruments have perhaps greater manoeuvrability in this area. Policy measures could be adopted through which these institutions will act as a countervailing force against the growth of inequality.

A number of steps have been taken in this direction. As for their impact, opinions would differ. It can be said that, at best, they have arrested to some extent the deterioration in the condition of the weaker sections. The Reserve Bank has stipulated that a minimum of 20 per cent of the total short-term loans advanced by the primary cooperative societies should be issued to the small/marginally weak farmers. In 1974–75, 28 per cent of the short- and medium-term loans were advanced to farmers with holdings upto 2 hectares. (The area operated by farmers cultivating upto 2 hectares constitutes 24 per cent of the total operated area.) Including loans to tenants and agricultural labourers, the percentage of loans to the weaker sections goes up to 32. The percentage of long-term agricultural credit provided by the land development banks to this category of farmers was 32 (Reserve Bank of India, 1976).

A recent study on financing of small and marginal farmers by cooperative societies in Maharashtra reports:

There is little evidence to suggest that very small and small farmers do not receive their due share in the total short-term credit dispensed through the cooperative credit structure. In fact, they seem to receive more than their due share in comparison with medium and large farmers.[11]

Their handicap is that the extent of their membership of the cooperative societies is much smaller than that of the medium and large owners. Cooperative laws are now being amended to provide automatic universal membership of cooperative societies. Multipurpose Farmers' Service Societies (FSS) have been established to cater mainly to the weaker sections. Two-thirds of the membership of the board of management of the FSS will be reserved for the weaker sections. Similarly Regional Rural Banks are being established to cater exclusively to the needs of small and marginal farmers, landless labour and small artisans in rural areas. State Governments have passed legislation for moratorium, discharge or scaling down of debts incurred by small and marginal farmers, agricultural labourers and rural artisans from private moneylenders. The resulting non-availability of non-institutional credit is sought to be made up by the provision of consumption credit by the (well-managed) cooperative societies and the FSS for purposes like medical expenses, education, marriage ceremonies, funerals, etc. Such loans will be issued against personal security with at least two sureties to borrowers who are not able to offer any tangible assets as collateral. It is estimated that Rs 170 crore would be needed to meet the requirements of consumption loans.

Other measures to help the weaker sections and backward regions include formation of Small Farmers' Development Agency (SFDA), agency for Marginal Farmers and Agricultural Labourers (MFAL), Drought Prone Area Programme (DPAP), Integrated Tribal Development Projects (ITDP) and Employment Guarantee Schemes (EGS). It is beyond the scope of this paper even to attempt to evaluate the achievements of these programmes. Official sources give an impressive array of statistics on the number of beneficiaries under the schemes, and the number of dugwell/tubewells, pumpsets, other minor irrigation works, dairy units, poultry units, etc., provided to the beneficiaries. It may, however, be mentioned that there is a widely shared view that most of the benefits under the scheme have been diverted and appropriated by better-off farmers with political influence. From this a general conclusion is drawn that in the absence of a radical change in property relations and socio-political power structure, such reformist measures as outlined here will make little impact on the conditions of the rural poor and in fact 'tend to be unproductive and as such add to the inflationary pressure in the economy'. The choice is wide open. Change the machine or the mechanic or the proprietor or any combination out of the three.

Summing up

In the preceding sections we have argued that some of the charges against India's agricultural policy such as neglect of agriculture, deliberate under-investment, under-pricing of agricultural commodities and urban bias need a more dispassionate appraisal. We have also contended that the Green Revolution, or more modestly the widespread adoption of HYVs, has helped to step up cereal production, stimulated investment and substantially increased the use of modern inputs. While it is accepted that technological change has led to a widening of the inter-regional and inter-class disparities, the price-restraining effect of higher foodgrains production—more than negatived by monetary inflation—has relieved to some extent the burden of poverty. As against these positive aspects, agricultural policy has not contributed significantly to the removal of rural poverty and unemployment or to making the agrarian structure more egalitarian. Thus, while Indian agriculture since Independence has been able to maintain, by and large, the level of per capita consumption of foodgrains, in spite of the addition of 251 million people over the 25 years since 1951, it has failed to provide land or employment to a large segment of the additional labour force. Only one question may be asked: Was it the sole responsibility of Indian agriculture to provide employment to all and as many people born in rural India, or atone for the failures of population policy or for that matter industrial and monetary policy? Our dissent is mainly with this fragmented view which looks at agricultural policy, isolated from the totality of economic policy.

As pointed out earlier, efforts have been made to help the weaker sections of the rural population through programmes like SFDA, MFAL, DPAP, Employment Guarantee Schemes, and the earmarking of a percentage of cooperative advances to small farmers. Apart from a few exceptions, their overall impact has not been very perceptible. The recent 20-Point Programme enunciated by the Prime Minister gives pride of place to agriculture and especially to the problems of the rural poor. The programme includes items like bringing under irrigation at least 5 million more hectares of land, provision of drinking water especially in drought-prone areas, implementation of (land) ceiling laws and redistribution of surplus land among the landless with redoubled zeal, a vastly expanded programme of providing house sites to the landless in rural areas, abolishing the practice of bonded labour, liquidation of rural indebtedness by stages, enhancement of minimum wages of agricultural labourers wherever necessary. It is too early to judge the performance of the programme.

The failure of agricultural strategy—and its economic policy content—to make any impact on rural poverty and unemployment or equitably distribute the gains from technological change has been variously attributed to socio-political factors such as the lack of political will, the elitist composition of political leadership and bureaucracy—no less than that of its critics—structural inequalities in the ownership of land and other assets, a bias in favour of big farmers, etc. There is a strong element of truth in each of these criticisms. Yet perhaps this is not the whole explanation. It is not as if only the projects meant for the benefit of the weaker sections have been frustrated. Even projects which would have benefitted the affluent farmers have performed poorly. Poor planning and poorer implementation appear almost endemic in developing countries. Are the answers outside the domain of the economists? Is this a sociological phenomenon, or is it associated with some sort of cultural traits or work ethics? We have yet to find an answer. While the economists know enough about stimulating growth, perhaps their knowledge and understanding are not adequate enough to suggest solutions to the problems of poverty and unemployment.

NOTES

1. Revised version of the paper presented to the XVIth International Conference of Agricultural Economists, 26 July–4 August 1976, Nairobi, Kenya. Reprinted from *Indian Journal of Agricultural Economics*, Vol. 31, No. 4, October–December 1976: 31–53.
2. 'Public sector outlay' should be distinguished from 'investment'. The latter excludes 'current outlay' but includes (estimated) private sector investment.
3. 'It has been estimated that farmers would benefit to the extent of Rs 1,050 million as a result of the cut in the prices of fertilizers' (*The Times of India*, 18 March 1976). Since then there have been further reductions in fertilizer prices.
4. Procurement during the 1975–76 season is estimated at 13 million tonnes.
5. Thamarajakshi has estimated the coefficient of flexibility of the price of rice with reference to changes in availability of the grain at 1.10 given other things equal (Thamarajakshi, 1977). Mellor and Dhar estimate price flexibility coefficient for all cereals at 2.0 (Mellor and Dhar, 1976).
6. In spite of the persistently steeper increase in the prices of pulses relative to wheat since 1960–61, production of pulses has declined over the years.
7. 'In a normal year, with the same quantity of measured inputs, the most

productive districts of Punjab produce about five times the average output for the entire sample while the least productive districts produce, with the same level of measured inputs; only about one-third of the sample output' (Mukhopadhyay, 1976: 61).

8. According to the Agricultural Census, 1970–71, there were 2.7 million operational holdings with 10 hectares and above; of them, 1.6 million were wholly unirrigated. The operated area under such large holdings was 50 million hectares, out of which 11.62 million were in Rajasthan, 8.7 million in Madhya Pradesh and 8.5 million in Maharashtra, states known for the preponderance of dry regions (Naidu, 1975).

9. A recent report in *The Times of India* gives a figure of 3.5 million acres as the expected surplus (*The Times of India*, 20 May 1976).

10. There are however a few exceptions. For example, in the coastal region of Western Maharashtra 'tenants became owners of nearly 70 per cent of leased land and on another 10 per cent tenants continued because the landowners were widows, minors or disabled persons' (Government of Maharashtra, 1974).

11. Maharashtra State Cooperative Bank: Report of the Committee (Chairman: Prof. V.M. Dandekar) on Financing Small and Marginal Farmers through Cooperative Credit Structure, Bombay, 1976.

CHAPTER 6

Growth and equity in agriculture[1]

Reviewing the state of the Indian economy, the Seventh Five-Year Plan refers to some of the salient achievements of planned development. There has been a marked decline in the incidence of poverty. Based on the information available from the National Sample Survey, it is estimated that during the period from 1977–78 to 1984–85 the percentage of population below the poverty level declined from 48.1 to 36.9. Agricultural performance has been particularly impressive, specially in foodgrains. (The foodgrains stocks at the end of June 1986 were estimated around 28.6 million tonnes.) The targets set under the Sixth Plan for the coverage of poor families under the Integrated Rural Development Programme (IRDP) and employment generation under the National Rural Employment Programme (NREP) and the Rural Landless Employment Guarantee Programme (RLEGP) were met. During the Sixth Plan, the targets for elementary education enrolment and for the provision of primary and subsidiary health centres were exceeded.

Based on this optimistic picture of performance, the Seventh Plan envisages that 'the percentage of population with a consumption standard below the poverty line is expected to come down from an estimated 36.9 per cent in 1984–85 to 25.8 per cent in 1989–90', and by the end of the century to just 5 per cent. 'In absolute terms, the number of poor persons below the poverty line is expected to fall from 273 million in 1984–85 to 211 million in 1989–90, the bulk of this improvement being in the rural areas.' As for employment,

Over the Seventh Plan, employment potential is expected to increase by 40 million standard `person years' against an increase in labour force of around 39 million persons. The bulk of growth in employment potential is in the agricultural sector, and within the sector, in subsidiary activities other than crop production (Government of India, 1985, Vol. I: 32, 33).

Out of the increase of 40 million standard person years, about 6.9 million person years will come from the crop sector and 11.0 million from the non-crop sector.

Growth of agriculture

The analysis of performance and potential of the agricultural sector made here suggests that the capability of the sector to contribute to the alleviation of poverty and unemployment is perhaps overestimated. Demographic pressure on land resources and environmental degeneration are the two main reasons for this caveat.

Despite wide fluctuations in agricultural production due to frequent natural calamities like droughts and floods, India's agricultural growth since Independence is indeed creditable. The annual rate of increase in agricultural production based on Index Numbers was 2.6 per cent between 1949–50 and 1985–86 (CMIE, 1986). Foodgrains production increased from a three-year moving average of 57.47 million tonnes in 1950–51 to 142.7 million tonnes in 1983–84, at an annual rate of increase of 2.55 per cent. In fact, the annual compound growth rate of major foodgrains has steadily gone up from 2.16 per cent during 1950–51 to 1967–68 to 2.62 per cent during 1967–68 to 1983–84 and to 3.00 per cent during 1973–74 to 1983–84.[2] Such sustained increases in a large country—or for that matter any country—like India are rare.

Demographic pressure on land

But all this achievement pales into insignificance when viewed in per capita terms, which indicate the stress imposed by demographic pressures on the economy. Between 1951 and 1981, India's population has increased from 361 million to 685 million, and by March 1986, is expected to go up to 761 million, more than doubling within 35 years. In another 15 years, by the year 2001, India's population will hit the 1000 million mark. These facts are well known, but their implications for the national economy and particularly for the agricultural sector have not been thoroughly analyzed and explained.

The data on per capita consumption, based on the estimates of net availability of foodgrains, computed as net production, (+) net imports, (-) changes in stocks with the Government provide a dismal picture. Dandekar (1986: A.91) has estimated that the per capita per annum gross consumption of foodgrains has increased from an average of 181.80 kg in 1954–58 to 185.18 kg in 1976–83, an increase of just 1.86 per cent in 30 years. The only relieving feature in this 'development' is the cessation of dependence on imports. Assuming a normal production of 150 million tonnes of foodgrains and population of 751 million in 1985, Dandekar (1986: A.93) has calculated that the net availability (allowing for seed, feed and wastage) of foodgrains from domestic production will amount to 175 kg per capita per annum, or 480 grams per day, with a caloric value of 1632. Taking into account additions to the calories available from vegetable fats and sugar, his estimate shows that the per capita per day supply of calories in 1985 would amount to 2054, against the recommended norm of 2300 calories. Assuming further that the small deficit of 250 calories will be made up by other items of food consumption, it may be said that in 1985, India's population had a diet which, on an average, was adequate in respect of calories. But he makes a pertinent point that 'in view of the known inequality in the distribution of purchasing power in the population, the conclusion is inescapable that at least half the population lives on diet inadequate even in respect of calories'.

Two points are emphasized in this observation. When agricultural performance is measured in per capita terms, i.e., with population as the denominator, much of the shine on it is wiped off. Second, unless inequality in the distribution of purchasing power is reduced, food for all will remain an unfulfilled objective. The question before us is to what extent agricultural development strategy can help to solve these problems? Obviously, the growth rate of production must not only be maintained but improved considerably. This will not be easy, but is certainly not inconceivable. A recent FAO study (1982b) has stated that by the year 2000, assuming that India's massive irrigation development plans materialize, and the contribution of irrigation to production increases from the present level of 56 per cent to 87 per cent, even with a 'low level of inputs', India's lands will have the capacity to support a population of 1298 million, against the assumed population of 1036 million in that year (vide CSE, 1985: 157–58).

Though it is difficult to share this optimism in view of the increasing degradation of India's lands through soil erosion, waterlogging, salinity, etc. and the rapid increase in the proportion of marginal operational holdings, to which reference is made later, let us assume that the overall availability of food will not be a serious problem for India in the years to come. That leaves the question of income distribution and provision of gainful employment for all, and the agricultural sector's responsibility in the matter. Before discussing this issue, let us refer to some other aspects of the country's agricultural performance during the past three decades.

Disparity in agricultural growth

Though the overall performance of our agriculture was satisfactory, there was considerable inter-regional inequality in growth. There is much concern over the fact that the bulk of the increase in foodgrains production has come from a relatively small area, the so-called Green Revolution belt, and consequently, as Dandekar and several other scholars have stated, 'the benefits of the increase in production remained largely confined to the farmers in this area'. The Seventh Plan has also stressed that

> while India's agriculture has taken massive strides during three and a half decades of planning, its growth and development has not been uniform all over the country. The differential pattern and pace of development, particularly the growth of foodgrains production, has led to regional disparities (Government of India, 1985b, Vol. I: 14).

The Plan document also bemoans the fact that less than 15 per cent of the area under foodgrains in the country (mostly the Green Revolution belt) contributed as much as 56 per cent of the increase in foodgrains production in the post-Green Revolution period (Government of India, 1985b, Vol. II: 2).

Several questions arise from these constant references to the accentuation of regional disparities in agricultural development. First, is it correct to say that the benefits of the Green Revolution have remained confined to the farmers in that area? Did not the whole nation benefit from the larger availability of foodgrains and its price-restraining impact? Had the Green Revolution been stifled on ideological grounds of being 'technocratic', the poor in the country would have been the worst sufferers from foodgrains shortages and their high prices. It should also not be forgotten that the entire nation was saved the humiliation of pathetic dependence on 'foreign food'—as one ideologue put it—thanks to the Green Revolution and the farmers who ushered it. Second, is it economically realistic to expect uniform growth of foodgrains production in all regions of this vast country? The agro-climatic environment varies vastly from region to region. Some regions are better suited for foodgrains production than others. It would be perhaps more realistic to expect overall agricultural production to be more uniform inasmuch as regions not suited for utilizing the available foodgrains technology—particularly irrigation—could grow non-foodgrains crops more profitably, or develop their horticulture and plantations, and make up the balance. Would it make sense to push Kerala, for example, into growing foodgrains when its advantage lies in developing its plantations? It would be another matter if the lag in foodgrains production growth in some regions were attributable to the neglect of effort to exploit their full growth potential. Incidentally, information available to us on coefficient of variations in State Domestic Product per hectare of net sown area indicates that the coefficient has, in fact, declined from 41.03 in 1970–71 to 38.43 in 1977–78.[3]

A regionally more balanced growth of foodgrains is certainly desirable but the pursuit of this objective should not be at the cost of pushing up the marginal cost of production of foodgrains. It would be economically more sensible to assist each region to make the optimum use of its development potential, instead of seeking product uniformity in the growth process. Even with the concentration of foodgrains production in the most favourable area, we are growing foodgrains at a cost and a price which millions in the country cannot afford, which no foreign buyer is prepared to pay, and which is therefore accumulating, perhaps rotting, in Government godowns and on open plinths. The Planning

Commission should calculate the cost-benefit consequences of regionally more balanced foodgrains production. The Seventh Plan has cautiously referred to the 'decline in productivity of inputs' (Government of India, 1985b, Vol. II: 2). Is this a consequence of pushing production to less and less fertile lands? There is evidence of decline in fallow rotation and grazing land being converted for crop farming. A recent study of cardamom plantation in Kerala has observed that 'productivity decline in cardamom has been a consequence of the large scale deforestation taking place in the Western Ghats' (CDS, 1986). The Study Report states: 'The policy of the government emphasized provision of cultivable land in the arable forest land of the state to land hungry peasants and landless labourers.' The Report adds: 'In the wake of large scale occupation of Cardamom Hill Reserve, even areas not at all suitable for raising cardamom happened to be encroached upon' and 'lands suitable for cultivation of cardamom have been converted for cultivation of seasonal crops'.

Paradox of growth

Another example of dwarfing of agriculture's performance by demographic pressure, observed by conversion of aggregates into per capita terms, is provided by Dandekar. He has pointed out that 'in spite of the per capita production of almost 200 kgs., the gross per capita consumption does not seem to rise above 185 kgs. per annum' (Dandekar, 1986: A.93). The anomaly is examined by reference to the increase in per capita Net Domestic Product (NDP) and its distribution among different sectors of the population. The share of agriculture in Net Domestic Product has declined from 58.7 in 1950–51 to 37.5 per cent in 1982–83. But the share of the population dependent on agriculture (cultivators and agricultural labourers) has not declined to the same extent. In fact, the decline during the period from 1951 to 1981 was only one percentage point, from 67.5 to 66.5. Due to the combined effect of the decline in agriculture's share in NDP and the near stagnancy of population dependent on agriculture, the *per worker* NDP in agriculture, forestry, fisheries' sector declined from Rs 1,305 in 1970–71 to Rs 1,293 in 1981 (Dandekar, 1986).

Dandekar has thus highlighted once again this paradox of growth in overall agricultural production and the declining per worker NDP in agriculture with well-marshalled statistical data. The task now is to unravel the analytical significance of this phenomenon for public policy.

In this connection, our first contention is that whatever has happened to the per capita production/consumption of food or to the per worker NDP in agriculture is largely attributable to the denominator (population, labour force), rather than to the numerator (agricultural performance). In other words, the failure is due to our inability to check population growth and to sufficiently diversify the rural economy to reduce the pressure of population on agriculture.

Indian planners have consistently underestimated the likely growth in population and overestimated the likely shift of labour force from the agricultural to the non-agricultural sector. As a consequence, agriculture has been burdened with supporting a much larger population and labour force. The First Five-Year Plan, which envisaged that the national income could be doubled by 1971–72 and per capita income doubled by 1977–78, had assumed, *inter alia*, that population would grow at the rate of 1.25 per cent per annum during the entire period to which the projections related. The Second Plan revised this assumption upward but still assumed that the population will grow at the average rate of 1.33 per cent per annum during the decade 1961–70 and at the average rate of 1.4 per cent per annum in the decade 1971–80. As it is, during the decade ending in 1971 the population grew at an average annual rate of 2.20 per cent and at the rate of 2.25 per cent in the decade ending in 1981. 'The Planning Commission had just put finishing touches to its Sixth Five Year Plan (1980–85), when the Registrar General of the Census announced that the country had some 13 million more people than the number estimated by the planners' (CSE, 1985: 157).

As for the distribution of the labour force, the Second Plan had assumed that the total working force will increase by 19 million between 1951 and 1961 and by 23 million between 1961 and 1971, i.e., by 42 million over a period of 20 years or by 33 million during the next three Plan periods. It was stated that

> if the economy develops at the sort of rates indicated in Chapter
> I, it is reckoned that the proportion of labour force engaged in

agricultural occupations 20 years hence [i.e., by 1971] will come down to 60 per cent in place of the present proportion of 70 per cent (Government of India, 1956: 317).

As it is, the percentage of the workforce engaged as cultivators and agricultural labourers was 70.1 in 1971 and 68.4 in 1981. Such serious differences between actual trends and the earlier estimates or assumptions about critical parameters such as population and labour force have imposed a heavy burden on the agricultural sector that is not fully recognized.

Impact of rural labour force on agrarian structure

Let us now see what the unrelenting pressure of the rural labour force has done to the structure of operational holdings. We believe that the most serious problem which India's agricultural economy will face in decades to come will be posed by what may be termed as marginalization of the structure of land ownership/operation. During a span of ten years, 1970–71 to 1980–81, the number of operational holdings has increased by almost 20 million, from 70.49 to 89.39 million. During this period, the area operated increased by just 0.67 million hectares. There can be little doubt that by 1990, the number of operational holdings will reach 100 million and the operated land will remain static, or in all probability decline, as it did between 1976–77 and 1980–81.

Obviously, those 20 million additional operational holdings (during 1971 and 1981) could not have been accommodated on the additional 0.67 million hectares of land. The additional holdings are a result of a severe and continuing process of sub-division into smaller operational holdings. Consequently, the percentage of marginal (below one hectare) holdings has steadily gone up from 50.6 in 1970–71 to 56.5 in 1980–81, and by 1990, their percentage is sure to reach 60.

At this rate, by 2001, the pressure of the rural labour force on India's rural economy will be unbearable. Sundaram has estimated that in that year, with a rural population of 720 million, the rural labour force will be about 342 million, a whopping increase of 100 million in a span of 20 years from 1981 to 2001 (1984: 1482). How many of these 100 million can be accommodated

on the shrinking cultivable land? What sort of land ownership/
operation structure will be needed to ensure both growth and
equality?

It should be admitted that there was considerable scope for
orienting agricultural development strategy more purposefully towards
the alleviation of poverty. This scope was not fully exploited.
While the accentuation of regional inequality in the process of
growth is perhaps unavoidable to a certain extent, the accentuation
of inter-class inequality within a homogeneous region could and
should have been checked directly through reform of the agrarian
structure and institutions. The most recent data from the 37th
Round of the National Sample Survey on Assets and Liabilities
of Households as on 30 June 1981 reveal that in the rural household
sector about 39 per cent of households with total assets of less
than Rs 10,000 each shared only five per cent of the value
of total assets. At the other end, about eight per cent of households
with assets worth more than Rs 1 lakh each accounted for 46
per cent of the value of total assets. Incidentally, inequality
in asset ownership is even more glaring in the urban household
sector, but the academicians have chosen to concentrate almost
exclusively on rural inequality, perhaps because there are no
easy academic solutions to the problem, such as land redistribution,
in the urban sector.

The abolition of *zamindari* and such other intermediary tenures
was indeed a radical reform, despite some loopholes. But beyond
this, the performance of land reforms has been dismal. The land
ceiling legislation was not sincerely implemented. Its wanton evasion
was knowingly ignored. The damage done is irreversible, forcing
this author to take a highly unpopular view that the land ceiling
legislation has now lost much—though not all—of its potential
to make a significant contribution to poverty alleviation. As for
the tenancy legislation, while some states, like Gujarat and Maharashtra,
utilized it to enhance social justice, a large number of other
states have connived at its non-implementation. Share-cropping
and concealed or fraudulent tenancy are still rampant. Given
the political will, there is still considerable scope for deriving
social justice from purposeful enforcement of tenancy laws. The
failure in speedily implementing the less spectacular but nonetheless
crucial land reforms such as updating and correcting land records
and consolidation of holdings indicates disorientation of priorities.

Last but not the least disturbing is the phenomenon of privatization of 'common land' to which some scholars have drawn pointed attention.

Common Property Resources (CPRs) play a significant role in the life of the rural poor. Based on data from over 80 villages in 21 districts in the dry region of seven states, Jodha's study reveals that 'the per year per household income derived from CPRs ranged between Rs 530 and Rs 830 in different states, higher than the income generated by a number of anti-poverty programmes in many areas' (Jodha, 1983). Regrettably, the area under CPRs and their productivity is declining. 'Large scale privatisation of CPRs has taken place mostly during the last three decades. Privatisation of CPRs was done largely to help the poor. However 49 to 86 per cent of CPRs ended up in the hands of the non-poor in different areas.' Kurien has elucidated the deleterious consequences of privatization of common property for the weaker sections.

> Traditional rural society was hierarchical and iniquitous, yet it was also of mutual obligations. But growing privatisation of resources and the commercialisation of economic activity have almost completely marginalised the weaker sections who find increasingly that they have to buy things which they formerly used to receive in the form of traditional claims. . . . Special mention must be made of the manner in which common property resources—grazing lands, waste lands, forests, water resources—are coming to be eroded through the interrelated processes of privatisation and marketisation (Kurien, 1986: 389).

Equity

The degradation of forests and the dwindling of grazing land are also hurting the poor most (CSE, 1985). The point we wish to emphasize is that while anti-poverty programmes are launched by the dozens, social and economic processes which continuously deplete the resources from which the poor derive their income and employment and make their traditional skills redundant are either not noticed or are ignored and effective action to stop such processes is rarely taken. Thus, what the Government gives to the poor through its anti-poverty programmes is taken away, not too unstealthily, by the social process dominated by the rich.

In the context of this scenario, what sort of agricultural development strategy can conceivably help the agricultural sector to contribute more positively to the objective of growth with equity? It is obviously beyond our competence to suggest something quite original in this regard. At best, we can refer to some of the major issues which have sprung up from an earnest debate on alternative strategies.

The Indian planners and policy-makers have been keenly aware of the stupendous problem of growth and reconciling it with equity. The approach to the problem has maintained its facade but not the weightages of its internal composition. It is not necessary to chronicle all the shifts in approach from plan to plan and over the three and a half decades of development planning. Much has been written on it. The Fifth Plan was perhaps more specific on development strategy and initiated what has come to be known as a direct attack on poverty, which however was not restricted to target-oriented special anti-poverty programmes. The Fifth Plan recognized that poverty abolition would entail a massive transfer of resources from the top three deciles to the bottom deciles.

In the Seventh Plan, the emphasis on asset and income redistribution is rather muted. There is hardly any search for new, imaginative and innovative approaches to reduction in assets and income inequalities. Since the poverty levels have come down significantly, according to the Planning Commission, what is now needed, in its view, is a more determined effort to push forward the current anti-poverty programmes and implement them more efficiently. The emphasis now is on science and technology for the solution of the poverty problem. To quote from the Deputy Chairman's Preface to the Seventh Plan: 'Recent experience suggests that by harnessing the forces of modern science and technology, it is possible, as never before, to ensure that chronic poverty need not be the inevitable lot of the majority of humankind' (Government of India, 1985, Vol. I: xiv). This is what is often derisively characterized as a 'technocratic' approach to development.

There is however one reference in the Preface which I must cite and endorse. Along with the reiteration of the need to sustain the tempo of modernization and social development, the Preface observes: 'Simultaneously, we must evolve new structures, new

attitudes, a new moral code, a new work ethic, a sort of cultural
revolution, if you wish, which lays emphasis on dedication and
commitment' (Government of India, 1985, Vol. I: xiv). Somewhat
rhetorical, but the reference to attitudes, moral code, work ethics
are very welcome and opportune. I only wish the contents of
the moral code and new ethic were spelt out in the context
of development strategy whose principal objective is social justice.

The Preface refers to 'the dream of Mahatma Gandhi to
wipe out the tears from the eyes of each and every individual
in our country' (Government of India, 1985, Vol. I: xiv). But
the Mahatma also spoke of Trusteeship, exhorting the capitalists
and the landlords to renounce the rights and privileges of ownership.
At the Round Table Conference he had proclaimed: 'When Independence comes, every title to property would be subjected
to scrutiny, and confiscation ordered where necessary.' The Plans
talk constantly about poverty and its alleviation but scrupulously
avoid even a mention of unmerited affluence. Do the planners
believe that poverty can be eliminated without touching affluence?
Is the ethics which permits poverty to be generated and sustained
different from the ethics which generates affluence?

Structural issues

This brings us to the major critique of the development strategy
pursued during the planning era. Let us first put it in moral
terms before it gets enmeshed in technical jargon. Briefly it
says: equity-oriented policies and programmes pursued within the
cast-iron iniquitous economic structure of ownership of assets
will not only be self-defeating, but may prove counter-productive,
through a 'trickle up'. More simply, a direct attack on poverty
without an equally direct attack on the structure, which has bred
poverty and continues to do so, is an illusion at best, fraud
at worst. The dilemma is of 'A Moral Man in an Immoral
Society' which the philosopher Neibuhr has posed!

A simulation model developed by Sinha et al.[4] (1970) shows
that 'a spill over effect of a net injection of one rupee to
the rural bottom class would result in an overall increase in
income of Rs 1.916 in the rural areas, distributed in Re. 0.213
to the bottom class, Re. 0.520 to the middle class and Rs 1.183
to the top class (apart from an income generation of Re. 0.640

in the urban areas)' (quoted by Kurien, 1986: 382). Another simulation model worked out by Adelman and Robinson (1978: 191), which I had cited in an earlier paper (Dantwala, 1983: 14), leads to a surprising conclusion that

> most anti-poverty policies eventually help the rich and the middle income groups more than they help the poor. This is so even when, as in our experiments, the rich are taxed quite progressively to finance the programmes, the programmes are designed so that their initial impact is quite specific in favouring the lower income groups, and there is no graft, corruption, diversion, or stupidity in their execution. This trickle up effect was evident in a great many different policy experiments and is difficult to avoid. Second, our experience with a wide range of policies indicates that it is much easier to make the income distribution worse than to improve it.

Summing up the findings of some of these studies and his own analysis, Kurien observes:

> What strategies such as target programmes attempt to do is to achieve through administrative interventions some redistributions in favour of those who do not have resource power. The interventionist strategy, therefore, is an attempt to correct the structural consequences without altering the structural characteristics (Kurien, 1986: 390).

What may be called the 'Sinha-Adelman-Kurien' thesis deserves a serious debate. The thesis, to repeat, is that given the structural milieu, policy interventions of the poverty alleviation type benefit the non-poor more than the poor. The essentiality of structural change cannot be questioned. It is, however, necessary to be more specific about the components of the alternate structure compatible with available resources. Second, since the existing power structure will not be interested in bringing about the desired structural change and would, in fact, do its utmost to prevent such change, who will accomplish this task and how? Economists should not evade this question on the ground that it is for the political scientists and activists to provide the answer. Lastly, will the altered structure endure and retain its benevolent character without a supportive change in the value system of the new power base? It will not be realistic to assume that the new economic structure will automatically generate an appropriate value system. We know that the structures have changed but the values needed to support the structure did not is an old structure-superstructure theme. If the change in ethics without the change in structure is futile, so is the change in structure without the change in ethics. Thus we are back to the stimulating structure-superstructure debate.

NOTES

1. First published in *The Economic Times Silver Jubilee Feature, 1961–1986*, 'Indian Economy: The New Phase', 19 December 1986.
2. Courtesy S.D. Sawant, Department of Economics, University of Bombay.
3. Courtesy S.D. Sawant, see also Dholakia (1985).
4. The models in the book are based on Indian empirical data.

CHAPTER 7

Technology, growth and equity in agriculture[1]

Dharm Narain's interest in agricultural prices predated his appointment as Chairman of Agricultural Prices Commission (1965). But it probably was his involvement in the determination of agricultural prices for the Indian Government's price policy that revealed to him the critical relevance of foodgrains prices to the incidence of poverty. It is therefore not surprising that at the first opportunity, which the International Food Policy Research Institute provided, he put his hunches and intuitive insights to rigorous statistical analysis. I, too, had speculated on this relationship and in a freewheeling mood had characterized lowering of food prices as 'instant socialism', transferring, as it does, real income from surplus producers to poor consumers. Thus, apart from mutual affection, this theme of prices and poverty led to our academic affinity.

This paper examines the impact of the new technology associated with high-yield varieties (HYVs) of seeds on agricultural growth and food production. If food prices are to be kept low without becoming unremunerative to producers, a technology that induces higher returns to inputs like irrigation and fertilizers must be used. This is precisely what the HYVs did.

India's agricultural performance since Independence, and particularly since the introduction of HYVs, has been faulted on the following grounds:

1. The growth of agricultural production has been unimpressive. Foodgrain production has barely kept ahead of population

growth, and per capita availability has remained stagnant.
2. Growth has been uneven. Since the technology associated with HYVs has favoured better-endowed regions and large farmers, inter-regional and inter-class disparities have widened.
3. Agricultural development has failed to alleviate rural poverty and unemployment, and both have probably intensified.

This paper examines whether the preoccupation with technology was responsible for the blemishes in agriculture's performance and whether more attention to 'institutional' change would have yielded better results. Or to put it differently, did agricultural development sacrifice equity to growth?

No single sector of the economy can fulfill all development objectives. Other sectors have to play supporting roles. The blame for failure should not be placed on any single sector. For example, a working group headed by Sukhmoy Chakravarty stated that a 2.7 per cent per annum growth rate of agricultural output between 1949–50 and 1973–74 was impressive compared with the secular rate of some developed countries or with the Indian economy's virtual stagnation during the first half of this century (ICSSR, 1980: 5). The net domestic production of foodgrains nearly doubled between 1951 and 1971. But per capita availability from domestic production changed little because of population growth. Had the population growth rate expected in the First Five-Year Plan been achieved, the nutritional level of India's population would have risen.

Similarly, the ICSSR group reported that the proportion of the labour force engaged in agriculture had remained at over 72 per cent of the country's total labour force since the beginning of planning (ICSSR, 1980: 17). While the number of workers in agriculture (including animal husbandry, fishery and forestry) increased by 64 per cent between 1951 and 1971,[2] the cropped area increased by only 26 per cent and per capita crop land dropped from 0.33 hectare to 0.25. The average size of an operational holding declined from 2.30 hectares in 1970–71 to 2.0 hectares 6 years later. A much faster decline in operational holdings is in prospect, since the labour force is likely to increase more than either the net or the gross cropped area. Noting that the number of agricultural-labour households had increased from 15.4 million in 1964–65 to 20.77 million in 1974–75, the ICSSR report stated: 'When this feature is read in conjunction with significant increase in the proportion of small owners and their declining position in per capita land, *one notices an unmistakable trend towards gradual proletarianisation of the agricultural economy*' (ICSSR, 1980: 39; emphasis added).

Agricultural strategy cannot be blamed for this progressive shrinkage in per capita crop land and the growth of landlessness. The slow growth of the non-agricultural sector failed to relieve the population pressure on the land. Historically, the process of development has meant a growing absorption of the labour force from the primary sector by the secondary and tertiary sectors. The Second Five-Year Plan (1956–61) had envisaged that the proportion of the labour force in agriculture would be lowered from 70 per cent at that time to 60 per cent over a 20-year period. This, however, did not happen.

In contrast, in Japan the total number of farm households remained remarkably stable—5.52 million in 1974, 5.49 million in 1939, and 5.51 million in 1908. Thanks to rapid industrialization, the number of permanent agricultural labourers *declined* from 1 million in the mid-Meiji period to 380,000 in 1920 and 165,000 in 1941 (Ishikawa, 1981).

Production

Although the ICSSR working group considered the 2.7 per cent growth rate of agricultural production from 1949–50 to 1973–74 impressive, it also observed that growth was accompanied by increasing instability and a slackening of agricultural income growth since the early sixties.

Studies on the stability of agricultural production and its relation to the new technology show mixed results. Sarma, Roy and George (1979) observed that the coefficient of variation in aggregate foodgrain production decreased from 0.14 in the period from 1949–50 to 1964–65 to 0.08 in the period from 1967–68 to 1976–77, the post-HYVs period. *The Economic Survey, 1981-82* seems to confirm this.[3] However, studies by Mehra (1981) and Hazell (1982) reach a contrary conclusion. Mehra attributes most of the variation to fluctuations in yield. In his foreword to this study (Mehra, 1981, Foreword), John Mellor suggests that 'there may well be a *causal relationship* between the observed instability and rapid application of new food production technologies', since the standard deviation for non-foodgrain crops did not increase. On the other hand, Mehra observed that 'wheat and rice show only a small increase in absolute yield variability' (Mehra, 1981, Summary). These are the crops on which use of the new technology has been widespread. In the Punjab, where the use of tubewells has increased dramatically, the yield variability of all of the six crops examined had remained constant or declined, although HYVs were used extensively.

Hazell's study confirms that the coefficient of variation of total cereal production increased from 4.03 per cent during the period from 1954–55 to 1964–65 to 5.85 per cent during the period from 1967–68 to 1977–78. He found 'enormous variability in production risks between crops and states' (Hazell, 1982: 15). The increase in risk was least for wheat (a 2.1 per cent increase in the coefficient of variation) and highest for *bajra* (225.2 per cent). Among the states, production variability decreased in the Punjab (–30.3 per cent) and Bihar (–21.1 per cent), and changes were marginal in Uttar Pradesh and Madhya Pradesh. All the other states showed increases. For all India the coefficient of variation in total cereal output increased by 45.2 per cent, but the yield increased by only 20.4 per cent.

Hazell rejects Mehra's argument that the new seed-cum-fertilizer technology was responsible for the increased instability in cereal production. According to his findings, only a minor part of the increased variance in total cereal production might be attributed directly to an increase in the variances of the individual crop yields and thereby to the widespread adoption of improved seed-cum-fertilizer technologies since the mid-1960s. Other important sources of increased production have shown more positive correlations between the yield fluctuations of different crops in the same and in different states and an increase in the variability of crop areas sown, which is itself now more positively correlated with yields. These fundamental shifts probably have less to do with the new technologies than with changes in weather patterns, the spatial allocation of cereal crops, and the more widespread development of irrigation.

The evidence for a slackening of the agricultural growth rate since the early sixties is far from conclusive, and various studies have not produced a consensus. However, it is clear that foodgrain production has fluctuated sharply in recent years, rising from 111 million tons in 1976–77 to 126 in 1977–78 to 132 million tons in 1978–79. It then fell disastrously to 110 million tons in 1979–80 but jumped to 130 million tons in 1980–81. Between 1978–79 and 1981–82—both years of good monsoons—foodgrain production increased by no more than 1.2 million tons. Although past performance belies a prophecy of catastrophe, it must not induce complacency, particularly in view of the fact that the nutritional requirements of the vast number of people living below the poverty line have yet to be met. There can be no doubt that agricultural production, particularly of pulses and oilseeds, has to grow much faster over the coming decade if it is to wipe out the nutritional gap and supply the raw materials needed by the industry.

Disparities

The unevenness of agricultural growth is a major problem. The Jawaharlal Nehru University—Perspective Planning Division (JNU-PPD) study (Bhalla and Alagh, 1979) revealed a large difference in yields across the country. Of the 282 districts studied, 69 accounted for 20.5 per cent of cultivated area in 1970–73 but contributed 36.4 per cent of the national output. At the other extreme, 83 accounted for 31.74 per cent of total cultivated area but produced only 15.68 per cent of the total output. During the period from 1962–65 to 1970–73, output grew at a compound annual rate of between 4.5 to 7.5 per cent in 48 districts, by 1.5 to 4.5 per cent in 102 districts, and by 0.0 to 1.5 per cent in 62 districts. The remaining 70 districts had negative growth rates of from –1.5 to –3.0 per cent and covered more than a quarter of the cultivated area.

A noteworthy feature of the period from 1962–65 to 1970–73, however, is a decline in the number of low-productivity districts and in the area covered by them, the number dropping from 106 to 85, and the area from 39.5 per cent to 31.36 per cent.

Certain patterns emerge from the JNU-PPD study. First, areas with high agricultural productivity levels are significantly associated with areas of high rainfall and assured irrigation. The opposite is the case in areas where the productivity is lowest. Similarly, high rates of growth are very positively associated with high productivity levels and/or increased irrigation. Negative rates have been recorded in the central and southern dry parts of India.

The JNU-PPD study has identified 49 districts that had a negative to 1.5 per cent growth rate between 1962–63 and 1970–73 and productivity of less than Rs 700 per hectare at the 1970–73 yield level. A majority of these 49 districts were either drought-prone or preponderantly tribal. While every effort should be made to upgrade their agricultural potential, research should ascertain the comparative cost of alternative development.

Of the approximately 142 million hectares of land cultivated every year, 104 million hectares have a mean rainfall ranging from about 350 mm to 1,400 mm. Most of the region is semi-arid, but substantial area in Rajasthan, Gujarat and between Sholapur in Maharashtra and Anantpur in Andhra Pradesh is arid, with rainfall of 500 mm or less falling in just one or two months. The soils are also unresponsive. It is in this area that research and extension need to be concentrated. Fortunately, the endeavours of the International Crops Research Institute for the Semi-Arid Tropics (ICRISAT) are beginning to yield promising results. According to Swindale (1981), Director General of ICRISAT, 'It is not difficult to believe that the low yields (below 800 kg/ha. in the rainfed region) can be increased by 50 to 100 per cent, with the technologies that exist.' Results from five separate experiments at ICRISAT over a four-year period are highly promising. The use of improved seeds and fertilizers with improved management, not beyond the capability of an average farmer, increased gross returns by Rs 3,086 per hectare. Average added costs amounted to Rs 327, yielding a benefit-cost ratio of 9.4. The use of supplementary water increased profits by an additional Rs 570.00. The technology is bullock-powered and based upon the concept of a small watershed as the basis of the resource management unit. Pilot-scale testing is being done in the fields. ICRISAT has demonstrated that rainfed areas 'can be major contributors to growth, and to *increasing employment and to the rapid reduction of rural poverty*' (Swindale, 1981; emphasis added).

Such technology would necessitate some structural changes, as well as adjustments in farmers' aptitudes. To reap full benefit from the ICRISAT technology, it is necessary to remove field boundaries to permit shaping the land into graded broadbeds and furrows to facilitate cultivation and surface drainage and building a common pond within a small watershed of about 12 hectares. Traditionally, the farmers in this area do not cultivate during the rainy season and take only a *rabi* crop from the residual post-monsoon moisture. ICRISAT technology has demonstrated the feasibility of harvesting two crops, and the farmers will have to learn to cultivate during the *kharif* season.

The HYVs technology favours well-endowed regions, particularly in regard to rainfall and irrigation and the better-off farmers who can bear—through their own resources or borrowing—the higher per-acre cost of cultivation and invest in fixed capital assets. Even in regions like the Punjab, where the yield per acre on small farms matched that on large farms, the larger land base of the latter resulted in inequality in income. Given this fact, the relevant questions to ask are: Did the Indian policy-maker make a mistake in encouraging the adoption of this technology *at the time he did*? What options were available at that time? Would it have been possible to mitigate the adverse effects of this technology? Did the Government of India take adequate measures to do so?

For satisfactory answers, one had to review the situation between 1961 and 1965, when it was decided to adopt the HYVs and associated technology. For four consecutive years, from 1960–61 to 1963–64, foodgrain production remained stagnant at the start and then began to decline. The excellent harvest of 1964–65 revived hopes of resurgence, but the two subsequent droughts dashed them again. The situation was desperate. Per capita availability of foodgrains was diminishing, despite imports of four to six million tons a year. The index of foodgrains prices rose by 30 per cent in five years. Observers abroad questioned the country's ability to feed itself.

In such a situation, the first priority for the Indian policy-maker was to grow more food as quickly as possible. Fortunately, around this time high-yield varieties of seeds became available. No apology is needed for the Government's decision to seize the opportunity offered by the HYVs quickly and sharply to augment food production. The wisdom of that decision was affirmed when two consecutive, unprecedented drought years—1965–66 and 1966–67—resulted in a drop of 17 million tons in foodgrain production. Without the Green Revolution, it would have been impossible to lift the production potential of Indian agriculture.

There was no alternative production strategy available *at that time*. Even awareness of the likelihood that gains from the new technology would not be distributed equally would not have justified a decision to forgo adoption of the new technology, which offered an opportunity to avoid widening food scarcities and the humiliation of accepting the conditions attached to US food aid.

If production and prices of foodgrains are considered in relation to poverty, the equity aspect of the adopted strategy was not as negative as has been made out. This is precisely what Dharm Narain was struggling to establish. Only a quick and substantial increase in foodgrains production or large imports could restrain the upsurge in prices occurring at that time. The production upsurge provided by the HYVs averted the crisis predicted by many.

Bardhan cites eight means by which the new strategy might have counteracted forces, such as high growth of output, that tend to improve the income of small farmers and wage labourers (Bardhan, 1986: 77–78). I have examined some of these forces, relying mostly on empirical data for the Punjab, where the new strategy has been adopted most widely and intensively.

1. *The labour-displacing effect of adoption of machinery induced by the new technology.* The Punjab probably makes the most extensive use of labour-saving machinery, especially tractors and pumpsets. Yet there is clear evidence that labour input has increased phenomenally and that the wage rate in real terms has improved since the adoption of the new strategy. According to a recent study (BISR, 1981: 22), the 'intensity of human labour used per unit of area was about 66 per cent higher in 1976–77 than in 1967–68'. The increase was shared by family members and hired labourers. Another significant development has been the diversification of the Punjab economy. Bardhan refers to the displacement of village artisans (Bardhan, 1986: 77). The Punjab is perhaps the only state in which the share of workers in the secondary and tertiary sectors, which was declining until 1971, has increased, rising from 37.32 per cent in 1971 to 40.85 per cent in 1981. The productivity of these workers is much higher than that of the 'displaced artisans'. The adoption of labour-saving machinery is not

an inevitable concomitant of the new strategy, though in certain situations it may become necessary in order to take full advantage of the new technology. In fact, expenditure on drought cattle is equal to 49 per cent (61 per cent in one region) of the total material cost of marginal farmers in the Punjab (Bhalla and Chadha, 1981).

2. *The increased profitability of self-cultivation by large landlords, leading to the eviction of tenants.* Eviction of tenants is not peculiar to the post-HYVs technology era. Probably a much larger number of tenants were evicted (legally and illegally) in the wake of early land reforms (the zamindari abolition) and other measures. It is alleged that even Operation Barga in West Bengal is inducing eviction. The increased profitability of self-cultivation under the new strategy offered great temptation to resume tenanted land and acquire land on lease from weak landholders. This resulted in a rather curious situation in which small farmers became 'landlords' and large farmers became tenants. However, resumption of land and eviction of tenants does not appear to be universal. According to the Bhalla-Chadha study (1981), in the Punjab and Haryana, the percentage of operated area leased in *declined* from 40 per cent in 1953–54 to 26 per cent in 1971–72, with all size classes sharing in the decline. Furthermore, the percentage of total area owned by large farmers (23 acres and above) declined from 37 per cent in 1953–54 to 23 per cent in 1971–72.

3. *Increasing dependence of small farmers on purchased inputs.* The proposition that increasing dependence on purchased inputs has driven small farmers with limited access to resources and credit out of cultivation and into a crowded agricultural labour market needs to be examined from several angles. First, with the growth of population, small-farm families became marginal farmers, and marginal-farm families became practically landless labourers. To what extent the inability to purchase (modern) inputs drove them into the ranks of landless labourers is a matter of conjecture. In the Punjab, small farms do not seem to have had much difficulty obtaining purchased inputs. Bhalla and Chadha show that differences by size-class in total bio-chemical

inputs per acre are not significant. As a result, for the Punjab as a whole, farm business income per acre does not show any significant size-class differences.

4. *The pre-emption of underground water by large farmers.* I share Bardhan's concern about the pre-emption of underground water by large farmers. More than a decade ago, I suggested socialization of underground water. The Gangetic belt has a large, unexploited underground water potential. Neither the rich nor the not-so-rich are exploiting it. Here is an area ripe for a multi-disciplinary probe.

5. *Poor maintenance of old irrigation channels.* It is somewhat farfetched to suggest, as Bardhan does, that the upsurge in tubewell irrigation, as an offshoot of HYVs technology is responsible for the poor maintenance of old irrigation channels. Neglect of irrigation channels and the resulting waterlogging and salinity of soil is an old story. It is not fair to blame the new technology. As a matter of fact, the dependence of HYVs technology on controlled water input has enhanced awareness of the importance of water management. The HYVs have increased the profitability of all irrigation.

6. *The decline in female participation in the agricultural workforce.* The NSS data do not suggest a significant decline in female participation in the agricultural workforce (Visaria, 1984). In fact, Sheila Bhalla's study (1981) on Haryana reports that 'the number of female labour supplied per household is relatively greater in the three more technologically advanced regions'.

7. *Pressure by the rural rich for higher administered prices of foodgrains.* The rural rich (farmers) have persistently put pressure on policy-makers to raise support and/or purchase prices not only of foodgrains but of all farm commodities. However, not all of the pressure comes from the rural rich. The Communist Party of India (CPM) and other leftist groups also support the agitation by farmers' organizations for higher administered prices. It is a matter of pride that Indian economists associated with the Agricultural Prices Commission did not succumb to the pressure and exercised a restraining influence. At least a part of the credit for this goes to the polite stubbornness of scholars like our dear departed friend Dharm

Narain, who served as the Chairman of the Agricultural Prices
Commission during the period when the pressures from the
farm lobby were gathering force.

To repeat, the question that we are examining is not whether
the proletarianization of Indian agriculture is accelerating—in all
probability it is—but simply whether the new agricultural strategy
is responsible. Every size-class of landholders/operators has felt
the pressure of the increasing population. This would be evident
if studies of the process related to the same set of families
over time. The stock profiles at different points of time do
not fully reveal this position. For example, if the size distribution
in, say, 1953–54 and 1971–72 indicates that the middle peasantry
(with 5 to 25 acres), retained its share in total area, this does
not mean that some families did not retrogress. Rather it means
that some families joined the ranks of 'small' farmers, while
some in the high size-class joined the middle group. The stock
profiles would not fully reveal this process, since they would
show retrogression only at the top and the bottom. The top
class becomes smaller, the bottom becomes larger, and the middle
remains the same, gaining from the top and losing to the bottom.

Land reforms and the agrarian structure

A comprehensive appraisal of the land-reform measures of the
Government of India is beyond the scope of this paper. The
following discussion is limited to the equity aspect of agrarian
development.

With all its limitations, *zamindari* abolition was a bold land-
reform measure. That the Constitution was amended to protect
the legislation from protracted litigation testifies to its genuineness.
Absentee landlordism was abolished on over 173 million acres
of land, though some large landlords retain large chunks of 'self-
cultivated' (or 'sir') land. The tenancy legislation also was a
progressive measure. While it led to resumption of land, resulting
in authorized and unauthorized eviction of subtenants, it also
conferred occupancy rights on the statutory tenants. The ceiling
legislation, though seemingly progressive, was probably never meant
to be implemented, at any rate not by the political leadership
at the state level.

The literature on India's agrarian structure is replete with references to the inequitable concentration of ownership and operational use of land. Some scholars are unable to resist the temptation to draw the Lorenz curve and prove inequity despite the fact that data on size distribution of owned and operated land do not take into account variations in productivity owing to soil and climatic conditions or availability of irrigation. This data deficiency cannot be wholly overcome, but a more rigorous analysis of the available data would reveal that the concentration ratio derived from the Lorenz curve greatly exaggerates the inequity.

The last available sample data on landholdings for 1976–77 at first sight seem to confirm concentration. In that year, 2.44 million large operational holdings (10 hectares and above), or just 3 per cent of the total, occupied 42.82 million hectares, or 26.3 per cent of operated area. At the other extreme, 44.53 million marginal holdings (less than 1 hectare) constituted 54.6 per cent of the total but operated only 17.50 million hectares, or less than 10 per cent of the total (Government of India 1981).

To determine whether such a distribution is inequitable, it is necessary to take into account the soil and climatic conditions under which the large holdings are operated. District information on this is not available, but the All-India Agricultural Census for 1970–71 (Naidu, 1975) provides circumstantial evidence that permits reasonable references.

In 1970–71, 2.6 million holdings, or 4 per cent of the total, were 10 hectares and above and covered 50 million hectares, or 31 per cent of the total. Of them, 1.6 million holdings (58 per cent), covering 22.74 million hectares (46 per cent), were wholly unirrigated. This group held 23 per cent of the wholly unirrigated area. By contrast, holdings of less than 1 hectare constituted 51 per cent of the total but had only 9.5 per cent of the wholly unirrigated land. The average size of holdings in the category of 10 hectares and above was 18.10 hectares, but the irrigated component was only 1.8 hectares. Its share in the net irrigated area was only 17.3 per cent. 52 per cent of the wholly unirrigated land was in Rajasthan (13 per cent), Gujarat (7.7 per cent), Maharashtra (15.4 per cent) and Madhya Pradesh (15.8 per cent).

The All-India Agricultural Census for 1970–71 makes the

following observations. The largest spread of the unirrigated areas is in the western and central areas of the country, characterized by semi-arid conditions. The vast region comprises the states of Rajasthan, Gujarat, Maharashtra and Madhya Pradesh along with the adjoining areas of the southern states of Karnataka and Andhra Pradesh. These states together account for 71 million hectares of unirrigated area, constituting about two-thirds of the country's total unirrigated area (Naidu, 1975: 57). Of the 12.4 million hectares of land available for cultivation but not being cultivated, one-half (6.4 million hectares) are in large holdings (Naidu, 1975: 40).

The above data clearly indicate that much of the land under large holdings is of poor quality or in a poor ecological environment. Though I unequivocally support a ceiling on excessive ownership of land, I would like to destroy the illusion that redistribution of land alone will make a significant contribution to the eradication of poverty in rural areas.

The arithmetic of the land-man ratio compels this conclusion. As mentioned earlier, per capita crop land has been declining as the rate of increase in cropped area has fallen and the workforce in agriculture has increased. Since these trends are likely to continue, obviously it will be impossible to accommodate gainfully the growing workforce on the available crop land either as cultivators or laborers. That viable holdings can be provided to marginal farmers and landless labourers by ceiling legislation that would limit maximum net income from farming to, say, Rs 25,000 per year—equivalent to the remuneration of a junior executive in a nationalized bank or a semi-skilled worker in a factory— is an illusion. At best, ceiling legislation, if rigorously enforced, may make available enough land to provide house sites to the landless.

Granting the inexcusable laxity of state governments in the implementation of land reforms, there is no evidence to support Joshi's view (1982) that giving priority to the production approach has resulted in a lower priority for land reforms. This view implies that food production is less important than reducing poverty. The lower priority of land reforms was evident before the new technology appeared and persisted even after the food crisis. It is unfair to blame this on the new technology. Are we to believe that prolongation of the food crisis would have spurred a more sincere land-reform movement?

Joshi's claim that the increase in production coincided with increases in inequality and poverty is at best a half-truth. In a particular region, the incidence of poverty may go up in spite of a high agricultural production growth rate. Sheila Bhalla has observed that 'the high average incomes of the "prosperous" Region II mask the serious incidence of grave poverty among the landless labour households there'. She hastens to add, however, that 'this must not be taken to imply that in Region II poverty is now worse than it was before the Green Revolution. That is almost certainly not the case' (Bhalla, 1981: 75, 77). It may also be conceded that since the landless poor have no proprietary claim in the increased production, they may not benefit directly from it. But there is no evidence of either reduced absorption of hired labour in agricultural production or reduced real wage under the new technology. The more likely explanation for the increased incidence of poverty is that prosperity led to in-migration from backward regions. If poverty has increased in spite of higher food production, non-agricultural factors, such as inflation, demographic pressure, and failure to diversify the rural economy and reduce the dependence of the growing labour force on farm land, should be held responsible. By increasing production, the new technology lifted many small farmers from subsistence farming. Further gains are possible with a more effective input delivery system (Vyas, 1982) and community action. To reduce my (painful) disagreement with Joshi, I fully endorse his statement that

> development of irrigation and of water management system, small farmer-oriented land reforms with strong support for community rather than private rights in resources structure necessary for modern agriculture, the pursuit of private gains within the limits of community welfare as the guiding motivation—these are the indispensable requirements of dynamic agriculture in labour surplus Asian countries including India (Joshi, 1982).

Equity

India's agricultural price policy has been severely criticized for keeping prices deliberately low, thus providing a disincentive to production. This has been dubbed as urban bias in the mistaken belief that the poor and the net purchasers of food live only in urban areas. The literature on the adequacy of agricultural prices, the effectiveness of higher prices in augmenting production, and the propriety of procurement at support prices or below market prices is abundant. My impression is that few Indian scholars accept the view that policy-makers deliberately keep prices of farm products low. The terms of trade have not been adverse to agriculture except since the oil crisis. Farm prices have rarely, if ever, been fixed in the sense that it was an offense to sell farm products in the open market at whatever prices they could fetch. Throughout the decades of planning, the prices of *manufactured* goods—cement, steel, coal, paper—have been subjected to severe controls, giving rise to a flourishing black market. There has been no black market in agricultural commodities.

My plea is that if you cannot provide employment to the unemployed poor or a fair 'remuneration' to the larger number of 'underemployed', give them food at lower prices, which would give a higher purchasing power to their rupee. And the only way to do this without adversely affecting the incentive to produce is to adopt cost-reducing technology or to subsidize consumption, which the Government of India has been doing on an increasing scale.

To the best of my knowledge, the only alternative to the HYV technology is more rapid expansion of public irrigation. No one would question the critical importance of expanded public irrigation and water conservation. Lack of funds does not appear to be a major constraint on the expansion of irrigation; however, there is evidence that lack of cement, steel, and bricks (coal) has hampered completion of irrigation projects. But in the absence of fertilizer-responsive varieties of seed, the contribution that irrigation can make to the augmentation of production is limited. The spurt in tubewell irrigation resulted largely from the introduction of HYVs technology. Water conservation also is remunerative if appropriate technology with drought and pest-resistant seeds is available, as demonstrated by ICRISAT.

In addition to the redistribution of crop land, land-reform measures that promote equity include social control of ground water, providing tenancy rights if not ownership to sharecroppers, consolidation of fragments, and equal distribution of gains from land improvement and development. These measures greatly strengthen the status of small farmers. The measures previously adopted—

the Small Farmers Development Agency (SFDA), the Integrated Rural Development Programme (IRDP), the National Rural Employment Programme (NREP), Minimum Needs, and so on—are in the right direction but need conceptual refinement and more faithful implementation.

If by equity we mean simply equal access to land, given the pressure of population, nothing short of collective or cooperative ownership of land can provide such access to everyone currently engaged in agriculture, either as small or large owners, tenants, sharecroppers, or landless labourers. But to suggest such a solution would be highly unrealistic. Equity measures probably would be more acceptable politically if more emphasis were placed on more equitable allocation of non-crop land assets and inputs such as irrigation, fertilizers, and for the weaker sections, credit and 'reservation' of further development in sectors allied to the agricultural sector. Further, all policy measures should be directed towards ensuring that the bulk of additional production in agricultural and allied industries is generated by small and marginal farmers. This would mean pre-emption of allocation of public expenditure for agricultural and rural development—whether in irrigation, land reclamation, animal husbandry, forestry, or fisheries—largely in favour of weaker sections of the population (Dantwala, 1979).

While gains from redistribution of crop land assets might be limited, those from the generation of additional assets and income from allied industries would be considerable. But even these might not significantly reduce poverty. Further action would be necessary to diversify the rural economy through generation of non-agricultural employment.

To sum up

A substantial increase in agricultural/food production is a necessary but not sufficient condition for alleviation of poverty. The impact of higher production must be reflected in lower consumer prices. The success of agricultural policies also depends, in large measure, on supporting policies in other sectors of the economy.

The adoption in the mid-sixties of the new technology, despite some adverse side effects, has helped to overcome chronic food shortages. It restrained the rise in food prices which was reducing the purchasing power of the poor. Of no less significance was the restoration of belief in the capacity of Indian agriculture to free its growing population and spare the country the humiliation of continuing dependence on food aid.

Even with labour-intensive, small-farm technology, Indian agriculture will not be able to absorb gainfully the growth in the agricultural labour force—more than 100 million in the last three decades.

The difficult task of diversifying the rural economy through the encouragement of allied industries—forestry, animal husbandry, and so on—and village industries will have to be undertaken.

To ensure that the gains of diversification are not pre-empted, some sort of 'reservation' of development in favour of the weaker sections would be necessary. If the political leadership is reluctant to favour the weaker section, which is quite likely, there is no alternative for the poor but to form a solidarity front and use their numerical strength to claim not only a larger share of existing assets and current income flows but a preponderant share in the additional assets and incomes generated through public expenditure and development programmes.

NOTES

1. First published in John Mellor and G.N. Desai (eds.), *Agricultural Change and Rural Poverty: Variations on a Theme by Dharm Narain*, Oxford University Press, 1986.
2. Planning Commission, in its Draft Five-Year Plan for 1978–83, estimated that the labour force in agriculture would be 213.8 million in 1983 (Government of India, 1978: 98).
3. 'It is noteworthy that fluctuations in paddy production have been higher in areas where new technology has not yet become fully entrenched. This is evident from the region level analysis of the decline in output during the drought years 1972–73, 1976–77 and 1979–80. During these three years, decline in paddy production due to below normal monsoon was the lowest in Haryana and Punjab. The most seriously affected states were the traditional paddy growing areas where the new technology is yet to make a significant mark. In the case of wheat, the production in Punjab and Haryana in fact increased during these years of drought' (Government of India, 1982, 1982b).

CHAPTER 8

Reconciling growth and social justice: Agrarian structure and poverty[1]

Many explanations are offered for the failure of special programmes for the weaker sections—IRDP, NREP, 20-Point Programme, etc.— to make any significant impact on the magnitude of poverty and unemployment. The failure is attributed to the technocratic approach, administrative inefficiency, lack of motivation and urban bias of political leadership and bureaucracy, organizational weakness, non-application of refined management techniques and faulty delivery system. A hesitant approach to the decentralization of planning and decision-making and the consequent absence of people's participation, an *ad hoc* and piecemeal approach, inadequate attention to forward and backward linkages and lack of coordination amongst implementing agencies at the local (district) level are also emphasized as being responsible for poor results. Several case studies have established the validity of one or all of the above explanations.

But a more substantive explanation which has gained wide academic acceptability and respect is the one which attributes the failure to the economic and political power structure which has vested interests in maintaining the status quo. The vested interests may not exhibit open hostility to the programmes, but resort to dubious ways to defeat the purpose, and divert the benefits to themselves. More fundamentally, it is contended that even without resorting to such manipulation, the iniquitous economic structure itself ensures that any development programme, even if it is targeted towards the weaker sections, would automatically bring more benefit to those who have resources than to those who have none:

> . . . since the interventions are into an ongoing structural process,
> their longer term impact, through spill overs and spin offs can
> be to reverse a favourable initial impact. For instance, interventions
> that raise the absolute level of income of some target groups
> initially, but which also add to the resource power of the better
> off sections simultaneously and thus increase the inequalities in
> resource power, may turn out to be self-defeating in the long
> run. Thus an interventionist strategy in favour of small farmers
> that enables them to cross the poverty line in one year is no
> guarantee that they may not be pushed down subsequently through
> loss of assets through the normal operations of the system which
> confer more resource power to the larger farmers in the meanwhile.
> In other words, the developmental processes within our structure
> strengthen the resource position of some, but undermine that of
> others. The structural processes generate both growth and poverty,
> and very seldom are interventionist strategies sufficiently aware
> of these longer term implications or able to combat them effectively
> (Kurien, 1986: 391–92).

If the iniquitous structural milieu is to be accepted as the
principal reason behind the failure of the anti-poverty programmes,
all other explanations such as faulty planning, and bureaucratic
ineptitude, would become irrelevant, or at best marginal. Assuming
that structural change is a prior condition for the success of
each and every programme for the eradication of poverty, a
few further questions will have to be answered.

I think it would be fair to say that what the structuralists
are contending is that structural change is a necessary pre-condition
for the solution of the poverty problem and not that it is a
sufficient condition. In other words, it is not contended that
once the structural change—primarily more equal distribution of
resources/entitlements—takes place, poverty, unemployment and
exploitation would disappear. There is ample historical experience
to show that a just ownership (cooperative or collective) of resources
does not necessarily create a just society or generate just attitudes,
just behaviour and respect for human dignity—goals which the
abolition of poverty seeks to achieve.

The first question is: if an equitable resource structure is
a necessary but not a sufficient condition, what are the other
supplementary or supportive conditions? Without waiting for an

answer from others, let us hazard an answer.

Poverty removal is not purely an economic or a social issue. We desire and struggle to eradicate poverty because we cherish certain values. We believe that it is 'wrong' to tolerate a situation which subjects a vast (or even a small) section of the society to 'sub-human' conditions of living. Words like 'wrong' and 'sub-human' connote a moral principle. This, it would be said, is obvious. Our contention is that it is not so obvious in the structuralist view. The word moral is rarely used in the structuralist argument. It may not be deliberate, but perhaps it is, because, words like morality—call it ethics, if you like—are believed to be an escapist stratagem to sidetrack the basic issue of iniquitous ownership of poverty and all the evils it generates. To come to the point, if structural change is to achieve some basic goals like the elimination of exploitation of man by man, it should be specifically linked to a value system from which it derives its urge. Devoid of its moral content, structural change may end up in a worse form of tyranny than we are witnessing today. Is it the fear of being dubbed un-Marxist or a sanctimonious reformist which inhibits us from introducing a moral dimension in the case for structural change?

The point does not end here. If a moral dimension is relevant to structural change, it is equally relevant to other components of the economic system, the bureaucracy, the management, and the institutions. All these need 'technical' or 'operational' improvements (I cannot find more appropriate words), but the outcome of all these improvements will not be what we desire it to be, unless they too imbibe the moral purpose of change. We have superb scientists, technocrats and managers, but the world is not any the better for it.

Let us come down to a more mundane level. Here the first question is: what precise structural change have we in mind? Mainly, if not solely, a more equal distribution of ownership of land. To put it bluntly, though necessary and highly desirable, the realization of equity through redistribution of land is no longer a viable option for more than one reason. The main reason is not the political infeasibility of the proposition. Though the prevailing political configuration is the major obstacle for redistribution of land ownership, we do not put it up as the main reason for not considering it a live issue. In fact, if the main obstacle were political it would make it very much a live issue.

Our reason for giving land redistribution secondary place is that even a radical redistribution of land will not materially alter the economic and political power structure if the degree of radicalism is determined by a common urban and rural norm. Even if the *exemption* limit—inclusive of the permitted deductions—currently applicable to non-agricultural income and wealth is considered as the maximum (ceiling) permitted income and wealth for the landowner, the amount of 'surplus' land which may become available, will be too meagre for its distribution to significantly reduce the inequality in the ownership of land. If the permitted post-tax non-agricultural income and wealth are accepted as norms for agricultural income and wealth, hardly any surplus will materialize. This line of argument will be questioned on two grounds. First, there is considerable concealed or *benami* land ownership. So is the case with non-agricultural income and wealth, perhaps with a much bigger dimension. Second, land is a very special asset from which a vast portion of the labour force derives its livelihood. As such, norms pertaining to it cannot be the same as those applied to non-agricultural assets. If land is such a special asset, why not advocate its nationalization as has been done for banking and life insurance. We honestly believe that even a semblance of equality in access to land ownership cannot be achieved without its collectivization. But if private ownership is to be permitted, we cannot have a double standard: one for agricultural income/asset and another, vastly generous, for non-agricultural income.

More important, land ownership is no longer the major source of economic and political power which it was in good old days. Count those who wield money power and political power. How many of them are big landlords? The sociology of power is still not clear. On the face of it, it seems that you need a lot of unscrupulousness rather than land to acquire political power and to a slightly less extent, money power. So, if we are concerned with the incubus of the economic and political power structure as a major obstacle to the success of anti-poverty programmes, we should look at least occasionally elsewhere instead of hammering only at iniquitous landownership. The changes over time in the pattern of landownership indicate de-concentration at the top and concentration at the bottom. The swelling (almost doubling in three decades) of the number of marginal farmers and of the ranks of landless labour is thus not related to increasing concentration of landownership at the top. Both the number of large landowner households and the area in their possession have in fact declined sharply. How do we relate the two phenomena—reduction in the magnitude of large land ownership and increasing poverty—in the analysis of the poverty problem?

The facts and the line of argument advanced do not imply a plea for the abandonment of the policy of imposition of a ceiling on individual/family holding. The legislation for imposition of a ceiling has been enacted, made more stringent by stages, and the concept has been socially and politically accepted. As admitted by the Planning Commission in plan documents and appraisals, the enforcement of the legislation has been lax and by and large ineffective. It would be wholly appropriate to expose the loopholes in the legislation, administrative lapses, the evasions, and extract the maximum possible surplus. The point we are making is that the redistribution of such surplus will make an insignificant contribution. This point needs amendment. Even if the meagre surplus land can be utilized to provide house-sites with a small farmyard to the landless, it will reduce their helpless dependence on the landowner and strengthen their capacity for resistance.

A more important point which we wish to emphasize is that land redistribution does not exhaust the range and scope of resource redistribution. There are other resources as important as land, whose 'privatization' has not been as total as in the case of land. One such resource is underground water. This resource is being privatized on an increasing scale, but even now considerable potential is lying untapped. I had pleaded for social control, if not socialization, of this resource some 20 years ago. The Government of India was moving in this direction (regulation of ground water use) and a Model Bill was drafted for the purpose as early as in 1970. But the move has been stalled. Why are our academicians not taking up this cause instead of flogging what, for all practical purposes, seems to be a lifeless issue—land redistribution?

Another resource is the economically degraded 175 million hectares of land. Prem Shankar Jha has suggested that even if

50 million hectares of such land is brought under fuelwood trees, it would not only provide an ecologically safe source of energy generation at a lower per unit cost than that of oil, but also generate '50 million additional full time jobs, or provide 100 extra mandays of work ·per year to 125 million underemployed people in the rural areas' (*The Times of India*, 24 July 1984).

Ways will have to be found to stop privatization of this ecologically degraded land and put it to community use for generating income and employment for the poor. Resources and their productivity are not static. Redistribution need not be thought of only in terms of the existing privatized resources. There are plenty of untapped dormant or low yield resources. It would be easier to stop and, if need be, reverse (socialize) their privatization. The attachment of the owners to such resources is much less than to the land under cultivation, because the yield from them is low and the cost of developing them for higher profitability is beyond their means.

Apart from the scope for redistribution of untapped or dormant resources, there is scope for 'reverse discrimination' in the deployment of development investment and incremental income in favour of the disadvantaged groups. The aim of anti-poverty programmes is the same. But many social scientists are convinced that these programmes are intrinsically incapable of eradicating poverty, not simply because they are being poorly conceived, badly managed, or maybe sabotaged or manipulated by vested interests to appropriate the accruing gains, but for a more fundamental reason. It is argued that

> what strategies such as target group programmes attempt to do is to act through administrative interventions [to enable] some *redistributions* in favour of those who do not have resource power [emphasis in original]. The interventionist strategy, therefore, is an attempt to correct the structural *consequences without altering the structural characteristics* [emphasis added] (Kurien, 1986: 390).

It is difficult to accept the argument. If the 'structural consequences' are *systematically corrected,* and distribution of incremental income is steadily deployed to build up the resource base of the poor, it is reasonable to expect that over a period of time, the 'structural characteristics' will not remain unaffected. It is something like quantity transforming itself into quality. Apart from this, the target group approach does not rule out the attempt to alter structural characteristics. On the contrary, we have suggested elsewhere that the ultimate aim of rural development should be to progressively change the asset structure and make it more egalitarian (Government of India, 1978c, *Report of the Working Group on Block Level Planning*). We differ with the structuralist view—if we understand it correctly—in that we do not accept the proposition that structural change *through* land distribution must precede all other measures for poverty removal, and that if this is not done the latter are doomed to failure.

Our goals are identical: an egalitarian and non-exploitative society which, we agree, cannot be achieved without a fully egalitarian ownership of productive assets and skills. We include skills, because the biggest privilege today, besides political power, is education and specialized knowledge. Those who possess this resource are not excessively shy to privatize it for personal gain and status. But such an egalitarian structure cannot be brought about instantly. We therefore suggest initiating a process of progressive erosion of the prevailing power structure through policy interventions which would start changing the 'consequences' of the structure, and simultaneously chip off the protruding edges of the structure itself, for example, by putting a ceiling on large landholdings.

We also believe that we should not leave the task to the political process. The ultimate objective is to change the social ethos. Capture of power may be a necessary instrument and therefore an intermediate goal. The trouble is that the intermediate goal often becomes the end. Having captured power, we lose interest in the ultimate goal. New vested interests replace old interests. The colour changes, the content remains the same.

It should also be emphasized that land ownership is not a major source of exploitation of the poor, nor the most lucrative source of gain from the development process today. The prime source for amassing wealth is trade and corruption in collusion with those in authority—political or administrative.

Many artisans have exceptional skills and yet are perpetually poor. Their legitimate earnings are laundered by middlemen who supply them raw material and credit and pre-empt the purchase of their products. Why is this phenomenon underplayed and land redistribution excessively emphasized? Is it contended that once you take care of the inequity in land ownership, all such ugly features of the system will disappear? Or the ugly features cannot simply be eliminated without first removing the inequality in land ownership?

I think the analysis of the processes which generate poverty on the one hand and affluence on the other has got stuck in an intellectual rut. It is necessary to pull it out and refine it with a more open-minded debate.

To avoid ambiguity about my stand on 'structural' change I should like to sum up by recording a few specific statements:

1. Elimination of poverty on a durable basis can be achieved only by ensuring that all rural households, especially those currently below the poverty line, have an entitlement to productive assets and skills which provide them gainful employment and adequate earnings to enable them to live above subsistence level.

2. The objective of providing such entitlements to the (poor) rural households can be achieved through

   a. redistribution of existing productive assets,
   b. adopting a deliberate policy augmenting the flow of income stream towards poor households and facilitating acquisition of assets generated by public investments, *and*
   c. plugging the sources of exploitation of the poor households by establishing non-exploitative institutions for providing tenure security, credit, supply of inputs and marketing of output, etc.

   In our view all the three are *equally* important and we should not underrate the contribution which (b) and (c) can make to the removal of poverty. We do not accept the view that (b) and (c) are mere corollaries of (a), and that unless (a) is achieved, gains from (b) and (c) will be illusory.

3. The most valuable asset in the rural economy is land. Its equitable distribution would thus involve transfer of land ownership from large owners to the small and marginal owners and the landless. The land ceiling legislation should therefore be strictly enforced. But a critical assessment of the composition of land ownership and quantum of surplus likely to be derived through enforcement of ceiling legislation suggests that the

surplus will be quite inadequate for the purpose of providing productive assets to all those who need them and insufficient to provide an above-subsistence level of living. This does not mean that the idea of land redistribution should be given up. The policy of imposition of land ceiling has gained a wide measure of acceptability. Its pursuit will serve two equity objectives. It will reduce inequality—in our view marginally—and even the inadequate surplus can be utilized at least to provide house-sites and workplaces to a large number of dependent poor. We, however, do not believe that such redistribution will break the existing power structure. At best, it will weaken it and/or strengthen the resistance of the poor to exploitation. Hence, other avenues which would facilitate removal of poverty or arrest the process of poverty removal need to be explored.

4. The importance of land as an input for agricultural production has diminished and that of other inputs such as irrigation, modern varieties of seed, fertilizers, etc. has correspondingly increased. It would be easier to redirect and augment their availability—through subsidies and physical controls—to the poor landowners.

5. There is an equally large scope for augmenting the income flows towards the poor from a strongly egalitarian—even socialistic—approach to the development of ancillary industries like animal husbandry, forestry, fisheries, etc. The vested interests are yet not firmly established in these fields, though the process has begun. There is an imperative need to reach an academic consensus on the policy in these fields which will benefit the poor and alter the income stream in their favour. Preoccupation with land distribution has resulted in the neglect of these potentially powerful instruments for building a more egalitarian economic structure.

6. Much of the poverty can be traced to an exploitative institutional network—land tenure (sharecropping tenancy), credit, marketing, input supply. It may be admitted that the structure and the institutions are offsprings closely interrelated. But this does not mean that the institutions cannot be reformed without a prior change in the structure. Besides, our experience shows that while the direct attempt to change the structure has been almost ineffective, establishment and strengthening of

countervailing non-exploitative institutions—credit in particular—is having some impact on the bargaining power of the poor, though even in this field a corrective action is halting and half-hearted.

7. Finally, I have been arguing that structural change without a change in social-ethical values will be superficial and short-lived. The form may change but the purpose (equity) for which it was changed may not be achieved, unless the change is supported by—or has the foundation of—internalization of values which the change represents. My plea is to see 'poverty' not simply as an economic issue, but essentially as a moral issue.

NOTE

1. Paper submitted to Asian Seminar on Rural Development: The Indian Experience organized by the Indian Society of Agricultural Economics and the Indian Institute of Management at Ahmedabad in December 1984 and published in M.L. Dantwala, Ranjit Gupta and Keith C. D'Souza (eds.) (1986), *Asian Seminar on Rural Development: The Indian Experience*, Oxford & IBH Publishing Co. Pvt. Ltd., New Delhi.

III
PLANNING FOR RURAL DEVELOPMENT

CHAPTER 9

The two-way planning process: Scope and limitations[1]

In spite of frequent refinements and revisions, the planning strategy in developing countries has failed to achieve its objective of growth with social justice. The heart of the growth problem lies in maximizing the creation of surplus—invest and reinvest it to accelerate production. The accelerated production is identified as growth. The pursuit of this policy did yield a somewhat higher rate of growth (GNP) in comparison with historical standards, but it had hardly any impact on the severity of poverty and unemployment. The disillusionment with the growth theory and per capita GNP as an indicator came rather suddenly and we were advised to 'stand economic theory on its head, since a rising growth rate is no guarantee against worsening poverty'. GNP was dethroned and a direct attack on mass poverty was prescribed as the most appropriate strategy of development. For more than a decade this precept for poverty elimination adorned the blueprints of the Five-Year Plans of several developing countries. Unfortunately, the results have not been very different from those when the GNP symbolized the hallmark of development.

This paper does not deal with the rise and fall of economic theories or their consequences. But it does seem that the repeated disillusionment with the strategies of planning has probably turned the search towards the mechanics of planning. After 'standing economic theory on its head' failed to produce expected results, it is being suggested that what is needed now is to 'stand the planning process on its head'. In other words, we should plan from below, or as a second best strategy decentralize the planning process. The failure of planning to meet the challenge of poverty, inequality and unemployment was attributed to the highly centralized nature of planning. Consequently, the emphasis is shifted to decentralization. Decentralization also has a record of more than a decade. After the initial enthusiasm, the sobering influence of the technical, administrative and political problems associated with decentralized development has rekindled the search for an appropriate methodology of planning.

There is now a better appreciation of the relevance of macro as well as micro planning to meet the challenge of poverty and unemployment. But 'the methodology to mesh in planning from top and planning from below through a two-way linkage in the planning process' is still in a formative stage. The process through which such a methodology can be developed should commence by setting down clearly the roles of the national level and the local level planning in the strategy of development, the imperatives by which these roles are determined, and the rationale as well as the limitations of the two processes. Second, some indication should be given about the nature of obstacles to the 'meshing in' process, whether they are political, technological, administrative or organizational. A tentative attempt is made in this paper to deal with these problems, based almost entirely on the Indian experience. It should however be recognized that several such attempts would be needed before an acceptable blueprint of a two-way planning methodology is developed. At best, our attempt will help to obtain some insights into the problems involved in evolving such a methodology.

We should like to start the discussion at the conceptual level by examining three major issues:

1. The rationale of decentralization,
2. Limitations of decentralization, and
3. Contribution of decentralization to the problem of eradication of poverty.

The central theme which emerges from this discussion is the critical importance of integration of sectoral plans and the difficulty of persuading the vertical command line, viz., the Ministries and Departments at the State headquarters to accept the discipline of planning which would permit the integration of their project at the horizontal (district) level.

Poverty and the planning process

Poverty is a complex phenomenon, a product of a system with interlocked political, economic and social components. As such, poverty cannot be eliminated by merely restructuring the planning process. At best, án appropriate planning system can play a critical supporting role in a comprehensive strategy of eradicating poverty.

It needs to be emphasized that decentralized planning is not a substitute for planning at the national level. The development strategy and the policy frame for poverty eradication have to be evolved at the national level. Laying down a set of priorities, the fiscal and monetary policy, transport, communication, energy, science and technology policies, to name a few, all belong to the sphere of macro planning and each of them has a direct or indirect impact on the poverty problem. For example, Government expenditure is known to affect income distribution. A study of the distribution of benefits of Government expenditure in India reveals that 'at the all-India level, the share of the poor in benefits [in 1975–76] works out to only one-third of that of the non-poor' (Gupta, 1980: 33). Since the share of the poor in the tax burden at 26 per cent is not much smaller than that in benefits from Government expenditure, the author comes to the conclusion that 'for a large majority of the poor the fiscal system turns out to be regressive'.

The macro plan not only sets a limit to the scope of feasible decentralization, it also conditions the effectiveness of decentralized development geared to eradication of poverty. For example, if inflation is not contained, poverty will be aggravated. But this in no way detracts from the necessity of decentralized planning, nor does it diminish its crucial role in the task of removal of poverty and improving income distribution. Assuming that the national plan has formulated appropriate policies for the removal of poverty and inequality, the operative part of the plan has necessarily to be carried out at a fairly decentralized level, a district, a block or a cluster of villages. Decentralization will not be of much avail if national policies for redistributive justice are inadequate or faulty, nor will appropriate policies bear fruit

if a proper mechanism is not evolved to disaggregate the problem
at the dispersed levels where it actually manifests itself.

Policies have to be translated into programmes and these
programmes have to be devised and their implementation organized
in the context of the differing local situations. The rather dismal
performance of the macro plans in regard to their objectives
of eradication of poverty and unemployment and improvement
in income distribution is in no small measure due to the imperfections
of the planning process and weakness of the planning and implementing
machinery at the district and the lower levels.

A clear perception of the problem of poverty and of the
process which generates and sustains it is necessary if planning
is to perform a useful role in its eradication. A comprehensive
discussion of the theme of poverty is beyond the scope of this
paper and the author's competence; yet a few observations which
depart from the usual analysis of the problem may be helpful.

There is no doubt that it is the socio-economic system that
generates poverty, and its inseparable counterpart affluence. But
whichever be the system, it cannot be sustained without the
backing of value judgements which implicitly, if not explicitly,
endorse the outcome of the system. The roots of these value
judgements are deeper than those of the system. Planning, reformist
or revolutionary, which proceeds on the assumption that the two
are irretrievably inter-related, and hence an attack on the prevailing
socio-economic system will automatically destroy values and attitudes
which sustain it, may achieve some outward results but the results
will not be enduring. Of all the Plan objectives, eradication of
poverty involves not merely a structural change but a more basic
change in the value system. Even radically altered structures
and institutions can be manipulated if the values which impact
esteem to affluence and view poverty as misfortune have not
changed.

No less a person than Chairman Mao has conceded that

> a more public ownership of production cannot usher in socialism,
> because such a change by itself does not rid men's minds of
> selfishness, personal concept or the desire to have the better of
> others, nor end workers' alienation arising from division of labour.

To this we may add Joan Robinson's observation: 'Soviet
experience shows that power, privilege, and access to education

can form the basis of class distinctions,' notwithstanding the structural change in the system's economic foundation (Robinson, 1969).

Rationale of decentralization

The merit of decentralized planning derives from its ability to discover dormant resources and skills and its endeavour to activize them. Structural, technological, institutional and organizational obstacles to overall growth as well as its equitable spread can also be better identified when viewed in the proximity of the specific area and the people. More importantly, every area, however small, has its inherited social and cultural ethos which the planner has to understand if he is planning for the people and not merely for the area. A better perception of the situation by itself may not be a sufficient condition for the effective removal of obstacles to growth and equity, but their exposure with empirical backing would certainly help to generate pressures which would become increasingly difficult to resist. There are numerous recorded instances, albeit isolated and not necessarily universally replicable, which show that when opportunities are revealed and technological-organizational inputs are provided, commendable results are achieved through community action. Awareness among the disadvantaged can also lead to clashes and conflicts, but this too should be viewed as a positive factor in the struggle against poverty.

To illustrate the point regarding perception, let us take the case of poverty and unemployment. For the central planner, poverty and unemployment are macro phenomena seen through a highly aggregated array of statistics. Such statistical information is necessary for formulating a national plan but not sufficient for devising programmes for poverty removal. With such technical coefficients as he may have access to, the central planner can estimate employment which would be generated in different sectors by the plan outlay. If the exercise reveals that employment generation through plan outlay is likely to fall short of publicized targets, he may incorporate in the plan a few special labour-intensive projects to narrow the gap, and deliver homilies on appropriate technology, product-mix, factor pricing and so on. But this is as far as he can go.

It is one thing to understand poverty, quite another to understand the poor. The central planner sees poverty in the abstract and

prescribes global solutions. What is however needed is to know
the poor, identify them, understand their social, economic and
cultural disabilities and above all understand the local setting
and its institutions under which poverty is generated and sustained,
before solutions can be conceived, concretized and put into action.
Employment generation and anti-poverty programmes therefore have
to be area and community specific, taking into account the differing
development potential as well as the constraints of each area
and each community. All this can be done with the full cognizance
of its attendant implications only at the local level of planning.
As the saying goes, you cannot tend a flock of sheep from
a camel's back, in the same way you cannot eliminate poverty
from the elevation of a central plan, however thorough and earnest.

Take a concrete case illustrated by a field study in Tamil
Nadu conducted by the Madras Institute of Development Studies.
The researchers

> were continually impressed with the fact that most of the tasks
> sought to be promoted under the DPAP and IRDP could not
> be accomplished, except on the basis of village level decisions
> and village level cooperation. Neighbouring farmers had to agree
> for field channels to be rationally aligned and excavated, and
> thereafter, in the equitable regulation of water. Contour-bunding
> and other soil conservation works, which extended across boundaries
> of private field ownership, could not be taken up without the
> consent and cooperation of all who were involved (Madras Institute
> of Development Studies, 1980).

Another aspect of rural development for which decentralization
would be helpful, indeed essential, is the integration of projects
launched by different ministries and their departments. There is
abundant evidence which establishes that one of the main factors
responsible for the less than optimal performance of rural projects
was the lack of inter-departmental coordination. Planners now
do understand the importance of linkages; nonetheless each ministry
is keen to launch its own project, and even a separate agency
to implement it with a ritualistic exhortation that the project
should be 'dovetailed' with the other ongoing projects. In fact,
what the concerned department really expects is that other agencies
or departments will dovetail their projects with the one it has
launched. This competitive zeal to regard one's own project as

central to rural development to which other projects should cohere inevitably results in sub-optimal performance. A paper, of the Planning Commission on Planning Machinery in the States admits that the integrity of district planning is seriously threatened by the multiplicity of decision-making agencies such as the *panchayati raj* institutions, cooperative and public sector enterprises (there are 22 State Corporations in Maharashtra), SFDA/DPAP/CAD, District Industries Centres, etc.

The point that is missed is that after departmental projects are finalized and commenced, the scope for effective inter-departmental coordination will be severely limited. Integrated development will have meaning only when project proposals of different departments are submitted to a departmentally unaffiliated technical team working under a specially constituted district planning authority. The team, under the guidance of the local planning authority, will scrutinize the departmental projects and mould them into a single development plan consistent with the local, regional and national priorities, and development potential of the area and available financial and material resources. The team would carefully assess the past experience of successes and failures and the factors behind them. This experience may also help persuade the state departments or other district representatives to alter or amend their proposals.

A close scrutiny of forward and backward linkages of the various project proposals may reveal an unsuspected scope for economy in resource use and cost reduction. The attempt would be to get the best return from the total area development plan rather than from each individual project. It is conceivable that the return from the integrated plan may fall short of the sum total of what was unrealistically projected in individual projects. But hopefully, there would be less of the phenomena of half-finished projects, extended gestation periods, and eventual cost escalation as has invariably happened in the past.

It hardly needs to be said that local-level planning does not connote 'doing in the state capitals or at district headquarters the same kind of exercises as are done at the national level'. The entire process of preparing an area plan has to have a distinctive character. Its perception of problems has a human dimension, its assessment of the achievable reflects historical experience, its design displays linkages, its action plan avoids reliance on vested interests and attempts to build up countervailing forces.

One other aspect of decentralization which has not received the attention it deserves is what may be termed decentralization of the talent hierarchy. Talent has a tendency to float to the top, denuding the lower strata of the sustenance needed for growth. Whether it is in the realm of politics, administration or profession, talent gets concentrated at the top. We have seen that area planning is not a job for a parvenu. Besides, it is easier to sit down and formulate a plan, be it for growth or for growth with social justice, than to set it in motion in remote areas and among remote people. People in rural areas, particularly the poor, have a protective suspicion of any outside intervention and it is not easy to make them understand the intent of the plan and elicit their cooperation. Within such an environment, if area planning is to succeed, it will need persons not only with talent but also with tact, patience, perseverance and above all empathy. Moreover, at the district level, the processes of plan formulation and its implementation are closer. Hence, the problem of matching performance with promise is more pressing for the district planner.

It is therefore necessary to equip the District Planning Authority with a multi-disciplinary planning team under the leadership of a person well-versed in the technique and discipline of planning. The main qualification for the membership of the planning team would be professional competence, but since the plan it produces has to have a high degree of acceptability by the implementing agencies, they too should be represented on the planning team. Further, since a substantial portion of plan expenditure is now met through institutional finance, the credit institutions must also be represented on the team.

Limits to decentralization

In a federal State like India, decentralization of planning authority and financial resources has to take place first from the Union to the State Governments and then from the State Governments to the district or the block. The legislative and fiscal jurisdictions of the Central and the State Governments are defined by the Constitution. There is a provision in the Constitution which enables periodical adjustment in the matter of sharing of tax revenues between the Centre and the States through the Finance Commission appointed once in five years. State Governments also receive 'Central Assistance' under the Five-Year Plans and Annual Budgets of the Central Government. While the details of these arrangements are of little interest for our theme, the point is that the States, towards whom the first move in decentralization is to be made, feel—rightly or otherwise—that their planning endeavour is constrained by the paucity of financial resources.

In the context of the decentralization debate, one somewhat curious feature of Indian planning may be noted. A large number of special programmes for the weaker sections—for example, Small Farmers' Development Agency (SFDA), Marginal Farmers and Agricultural Labourers (MFAL) Development Agencies, Drought-Prone Area Programme (DPAP), the Accelerated Rural Water Supply Programme (ARWSP), House Sites for the Landless and Food for Work—were and many of them still are 'Centrally sponsored'.

The device of Centrally Sponsored Schemes (CSS) illustrates sharply the sort of contrary pulls which affect the process of decentralization. While successively a larger share of development outlays has been allotted to the States, the Planning Commission and the Central Ministries have expanded the coverage of the CSS. Thus the expenditure on CSS has increased from Rs 2860 million during the entire Second Five-Year Plan to Rs 8740 million in a single year, 1978–79. We cite at some length the justification for this arrangement as the same has been provided by a former Deputy Chairman of the Planning Commission. 'There are problems of national concern which cannot be left to [the] State because of their inter-State implications like population planning, inter-State power transmission lines, etc.' (Lakdawala, 1979: 8). Apart from this argument which has some validity, it is further stated that

> There are other plan priorities where the States should be interested but because of their *power structure or because of limited vision* or lack of resources, they have to be specially spurred and induced. Many of the interesting experiments in agricultural planning like SFDA, MFAL and CDA, etc., have come through centrally sponsored schemes [emphasis added] (Lakdawala, 1979: 9).

The statement raises some important issues. Is the power structure in the States more reactionary than at the Centre? As for the limited vision, is it suggested that the concern for the poor is more pronounced at the Centre than at the State level? Though *prima facie* such presumptions may appear unwarranted and may be viewed as an affront to the State leadership, if idealistic perceptions are tempered by stark realities as they prevail in many of the Indian States, the Deputy Chairman's view may not be all that objectionable. Besides, there are concrete instances which confirm the apprehensions of the Planning Commission. Some of the Centrally Sponsored Schemes are entirely (100 per cent) financed by the Centre and for others the expenditure is shared usually on a 50:50 basis. When it was explained to the States that assistance under CSS was additional and the unavailed amount would not be available as general Plan assistance, there was pressure from several States to augment the scope of CSS and expenditure on them. The relevant State Departments exercised pressure on their Government and Central Ministries also joined the game with a view to extending their own sectoral empires. On the other hand, 'A study of the use of centrally planned schemes would reveal that these have not been used [implemented] by some States and money allotted to them surrendered, even when there was no sharing involved' [Lakdawala, 1979: 19].

The former Deputy Chairman asks a very pertinent question: 'Which authorities should move first in an attack on backwardness [and let us add poverty] and how far can one push the other?' He does not give a categorical answer, but from his unquestionable intimate knowledge, he laments,

> State plan priorities themselves are different from what their interest requires. Higher educational institutions, large prestigious industries, etc. are preferred to new primary schools, adult education classes, village industries centres, extension work, etc. . . . On a problem like consolidation of holdings and land reforms which in many ways is the essence of agricultural development, some States have lagged behind others (Lakdawala, 1979: 18).

It is a well-known fact that in one State even the recording of land rights was suspended under pressure from the landlords.

At the other end, there are States which consider themselves as more progressive than the Centre and they probably are. They not only question the presumption by the Centre of greater concern for the poor but consider it as a stratagem to obstruct the radical orientation of State leadership and to preserve the balance of power in their (the Central leadership's) favour.

Be that as it may, at what level the power structure reflecting the vested interests is more assertive and pernicious is a question which the social scientists have to investigate. On their findings will depend the extent to which decentralization will be in the interest of the poor. One observation, however, can be made. The manipulative power of vested interests over the State apparatus concerned with planning (for the poor or the rest) and implementation increases as the area becomes smaller. But this is no reason for withholding decentralization because the potential for mobilization of countervailing forces also is greater when issues are more area specific.

The second stage of decentralization is from the States to the district. Here, the pattern of devolution of planning functions and financial resources to the districts varies a great deal. In some States like Maharashtra and Gujarat, a prescribed share— 30 to 40 per cent—of the State's total Plan outlay is allocated for district level schemes though a large part of it (80 per cent in Gujarat) is set aside for 'normal schemes to be proposed [at the State level] in the light of priorities and guidelines given by the State'.

The composition of the district planning authority also varies considerably from State to State. In Maharashtra, for example, the District Planning and Development Council has as its Chairman a 'Designated Minister' in the State Government. Another Minister and the Divisional Commissioner serve as Vice Chairmen. In Gujarat, on the other hand, the District Collector acts as the Chairman and the District *Panchayat* President as the Vice Chairman. In West Bengal, the *Zilla Parishad* (the District *Panchayat*) is put in charge of planning but more so for implementation of the district projects. This brief information may be of some relevance in judging the nature and extent of the decentralization process prevalent in the States.

Local planning has to operate within the scope defined for it from above. Even so, the local planning authority need not view itself as a passive recipient of projects and programmes handed down to it by the State or Central Government. If it takes such a view or the planning authorities at higher levels so restrict its operational role, the contribution of local-level planning by way of a more perceptive planning and more purposeful implementation would be at best marginal. Precisely how much autonomy should be given to the local planning authority, in which fields and with how much financial resources is an issue which would require an elaborate discussion. One point may however be stressed. The local planning authority should be given maximum latitude in regard to the development and welfare programmes concerning the target group which would obviously consist of the weaker sections of the population. This is necessary because it should be laid down that the performance of the local planning authority and implementing agencies will be judged primarily by the extent to which they succeed in augmenting and strengthening the skill and the asset base and hence the productivity and income of the weaker sections of the population within its jurisdiction.

Planning from below

'Planning from below' as a logical extension of the principle of decentralization has considerable ideological appeal. It is however necessary to view it in a proper perspective and recognize its limitations. Presumably, planning from below would mean that the planning process should begin at the level of the village or a cluster of villages. Such village plans will be assembled and suitably dovetailed at the *taluka* or block level and would become block plans and through a similar process during upward journey would assume the status of the district and ultimately the State plan. Such a plan, it is contended, will reflect peoples' aspirations and felt needs as distinct from the technocrat's and bureaucrat's perception of the content and direction of development.

Though the idea has an idealistic appeal, it has several flaws which cannot be ignored. All the problems of an area— a village, a block or a district—even such obvious ones as poverty, ill-health, etc., do not necessarily originate in the concerned area inasmuch as their causes lie outside the area and therefore their solutions have to be found outside the area. Drought-prone areas, waterlogging or soil depletion are instances in point. River valley projects or soil conservation schemes have to be planned on a watershed basis which may transcend more than one area. Power generation and the transport system too have to be planned on a larger canvas. No doubt, all such projects have an area content even at the planning stage but more in the process of implementation. As noted earlier, consultation with local authorities and the local people and their informed judgement must find a place in trans-area planning.

The proposition that the plan should reflect people's aspirations and felt needs assumes a harmonious society. In an unequal society, more often than not, a planner will be confronted with conflicting aspirations; the deprivations of one section may be a consequence of the privileges enjoyed by another section. Unless it is specified that he should consider removal of poverty as the supreme felt need and aspiration, a question will arise as to whose aspirations and felt needs should the planner endeavour to fulfil.

In spite of such a dilemma, if a planner is put under pressure to devise a plan tailored mainly to the fulfilment of an assortment of felt needs, he will be driven to finding cosmetic solutions, appeasing instead of planning. This is precisely the process through which populism takes hold of the politician, from which the planner at least should be saved.

There are many felt needs which reflect convergence of all interests which no planner can ignore, nor does he have the privilege of replacing people's perception with his own perception of felt needs. But if there is anything like a science of planning which would justify making a distinction between a planner and a politician, the planner should have the freedom to chart out the path for the fulfilment of the felt needs of the deprived people. This path may not be the shortest or the quickest, but within the limitations of socio-economic parameters and his own professional competence, the surest. The political leadership will of course have the final authority to accept or reject the planner's plan.

All in all, if a wholly or largely centralized planning has its infirmities, a fanatical advocacy of planning from below is not free from them. Planning, especially in a big country like India, has to be a two-way process at more than one level: between the Centre and the State (or a Region), between the State and its districts and between the district and the block or a cluster of villages. Given the commitment to the principle of decentralization, the modalities of the process should better be evolved through trial and error rather than prescribed as a blueprint. The question of sharing of authority and financial resources will never be free from controversy. Power equations will dominate the controversy, aggravate regional feelings, for example, on sharing of inter-State river waters, or the location of a steel plant. But this is a part of the game in a democracy.

As already stated, it is primarily at the national level that major policy decisions are taken; in one way or the other they affect the effectiveness of measures for the eradication of poverty and unemployment. Only if these policies are in consonance with the policy needed for poverty eradication, would a discussion on restructuring of planning machinery be useful. The whole plan and not just a part of it under the caption 'special programmes for the weaker sections' must reflect a commitment to poverty eradication. No policy, no project should be inconsistent with the objective of poverty removal. If the commitment of the national leadership to poverty eradication is lukewarm, it will severely hamper effective action at the State or local levels. In a federal structure, if some of the constituent States are governed by a party with a more radical orientation, a somewhat more energetic action for poverty removal can be initiated, but in the short run of say 5 to 10 years, the achievements in these states and the rest will not be outstandingly different. Thus the scope for the (decentralized) local authority to formulate plans for eradication of poverty and implementing them will be determined to a considerable extent by the latitude permitted by the State and Central Governments to the local planning authority.

The hope belied

It is now generally admitted that the expectation that decentralization of planning will help to improve performance, particularly in respect of achievement of social justice, has not been realized. Many explanations are given for the failure of decentralization to provide a stimulus, as was hoped, to rural development whose primary objective is to eradicate poverty and unemployment. A full discussion of this theme is beyond the scope of this paper. Briefly, we shall contend that though poverty cannot be eliminated altogether without a total social reconstruction or structural change involving property relations, considerable ground can be gained in the struggle for poverty eradication through a better planning process and planning mechanism. To put it differently, not all failures of anti-poverty programmes can be attributed to the opposition of the vested interests. A good many of them have failed through sheer inefficiency, bad planning and unintelligent mechanisms of implementation. If this were not so, projects and programmes such as power generation, major irrigation, soil conservation, production of fertilizers, cement and steel, which are demonstrably in the interest of the 'haves' would not have performed as poorly as they have done.

Let me cite a typical example.

Acute coal shortage has severely hampered work on the second phase of the Rajasthan Canal . . . The main work of lining the canal and water course in the command area has come to a virtual standstill . . . The problem of coal supply has been persisting for the last two years . . . Against the requirement of 90,000 tonnes of coal for 1980–81, the supply so far—mid-January 1981—was only about 8,000 tonnes . . . The nation is in fact losing Rs 5,000 million annually in terms of food production because of the delay in executing the projects (*The Times of India*, 1981).

Much of such mismatch can be traced to the compartmentalized system of decision-making at the Centre and the corresponding absence of a competent machinery to formulate an integrated area plan at local levels. If steps are taken to decentralize decision-making in areas appropriate for each level of the decentralized system and if the implementation system is revamped, there is reason to believe that many of the failures on programmes for the benefit of the weaker sections can be avoided. We would go further and stress that in the absence of such a reorganization of planning and implementation system, with the best of intent, these programmes will not succeed.

The major shortcoming of the decentralization experiments (most of them are still in the experimental stage), as they are being conducted in India and in most of the Asian countries, is, apart from their half-heartedness, the lack of appreciation of the necessity (or unwillingness) to constitute a planning authority at the local level with a high enough status assisted by a multi-disciplinary planning team. And the major obstacle in establishing such a planning apparatus is the training, tradition and culture of the administrative system which is accustomed to the one-way hierarchical line of command from the State to the District, the *taluka* and village levels.

Confirmation of the futility of the piecemeal approach to anti-poverty programmes comes from a more prestigious source, a World Bank research publication. Adelman and Robinson (1978) have constructed an economy-wide computable general-equilibrium model as a laboratory to test the impact of policy measures aimed at poverty elimination and better income distribution over the short to medium run. The model is rooted in the economy of South Korea. As their findings have received wide publicity and are likely to figure prominently in the animated debate on the problem of poverty, we take the liberty of quoting them at some length.

The Adelman-Robinson model reveals that 'policy instruments in current use are largely ineffective when used singly because the effects of even substantial government intervention are quickly dissipated over time, with a few of the trickle-down effects'. However, it also shows that 'with an integrated well-balanced, mutually reinforcing selection of development strategy and anti-deprivation policy packages, substantial improvement is possible over relevant time periods'. The authors contended that such coordinated packages are feasible within the existing economic structure, but warn that 'they [will] have a major impact on the relative position of different socio-economic groups and hence on the balance of power within the country' (Adelman-Robinson, 1978, on blurb and page 201).

The model simulated half a dozen programmes for rural economy individually and in combinations: Land reform, Cooperatives, Productivity and Marketing, Public Works and Industry, Consumption Subsidy, Education and Demographic Change. Without going into details, we may highlight two major outcomes from the model. Rural development including land reforms yields the best result in terms of both growth and income distribution. The package dramatically reduces the extent of poverty and is very favourable for overall income distribution. However, the programme which excludes land reform is noticeably less effective. 'Total production and income drop off somewhat, the size of poverty population increases substantially and the overall distribution is more unequal . . . the average incomes of the bottom two deciles are down 7 per cent' (Adelman and Robinson, 1978).

The contribution that redistribution of assets (land ownership, for example) can make is difficult to quantify. But the case for redistribution does not depend on such measurement. Inequality, particularly glaring inequality such as is seen in the coexistence of poverty and affluence, besides being indefensible as an economic phenomenon, is morally repugnant. Yet if it is contended that redistribution is the sole or major solution to the problem of poverty, the case for decentralization would lose much of its force, for the simple reason that policy decisions and legislative action for any worthwhile redistribution will have to be taken at a much higher level. Decentralization can play a positive role in poverty eradication mainly in two ways. A planning authority at the district level equipped with adequate sanctions and resources is in a better position to arrest the process of impoverishment through more specific identification of exploitative instruments, such as rents, interest rates, trading margins, etc., which generate and sustain poverty. It can initiate countervailing action by more effective enforcement of legislative sanctions and strengthening non-exploitative arrangements, such as institutional credit, cooperative marketing and public distribution. Additionally, it can help to channel a larger than proportionate share of public, private and institutional investment with supportive services—extension, training, technology upgradation, input supply marketing—to the weaker section of the population. It can also prevent the trickle up in the special programmes for the weaker sections and improve their performance. The total impact of this course of action may not be dramatic but it will definitely change the course of the income stream in favour of the poor. In any case, if such a reorientation is to be achieved, it can be done only through authentic decentralized planning and implementation machinery.

NOTE

1. This paper forms part of the study on 'Two-Way Planning: Logic and Limitations— A Critical Review of Indian Experience' prepared for the FAO Regional

Office for Asia and the Pacific, Bangkok, Thailand in 1981 and revised subsequently. The study was presented at the Expert Consultation on Two-Way Process in Agriculture and Rural Development Planning, organized by FAO in Bangkok from 1 to 4 February 1983. The author is grateful to the FAO Regional Office for sponsoring the study and for providing financial support as well as giving permission to publish this paper in the journal.

Reprinted from the *Indian Journal of Agricultural Economics*, Vol. 38, No. 2, April–June 1983.

CHAPTER 10

Rural development:
Investment without organization[1]

'Errors, false starts and dead ends in the development story of the last three decades' (Streeten, 1983) have brought about a fair degree of acceptance among scholars of the view that growth should be judged by the contribution it makes to reduction of poverty, inequality and exploitation. The growing emphasis on rural development can be traced to this delayed awareness reflected in the special programmes for the weaker sections of the rural community and backward areas like the SFDA, MFAL, NREP, IRDP, Minimum Needs, DPAP, etc. now incorporated in the new 20-point Programme.

The decade-old strategy of direct attack on poverty also does not appear to have succeeded in achieving the development objectives specifically entrusted to it. The special programmes launched under its banner, though frequently redesigned and renamed, have been in operation for more than a decade. Yet their impact on the problem of poverty and inequity is unimpressive. There are no doubt a few 'success stories' and even some 'high performers' here and there. But, on the whole, they have not perceptibly altered the poverty map.

The debate on the factors responsible for this failure is as extensive and animated as earlier debates which dethroned the GNP as the main indicator of growth. The debating camps are often classified and labelled according to the school of thought they are supposed to represent. In what follows we shall keep our distance from this high debate and restrict ourselves to a few operational aspects of rural development programmes and emphasize the preconditions necessary for their success.

It would be but fair to mention that there is recognition of the shortcomings of these programmes in official quarters, though there is a natural tendency to highlight the success stories. But the typical response of policy-makers to the inadequate achievement is to allot larger public funds for these programmes and urge credit institutions to deploy more credit for their implementation. While more funds are certainly needed to make the special programmes more effective and extend their coverage, the more important desiderata lie elsewhere. It will be argued with concrete illustrations that apart from mis-utilization and quite often non-utilization of these funds, the administrative machinery and the organizational arrangements needed for their optimum use are ill-conceived, weak, inefficient and often non-existing.

Official response

Before we proceed with this theme, let us revert briefly to the typical official response to the weak impact of the special programmes mentioned above. In his recent Budget speech, the Finance Minister while rightly emphasizing 'the importance of obtaining the maximum returns out of existing investments' (Government of India Budget for 1983–84) announced a hefty increase in allocation to the 20-Point Programme.

> The outlay for the New 20-Point Programme in the Central Sector Plan for 1983–84 is Rs. 2,747 crore, representing an increase of 26.6 per cent over the outlay in the current year's [1982–83] plan. The provision for these schemes in the approved Plan outlay of the states and Union Territories for 1983–84 will be Rs. 7.332 crore. Hon'able members will be happy to know that the total provision for the 20-Point Programme next year will thus exceed Rs. 10,000 crore.

The Hon'able members, we presume, did feel happy.

The Working Group on the Role of Banks in the Implementation of the New 20-Point Programme, appointed by the Reserve Bank, also adopts a similar approach in its recently released report. Its recommendation is that 'advances to weaker sections' should reach 25 per cent of priority sector advances (40 per cent of total bank credit to be achieved by 1985 or 10 per cent of total bank credit by the end of March 1985). This would imply that 'advances to the weaker sections would reach a level of about Rs 4,000 crore by March 1985, the increase envisaged during the two-year period from 1983 to 1985 being of the order of Rs 3,000 crore.

While the Government of India is still to take a firm view on the question of appropriate administrative structure and modalities for formulating and implementing the 20-Point Programme, the RBI has repeatedly urged the Government of India, the Planning Commission and the State Governments to bring about a better coordination between the district development plans and bank credit. The Working Group has also reiterated the same point. It says,

> From the experience of bank lendings to the weaker and poorer sections of the society, it has been increasingly realised that unless credit is provided in an integrated manner with other developing agencies providing support by way of extension work, inputs, marketing, infrastructure, etc. the result is generally infructuous lending (Reserve Bank of India, 1983).

The Working Group pins its hope on 'closer and effective coordination between financing agencies and state governments, their agencies and other development functionaries at the district and state levels' and relies on the 'detailed guidelines issued by the RBI' for preparation of District Credit Plans.

The gravamen of our critique is that, by and large, the RBI Guidelines and those issued by the Planning Commission for establishing an adequate planning and implementation machinery at the district level, which could ensure coordination between programmes and multiple agencies, have also proved infructuous. We shall cite ample evidence to substantiate this point. It is reported that of late there has been some improvement in the functioning of the DCCs and DDCs. One would like to know: in how many states and districts?

Non-utilization and non-recovery

Before we deal with infructuous lending and its root cause (dithering on decentralization on the part of the State Governments and

innate unwillingness of sectoral department agencies to accept
dilution of their authority implied in the coordination and integration
process) let us refer to the bewildering experience of non-utilization
of funds sanctioned for the special programmes. The Public Accounts
Committee of the Maharashtra Government in its report presented
to the State Assembly revealed that 'an enormous amount of
Rs. 1,100 crore provided in the budgets and supplementary demands
for the years 1977–80 lapsed as it remained unspent on the
concerned works'. A more pertinent observation in the report
is: 'some of the allocations made every year for the welfare
activities such as rural development under social and community
services such as water and power development, agriculture and
allied services, etc., remained substantially underutilised' (*The Times
of India*, 1982a).

A UNI release from New Delhi dated 15 October 1992
reports that 'the Centre has taken a serious view of the tardy
and unsatisfactory implementation of the drinking water scheme
for problem villages and has directed the states to exercise proper
control over allocation of funds' (*The Times of India*, 1982b).
According to the same report, a recent central study has revealed
that

> allocation of wells is not being done on the basis of actual local
> requirements. For instance, in one state it was noticed that 41
> wells had been dug in a district which does not have acute water
> problem, while only ten wells were dug in a chronically drought-
> hit district abounding in problem villages.

A more ominous aspect of the scene is that 'in most states,
influential farmers manipulated allocation of wells in their favour
and the poorer sections are not getting the attention they deserve'.
An earlier PEO Report had confirmed that the Scheduled Castes
and weaker sections have not gained proportionately from the
safe drinking water supply scheme (Government of India, 1980).
In another unpublished report it was pointed out that Harijan
bastis were being bypassed under the rural electrification programme.
Are we to believe that the reiteration of the earlier RBI Guidelines
by the Working Group on the New 20-Point Programme will
be adequate to plug these loopholes and reform the State Governments?
The situation is however different regarding credit for 'special'
programmes for the weaker sections, irrespective of the number

of points they contain. Though there are some similarities, for example, in regard to diversion of funds meant for the poor to the non-poor, the problem in the case of credit is not non-utilization but non-recovery.

Missing 'conditionality'

Exasperated by the lethargy of the State Governments in providing supportive infrastructure, an editorial ('IRDP in a Mess') in *The Economic Times* (Bombay) dated 3 November 1981 was constrained to suggest that 'Blocks where the infrastructure does not exist should have no claim to IRDP funds'. With a more direct experience which the RBI has on these matters, one wishes that the Working Group on the New 20-Point Programme had been a little more forthcoming in regard to 'conditionality' for providing more credit for the programme. On its own shelf, the RBI has a report which says 'one of the major constraints in the formulation of the District Credit Plans (DCPs) has been the absence of proper District Development Plans'. Some of the important findings of the study are:

1. A separate planning machinery for formulation of district development plans did not exist at the district level except in a few states.
2. Annual (district) Plans are formulated by the State Planning Department at the State level. These plans are based on the proposals received from the state/district level development departments.
3. In most states, the disaggregated plan outlays are not available before April/May every year, in some cases much later.
4. In most States there is no focal point officer who is in a position to supply required comprehensive data regarding Government development schemes to the lead banks.

In what follows, we shall cite findings from some of the studies conducted by the ARDC (now NABARD), nationalized banks and research institutes to evaluate the performance of the projects which now fall within the scope of the New 20-Point Programme. The scrutiny of these randomly selected evaluation reports is undertaken with the purpose of ascertaining the efficiency with which these projects are executed and more particularly to find out the extent to which they have succeeded in achieving their avowed objective of helping the weaker sections of the society. The findings cited may not be typical, but it can be asserted that they are not exceptional. Despite the adverse findings, we do believe that the commercial banks did make a sincere effort to finance on an increasing scale the projects for rural development, but for a variety of reasons, they failed to achieve commensurate results.

Our purpose in highlighting the lapses is the same as that of the RBI and the Planning Commission, namely, to emphasize that in the absence of a competent planning body to formulate an integrated development plan at the district—or any other decentralized level—and an appropriate development administration, credit will continue to be sub-optimally utilized, if not misutilized. This is perhaps obvious, but if so, is it prudent to prod the credit institutions to deploy a larger and larger share of their advances for such projects without insisting on certain 'conditionality' to ensure their proper use? The rub is that the credit institutions do not have much option and have to follow the directives issued from above. The irony is that even the RBI has not taken a firm stand on preconditions for larger lending to a wide variety of special programmes. It did draw the attention of the State Governments to their responsibilities in regard to the IRD programme. But it did not categorically state that credit will be available only for a well-designed integrated development plan— and not an assorted bundle of programmes—backed by an equally well-integrated implementing authority.

Hold of sugar lobby

Coming to the evaluation reports, let us begin with the NABARD report on the River Lift Irrigation Schemes in Pune District, Maharashtra (NABARD, 1982a). Though 54 per cent of the beneficiaries under the scheme were small farmers, their share in the total area benefitted was only 22 per cent. Sugarcane cultivators were the main beneficiaries: sugarcane crop alone accounted for 94 per cent of the gross value of incremental production. (What about Point 2: 'Make special efforts to increase production of pulses and vegetable oilseeds'.) Discrimination in favour of sugarcane cultivation was even more blatant. The lift water was deliberately underpriced for sugarcane cultivation. As against the 'Economic Water Rate' of Rs 948 and Rs 834 per acre under sugarcane respectively in 1978–79 and 1979–80, the actual rates charged were Rs 600 and Rs 225. For wheat, however, the actual water rates charged were higher than the economic rates in 1979–80. As a result of underpricing for sugarcane, the irrigation society incurred a loss of Rs 21,874 in 1978–79. The society was in fact accumulating losses year after year. The outstanding recovery on water charge account over the period from 1976–77 to 1978–79 was Rs 59,841. Even the ARDC refinanced scheme could not escape the hold of the sugar lobby.

The Pune Society was not an exception in discriminating in favour of sugarcane cultivation. The Kolhapur District Lift Irrigation Scheme did the same. It charged Rs 600, Rs 240 and Rs 60 respectively for sugarcane, *rabi* crops and *kharif* crops as against the respective, 'economic' cost of Rs 630, Rs 100 and Rs 10 (NABARD, 1982b).

The irrigation scheme did result in increased sugarcane production, but thanks to serious rise in salinity caused by the scheme, the productivity of the 'beneficiaries' was lower than the village average—330 quintals per acre under sugarcane grown by the beneficiaries against the village average of 422 quintals and 5.3 quintals per acre under cotton against the village average of 8 quintals. This is how Point 1 of the New 20 Points—'increase irrigation potential'—is implemented.

Let us cite one more example of ARDC-financed ground water irrigation scheme—in Kota District, Rajasthan—to illustrate the prevalence of 'infructuous' investment and frustrating experience of lack of inter-departmental coordination. The sample survey covered 111 wells of beneficiaries under the scheme. Out of these, only 22 (29 per cent of the total) wells were classified as 'relatively successful', 61 wells (55 per cent of the total) were classified as 'incomplete' with an average depth of 8.5 metres (against 15 metres envisaged in the scheme) 'which had struck some water but which was inadequate to make the investment financially viable', the remaining 18 wells were classified as 'failed' as they had 'struck no water at all at the average depth of 7 meters' (ARDC, 1982).

The Evaluation Study reports:

As of end-December 1979 [the scheme was sanctioned by ARDC in March 1969, and was closed in June 1973] the incidence of default in the repayment of investment loans was very high. Two-thirds of the sample borrowers were defaulters, the amount overdue being 80 per cent of demand (ARDC, 1982).

Amongst the many reasons behind this dismal performance, a few are mentioned (ARDC, 1982). 'Though the Rajasthan Ground Water Directorate was supposed to provide the necessary technical guidance, it did not fulfil this responsibility.' 'Though the Project Officer was required to be posted by the state government well in advance to coordinate the work of different agencies and ensure successful implementation of the scheme, he was actually posted one year after the scheme' 'The relative high incidence of failed/incomplete wells may be attributed to misutilisation of loans, under-financing of investment and technical factors.'

Vanishing artisans

Point 7 of the New 20-Point Programme pertains to the acceleration of programmes for the development of Scheduled Castes and Tribes. Let us therefore review the findings of a study series titled 'The Nature and Causes of Poverty of Rural Artisans in Maharashtra'. One study deals with cane and bamboo workers in Ratnagiri District (Vaikuntha Mehta Smarak Trust, 1982). All the 50 households selected for the study, from two *talukas* of the District, belonged to the 'Mahar' caste officially classified as Scheduled Caste. If the number of agencies involved in assisting the artisans and the Scheduled Castes among them can be viewed as indicative of our concern for their lot, there was no dearth of them. In Maharashtra, there is an Artisan Employment Guarantee (AEG) Scheme, introduced in 1972–73 by the State Government at the initiative of the Maharashtra Khadi and Village Industries Board. An attempt is made to bring the artisans within the fold of Block Level Village Artisan (Balutedar) Multipurpose Cooperative Society. The District Central Cooperative Bank finances the Balutedar Societies, while the District Village Industries (DIC) Officer looks after the implementation of the AEG scheme. The Mahatma Phule Backward Class Development Corporation, the Sanjay Gandhi Swavalamban Yojana and the Lead Bank are also assisting the artisans. The IRDP is another agency which assists artisans falling below the poverty line. In addition, there is a Tertiary Scheme under which cash credit is provided by the banks on the recommendation of the BDO.

In spite of this wide but highly complicated—somewhat crazy—network of agencies and a bundle of schemes, programmes and projects for the benefit of village artisans, the cane-bamboo industry is shrinking to almost vanishing point and along with it the Mahar artisans. The Balutedar Societies which were designed to be the primary agency for regenerating the industries and uplifting the artisans, in turn, have themselves become bankrupt and have placed a heavy load of indebtedness on the artisans.

Let us briefly note the confluence of forces which frustrated this well-intentioned and many-pronged effort to support and revive the vanishing cane-bamboo village industries pursued predominantly by the Mahar community. The main factor responsible for the ruin of the industry was the non-availability and high prices of the raw material—bamboo. This was not a consequence of fortuitous circumstances.

The main suppliers of bamboo are the larger peasant households and landlords who own large chunks of 'uncultivable' land on which bamboo can be grown in clusters, and the Forest Department. Let us forget the first category which is primarily concerned with private gain and not expected to worry about social losses. But the Forest Department, which we hope will be involved in implementing the New 20-Point Programme—specifically Point 12 which enjoins vigorous pursuit of programmes of afforestation, etc.—has been totally unconcerned about the need of the cane-bamboo workers for this raw material. The study cited above reports: 'Permits during the year 1980–81 were given to 15 contractors to cut and transport a total quantity of 12,900 bamboos. The average price at which contracts were given was approximately Rs. 60.27 per 100 bamboos.' Considering that the price paid by the Mahar artisans was Rs 4 per bamboo, 'it could be inferred that the forest department permitted the contractors to make large profits and was totally apathetic to the requirements of the artisans' (Vaikunth Mehta Smarak Trust, 1982).

Not by credit alone

These findings cited from evaluation studies are in no way non-typical. We have examined scores of evaluation reports on a variety of schemes—minor irrigation, dairy, rural electrification, village artisans, etc.—and practically each of them has found similar weaknesses, shortcomings and failure. It is not that the authorities concerned are unaware of these findings. But for reasons as yet unclear, no concrete steps have been taken to establish a planning authority at decentralized local levels capable of formulating a single 'integrated' rural development plan with professional competence, evoking the people's participation and with its prime accent on reduction in poverty and elimination of exploitation of the weaker section. A few States do have the usual paraphernalia of DDPB, DCCs and such other acronyms, but none to our knowledge, possesses the authority, competence and orientation needed for rural development planning of the type defined above. In regard to the administrative and organization system which would faithfully and efficiently implement the plan, thinking is still vacuous and the outmoded system with hierarchies and compartmentalism still persists.

No one grudges more public expenditure and liberal institutional credit for rural development or for the 20-Point Programme whose main objective is to remove poverty and inequity through growth. But simply pumping more money or credit will not accomplish this task. We know this and we believe we also know why. Yet the 'why' remains untackled.

NOTE

1. Reprinted from *Economic and Political Weekly*, Vol. 18, No. 18, 30 April 1983.

CHAPTER 11

Innovative approaches to the revival of village industries[1]

In the process of economic development, shifts in the inter-sectoral and intra-sectoral employment are to be expected and are even desirable, provided they are accompanied by an overall increase in the productive employment. Unfortunately, there has been an overall decline in employment growth from 2.82 per cent per annum during the period from 1972–73 to 1977–78 to 1.55 per cent during 1983 to 1987–88 (Economic Advisory Council, 1990). During this period the growth rate of employment in agriculture declined from 2.32 per cent per annum to 0.65 per cent. That agriculture is losing its capacity to absorb additional labour is further confirmed by the fact that in the rural area, in the industry group 'agriculture, forestry, hunting and fishing' the percentage of male workers declined from 83.3 to 74.5 and that of female workers from 89.7 to 84.7 during this period. The percentage of workers engaged in agricultural production to total workers in selected industries has continuously declined from 77.1 per cent in 1972–73 to 69.9 per cent in 1987–88 for males and from 80.4 to 70.0 per cent for females (Visaria and Minhas, 1991).

As for the household sector, which is the main concern of this article, employment in this group of industries has declined from 9.9 million persons in 1961 to 7.7 million in 1981. Eleven out of the 17 major industry groups (as per 2-digit NIC Classification) recorded a fall of 3.5 million in the household industry employment (Vaidyanathan, 1991).

The fall in household sector employment in all these groups is concentrated in the traditional industries—notably non-mill spinning, handlooms, khadi, hand printing, grain milling, oil crushing, gur making, leather and leather footwear and earthenware. Substantial expansion of household industry activity [creating an additional 1.2 million jobs] has taken place in a few industry groups notably beverages, bidi making and repair service (Vaidyanathan, 1991).

The distinction between the employment record of the agricultural sector and that of the household sector is that while the decline in the former is in the rate of increase, that in the latter is in the absolute number of employed workers. A more disconcerting aspect of the decline is that the female workers have suffered more from this displacement. While the total number of workers in the five major village industries—grain milling, *khandsari* and *gur*, edible oils, spinning and weaving in handlooms and powerlooms— declined from 28,00,672 in 1961 to 9,97,106 in 1981 or by 64.4 per cent, the proportion of the female workers in the total declined from 56.3 per cent to 25.5 per cent during this period (see Table 11.1). Employment of female workers is location and enterprise specific because of compulsions of domestic work. The employment policy has therefore a responsibility either to endeavour to make their work in the enterprises in which they are currently employed more productive and competitive or provide alternative congenial work opportunities.

Field investigations provide further confirmation of the weak impact of the self-employment schemes such as IRDP on the traditional industries. V.M. Rao who has extensive experience of field investigation reports: '. . . reduction in the extent of poverty was the least among those taking up village industries' (Rao, 1987: A.4).

That this decline in employment in household industries, particularly in the so-called traditional groups, has occurred in spite of the numerous wide-ranging protective and promotional measures by the State—excise duty concessions, sale rebates, reservations grants, and loans at concessional rates of interest, preferential purchases by Government Departments—raises serious doubts about the viability and survival of the household industries. Several questions arise which should be squarely faced.

The decline in the rate of growth of employment is not the only matter of concern for employment policy. The shifts

TABLE 11.1

Number of workers in rural household industries

Industries	1961			1981		
	Male	Female	Total	Male	Female	Total
1. Grain mill products	1,03,006 (38.24)	1,66,380 (61.76)	2,69,386 (100.00)	70,608 (86.17)	10,833 (13.30)	81,441 (100.00)
2. Production of indigenous sugar *boora, khandsari, gur* from sugarcane and *palmgur*	66,882 (52.76)	59,891 (47.24)	1,26,773 (100.00)	19,693 (72.03)	7,647 (27.97)	27,340 (100.00)
3. Edible oil	1,23,106 (58.53)	87,208 (41.47)	2,10,314 (100.00)	23,691 (81.19)	5,490 (18.80)	29,181 (100.00)
4. Handloom sector	9,17,762 (42.19)	12,57,630 (57.81)	21,75,392 (100.00)	6,16,583 (73.04)	2,27,638 (26.96)	8,44,221 (100.00)
5. Powerloom	12,872 (68.44)	5,935 (31.56)	18,807 (100.00)	12,328 (82.61)	2,595 (17.39)	14,923 (100.00)
Total	12,23,628 (43.69)	5,77,044 (56.31)	28,00,672 (100.00)	7,42,903 (74.51)	2,54,203 (25.49)	9,97,106 (100.00)

Note: Figures in parentheses show the percentages of male and female to total workers in the specified industry.

Source: Government of India (1964), Census of India, 1961, Vol. I, India, Part-II B (i), General Economic Tables; Government of India (1983), Census of India 1981, Series I, India, General Economic Tables, Tables B-12 to B-17, Part III-B (ii) of 1981, Office of Registrar General, Ministry of Home Affairs, New Delhi

in employment which are occurring in the process of economic growth also affect the quality of the structure of employment. Over the years, we observe a continuing decline in self-employment and a corresponding increase in wage labour. In the latter category, the increase is sharper in the proportion of casual labour. These shifts in the structure of employment are regressive inasmuch as the incidence of unemployment as well as that of poverty is markedly higher in the wage labour households and more so among the casual worker households. The latest NSS data reveal that the agricultural labour households constituting 30.7 per cent of all the rural households accounted for 45.6 per cent of the households in poverty and 59.5 per cent of the unemployed person-days. In contrast, 40.7 per cent of the self-employed households accounted for 32 per cent of the households in poverty and only 16.3 per cent of the unemployed person-days (Mahendra Dev et al., 1991).

Vaidyanathan has also raised the same question as to 'whether protection of traditional industry should continue to be a major concern of policy, on grounds of employment'. He has taken a view that 'In so far as workers engaged in traditional industries, who lose their employment due to competition from same or similar products manufactured through improved technology, are able to benefit from the expansion of employment in other areas', we need not worry. The examples cited are the handloom weavers shifting to powerlooms and the traditional potters to brick-making. The shift of production from handlooms to powerlooms and from pottery to brick-making may not have led to reduction in the overall employment in the household industries, but the shift has changed the status of the handloom weavers and the traditional potters from self-employment to wage employment. The powerloom sector is owned and managed by a new class of businessmen whose aim is to earn profit from the labour of the weavers. The quintessential characteristic of household industries is self-ownership and self-employment, not the size alone.

Vaidyanathan recognizes that though such shifts are taking place, their scale is not adequate. Citing data for handloom and leather industries, he estimates that between 1961 and 1981, over two million workers could be said to have been displaced from these industries. This estimate is based on the assumption of normal growth in employment. 'In view of the magnitudes involved, the social case for intervention to prevent further reduction in employment in some of these large traditional industries . . . is very strong indeed' (Vaidyanathan, 1990).

In so far as the cottage and village industries are concerned, the nation has a very high stake not just in their moribund survival but in transforming them into a source of creative employment and decent income. Persons and communities currently employed in them—the so-called backward classes, Scheduled Castes/Tribes and women—are too numerous to be driven into the ranks of landless manual labourers. More importantly, they possess skills—often dormant—which are precious and unique in some ways.

There is reason to believe that the cottage and village industries have inherent potential to provide gainful employment and become a self-reliant integral part of the country's industrial structure. To achieve this status what they need is a new policy frame, dedicated leadership and a package of innovative approaches. This conviction is based on the experience of several highly successful endeavours of individuals and voluntary groups. We shall cite a few examples of successful experiments.

Potters in Bhadravati, a small township 60 km from Chandrapur in Maharashtra, slogged, at times working 16 hours a day, but they earned barely Rs 20 to 25 per week, with large families to feed. There was neither a school nor a primary health centre. As a result of persistent efforts of Sarvodaya worker, Krishnamurthy Mirmira, to revive the industry, the same potters now exhibit every year at the Bajaj Arts Gallery in Bombay their decorative and ceramic wares and utility articles like roofing tiles and glazed earthenwares. In 30 years the Kumbhar Cooperative Society has an annual turnover of Rs 8 lakh. The social transformation is equally remarkable. There is Balwadi and the students get free textbooks from the profits of the Society. Moin Qazi reports: 'The Bhadravati project is a synthesis of tradition and modernity and aims at refining the traditional craftsmanship of the local population for making a valuable medium of permanent livelihood' (*The Times of India*, 28 November 1986).

More well known than the potters of Bhadravati are the craftsman of Tilonia, near Ajmer in Rajasthan. Set up some 20 years ago by Bunker Roy, the Social Work Research Centre (SWRC) has been interacting with artisans and working out with them ways of adapting their products to the taste of urban consumers.

Shri K.P. Singh of SWRC says: 'Five activities—patchwork, leather craft, weaving, wooden chairs and parrot mobiles which are a popular export item—fetch us a turnover of Rs. 10,000 a day.' This was in 1989.

> Tilonia Bazar comes to Bombay again (this time in Jehangir Art Gallery) with its chairs and its chappals, apart from other characteristically embroidered, handicrafted leather goods. What is also on sale this time is a range of patchwork articles (Chadars and Kashida work) made by the women of the less exposed Barmer District in Rajasthan (*The Indian Post*, Bombay, 21 June 1989).

In Pabal, a village 60 km from Pune in the drought-prone region of Western Ghats, Dr S.S. Kalbag is training schoolchildren in the 9th and 10th standards to perform tasks involving sophisticated technology such as 'land surveys' using plane tables, dumpy levels and theodolites. Students are trained to use vertical electric soundings for prospecting ground water. All the construction on the campus, residential, office, workshop, etc. has been done by the trainees. They have also made sinks, wash basins, W.C. pans and water tanks with ferrocement. They get jobs of repairing bicycles, tractors, trucks, agricultural implements, poultry cages, feeders, etc. They have fabricated racks, tables, chairs, stools, school desks, window frames and grills. The trainees have built handcarts-cum-bicycle trailers and pneumatic wheeled bullock-carts.

In agriculture, Kalbag is concentrating on drip irrigation for high value crops (example, seedless grapes), pest management and social forestry. He is advocating a Rural Technology Course for the 8th, 9th and 10th standards in technical schools located in the rural areas. The entire effort is to build a prototype institutional structure that will integrate the educational and development activities (Kalbag, 1989).

The technical/development education centres will be the most appropriate agencies for the transfer of new technologies and bringing feedback for development proposals based on local perception and needs.

There is an assured demand for all these enterprises. Their capital requirement is modest and the requisite skills are not difficult to impart. The children of the artisans would surely prefer skilled self-employment to joining the ranks of wage-seekers on public works.

Technological innovations can become more effective when they are supported by a responsive extension and delivery system. Here again the stereotype departmental agencies have a disappointing performance record. Hence, diversification of rural economy through decentralized industrialization needs innovative approaches. In this connection, the Block Adoption Programme initiated by the Industrial Development Bank of India (IDBI) is worth noting. The IDBI, in cooperation with some other financial agencies like IFCI and ICICI, has set up State Technical Consultancy Organizations (TCOs) with the purpose of providing professional consultancy services to medium and small industries. 'They undertake on behalf of the entrepreneurs market surveys, supply market intelligence, prepare feasibility studies and project profiles.' The IDBI decided to utilize the services of the TCOs for their Block Adoption Programme of rural industrialization. The TCOs were permitted to appoint specialized professional teams to assist them as they function in diverse economic and social environments. In 1989, the IDBI assigned the task of evaluating this programme to the Centre for Studies in Decentralized Industries. The Centre conducted a survey in twelve blocks and its Report has been published under the title 'Rural Industrialisation: A Catalyst in Action' (Acharya, 1990: 22). The survey found that the block development programme initiated by the IDBI has

> succeeded in a large measure in augmenting the existing delivery system and blending it with professional temper and dedicated approach. The small professional team at the block level, acting as an effective intermediary, was able to bring together different organizations such as the financial institutions, DRDAs, DICs, etc. for delivering a well-integrated package of schemes and services for rural enterprises in backward areas where no governmental or non-governmental agencies had made effort.

Not that there were no shortcomings in their approach, organization or working but these could be easily remedied. (For details see Acharya, 1990: 72.) It is heartening to find that 'The stimulus to growth came from rural youth and women in majority of blocks' (Acharya, 1990: 74). The Nehru Yuvak Sanghs in Borigumma block in Koraput District of Orissa took the lead role in the effort to impart new skills and diversify rural enterprise. As a consequence, not only in Borigumma but in a few other blocks also, women, both young and old, formed a sizeable proportion of the beneficiaries.

Our purpose in citing this example of an innovative approach is to dispel to some extent the prevalent pessimism about the scope for the revival of cottage industries. There is ample dormant talent, mainly amongst women, even in distant tribal villages, but in our zeal for rapid industrialization through modern large-scale industries, we have ignored indigenous traditional enterprises. Large-scale industries are undoubtedly necessary, but while encouraging their establishment, we should have attended with equal zeal to the task of upgradation of skills and technology in the traditional enterprises and their institutional infrastructure. There is, no doubt, a plethora of income- and employment-generation programmes. Substantial financial allocations are made, supplemented by subsidies, rebates, and reservations for these programmes. But as we have seen, these interventions have failed to stem the decline of household industries. Indiscriminate, if not excessive, protection has perhaps done more harm than good to the traditional sector. What is needed now is more dedication and some innovative ideas.

The innovative approach we are talking about comprises many components of an integrated package. Adopted in isolation, each component can make some contribution to the effectiveness of the preferred pattern of employment generation, but its worth will be considerably enhanced when linked to other components. For example, training under trysem (training of rural youth for self-employment) will be of no use if the jobs for which the persons are trained produce goods or services for which there is inadequate demand. But this is precisely what is happening in several cases.

The components of the new approach include market survey, product diversification, technological upgradation, extension geared to elicit workers' participation in decision-making, training in skill formation, in design orientation, entrepreneurship and management, cost reduction through elimination of exploitative intermediaries and their substitution by institutional (cooperative) agencies for credit, marketing and input supply and establishment of community service centres. The existing agencies like Khadi and Village Industries Commission, Centre for Development of Rural Technology, Council for Advancement of People's Action and Rural Technology (CAPART), District Industrial Centres (DICs) should be persuaded to adopt such a comprehensive approach, constitute coordination and consultative committees and mutually support each other's work.

It is not our intention to suggest that the revival of cottage and village industries will solve the problem of unemployment in the country. The unemployed and the underemployed constitute a heterogeneous group. At one end are those who have neither any assets nor any skill. For them well-planned and well-organized wage employment schemes, preferably for building community assets, are necessary. Our plea is primarily to arrest the decline of employment in the household sector by improving its productivity and competitive capability. Apart from providing employment, these industries help to preserve our artistic heritage. Self-employment has its own rewards, especially for women. But it is rapidly losing ground to wage employment. The largest contribution to the sharp increase in the number and proportion of casual workers in the labour force has come from marginal farmers and artisans. We believe that it is possible to stem this exodus by a more appropriate public intervention. But it seems that the policy-makers as well as the academicians are interested more in debating and devising poverty alleviation programmes than in devising poverty prevention strategies. Insights gained from the successful experiments in augmenting self-employment should be utilized for devising a policy package that will help to spread and strengthen the process of generating rural employment and retain its diversity.

The first and the foremost requirement of successful rural development or any of its components is that of a catalyst. Centuries of deprivation and exploitation have made the poor lethargic and distrustful of any outside intervention. By and large they are interested only in receiving aid in cash or kind. The role of the catalyst is to change this attitude of dependency, awaken them from the engulfing torpor and instil in them a sense of self-confidence and a desire to improve their lot.

Almost all the successful experiments that we have narrated and many more we know owe their success to an individual or a group of 'volunteers' or activists, as they would like to be called. Besides Shri Mirmira of Bhadravati and TCOs of IDBI mentioned above, we should like to relate one other example of unusual leadership. It is essential that leadership also ought not to be self-perpetuating. The most successful leadership—or

even a policy intervention—is one which makes itself dispensable
in course of time by building up local leadership at different
layers—youth and women—and spheres such as health, education,
etc.

In 1975, the late Professor Ravi Matthai of the Indian Institute
of Management, Ahmedabad (IIMA), initiated the Rural University
Experiment in Educational Innovation in Jawaja (Rajasthan) 'on
the assumption that sustained development of Rural India is feasible
only if it is based on people learning to be self-reliant by learning
to generate their own opportunities and resources' (Gupta, 1988:
3). The Jawaja experiment unravels all the obstacles and frustrations
in persuading the rural poor to help themselves and others. Ranjit
Gupta and some faculty members of IIMA who joined Ravi
Matthai in this experiment scrupulously avoided assuming a paternal
role and relied predominantly on the artisans to assume responsibility
for decisions they took. Matthai and his colleagues were committed
to restricting their role to teachers, advisors and helpers in the
last resort. The artisans committed many mistakes in their endeavour
to be self-reliant but in the end they did succeed through trial
and error. The one distinguishing feature of this experiment is
that the IIM team was not anxious to achieve quick results,
no targets were set, it did not mind the target group committing
mistakes, while learning to manage its enterprises, whether in
the use of upgraded technology or in the field of purchase of
inputs and sale of its products, accounting and fund management.

The Jawaja experiment started with two groups of villagers,
a group of weavers and a group of leather workers. Both these
groups belong to the under-privileged sections of the village society.
The two groups have founded their own organizations: the Jawaja
Weavers' Association (JWA) and the Jawaja Leather Association
(JLA). Economically, from the time they started, the members
of the JWA have moderately improved their earnings by Rs
2500–3000 per member on an average per year. But as Gupta
points out, the real test of success is provided by the process
of learning by the target group as well as the experimenters
and agencies such as the National Institute of Design (NID)
associated with them. Both groups—the weavers and the leather
workers—have achieved a fairly high level of self-reliance. They
handle virtually all functions themselves. If they consult the
experimenters or, in some sense, depend on them, it is in relation

to such vexing tasks as annual auditing of books of accounts
. . . or obtaining sales tax licence. Barring these, *'they have
made the experimenters dispensable'* (emphasis added) (Gupta,
mimeo).

The IIM team's more recent outstanding success is in the
field of School-based Plantation Programme in which schoolchildren
played the role of catalysts. From a beginning made by a schoolboy
of about 10 years who

> collected seeds of whatever species he could lay his hands on
> and planted them on a plot of wasteland adjoining his house,
> the activity expanded to 20 more villages adjoining those covered
> by the non-formal educational centres where it was already in
> operation. . . . The activity thus acquired the overtones of 'social
> forestry' (Gupta, 1988).

While the spread of the experiment and physical achievements
are commendable, Gupta says that the success of the experiment
lies not only in physical results.

> More important is the process initiated to motivate and develop
> the villagers' capability to think and act for themselves with minimum
> institutional support from outside. The process has not been due
> to any single intervention, not a package of inputs from a particular
> organization during any particular period. The process evolved out
> of years of patient, seemingly unrewarding efforts by various groups,
> both villagers and outsiders. The interest, enthusiasm of villagers
> and its spread is an index of the potential of such approaches
> to development (Gupta, 1988: 7-9, 15).

As a tailpiece, he adds:

> Nothing illustrates the emotional involvement of the community
> better than a unique attempt on the part of school children in
> a cluster of adjoining villages in Jawaja. On their own initiative,
> they have built a 15-acre forest in the midst of totally barren
> hilly region and named it the Matthai Vana (Gupta, 1988:15).

Realization of one's potential to earn a decent living through
creative work is just the first step. Without the backing of a
supportive organization, the realization will end up with a deeper
frustration. The most important ingredient of such an organization

is substantial improvement in the marketability of the products of the cottage and village industries. The successful experiments referred to earlier have done this, to a great extent, by upgrading technology and processes, design adjustment, diversification of traditional production, elimination of middlemen in input supply and product marketing the liaison with credit institutions. The aim is to reduce the cost of production and marketing, improve the quality of products and make them competitive with products of factories. Quite often, handicrafts do not face competition from factory production.

We shall cite one final example of what an imaginative marketing strategy can accomplish. The experience of the Khadi and Village Industries Board, UP, in attempting to introduce a more sophisticated and modern marketing system for the products of rural industries in worth noting (Taori and Singh, 1991: M-21). It is not simply a story of success, but also of failures and frustrations it encountered mostly from the unresponsive bureaucracy. Whatever success it has achieved is mainly due to the assistance it sought and received from professional bodies and voluntary organizations. It also draws attention to the 'complacency [generated by] easy and assured market with scope for manipulation and unfair trade practices in respect of the supply to the government, the prevalent features of reservation' (Taori and Singh, 1991: M-22).

> The Board has been supplying file covers, file boards, cadaks and drawing paper to the State Government for the last 20 years. The arrangement, was doing more harm than promoting the cause of the industry by breeding malpractices and leading to the deterioration in quality as the units were certain that whatever they produce would be accepted. This completely blocked innovative ideas, competitive attitudes and diversification of products (Taori and Singh, 1991: M-23).

The UP Board broke away from the traditional approach and attitudes, consulted the technical and management institutes for product diversification and improving their marketability. With guidance from the Institute of Marketing Management, Lucknow,

> the Board printed 80,000 (greeting) cards in eight designs. The experiences gained are rich and rewarding, indicating that products

of the decentralized sector if they go in the hands of professionals can be successfully marketed, which if done in government departments with number of snags would be an utter failure (Taori and Singh, 1991: M-23).

A similar experiment was made to convert *khadi* into garments with the assistance of designers to introduce design inputs and ethnic appeal. The Board organized

> an exhibition-cum-sale in schools and colleges to attract the new classes of discriminating buyers like students, the neo-rich and the fashion conscious. The results were amazing. An exhibition for three days organized in the Hotel Clarks Awadh during the off-season, i.e., the non-rebate period, had a grand success recording sales of Rs. 3 lakhs (Taori and Singh, 1991: M-25).

This shift from the (poor) rural to the (affluent) urban customers may not meet with the approval of the old guard, but if village industries are to survive and continue to provide gainful employment to the artisans, such orientation is necessary.

Finally a word about training. The training of artisans has to be broadened to include lessons in entrepreneurship and management. The trainer's role should be correspondingly expanded to stimulation of initiative, self-reliance and responsiveness to innovations in product—mix, designs and salesmanship. To reduce the cost of training by a team of highly empathetic personnel, the team should be peripatetic, camping in one village after another, acquainting itself with the social and cultural background of the trainees, their preferences and constraints. The team should be well acquainted with the market demand for products in which training is being imparted and its aim should be improving the overall marketability of the products.

Experiments by a few dedicated individuals and voluntary organizations cannot of course cover the entire country. But the policy-makers can certainly benefit from them if they wish to. If they do, the thrust of the policy for the revival and rejuvenation of cottage and village industries would shift from protection and pampering of the artisans with rebates and reservations to en-couragement of innovative approaches to technological upgradation, marketing and above all self-reliance. To start with, it would be more rewarding to train those who have some experience and skill in the profession rather than those whose aptitudes are untested.

NOTE

1. Reprinted from the Special Commemorative Issue of *Cooperative Perspective*, 1991.

IV
AGRICULTURAL PRICE POLICY

CHAPTER 12

Incentives and disincentives
in Indian agriculture[1]

The charge sheet

The slow pace of growth of agricultural production in India, further retarded by two successive disastrous harvests, has cast a shadow on the entire agricultural policy of the Government and the planning authorities. Nothing fails like failure and the chorus of criticism from the lengthening queue of critics has risen to a crescendo. The belief that the slackness in agricultural production was a consequence of wrong policies has been strengthened by the relatively better performance in Pakistan, presumably a result of a radical revision of its agricultural policies since 1960. The issue of agricultural policies in the developing countries has an importance and relevance over a much wider area than India and Pakistan. As such, it is of utmost importance that the successes and failures in agricultural production are properly evaluated and their relationship with particular agricultural policies clearly established.

Several eminent foreign and Indian scholars have recently commented on India's agricultural policies. Professor Theodore Schultz, writing in the context of a wider canvas of 'the poor performance of agriculture in so many poor countries' has advanced a comprehensive thesis which deserves close attention (Schultz, 1964). To begin with, he absolves some popular villains of the piece who are generally held responsible for the poor performance of agriculture. He observes:

It has been convenient to conceal the mistakes in economic policy that account for the failure in modernising agriculture by blaming the poor performance of the agricultural sector in poor countries on the adversity of Nature, or the perversity of farmers, or the fecundity of man (Schultz, 1966).

Regarding Nature, he says:

As one who was reared in the Dakotas with its volatile weather, I look upon this aspect of Nature as perfectly natural, and as such should be considered as an integral part of any normal expectations with respect to agricultural production.

We should agree with him that in South Asia, bad monsoon should be considered as an integral part of normal expectations, but it would be highly misleading to equate crop failures in Dakota in the agriculturally surplus and affluent USA with a succession of bad harvests in a country like India living at a barely subsistence level. What may be a setback in one case would be a disaster in the other. As for the perversity of farmers, there need be no dispute with Professor Schultz. Apart from 'some economists and urban-oriented intellectuals', no public leader of any stature has blamed the poor performance of Indian agriculture on the perversity of farmers. This does not, however, mean that there are no problems of education and extension in modernizing agriculture. Let us agree that even a subsistence farmer would respond to innovation if it is demonstrably profitable, and he has the resources to adopt it. The fecundity of men, however, is a much more complex problem than Professor Schultz would have us believe. For one thing, it is the timing of the excessive growth of population that is crucial. If it synchronizes with the early developmental effort, it may constitute a serious drag on growth. India's population has grown by 150 million since the planning effort began in 1951. During this period, the workforce in agriculture has increased probably by 50 million.[2] It would be a folly to ignore the impact of such a massive growth on the efficiency of organization of Indian agriculture. It is not only the need for more food, but also for more land and more work, which may bedevil the development in agriculture.

Having absolved the spurious villains, Professor Schultz makes a positive identification of the culprit. The root cause of the trouble according to him is

> the policy preference for industrialization, agriculture's contribution to its attainment being cheap food, as a source of cheap labour and public revenue. . . . This policy preference implies a low regard for agriculture as a source of economic growth. It means that low farm product prices and cheap food are an integral part of this type of economic policy. . . . When countries such as Nigeria, Chile or India want to keep their farm product prices low, the investment incentive for increasing the capacity of agriculture is thereby reduced.[3]

He illustrates this more elaborately by referring to the pricing of inputs. Observing that the necessary economic requirement in modernizing and increasing the capacity of agriculture in poor countries is a system of efficient prices, he asserts that most of the less developed countries have an inefficient system of pricing. 'The input prices are not only high, but they are also distorted one to another in most poor countries' (Schultz, 1966).

Professor Edward Mason writing on the Economic Development in India and Pakistan endorses most of Professor Schultz's criticism. He states,

> Both countries (India and Pakistan), despite appropriately worded paragraphs in their Five Year Plans assigning high priority to agriculture, neglected this overwhelmingly important sector. . . . Agricultural development in both countries was characterized during this early period, by declining incentives to farm output as the internal terms of trade moved against agricultural products . .
>   as prices of farm inputs and of consumer goods used by the agricultural population rose, the prices of foodgrains and of some other farm outputs were *held down by government action* [emphasis added] (Mason, 1966: 7, 8).

Both Professor Schultz and Professor Mason believe that the ready availability of agricultural surpluses from the United States has something to do with maintaining cereal prices at a low level and has contributed to postponing of serious attention to the question of agricultural productivity. Professor Mason repeats, 'PL 480 shipments had something to do with reducing farm incentives and in quantifiable degree must share the blame for the relative stagnation of agricultural output' (Mason, 1966: 52).

More importantly, he believes that the better performance of Pakistan since 1960 in promoting growth in the agricultural sector should be attributed to the reversal of the policies followed during the 1960s, the major departure from the earlier policy being the restoration of free market mechanism.

Production performance

As the critique of India's agricultural policies has been based on the production performance of Indian agriculture, it is but proper to note a few facts about it.

Prior to the disastrous failure of the monsoon in 1965–66, foodgrains production in India had increased to 89 million tonnes from 52 million tonnes in 1951. As a part of this increase is accounted by the enlarged statistical coverage and possibly by the change in the method of estimation, a better idea of the magnitude of the increase is provided by the index numbers of production from which the influence of these two factors has been eliminated. Table 12.1 gives the index numbers of agricultural production.

It is often suggested that much of this increase in production was due to the increase in acreage (as distinct from the increase in statistical coverage), and since the scope for further expansion in acreage is limited, agricultural production may not increase at the same rate in future. The facts are that between 1955–56 and 1964–65, acreage under all commodities increased by about 8 per cent and production by 34.8 per cent (Table 12.1).

Table 12.2 gives the growth rates in agricultural area, production and productivity between 1949–50 and 1964–65. The rates of growth in production, though not adequate in the context of

TABLE 12.1

Index numbers of agricultural production and area in India
(agricultural year 1949–50 = 100)

Period	Foodgrains		Non-foodgrains		All commodities	
	Production	Area	Production	Area	Production	Area
1950–51	90.5	97.9	105.9	110.8	95.6	99.9
1955–56	115.3	111.9	119.9	130.7	116.9	115.0
1960–61	137.1	116.9	152.6	141.2	142.2	120.8
1964–65	149.1	118.8	174.9	152.7	157.6	124.2

TABLE 12.2

Compound growth rates of agricultural area, production and
productivity, 1949–50 to 1964–65

(1949–50 to 1951–52 = 100)

	Area under crops (%)	Production (%)	Productivity (%)
Foodgrains	1.34	2.98	1.61
Non-foodgrains	2.52	3.61	1.06
All commodities	1.55	3.19	1.60

Source: Growth Rates in Agriculture 1949–50 to 1964–65, Ministry of Food and Agriculture, Government of India, 1966 (mimeo).

the rapidly rising population and money incomes, do not compare unfavourably with world averages or the averages for South-East Asia.

Price trends

The major count on which the agricultural policy of the developing countries has been criticized is the alleged attempt on the part of the policy-makers to keep farm product prices low. We may, therefore, examine this question in some detail. To begin with, we may acquaint ourselves with some of the basic facts about agricultural prices. Table 12.3 gives the index numbers of the wholesale prices of various commodities and commodity groups. While analyzing these price data it is necessary to note a few points. Firstly, the base year of the current price series is 1952–53, on the assumption that this was a normal year. It should, however, be noted that according to the earlier series with the base year 1939, the index number of cereal prices in 1952–53 was 444, with the general price index at 380.6. Thus, cereal prices were not only 4½ times higher than the pre-war prices, they were also relatively higher than the prices of manufactured articles, broadly indicating favourable terms of trade for agriculture. The shift in the base year of the new series, in a way, obliterated this phenomenon and also gave to the high prices an appearance of normalcy. This would, perhaps, explain why in January 1957, when the cereal price index stood at 95, the Government of India thought it fit to set up a high-powered committee 'to examine the causes of the rise in prices and to suggest remedial

TABLE 12.3

Index numbers of wholesale prices for selected commodity groups,
1951–52 to January 1967

Year	General index	Food articles	Cereals	Industrial raw materials*	Manufactures
		(Base: Year ended August 1939 = 100)			
1952			444.5		371.3
		(Base: 1952–53 = 100)			
1951–52	111.8	112.5	94.7	130.9	103.3
1955–56	92.5	86.6	75.5	99.0	99.7
1960–61	124.9	120.0	104.4	145.4	123.9
1965–66	165.1	168.8	148.1	189.1	149.1
Jan. 1967	198.3	209.7	190.0[†]	237.1	167.2

* In the total weight of 155 for this group, fibres and oilseeds account for 121; other agricultural commodities included are lac, rubber, etc.

[†] Last week/week ended Saturday.

Source: Report on Currency and Finance, 1965–66, Reserve Bank of India, Bombay, 1966.

measures, which would prevent speculative hoarding and arrest undue rise in prices'.

Another fact which may also be noted is that for some commodities like cotton, there has been a statutory ceiling on prices, and though in reality the ceiling has never been operative, the Office of the Economic Adviser, which prepares the index series, records only the ceiling prices. Thus, for commodities like these, the index number underestimates the rise in prices.

The price data for the past 15 years—or for that matter for the entire war and post-war period—do not indicate a situation of low farm prices. In fact, for the last five years, farm prices have been spiralling upwards and have caused extreme consumer distress, which was probably responsible for the severe reverses suffered by the ruling party in the recent general elections.

In terms of the new series, around 1955–56, there was a severe fall in the prices of agricultural commodities, and foodgrains prices suffered most. The decline in prices was not however brought about by any deliberate policy of the Government to keep down the prices, but was a consequence of a general slack in the economy and a series of good harvests. The Government could, however, be legitimately criticized for not taking adequate steps to prevent such a drastic fall in prices.

A few half-hearted attempts were made to support prices through government purchases, but these had little impact on the price trend. The developmental expenditure under the plan was considerably stepped up from 1954–55. Deficit financing, bank credit and money supply started on the upgrade from about this time. Food imports and withdrawal from Government stocks were cut down to the barest minimum. The embargo on foodgrains was lifted for the first time after the decade (Government of India, 1957: 9, 10).

However, as a result of these measures and the relatively poor crops in the subsequent seasons, prices started rising once again. By 1957, cereal prices were 54 per cent higher than those during the trough of 1955. Between 1961 and 1966, there was a further rise of about 50 per cent and in January 1967, the prices of cereals were 150 per cent higher than in 1955–56. The rise in the prices of agricultural commodities other than foodgrains has been even steeper.

Probably, what the critics have in view is not the absolute level of farm prices, but the relative prices and the farmers' terms of trade. The usual method used to determine the terms of trade is to study the relative movements in the prices of agricultural and non-agricultural commodities and the ratio between the two. This should not be strictly called terms of trade inasmuch as the weights used in the composition of the wholesale prices would be very different from the weights of the commodities entering into the trade between the two sectors. In any case, information regarding the movement in the prices of these two groups of commodities is of some interest and is given in Table 12.4.

By and large, the movement in the prices of the agricultural and non-agricultural commodity groups has been similar. In 1955, however, the index for agricultural commodities declined by as many as 12 points from the base year but that for the non-agricultural commodities fell by only 1 point. Thereafter, the rise in the price index of the agricultural commodities has been somewhat steeper than the rise in the non-agricultural commodity

TABLE 12.4

*Index numbers of wholesale prices of agricultural
and non-agricultural commodities, 1950 to 1966–67*

(Base: 1952-53 = 100)

Year	Agricultural commodities		Non-agricultural commodities	All commodities
	(680)*	(461)	(320)	(1000)
1950	113		99	109
1951	122		117	120
1952	102		104	102
1953	107		99	104
1954	99		100	100
1955	88		99	92
1956	102		105	103
1957	109		108	109
1958	112		109	111
1959	118		111	116
1960	124		121	123
1961	126		127	126
1961–62		122.9	–	125.1
1962–63		123.3	–	127.9
1963–64		131.5	–	135.3
1964–65		155.8	–	152.7
1965–66		169.3	–	165.1
1966–67		199.0	–	191.1

* The figures in parentheses show the weights.

Sources: *Economic Survey of Indian Agriculture 1960–61*, Directorate of Economics & Statistics, Ministry of Food & Agriculture, Government of India,
New Delhi, 1961: 56; and *Reserve Bank of India Bulletin*, Vol. XXI, No.
4, April 1967.

price index. In 1961, the two indices stood almost at the same
level. Since then the prices of agricultural commodities have
risen more rapidly than those of non-agricultural commodities.

An analysis of the data relating to the percentage change
in price levels for all commodities, agricultural commodities and
their sub-groups during the period 1953–66 confirms these observations. Except for the quinquennium 1951–56 when the decline
in agricultural prices was somewhat more than that in the prices
of non-agricultural commodities, the subsequent rise in the prices
of the former, especially commercial crops, has been consistently

higher than that in the prices of non-agricultural commodities.

Information regarding the ratio of prices received to prices paid by the farmers is available only for a few regions. The Punjab Board of Economic Inquiry has been compiling this information for the last 25 years. Similar information is available for the last decade in some other States like Assam, Kerala, Orissa and West Bengal. Extreme caution has to be exercised in making use of this information without a detailed scrutiny of the methods and techniques used in the construction of the index. The differences in the crop patterns of these regions are significant. Orissa, Assam and West Bengal are predominantly rice-growing areas, while the major crops in the Punjab are wheat and gram. Kerala's agriculture is dominated by products like coconut, tapioca and pepper. Weights given to different commodities in the construction of the indices of prices received naturally vary, as they should. But the marked variations in the weights given to commodities entering into the indices of prices paid, particularly in regard to family consumption—for example, 48 per cent for clothing in the Punjab and 8 per cent in Bengal—are difficult to explain. Similarly, the basis for weights given to commodities purchased for farm production is quite arbitrary in some cases. Apart from the technicalities of the construction of the index numbers, the method of collection of the data and their dependability leave much to be desired.

Price policy statements

Thus, contrary to the general impression, the analysis of the relevant data on agricultural prices does not (with the exception of the quinquennium 1951–56) indicate either absolute or relative low levels and adverse terms of trade for agriculture during the last 15 years. We will now see whether the policies announced or implemented by the Government indicate any deliberate bias to keep farm prices low. The various Plan documents are the best sources for acquainting ourselves with the thinking of the policy-makers. The First Five-Year Plan document contains a very comprehensive statement on food price policy. It may be noted that when the First Five-Year Plan was formulated, the prices of wheat and rice were 5 to 5 1/2 times higher than the pre-war level. It is, therefore, not surprising that the planners were

concerned about ensuring that the prices of foodgrains are held
stable at levels within the reach of the poorer sections of the
community. But the Plan document hastened to emphasize that.

> This does not, of course, mean that the producer of the foodgrains
> should not get a reasonable return. On economic as well as social
> grounds it is vital that he does. But, the real return that he
> gets does not depend only upon the prices he obtains for his
> produce; it depends as much upon the prices he in turn has
> to pay for what he buys. If any increase in food prices raises
> the latter, he may be no better off in the end, and may even
> be worse off. In the final analysis, what limits the real income
> of the primary producer is low productivity. To increase this,
> what is needed is a programme of public investment, which will
> give him the water, the power, the seeds and the manures he
> needs. A policy which might raise prices all round and jeopardise
> the investment programme is therefore of no ultimate benefit to
> the producer (Government of India, 1953: 173).

This was further elaborated in the following statement.

> A policy of price stabilisation must have in view certain maxima
> as well as certain minima. At a time when the economy is subject
> to inflationary pressures, the emphasis is inevitably on the maintenance
> of the maxima. But if the trend of prices is persistently downward,
> a system of controls with defined procurement prices can be used—
> and indeed should be used—to safeguard the interests of producers
> by preventing prices from falling unduly. Judicious purchases by
> Government at defined prices are thus an excellent device for
> stabilising prices and for evening out to some extent inter-State
> disparities.
>   It is sometimes argued that controls act as a disincentive
> to production and that if free market conditions are restored, production
> will be stimulated, and even though prices rise in the process,
> the consumers will, in the long run, stand to benefit. To what
> extent controls are a disincentive depends on two factors: (a)
> prices paid to producers for controlled commodities, and (b) the
> efficiency and fairness with which the controls are administered.
> This latter aspect of the problem has, of course, to be constantly
> kept in view. As regards prices, the problem is to define a level
> which may be considered reasonable under given circumstances,
> and to ensure through direct controls or through fiscal and other
> devices that the producer of foodgrains is not placed at an undue

disadvantage. The difficulty about the incentive which might be given by the unregulated operation of the free market to production in a particular line is that expansion in this line takes place at the expense of output in some other line. A general increase in output cannot, obviously, be secured by merely increasing the money reward for each unit of work. The great advantage of a system of controls is that under it the measure of incentives to be given can be regulated (Government of India, 1953: 180).

Subsequent Plan documents have reiterated this policy with only some minor changes in emphasis. The Third Five-Year Plan stated:

The producers of foodgrains must get reasonable return. The farmer, in other words, should be assured that the prices of foodgrains and other commodities that he produces will not be allowed to fall below a reasonable minimum. The farmer should have the necessary incentive to make these investments and to put in a larger effort. The policy designed to prevent sharp fluctuations in prices and to guarantee a certain minimum level is essential in the interest of foodgrains production. . . . The other objective, no less essential, is to safeguard the interest of the consumer, and, as has been stated earlier, it is particularly necessary to ensure that the prices of essential commodities such as foodgrains do not rise excessively (Government of India, 1961: 130).

In January 1965, the Government of India constituted the Agricultural Prices Commission. The Commission is to advise the Government on

the price policy of agricultural commodities with a view to evolving a balanced and integrated price structure in the perspective of the overall needs of the economy and with due regard to the interests of the producer and the consumer.

While recommending the price policy and the relative price structure, the Commission was enjoined to keep in view amongst other things,

the need to provide incentive to the producer for adopting improved technology and for maximizing production and the likely effect of the price policy on the rest of the economy, particularly on the cost of living, on wages, industrial cost structure etc. (Government of India, 1965: 47).

As will be evident, the various policy statements do not
indicate any deliberate intention to keep farm prices low, though
the need to protect the consumers from the consequences of
an inordinate rise in prices has been necessarily kept in view.
It has been amply made clear that the concern for consumer
interests should not be allowed to take away the farmer's incentive
to adopt improved technology and make the necessary investment
for the purpose.

Operational price policy

It may be argued that, as in other spheres, the policy statements
of the Government have been invariably unexceptionable, but
little of this wisdom is reflected in the actual implementation
of the policies. We shall, therefore, now examine in some detail
the operational aspects of the price policy. At the very outset,
it may be admitted that, as in other spheres,. the Government
has not been wholly successful in realizing the objectives of
its price policy, but as we shall presently see, the failure has
been more in respect of curbing the inflationary rise in prices
than in maintaining what may be termed as incentive levels
of prices.

In reviewing the operative part of the price policy, it should
be noted that except for sugarcane sales to the sugar factories—
which amount to about 25 per cent of the sugarcane production—market
prices are not fixed for any agricultural commodity. Floor and
ceiling prices have been announced for raw cotton since 1943,
but both the levels have been raised several times. It is, however,
common knowledge that the ceiling levels have never effectively
checked the rise in prices. Some State Governments did, off
and on, announce maximum prices for foodgrains, but they have
never been able to enforce them effectively. On the other hand,
the Government has supported the prices of foodgrains as well
as commercial crops, particularly jute at floor levels. The actual
purchases, however, were limited because the prices soon rose
above the support level. Thus occasionally even when the avowed
intention of the Government was to check excessive rise in prices
of agricultural commodities, it did not succeed in controlling

farm prices.

Operationally, the only prices fixed by the Government—and effectively implemented in recent years—are the minimum guaranteed support prices. It has been explained that these are floor prices, calculated to provide a sort of insurance against the contingency of a severe fall in price, such as had occurred during 1955–56. Though no rigid formula has been accepted to determine the levels of floor prices, the criterion followed is that progressive farmers should find these levels adequate to encourage enterprise and investment to augment production through the adoption of improved technology with all its risk and uncertainty. The actual market prices have been higher than the statutory floor levels, and it can be safely asserted that for the last several years, no progressive farmer has been inhibited by the price factor in adopting improved technology.

Procurement

Besides the guaranteed minimum support prices, the Government fixes from time to time prices for procurement of foodgrains needed for its system of public distribution through fair price or ration shops. These prices are higher than the minimum support prices by a fair margin.[4] Only in 1963–64 was the difference between the two rather small. Procurement prices have been successively revised upwards in keeping with the market trends, but they are certainly lower than the prevailing open market prices. The fact that the Government procures foodgrains which has an element of compulsion and that the procurement is made at below market prices, has been criticized as constituting a disincentive to production. As in respect of other policy matters, the facts of the situation are probably not fully known. The average annual foodgrains procurement over the decade ending 1961 comes to 1.16 million tonnes from the average production of 68.6 million tonnes—which would amount to less than 1.7 per cent of annual production (see Table 12.5). If we exclude the procurement in the first two years (1951–52 and 1952–53) of the decade, it amounts to less than 1 per cent of the domestic production. Incidentally, it may be noted that during these years not all procurement has been made at below the market rate. A part of it was in support of the floor prices.

TABLE 12.5

Foodgrains production and procurement, 1951–52 to 1965–66

(in million tonnes)

Year	Production	Procurement	Per cent of (3) to (2)
1	2	3	4
1951–52	52.02	3.48	6.68
1952–53	59.24	2.09	3.52
1953–54	69.82	1.43	2.04
1954–55	68.07	0.13	0.19
1955–56	66.85	0.04	0.06
1956–57	69.85	0.29	0.41
1957–58	64.31	0.53	0.82
1958–59	77.14	1.80	2.33
1959–60	76.67	1.27	1.65
1960–61	82.04	0.54	0.66
Total years (1951–52 to 1960–61)	686.01	11.60	1.69
1961–62	82.71	0.48	0.58
1962–63	78.45	0.75	0.95
1963–64	79.43	1.41	1.77
1964–65	89.00	3.23	3.62
1965–66	72.30	3.72	5.14

Source: Bulletins of Food Statistics, Ministry of Food & Agriculture, Government of India.

The step-up in procurement commenced from 1963–64 and was mostly confined to paddy and rice. The procurement of wheat has never exceeded half a million tonnes and most of it was procured in the Punjab in the open market—subject, however, to the ban on movement beyond the Punjab Zone. In 1964–65, the procurement of 2.9 million tonnes of rice amounted to some 8 per cent of rice production or 25 per cent of the marketable surplus. This, no doubt, was a substantial proportion. But what exactly is the effect of this procurement on the average price received by the rice grower for his production or marketed surplus? It may be noted that with the exception of Maharashtra, which has introduced during the last two years, the so-called Government monopoly of rice and jowar purchase, the farmers are free to sell what is not procured by the Government—something like 75 per cent of the marketed surplus—in the open market. It is well known that whenever there is procurement by the Government, open market prices go up steeply and disproportionately to the quantum withdrawn by the Government from the open market. As such, it would be reasonable to hold that the weighted average price received by the producer for the total sales (to the Government and in the open market) will be no less than what he would have received in the absence of procurement. While this large-scale procurement was being undertaken, the index number of wholesale prices of cereals has gone up from 101 in March 1963 to 190 in March 1967. In the face of such spiralling prices, the Government could not adopt a *laissez-faire* attitude; and the least it had to do was to maintain a system of public distribution of foodgrains at reasonable prices. For this purpose, wheat was available under the PL-480 programme, but rice had to be internally procured.

It is often suggested that the Government should purchase foodgrains, if it must, through the Food Corporation at competitive market prices. But to anyone with a little knowledge of market psychology it should be obvious that such action would instantaneously push up prices in the open market. It has been found that at the very appearance of the agents of the Food Corporation as buyers in the market, prices go up, compelling the Corporation to bid at higher and higher prices or go without purchase. This happens because the market knows that the Government, unlike the ordinary trader, has definite commitments to supply foodgrains for its system of public distribution and comes to the market in the given period only to buy and not sell. Besides, a system under which the Government purchases foodgrains at soaring market prices and distributes them at reasonable prices, would involve a heavy subsidy on consumer prices, at the cost of the State exchequer. We have not made any precise estimate of the financial cost to the Government of a scheme under which the Food Corporation would buy at the going rates and supply to the consumers at reasonable prices. But it is obvious that the scheme would impose an intolerable burden on the finances of the Government.

The Foodgrains Policy Committee (1966) had examined the question of open market purchases by the Government and observed:

> Such a system will, no doubt, involve very little disturbance to the working of the market economy. What is overlooked, however, is that prices will unduly rise. When Government enters the foodgrains

market as a buyer in competition with private traders, the latter will push the prices up in order to command sufficient stocks so that they can continue to remain in business. Moreover, it has to be remembered that purchase operations by a single large buyer tend to raise prices much more than by a large number of smaller buyers. Government's purchase prices are likely to turn out to be so high that neither the objective of holding the price line, nor that of equitable distribution to all, including the low income groups, can be expected to be achieved (Government of India, 1966: 37).

While this is generally admitted, Professor V.M. Dandekar suggests that

there exists a method of buying whereby the government may buy at the going market price without itself entering competitive bidding. This is called purchase by pre-emption. It has been successfully practised in the Punjab. In this method, the government or the public marketing agency does not directly participate in the formation of price in the market. The market price is allowed to form through the normal processes of competitive bidding and bargaining in the market. However, after the price is fixed and the deal is settled, the government reserves the pre-emptive right to step in and buy the given quantities at the price settled in the market. As the government does not enter the competition with other buyers in the market, it does not give a push to the price as it would otherwise. Nevertheless, it is able to offer the producer a price in accordance with the market situation (Dandekar, 1967: 41, 42).

The system of purchase by pre-emption has much to commend itself. But such purchases can be made only in markets which are 'regulated' and have introduced a system of sale by auction. Very few up-country markets are so organized and regulated. Dandekar accepts this fact and suggests that 'one of the first measures necessary is to organize and rationalize the marketing of foodgrains in the country so that a structure of market prices would emerge, from day-to-day, by normal market processes which are competitive and public' (Dandekar, 1967: 42).

Dandekar suggests that within each district, a Foodgrains Marketing Board should be established endowed with a monopoly of inter-district trade. It should be a representative body of foodgrains producers, traders and the *Panchayati Raj* institutions, with a Government-nominated chief administrative officer and accountant. The Marketing Board will purchase foodgrains in the open market in competition with other traders and marketing agencies. All inter-district purchases and sales will be restricted to the agency of District Marketing Boards. 'Thus, the inter-district trade will be reduced to mutual trade between the 300 odd District Foodgrains Marketing Boards.' 'All deals settled between them will be promptly publicized giving particulars of quantities, quality and prices at selling points.' (Large districts could have more than one Board as 'there is no harm even if the number of Boards is increased to thousand or even two thousand'.) Once the foodgrains market is thus 'reorganized', the Government (State or Central?) would exercise its right of pre-emption. 'All contracts for interdistrict sale or purchase . . . should be immediately notified to the respective state governments and permits for the necessary movement of the foodgrains sought.' If the Government finds the price attractive, it would exercise 'its pre-emptive right and ask the District to surrender not more than half the quantities contracted for, at the contract price'. 'In this manner the state governments will acquire stocks of foodgrains adequate to conduct their food policy' (Dandekar, 1967: 47–49). There will thus be 300 or 1000 food budgets, 300 to 1000 monopolies of inter-district trade and as many food zones: all in the interest of 'free market' prices and incentives to production! Food and Freedom is the title of Dandekar's brochure.

Apart from this, is it reasonable to suggest that anything less than the market price—whatever the state of scarcity, hoarding and speculative manipulations—necessarily constitutes a disincentive to the farmers? Is such absolute reliance on the 'reincarnated dogma of the market' necessary, or desirable? What seems reasonable to posit is that as long as prices are well above the cost of production (inclusive of the risk margin), the farmer will spare no effort to increase his income through the largest possible production, within the constraint of his own and national resources.

PL-480 imports:
Impact on prices and production

We may now examine the repeated assertion that PL-480 imports

have had the effect of depressing farm product prices within
the receiving country and impairing the economic incentives to
farmers to increase agricultural production. Let us first record
a few facts. During the decade 1951–61, imports of cereals averaged
3 million tons per year. Table 12.6 indicates that they varied
from 1.3 to 11 per cent of domestic cereal production,[5] the
variation being related to the domestic supply position. During
the triennium from 1954–55 to 1956–57, when the crops were
moderately good, but the foodgrain prices declined sharply, imports
were only marginal, being less than 2 per cent of the net domestic
production.

It is obvious that in the absence of PL-480 imports, foodgrains
prices would have risen higher. We may assume that high prices
are not considered as an end objective, but are deemed to be
crucial from the point of view of their impact on production
and the farmers' incentives. For the discussion of this issue,

TABLE 12.6

Gross imports on Government account, 1951 to 1966

(in thousand tonnes)

Year	Imports of wheat	Total cereal imports	Total cereal production	Col. (3) as % of Col. (4)
1	2	3	4	5
1951	2970	4800	45740	10.50
1952	2459	3930	46400	8.46
1953	1612	2040	51350	3.97
1954	197	830	61080	1.35
1955	435	600	58970	1.01
1956	1095	1400	57530	2.43
1957	2898	3630	60200	6.03
1958	2716	3224	56410	5.71
1959	3553	3868	65490	5.90
1960	4386	5137	64873	7.91
1961	3092	3495	69310	5.04
1962	3250	3640	70951	5.13
1963	4073	4556	67008	6.80
1964	5621	6266	70188	8.92
1965	6583	7450	76560	9.73
1966	–	10340	62250	16.61

Note: 1951 refers to agricultural year 1950–51 and so on.

Source: Economic Survey, 1966–67, Ministry of Finance, Government of India,
New Delhi, 1967.

it would be relevant to determine whether the foodgrains imports would affect the prices of foodgrains alone or those of all other crops as well. The major component of PL-480 imports was wheat and it is reasonable to assume that these imports affected the prices of wheat or at best also of other substitutable cereals from the consumer point of view, but could not have had much impact on the prices of commercial crops. The expected consequence of this relative shift in prices in favour of commercial crops would be a shift of agricultural inputs to their production. Assuming that this is exactly what happened, would such a development be necessarily injurious to Indian agriculture or the Indian economy as a whole? It is, of course, true that higher foodgrains production is very vital to India's economy, but a stimulus to the growth of non-foodgrain crops is of no less importance for the overall national economy, particularly in regard to the international balance of payments.

Reverting back to the price effect of PL-480 wheat imports, we do find that prices of wheat remained relatively lower than the prices of several other agricultural commodities. It may, however be noted that in the years of very low cereal prices (1954–56), PL-480 imports were negligible and the prices of all agricultural commodities had declined sharply. This would indicate that there were more potent economic factors than PL-480 wheat imports which determined the trend in agricultural prices. It is indeed difficult to discern a consistent correlation between the prices of agricultural commodities and domestic production or the total availability (production—imports). The per capita availability of foodgrains in 1954–56 (15.7 ounces per day) when foodgrain prices crashed was in fact no larger than that in the years 1963–65 when prices were sky-rocketing, in spite of the enormous PL-480 imports. The price impact of PL-480, if any, was evidently drowned by more powerful monetary factors.

We may now assess the impact of PL-480 imports on the production and productivity of different crops. Wheat was the major component of these imports. As such if the assumption regarding the depressing effect of these imports on domestic production were valid, one would expect that the commodity whose production would suffer most would be wheat. As a matter of fact, this did not happen. The study of growth rates of different crops in India shows that wheat fared better both in area and production compared to all other foodgrains, and the growth of wheat production was at par with that of commercial crops like cotton—though not with groundnut, jute and sugarcane (Table 12.7).

In assessing the price effects of PL-480 or any other imports, it is necessary to ascertain critically, both theoretically and empirically, the factors which influence farm prices. While it is clear that on the supply side the main factor is availability (domestic + imports), on the demand side the relative importance of population growth and increase in money incomes is inadequately taken into consideration. In fact, in the entire analysis of the problem by Western critics, the price effect of the rise in money incomes has been completely ignored. By exclusively pinning attention on the *agricultural* policy of the developing countries, instead of viewing it as a part of the total economic policies, they have been led into a serious error of economic analysis.

In a recent study analyzing the inter-relationship between the change in price on the one hand and changes in Government spending and commodity output on the other, it was found that 'a 10 per cent increase in plan outlay and non-plan expenditure will increase the price index by 2.6 per cent, and a 10 per cent increase in commodity output will result in a decrease in price of only 0.7 per cent' (Economic and Scientific Research Foundation, 1967). Commenting on this inter-relationship, the authors observe:

> The most striking fact is the very small effect commodity output has on price: commodity output has to increase nearly four times as fast as Government expenditure to offset the sharp increase

TABLE 12.7

Compound growth rates of production of and area under different crops, 1949–50 to 1964–65

Crops	Production (%)	Area (%)
Rice	3.37	1.26
Wheat	3.97	2.70
Jowar	2.50	0.91
Cotton	4.44	2.42
Groundnut	4.18	3.81
Sugarcane	4.59	3.26

Source: Growth Rates in Agriculture 1949–50 to 1964–65, op. cit., Table 3.3.

in prices induced by the latter. If, for instance, total Government expenditure increases at a rate of about 15 per cent per year, the price index will be expected to rise by 3.9 per cent annually. If we wish to limit the net price increase to 3 per cent annually, the difference between 3.9 and 3 will have to be offset through an increase in output amounting to a rate of 13 per cent annually.

In another study, analyzing factors affecting agricultural prices in India, the conclusion was that 'the national income/money supply played a more significant role in explaining the variance in foodgrains prices as compared to the per capita availability' (Krishna and Radhakrishna, n.d.).

The Indian planners have repeatedly emphasized that 'a major constituent of price policy in this situation is fiscal and monetary discipline': unfortunately this precept was observed only in its breach. The sins of the policy-makers, if any, were in following a highly inflationary policy, which compelled the devaluation of the rupee in June 1966, and by no stretch of imagination those of keeping farm prices low. When the attention of Western critics was drawn to the fact that 'the PL-480 imports were meant as a countervailing force to the inflationary pressure in the economy generated by deficit financing and development expenditure' (Dantwala, 1963) a typical reaction was that

> This may indeed be so. However, while there may be no pronounced negative effect on domestic agriculture [because of the existing upward pressure on farm prices], if farmers are at all sensitive to prices, then agriculture will not expand to the extent that it would have done in the absence of the imported surplus.[6] The signal from the price mechanism that *more* resources are needed in domestic agriculture will not get through because of the effects of the surplus (Fisher, 1963: 868).

If this rejoinder is to be taken seriously, it would imply that

1. under no circumstances, however grave, should the domestic imbalance in production be corrected through imports, since they depress prices and destroy producers' incentives;
2. the process of higher prices-higher production could go on *ad infinitum*, notwithstanding the resource supply constraint;

and

3. the only valid guide for the allocation of resources is the price mechanism, whatever be its observed functional deficiency in a given situation.

One would wish that the strategy of economic development was as simple as this, for under it, all that the planners would have to do is to ensure an uninhibited price rise. Surely, more understanding is needed of the factors which inhibit agricultural growth in poor countries.

Input prices and policies

We have examined the criticism that in India the policy has been to hold down product prices. We will now turn our attention to the criticism that input prices have been kept very high and this has prevented the farmers from modernizing their agriculture. Professor Schultz observes:

> It should be obvious that where the price of fertilizer is too high, relative to the price of farm product, no extension programme can be devised that will induce farmers to use more fertilizer. . . . In Japan where farmers are applying a hundred times as much fertilizer, it is vastly lower in relation to the price of farm product. It takes less than half as many pounds of wheat in Japan to buy a pound of nitrogenous fertilizer as it does in India. Rice farmers in India pay between three and four times as much for the fertilizer as do farmers in Japan in terms of the price that they receive for rice (Schultz, 1966: 49).

Mason endorses this view when he states,

> If the potentialities of growth of Indian agriculture are to be realised, much greater attention than has been evident in the past will have to be paid to the relation between the prices of farm inputs and the prices of farm outputs (Mason, 1966: 59).

Both Schultz and Mason quote the ratios of fertilizer-product prices to illustrate the point. There is no gainsaying the fact that the price of fertilizer in India is very high, and to the extent the Fertilizer Pool operated by the Government sought to earn a profit from fertilizer distribution, it could be said that the policy contributed to a small extent to high prices. We can expect some reduction in the price when, as proposed, new large-sized fertilizer factories based on modern technological processes are established leading to a substantial reduction in the cost of production. Pakistan, we know, has been heavily subsidizing fertilizer use, but this has been possible mainly because of, as Mason points out, the rapid growth in foreign assistance, 'which in the last two years of her Second plan amounted to 6 per cent of GDP and some 40 per cent of total development expenditure' (Mason, 1966: 53).

The real bottleneck in the further extension of fertilizer use in India is its availability and, till the introduction of the high-yielding varieties, a relatively low technical coefficient of output response at higher levels of fertilizer application. The fertilizer production programme in India makes a poor showing and the Government cannot be absolved from the blame for this poor performance. In this connection, it would be pertinent to note the recent liberalization of Government of India's policy on fertilizer. New units obtaining industrial licence before 31st December 1967 will not be subject to restrictions as to price or marketing for a period of seven years. As yet, the response of foreign collaborators to the new policy has not been very encouraging.

It should be readily agreed that factor prices must not be so high as to discourage optimum use of inputs for augmenting production. This condition is satisfied as long as additional expenses (including the risk premium) involved in the use of any technical input are fully covered by the expected increase in receipts at current product prices. Under these conditions there is no conceivable obstacle to the use of the input by progressive farmers. To the best of our knowledge, at no stage is the farmer in India known to have refrained from the use of fertilizer because of its high price. The Committee on Fertilizers (1965) which looked into this problem has stated that:

> Except in the rain-fed areas where certain risks related to the dependency on seasonal rainfall exist, the field results appear to indicate that at present levels of fertilizer application, the farmer in India finds adequate profitability in fertilizer use even at present prices (Government of India, 1965: 30).

The Committee cites the studies conducted by the Indian Institute of Agricultural Statistics and observes that 'net return on fertilizer investment can go up to 400 per cent'. It categorically states that 'in the current context of short supply of fertilizers in relation to the demand, it cannot be said that fertilizer prices are inhibiting the growth of fertilizer use'. In fact, there is an active black market in fertilizers and the problem is how to check the diversion of fertilizers from contemplated uses.

Data derived from a large number of fertilizer trials conducted on farmers' fields indicate that a 20 kg application of nitrogen per hectare increases yield of rice by 259 kg and that of wheat by 350 kg With the price of N at Rs 1.66 per kg and of rice and wheat at Rs 60 and Rs 50 per quintal, respectively, at the level of optimum doses, the profit per hectare would be Rs 173.8 for rice and Rs 221.3 for wheat. In other words, one rupee worth of nitrogen gives a profit of Rs 2.4 for rice and Rs 2.6 for wheat.[7] The fertilizer response of the newly introduced high-yielding varieties is much larger, making higher doses of fertilizer application distinctly profitable.

> It is over 18 months since the new high-yielding varieties of 'dwarf' Mexican wheat outgrew the experimental stage and were first distributed to a large number of cultivators in the major wheat-growing areas of Punjab, Haryana, Western Uttar Pradesh and Northern Rajasthan. Their results are now available. Their yields in 1965–66 have averaged 5,340 kilograms per hectare as against 3,330 kilograms of the best local varieties. The gross return per hectare is assessed respectively at Rs 3,500 and Rs 2,200. The cost of fertilizers has been assessed at Rs 300 for the former and Rs 130 for local varieties. This gives an increase of 54 per cent in net returns in favour of the 'dwarf' varieties with applications of fertilizer that are still below maximum yield levels.[8]

This is a sufficient condition for as extensive a use of fertilizer as may be desired—subject to availability. We should accept Professor Schultz's proposition that the farmer's acceptance of the new input would depend upon the profitability of its use; but it is not logical to suggest that the acceptance is proportional to profitability. The incentive or disincentive for the use of fertilizers in India does not depend upon profitability of its use in Japan,

Taiwan or Pakistan. The Indian farmer does not decide the quantum of fertilizer use on his farm in India by reference to the profitability of fertilizer use in Japan. It is therefore difficult to understand the relevance of the citation of fertilizer-rice or wheat price ratios in other countries to the economics of farming in India. Progressive farmers in India are satisfied that fertilizer use is currently profitable and would like to use as much of it as they can obtain. They and everyone else concerned would desire a reduction in fertilizer prices, but even today, farmers do not mind buying it in the black market. 'There was a time when the extension agencies used to go with a message of greater use of chemical fertilizers and pumping sets. Today, the farmers go money in hand to purchase these commodities but they are not available to them' (Punjab Agricultural University, 1966).

Most of the improved varieties of seeds in India were earlier developed to have a drought-resisting quality. This was perfectly natural under Indian conditions where the major risk in farming arose from the failure of the monsoon. But the response of these varieties to high fertilizer doses was somewhat meagre. It considerably reduced the profitability of intensive fertilizer use. A major breakthrough in Indian agriculture is now occurring as a result of the introduction of high-yielding varieties which have a very high fertilizer response. With this, fertilizer use which was already profitable, will become much more so.

A word may be said about Professor Schultz's view about investment in irrigation. He observes, 'India already has three times as much land under irrigation as Japan—measured on a per capita basis. Yet India has invested large sums during recent years in still more irrigation' (Schultz, 1966: 45–46). It is absurd to measure irrigation requirement on a per capita basis. The only sensible basis of judging the requirement is the soil-climate complex. Fifty-five per cent of Japan's arable land was irrigated in 1962 as against only 15 per cent in India. In a country where the major threat to farming is drought, irrigation must have the highest priority. A few more tubewells in Bihar would have avoided the major disaster it is facing today. But more importantly, the high pay-off to what Professor Schultz calls modern inputs depends primarily on assured water supply. It is not just a whim of the policy-makers in India that the new strategy of agricultural development and India's only hope of a breakthrough in agricultural production is sought to be concentrated in areas of assured rainfall or irrigation. Assured water supply is essential to the success of high-yielding varieties of seeds. In a recent enquiry conducted by the Agricultural Economics Research Centre, University of Delhi, in the IADP district of Aligarh (UP), 53 per cent of farmers gave 'lack of timely and adequate irrigation' as the reason for not using chemical fertilizers, and another 10 per cent mentioned lack of financial resources. The main conclusion of the study was:

> The most important pre-condition (for the breakthrough in agricultural production) is the creation of an assured and adequate irrigation, followed by improvement in farmers' knowledge about the technical and also economic aspects of the new inputs which they are expected to adopt (*The Economic Times*, 12 April 1967).

When we are thinking about agricultural production at the national level rather than at the level of an individual farmer, the overall availability of critical inputs, rather than an individual farmer's capacity (income) to offer higher prices, becomes a more crucial factor in augmenting production. It could, of course, be argued that availability is a function of price. But this is not invariably so in developing economies. Take the case of high-yielding varieties of seeds. Their discovery and adaptation to local conditions, agronomic trials, preparation of nucleus and foundation seed, the first stage of seed multiplication and the extension work associated with their adoption by the farmers: all these activities depend to a very large extent on Government initiative and sponsorship. The farmers' capacity to offer adequate price for the high-yielding varieties is largely irrelevant to the development of the activities listed above. In other words, one would not get the needed quantities of improved varieties of seeds merely through the functioning of the price mechanism.

The question is not whether India's agricultural economy should be run by the market or the planners. It is simply whether at this stage of India's agricultural development, public investment in socio-economic infrastructure—agronomic research, soil-testing laboratories, fertilizer trials and demonstrations, seed farms, well-trained extension personnel—would be more rewarding than high prices, which perchance may result in dispersed and rather uncertain investments by a large number of farmers. Neither is it a question of either-or, i.e., the market or the planner. A judicious balance has to be struck. The fact that more resources are needed for agriculture need not wait for the signal of inordinately high prices. In our context they are at best a danger signal. All that needs to be ensured is that the price does not act as an inhibitive factor to the flow of resources to agriculture.

Prices and income

The persistent campaign for the recognition of price as the most crucial factor in production compels a close examination of the issue of the price effect on production. To clear the decks, it should be conceded straightaway that farmers, even in a subsistence economy, do respond to prices in the sense that they adjust production to the most profitable cropping pattern. Nor need it be disputed that farm prices should be remunerative. But the view that 'the higher the prices offered to farmers, the more they will produce and bring to the market' needs a closer examination.

First and foremost, for a critical analysis of the price effect on production, it is important to distinguish between

1. shifts in land and other resources in response to changes in inter-crop price relationship, and
2. an overall increase in agricultural production through the input of additional resources.

The price factor is quite effective when a shift is desired in the relative production of two competing crops—say, between jute and rice. Its effectiveness is considerably reduced when a simultaneous increase in the production of almost all agricultural crops is desired—as is the case in India.[9]

Even in regard to shifts in resource use, particularly of land, there are severe agro-climatic constraints. In a recent study, an attempt was made to ascertain whether the changes in the cropping pattern were influenced by the relative price/returns of selected competing groups of crops. The results did not indicate any uniform pattern. In a number of cases, the relative area, price and returns are found to move in the same direction while in a number of other cases they moved in contrary directions. The final conclusion of the study is that 'it is not possible to choose a set of factors which have uniformly influenced changes

228 Dilemmas of growth

in cropping patterns with regard to all the crops in the State as well as in the district' (NCAER, 1966).

Another study has shown that in the allocation of area between rival foodgrains, price was not a vital consideration.

> In respect of foodgrains, price relative to weather becomes a feebler consideration, except and to the extent that foodgrains compete with crops other than rival foodgrains for area. Thus rainfall assumes that status which price does in the case of cash crops (Dharm Narain, 1965: 158).

The increase in rice production in Punjab is primarily due to the increase in the water-logged area where rice is the most appropriate crop to grow. In Gujarat, where groundnut-*bajra* price parity moved in favour of the former, groundnut production increased at a compound rate of 9 per cent per year through the increase in area at the rate of 10 per cent, productivity decreasing at the rate of 0.97 per cent. The area under *bajra* decreased at the compound rate of 5.14 per cent, but its productivity increased by 4.88 per cent (Government of India, 1966). A judgement on the economic gain from such a change in the cropping pattern is not easy to make.

Thirdly, for some crops, the relative price change has to be quite substantial so as to reverse the relative profitability of the competing crops. In a recent study, it was found that there was not much meaningful association between the prices of rice and sugarcane on the one hand and the acreage of the two crops on the other.

> The acreage of sugarcane as compared to paddy continuously increased during this period, but no such systematic trend was found in their relative prices. One important factor which determined the trends was that the net value of sugarcane output per acre was more than four times that of paddy (Gupta and Majid, 1962: 51).

Such profitability cannot be negatived by merely a shift in the price parity of the two commodities.

Fourthly, for operational purposes, which economic devices would one use to deliberately alter the inter-crop price relationship? Assuming we could deliberately push up foodgrain prices, would this necessarily alter the food-non-food price ratio in favour of the former? For this to happen, it would be necessary to prevent a rise in the prices of non-food crops which is bound to take place as a consequence of the shift in resources in favour of the food crops, because the supply of commercial crops is already lagging severely behind demand. Assuming that it would be right to hold down the prices of non-food crops—but not of foodgrains— how does one do this? The only known economic devices are buffer stocks and imports—PL-480 or others. Prospects for neither are bright, of buffer stocks in view of the continuing shortages, and of imports because of the stringency in foreign exchange.

Apart from this, it is income rather than price which is more relevant to the issue of the incentive. In many developing economies, agricultural productivity is very low. The greatest disincentive in farming is low income. And at the root of low income are the scanty resource base of the cultivator and its low productivity. Increase in productivity will therefore be more rewarding than the increase in price in augmenting farmers' income. To stress the price factor beyond a point is to seek an easy way out, and sidetrack the main issue.[10] An excessive emphasis on the price factor may even weaken the incentive for the adoption of improved production practices by making existing practices more profitable. It is indeed surprising that the crusaders for incentive prices do not simultaneously mention the contribution which higher productivity can make to higher incomes—without an increase in product prices. The high-yielding varieties of seeds recently introduced in India have a much greater potential for augmenting farm incomes than merely higher product prices. The relationship between prices of farm products and prices of purchasable inputs is, no doubt, important. But *more important* is the output response to the inputs, which can be greatly increased by technical research and better farm management.

Non-price incentive

It is somewhat surprising that the discussion on production incentives is restricted to prices and the prevalence of a free market mechanism. There was a time when the developing countries were told that defects of the agrarian structure—absentee landlordism, exploitative tenancy, usurious credit and inefficient marketing—were major obstacles to agricultural development. India has carried out a fairly radical programme of land reforms. In spite of the many admitted imperfections in the implementation of the programme, the agrarian structure is today more rational and equitable. *Zamindari* and other intermediary tenures have been abolished from 170 million acres, or about 45 per cent of the total land under cultivation. As a result of this, 20 million tenants have acquired occupancy rights. According to the 1961 Census, the percentage of land under pure tenancy (of the landless) was 4.2 and that under mixed tenancy (owner-cum-tenant) 18.2 per cent of the cultivated land. Though there is a good deal of concealed tenancy, the area under recorded tenancy is less than 12 per cent. If land to the tiller is a production incentive, Indian policy in this direction, at least, deserves a mention. Perhaps the critics have some second thoughts on the relevance of the agrarian structure to agricultural production, because many of the countries which have earned praise for their production performance and restoration of the free market mechanism have shown no conspicuous achievement in the sphere of the reform of the agrarian structure.

The total public sector outlay on agriculture, community development, major and medium irrigation projects during the three Five-Year Plans comes to Rs 3530 crores. It has been suggested that this was not enough and much of the investment has not yielded expected returns. Yet, the point is that this effort is in great contrast to what was being done for Indian agriculture under colonial rule.

But the one aspect of incentives to which we wish to draw special attention is agricultural taxation. Indian agriculture has received exceptionally favourable treatment in this regard. It is estimated that direct agricultural taxes amount to no more than 2 per cent of the value of agricultural production. And even so, one state government after another is announcing a partial or complete withdrawal of the land (revenue) tax. It should suffice to quote a few notable findings on the subject from a recent study on tax burden on Indian agriculture (Gandhi, 1966). The overall conclusion of Ved Gandhi's study is that 'the agricultural sector of the Indian economy is being favoured over the non-agricultural sector as far as the fiscal operations of the government are concerned' (Gandhi, 1966: 199). It also notes that there was—and has been since 1950–51—a net outflow of funds from the non-agricultural to the agricultural sector via the capital budget of the government. In 1962, for example, the agricultural sector received about Rs 250 crores of capital expenditure by the government, whereas it contributed only Rs 75 crores to the capital budget' (Gandhi, 1966: 116–119).

Surely, anyone concerned with the problem of incentives in Indian farming should note some of these features of the Indian economy, and not just keep hammering on product prices.

A summary

Our review of the agricultural price policies—announced and implemented—does not reveal a deliberate attempt to keep farm product prices low. On the contrary, farm prices have been continually rising from 1956 onwards and are at present 100 per cent higher than in 1952–53 (the base year of the Wholesale Price Index Series), when they were 4.5 times higher than those before the war. In fact, the most serious problem of the national economy today is the steep rise in prices of food and agricultural raw materials. There was a brief period around 1955 when there was a sharp drop in prices of agricultural commodities. The policy-maker can be blamed for not following a more imaginative price policy during this period. Since then the failure is in restraining the rise in the prices of food and raw materials. There is also no evidence of consistent adverse terms of trade for agriculture.

For the bulk of the agricultural produce, there is—and has been—an effective free market. Procurement below the market rates has been insignificant, except in recent years when for rice in 1964 and 1965, it reached 25 per cent of marketable surplus. Nor does the review show that input prices have been kept high as a policy measure. Compared to world prices, the prices of fertilizers in India are no doubt high, but there is no evidence to suggest that this factor has inhibited the use of fertilizers by the farmers. But the policy-maker must take the blame for the tardy development of an efficient fertilizer industry.

We have shown that neither the production nor the productivity of wheat—which was the main PL-480 commodity to be imported on a large scale—suffered because of the relatively lower prices.

Growth rates of other agricultural commodities not affected by PL-480 imports—rice, for example—are not better than those of wheat.

Lastly, the review shows that the analysis of the price effect on production needs more sophistication. A distinction needs to be made between what may be called a 'shift' effect of prices— shift of acreage and other resources from one crop to another—and the 'overall' effect on the aggregate agricultural production. Regarding the input-product price relationship, it is axiomatic that this should be demonstrably favourable for expanding the use of modern technical inputs, but a more rewarding approach to the problem is by way of cost reduction, through improved technology and productivity-raising research and management. The supply inelasticities in the factor market must also be borne in mind, because in such situations, the immediate effect of the increase in product prices would be an increase in input prices. Loosening of inelasticities requires action on a wider front than that of price mechanism.

Finally, in the discussion on incentives it is but proper to consider the totality of economic policy. Each specific policy can be meaningfully interpreted only in the context of other ancillary policies and the developing economic situation. When the price policy—if such there was—or the actual price situation for agriculture in India is examined within a comprehensive focus, the impression that product prices were deliberately kept low or that the high input prices inhibited adoption of modern technology appears to be based on partial and selective evidence. In any case, low agricultural prices have never been a constituent of economic policy. It is, however, possible that efforts to check exorbitant prices have been misunderstood as preference for low prices.

India's agricultural growth undoubtedly has been disappointing. This is perhaps at the root of her many economic troubles today. It, however, does not follow that the 'failure' of Indian agriculture was *mainly* a consequence of wrong policies in the field of agriculture. In hindsight, many errors of judgement can be discovered. More often, even the right policies were not effectively implemented. This does not, however, justify the verdict that agricultural development was neglected or that there was a policy preference which implied 'a low regard for agriculture as source of economic growth'. True, agriculture has responded poorly to the developmental effort of policy-makers. In retrospect, it appears that the problem of agricultural development is more complex than what either the economists or the policy-makers think it to be.

NOTES

1. Reprinted from *Indian Journal of Agricultural Economics*, Vol. 22, No. 2, April–June 1967.
2. The total labour force of USA in 1960 was 71 million and that of Japan 45 million.
3. It is surprising that in these discussions, no mention is made of international pricing of primary commodities of developing countries.
4. The Agricultural Prices Commission has recommended that for the 1967 Rabi season, procurement price of wheat should be Rs 8 or about 16 per cent above the minimum prices fixed in the wheat producing areas.
5. Excludes pulses.
6. It is not clear whether the objection is to concessional imports or to any imports.
7. Response of rice and irrigated wheat to graded doses of N (Nitrogen), under Indian farming conditions is as follows.

Crop	Doses of N (kg per hectare)				
	20	30	40	50	60
Increase in yield of rice (kg per hectare)	259	343	397	420	412
Increase in yield of wheat (kg per hectare)	350	472	559	611	628

Profitability of fertilizer use (N) at current prices

Crop	Optimum dose (kg per hectare)	Cost of ferti- lizer (Rs per hectare)	Value of additional yield (Rs)	Profit (Rs per hectare)
Rice	43.5	72.2	246	173.8
Wheat	50.4	83.7	305	221.3

Note: Prices assumed are Rs 1.66 for 1 kg of N and Rs 60 and Rs 50 per quintal of rice and wheat. Current prices for rice and wheat are substantially higher.

Source: V.G. Panse, 'Fertilizer Recommendations' in Proceedings of National Seminar on Fertilizers, Fertilizer Association of India, 1965.

8. *The Times of India*, 17 April 1967.
9. This is exemplified in a recent study in the Philippines. While prices of rice and corn in the Philippines have apparently been fairly efficient in

their resource allocation functions, there is little evidence to indicate that price changes are an effective device for influencing aggregate agricultural output. In spite of the micro-economic evidence that prices are an important incentive for the purchase of yield-increasing technical inputs such as fertilizer, insecticides, and herbicides, no measurable yield response to price was obtained . . . most of the increase in the output is a result of shifting of land from other crops to rice or bringing new land into production. This implies that we should be less optimistic about the role of price as a development tool at least for the present, than would be the case if the price changes included yield responses in addition to area shifts.' See Mahar Mangahas, Aida E. Recto and V. W. Ruttan, 'Price and Market Relationships for Rice and Corn in the Philippines', *Journal of Farm Economics*, Vol. 48, No. 3, Part I, August 1966: 702.

10. No wonder, the politician finds the price incentive advocacy most palatable. According to press reports, the Food Ministers' Conference recently held in Delhi voted for 20 to 25 per cent higher price for wheat procurement than was recommended by the Agricultural Prices Commission, which by its terms of reference is enjoined to consider the effects of its recommendation on the entire economy.

CHAPTER 13

Principles and problems of agricultural price determination[1]

This Annual Conference of the Agricultural Statistical Society is meeting under the shadow of an unusual drought, which has drastically slashed agricultural production this year. Even a casual look at the meteorological map reveals that this is perhaps the worst weather year in the last 25 years. Even otherwise, the growth of agricultural production during the last decade has been far from satisfactory; and this has cast something like a gloom over the Indian economic scene. But, as they say, every cloud has a silver lining. The serious challenge posed by the agricultural situation in the country has kindled a new awakening in our thought and action. The scientists, technicians, administrators and politicians are all re-checking their diagnosis and searching for more effective remedies. What is really significant is that the new ideas, whether they be in the field of agricultural technology or agricultural institutions, are becoming operational. Altogether there are fewer inhibitions, less hesitation in discarding old beliefs, a new respect for science and technology and more confidence in the organizational machinery. It would perhaps not be an exaggeration to say that we are on the threshold of an agricultural revolution. This agricultural revolution will impinge on many disciplines. Agricultural scientists with their many specializations in plant breeding, plant protection, soil chemistry, etc., agricultural economists and statisticians, rural sociologists, organization personnel and administrators, each will have to play a critical role in ushering in this revolution.

Though there is still a lurking belief that agriculture in India is a way of life, nobody seriously holds that it is immune from even the simple laws of economics. If so, agricultural economists and statisticians have to share with other scientists the responsibility of assisting in the process of agricultural development. It is felt that one of the factors relevant to this process is the level and structure of agricultural prices. Early this year, the Government, therefore, appointed the Agricultural Prices Commission to advise on the agricultural price policy and price structure in the context of the need to raise agricultural production and give relief to the consumer. One of its major terms of reference was to evolve a balanced and integrated price structure in the perspective of the overall needs of the economy and with due regard to the interests ,of the producer and the consumer. For the last one year, I have had the opportunity, in collaboration with my colleagues in the Commission and its research staff, to grapple with the real world of the working economy. I thought that I would take this opportunity to share with my professional colleagues my brief experience of this sojourn into the realm of economic administration. This experience has indeed been quite rich and varied. On the present occasion, however, I shall relate only that part of my experience which may be of some interest professionally.

At the very outset the Commission had to make sure what exactly was meant by the phrase 'balanced and integrated price structure' mentioned in its terms of reference. Although the phrase has been used frequently in economic discussion in India, I have not come across a wholly satisfactory formulation of the concept of balance and integration in terms which would be operationally meaningful.

It would be helpful to differentiate between the definitional aspect and the estimational problems relating to the concept. The concept can perhaps be split up into two components: (*a*) balance and (*b*) integration. One type of *balancing* could be between the interest of the producer and that of the consumer, though how much of economics would be relevant to the determination of the balancing point is a moot question. As for *integration*, presumably the reference is to the relationship between the prices of different agricultural commodities and also between the price aggregate of all agricultural commodities and the price aggregate of the products of other sectors.

Several sets of guidelines for deriving such a balanced and integrated pattern can be thought of. It is sometimes suggested that the price structure which prevailed during a reasonably recent historical period considered as 'normal', could form the basis for deriving a 'balanced and integrated' price structure. This idea is perhaps rooted in welfare economics, the hypothesis being that the relative income[2] patterns in the base period were of the right type, economically, socially, and politically and should, therefore, be maintained. In the dynamic world of today, with the rapidly changing technology of production affecting the cost-return ratios, and the fact that there is a continuous pressure for increased supply levels, reference to a historical normalcy would be wholly inappropriate. Moreover, the fact that demand elasticities with respect to price and income differ widely for different commodities, greatly reduces the utility of past experience. The exercise for evolving the integrated pattern of prices has to be forward-looking.

The task of evolving a balanced and integrated price structure, that has been entrusted to the Agricultural Prices Commission, would in a sense require it to anticipate the 'equilibrium' or 'pivot' prices. The equilibrium price structure for the agricultural sector should, *inter alia*, equate

1. marginal productivities of inputs in agriculture with their prices,
2. demand for factors of production (individually and in aggregate) with their supply, and
3. demand for agricultural commodities (individually and in aggregate) with their supply.

The realization of the first objective, i.e., equality of input productivities with their prices would depend on the degree of mobility of inputs and the existence of full or near-full employment conditions. The second and third criteria, in a sense, are equivalent to a constrained production maximization model for the agricultural sector, the constraints being resource availability and the demand targets. If equilibrium prices are anticipated and announced in advance of the production period, the producers may be expected to optimally allocate the resources in a manner that would meet these three criteria. However, the ability of the price-fixing authority

to correctly anticipate the equilibrium price structure depends
on the formulation of the relevant economic model and availability
of requisite data.

A number of economic models have been developed and
tested by economists. I need not go into the details of their
work with which, I am sure, most of you will be familiar.
In order to anticipate the 'equilibrium' or 'pivot' prices, the
price-fixing authority would primarily be interested in models
aggregating demand and supply relations for agricultural commodities.
The economic function of prices (of outputs and inputs) is nothing
other than that of equating demand and supply with the given
resource constraints, technical coefficients of production and demand
and supply elasticities.

While it is possible to conceive of such a model as a
theoretical abstraction, there exist a host of difficulties in relating
it to real-world situations. There are many assumptions on which
such a model has, of necessity, to be based, e.g., perfect mobility
of inputs within the agricultural sector, absence of imperfections
in the working of the market mechanism, etc. Even if we ignore
these assumptions, it is problematic whether we have reliable
information on

1. income and price elasticities of demand for various agricultural
    commodities and their cross-elasticities,
2. price as well as income elasticities of supply of these commodities,
3. technical coefficients—current and potential—of production
    in agriculture, and
4. elasticities of demand for and supply of inputs. There is
    also the problem of aggregation over space, which has brought
    into focus the inter-regional variance in resource endowments,
    quality of inputs and outputs, production technology, consumption
    patterns, etc.

Moreover, in order to envisage the equilibrium price structure,
the price-fixing authority has to assume the expected level of
demand for agricultural commodities. The plan targets may perhaps
be taken as adequately reflecting the expected level of demand.
Strictly speaking, the magnitude of neither demand nor supply
can be taken as given, because both would change with changes
in prices. But the formulation of plan targets is based on the

assumption that the level and structure of prices will remain unchanged during the plan period. In estimating demand, its elasticity with respect to price is not taken into account. The estimated equilibrium price structure may not always be the same as that assumed by the planning authority while working out the demand estimates or production targets. To the extent that the new structure of equilibrium prices is at variance with the price structure initially assumed by the planning authority, the time paths of targeted demand and supply levels would undergo a change. The magnitude and direction of the difference would depend on the price elasticity of demand and cross-elasticities.

Even if we assume that these problems are somehow overcome, how much faith can be put in the predictive power of the model? In an economy where rapid technological and structural changes are taking place, the parameters of models might change (even if the model specification remains unchanged), and thereby vitiate the predictive ability of the model. Moreover, in an economy like ours, where the aggregate agricultural production even today is to a large extent dependent on weather, deviations from normal weather conditions may throw the equilibrium price structure out of gear with the ex-post structure of realized prices.

If this is generally accepted, can a price advisory authority predict a unique structure of integrated and balanced prices and ensure that it will stay put during the plan period? Given the present frontiers of our knowledge in this field and the available tools of analysis, the answer, in my view, cannot be a confident affirmative. But, perhaps, there is no need to adopt such a perfectionist stance. It should really suffice if it can specify a range within which the ex-post realized prices might move, and the system can still be 'balanced and integrated'. In fact, as discussed later, operationally also there seems to be no choice but to opt for a range.

This concept of range, therefore, provides a starting point for our price policy. By definition, a range has two points— the lowest and the highest. Even those who implicitly trust the free market mechanism generally accept the necessity of a minimum support price as well as the desirability of avoiding excessive fluctuations in commodity prices. In developed economies, the genesis of the price policy lies in abnormal situations like the Great Depression or the World Wars. Where such a policy is continued even during normal times, the main objective is to sustain farm incomes at levels which are considered as socially irreducible. The need to protect minimum farm incomes exists even in developing countries, though at times like the present in India, with prices soaring high, the relevance of such a concern may not be quite apparent. But even in a situation of soaring prices, there may be several pockets where the post-harvest prices reach distressingly low levels. A programme under which the Government stands ready to purchase all quantities offered at the minimum support price could, in such a situation, be quite valuable in preventing distress.

It is, however, felt that the objective of the minimum support price policy should not merely be a negative one of protecting incomes at distress levels. The price policy in developing economies should be—as the terms of reference of the Agricultural Prices Commission emphasize—production-oriented and should have an element of incentive in it. This, however, need not necessarily mean a cost-plus price. The incentive element must be tied to the adoption of improved practices. The Agricultural Prices Commission has, therefore, in its report on price policy for kharif cereals, observed that 'the progressive farmer should be assured that his effort to augment production through the adoption of improved technology will not become unremunerative because of the price factor' (Government of India, 1965: 1).

There is the other point in the price range, i.e., the maximum, at which the Government's intervention has become necessary because of the continuing and often quite acute pressures of demand for different agricultural commodities. Safeguarding the interests of consumers has been a very important force behind this policy. It is now an accepted policy of the Government, for example, to maintain a system of public distribution of foodgrains— through fair price shops and informal or formal rationing.

There is, however, one difficulty in the range approach. As already pointed out, the minimum price carries with it a long-term guarantee or assurance of unlimited purchase by the Government. As such, it has to have a certain degree of stability. It would lose its insurance value if the minimum price level is allowed to fluctuate, especially downwards. But fluctuation is the very essence of the price mechanism.

Agricultural production varies from year to year and the

variations are caused by non-economic factors like the weather. If market prices are not allowed to fluctuate according to variations in production, farm incomes will fluctuate, declining when the crop is small and rising when the production is large. And more than price it is the income that we would like to stabilize. The minimum price—the lower end of the range—can be moved only by reference to the secular (long-term) trend. Its comparative stability will have to be reconciled with the year-to-year fluctuations of the market price in response to fluctuations in production.

Again, there is the question of the width of the price range. On economic grounds, this would depend on the predictive ability of the model employed. Political and social considerations also sometimes become important determinants of the width of the range. Whatever be the approach and the dimension of the range, it is clear that the price policy will have to be related to a price interval rather than a point estimate of price.

Thus, the lack of precise predictive capacity of the equilibrium model as well as the policy requirement of ensuring minimum support and maximum consumer tolerance prices lead to the price range approach. Now the problem is of reconciling the two approaches in the more difficult task of deriving the actual figures of either the pivot price and/or minimum-maximum prices for a given commodity. The criteria for determining the level of minimum (or maximum) prices—which we discuss hereafter—cannot be the same as those which determine the pivot prices, for the simple reason that the economic purposes of these two price concepts are somewhat different.

There are two possible ways in which the equilibrium approach and minimum price approach can be reconciled for actual price determination. We may first determine the 'equilibrium' price point (which can only be a rough approximation to the ex-post 'equilibrium' price) and allow for a certain percentage of off (minus) and on (plus) to determine the minimum and the maximum points in the price range. In the alternative, we may derive the minimum (or the maximum) point and fix the other at a suitable distance, accommodating the equilibrium price in between.

Although the first alternative, i.e., the specification of the minimum and maximum prices in relation to the 'equilibrium' or 'pivot' price structure is more appealing, at least on the theoretical plane, the problems associated with the anticipation of the 'pivot' price structure are many and complex and have already been discussed. As such, we may have to opt for the other alternative of deriving the range from an independently determined minimum price.

This leads us to the search for the criteria which would be appropriate for the determination of the level of minimum prices. This too is not easy and there are as many imponderables as in the search for a model for equilibrium price. It is obvious that the three criteria specified here will have to be taken into account, though not rigidly adhered to in the specification of the structure of minimum prices. The task of the price-fixing authority would be not only to suggest price levels for individual crops, but also inter-crop price relationships which would tend to bring about the desired pattern of production. In this context, the cost of production—specially of those farmers who adopt improved technology—and inter-crop price parities become relevant.

It has been suggested that the cost of cultivation should form the basis for the fixation of prices. If, by this, it is meant that the price should cover the cost of each and every producer, it is obvious that such an attempt would totally ignore the demand factor in price formation. In a way, price itself has to perform the function of determining the cost. Production takes place within varying degrees of efficiency (levels of cost). Price has to indicate the minimum level of efficiency which the producer has to attain in order to remain in business, especially in the long run. This is obvious in the sphere of industrial production.

Even so, the price advisory authority may not altogether neglect the cost aspect of production. But when it starts looking at the cost aspect, the difficulties of bringing it within a meaningful focus turn out to be quite formidable. Two main questions arise which may be briefly phrased as 'which costs' and 'whose cost'.

To a student of farm management, the question 'which costs' will not appear as unusual. The concepts of cost developed in farm management in India are by now quite familiar.[3] The main point for consideration is: should the imputed cost of family labour expended on production be included in the cost? Prima facie, there is no reason why it should not be included; for, after all, without the input of family labour, production would not have taken place. Had all that production been obtained through the employment of hired labour, no such question would have been asked. Why then does such a question arise when family labour is used in the production process? It would appear that the question arises firstly because the imputed cost of family labour, viewed from another angle, constitutes the income of the family; and as such, if the principle of fixing prices on the basis of total costs is accepted, we face the paradox of 'higher the cost (of family labour) higher the income'! This would not perhaps matter if we were sure that at every point in the range of family labour input, its marginal productivity was equal to the wage rate at which the input was evaluated. There is, however, reason to believe that, on small farms in particular, the input of family labour is pushed up to a point where its marginal return is much below the wage rate. This is not surprising. From the point of view of the small farmer this is perhaps the most rational use of his labour, and the only available way of adding to his meagre income. He knows that the opportunity cost of his additional labour beyond a point is quite low. In spite of this, if the cost analyst chooses to evaluate the family labour at the going wage rate, it is obvious that the cost of cultivation would get inflated. In view of this, the question really is not whether the imputed value of the family labour input should or should not be included in the cost, but whether the cost of the cultivation figure arrived at by valuing at the current wage rate (either of the casual labour or the permanent labour) is a true indicator of the cost or not. It may, therefore, be suggested that while cost 'C' should be the appropriate cost as a frame of reference for the price-fixing authority, the actual figure would need to be discounted because of the limitations of the valuation procedure.

We may now see whether there is any empirical evidence in support of this reasoning. As you know, we have a fairly large number of farm management surveys. The Agricultural Prices Commission is at present engaged in analyzing all the available data from these surveys. The data, no doubt, suffer from many limitations. One methodological limitation is the absence of differentiation in the quality of the inputs. In spite of this, we felt that it should be our endeavour to extract the most from these data, without compromising with the strict requirements of scientific analysis.

TABLE 13.1

Correlation between the size of holding (in acres) and cost of production per maund for paddy and wheat

State/Year/Crop	Correlation with			
	Cost A	Cost C	Operational cost	Fixed cost
1	2	3	4	5
PADDY				
West Bengal (1954–57)				
Aman	0.55*	−0.47	−0.23	−0.62*
Aus	−0.005	−0.30	−0.068	−0.05
Madras (1954–57)				
First season	−0.52	−0.42	−0.61	−0.42†
Second season	−0.04	−0.02	−0.73†	−0.84‡
Third season	0.04	−0.85‡	–	–
Orissa (1958–60)				
Aman	0.94‡	−0.87‡	−0.83	−0.31
Andhra Pradesh (1957–60)				
First season (irrigated)	0.60*	0.16	−0.41	0.31
Second season (irrigated)	0.54	0.10	−0.29	0.23
Kerala (1962–63)	0.16	−0.51	–	
Madhya Pradesh (1962–63)	0.14	−0.83†	−0.56	−0.70†
WHEAT				
Punjab (1954–57)	−0.95‡	−0.95‡	N.A.	N.A.
1961–62				
Irrigated	0.66†	−0.20	N.A.	N.A.
Unirrigated	−0.87‡	0.34	N.A.	N.A.
Bombay (1954–57)				
Nasik Irrigated	0.60*	0.74*	0.09	−0.10
Dry	−0.42	−0.58	−0.52	−0.49
Ahmednagar Irrigated	−0.56	−0.73†	−0.67	−0.54
Dry	0.14	0.18	–	–
Uttar Pradesh (1954–57)				
Irrigated	–	0.63*	−0.29	−0.37
Unirrigated	–	0.47	0.30	0.31
Rajasthan (1962–63)	0.66*	0.51	0.75	−0.56

* Significant at 10% level.
† Significant at 5% level.
‡ Significant at 1% level.

Table 13.1 gives the correlation between the size of the farm and cost of production per maund of paddy and wheat. The correlation of cost 'C' (which includes the value of family labour) with farm size indicates broadly that the cost decreases with the increase in the farm size. A more direct correlation between family labour input per acre and farm size also reveals a high and statistically significant negative relationship (Table 13.2). There is also evidence to show that the return per labour day of family members on small farms is generally lower than that on big farms. However, whether, and if so to what extent, the cost of production gets inflated by evaluating the farm-family labour on small farms at the going wage rate can be conclusively established only by reference to the marginal productivity (and its relation to the imputed wage rate) of family labour on these farms. Even if the marginal productivity of family labour on these farms is found to be lower than the imputed wage rate, this by itself would not mean that the labour input is inefficiently utilized on small farms insofar as it is used in substitution for other inputs.

The question of 'whose price' is equally complicated. As is well known, cultivation costs vary from farmer to farmer. What is generally not known is the large range of the variation, both within and between regions. This gives rise to the problem of aggregation of widely varying cost estimates. Taking a random example, we find that in two districts of West Bengal, the cost of production of Aman paddy during 1955–57 varied from less than Rs 6 a maund (for the first 10 per cent of production in the least-cost order), to more than Rs 15 per maund (for the last 10 per cent of production). Two extreme cost points were, in fact, less than Rs 13 per maund and more than Rs 23 per maund. Given such a wide scatter, the average cost of cultivation will have little operational significance. The average cost in this case came to Rs 10.25 per maund. This would not cover the cost of 37 per cent of production, 44 per cent of farms and 38 per cent of area under cultivation. Similar instances can be cited in respect of other crops and regions (see Table 13.3).

So long as these facts are not generally known, the lay opinion would perhaps consider the average cost criterion as reasonable. When, however, the facts become widely known and are discussed,

TABLE 13.2

Correlation of size of holding (in acres) with human labour input

State/Year/Crop	Correlation with human labour		
	Hired	Family	Total
1	2	3	4
Bombay (1954–57)			
Irrigated wheat			
Ahmednagar	0.81[†]	–0.56	–0.20
Nasik	0.67[†]	–0.82[†]	–0.73[†]
Unirrigated wheat			
Ahmednagar	N.A.	N.A.	0.13
Nasik	N.A.	N.A.	–0.65*
Uttar Pradesh (1954–57)			
Wheat	N.A.	N.A.	-0.92[‡]
Rajasthan (Pali) (1962–63)			
Wheat	0.3	0.2	–
Andhra Pradesh (1957–60)			
Paddy:			
I Season	0.74[†]	–0.88[‡]	–0.31
II Season	0.81[†]	–0.74[†]	–
Orissa (1957–60)			
Aman	0.98[‡]	–0.96[‡]	–0.88[†]
Kerala (1962–63)			
Paddy	N.A.	N.A.	–0.35
Madhya Pradesh			
Paddy	N.A.	N.A.	–0.66

* Significant at 10% level.
† Significant at 5% level.
‡ Significant at 1% level.

the price-fixing authority will be under pressure to fix the price
at a level which would cover the cost of the last ounce of
foodgrain, however inefficiently produced, under the plea that
not only that last ounce but many more are needed to meet
the consumer demand. On the other hand, if the economic purpose
of price regulation is to stimulate production, the policy should
be to ensure that the cost of production of the progressive farmer,
who is prepared to adopt improved technology, is covered through
a price guarantee. To bridge the gap between these two polar
approaches, it is suggested that the guaranteed price should cover
the cost of cultivation of the bulk of the more efficient production.
Assuming that 85 per cent of such production is considered eligible

TABLE 13.3

Cost per maund on the basis of different concepts

Crop/State/ Year	Cost C (Rs)			Bulk-line con-cept	Efficiency concept			
	Mini-mum	Maxi-mum	Aver-age		Least-cost production		Highest cost production	
					% produ-ction covered	Cost/ maund	% produ-ction covered	Cost maund
1	2	3	4	5	6	7	8	9
WHEAT								
Bombay (1954–57)								
Ahmednagar	10.1	23.8	15.9	24.2	14.7	5.0 (N.S.)	12.5	25.0
Nasik	17.8	36.3	21.3	30.25	7.8	10.0 (N.S.)	15.7	36.0
Punjab (1954–57)	8.65	14.92	12.42	17.33	14.71	9.0 (5.00)	10.0	19.0
Uttar Pradesh (1954–57)	9.9	15.7	11.2	17.00	10.5	8.0 (Below 6)	10.5	18.0
Rajasthan (1962–63)	18.37	18.37	25.05	26.60	16.62	8.0 (6.0)	9.3	32.0 and above
PADDY								
West Bengal (1954–57)								
Aman	9.36	11.41	10.25	13.81*	10.0	6.0	9.0	15.0 and above
Aus	8.49	15.24	11.85	N.A.	N.A.	N.A.	N.A.	N.A.
Andhra Pradesh (1957–60)								
I Season	11.57	12.74	12.29	14.67	5.71	7.0 (Below 7.0)	15.2	15.0
II Season	11.45	13.81	12.86	14.87	16.95	9.0 (7.01)	18.5	15.0
Orissa (1957–60)	7.93	8.86	8.25	11.20	14.00	5.0 (4.0)	13.0	12.0 and above
Kerala (1962–63)	8.58	14.67	9.83	14.41	12.6	6.0 (Below 1.0)	17.0	14.6
Madras (1956–57)								
I Season	9.5	21.4	12.4	17.56	N.A.	N.A.	N.A.	N.A.
II Season	5.6	14.6	7.4	10.52	N.A.	N.A.	N.A.	N.A.

N.S : Not Specified.
N.A.: Not Available.
  * Relates to 1955–57.
Note: Figures in brackets under Col (7) indicate the lowest cost per unit at which some output has been produced.

for protection, it may be pointed out that in the case of West Bengal, the bulk-line cost will cover the cost of 73.8 per cent of farms and 80.2 per cent of the area under Aman paddy cultivation.

The disparity in the costs of cultivation between different regions is as glaring as that within the region. For example, average cost 'C' for wheat in the Nasik District of Maharashtra during 1954–57 was Rs 21.3 per maund as against Rs 11.2 in Uttar Pradesh during the same period. Similarly, the average cost in the second season paddy in Madras was Rs 7.4 per maund, (1956–57) as against Rs 11.85 for Aus paddy in West Bengal during 1954–57. The variations in the bulk-line costs are equally glaring.

It would thus appear that till more refined and accurate cost data become available the price-fixing authority will have no alternative but to use its best-informed judgement in recommending levels of minimum prices. The Agricultural Prices Commission has already suggested a scheme for obtaining more meaningful cost data.

Another relevant factor in determining the levels of minimum prices is the need to maintain a relationship amongst prices of competing crops that would bring forth the desired levels of their output. As is well known, the increase in production is obtained either through an increase in acreage and/or increase in productivity through the use of more and better inputs and good husbandry. When increase in production of almost all competing crops is desired, shift in acreage from one crop to another as a result of the price policy may not be of much use. But, if shifts are taking place and if a modification in the trend of the shift is desired, price policy can, at best, take some correctional steps. However, if new land is brought under cultivation, the relative prices and profitability will have a definite influence on the cropping pattern of the reclaimed land.

It should, however, be noted that at the micro level where the ultimate decision regarding land use is taken, the farmer will have to contend with constraints of agronomic conditions—soil, rainfall, irrigation, etc.—as well as those of his resources and skill. The price factor is, therefore, not wholly decisive. More importantly, the extent to which the price impact is retarded by non-price factors cannot be assessed in quantitative terms.

Further, whereas the impact of the price factor is general, that of non-price factors is specific to an area. As such, the effect of the price factor on production would vary from region to region. This fact of regional variability of the production response considerably reduces the utility of price administration as an instrument for bringing about specific production increases.

Response of inputs other than land would perhaps be more elastic to the product price. But here too in order to bring about the desired shift in the use of, say, fertilizers from sugarcane or cotton to wheat, the price adviser would have to know the precise quantum of increase in the price of wheat that would be needed to enable wheat cultivators to outbid sugarcane or cotton cultivators in the purchase of fertilizers.

For a realistic appraisal of the impact of the shift in the price parity of substitutable crops on production response, we must work only within a regional context, since substitutability between crops varies from region to region. As for the prices, the all-India index number of wholesale prices would be misleading for studying production responses. The prices of cotton in Punjab may not have necessarily moved up or down in the same proportion as those of cotton in Maharashtra. With the prevailing disparities in the prices of foodgrains—an unfortunate consequence of the zonal restrictions—the all-India index of wholesale prices has lost much of its relevance for the sophisticated analysis of production response to price.

Secondly, with the rapidly changing technology and its impact on input-output ratios, price movements over time may not faithfully reflect the relative changes in profitability of different crops, and in the ultimate analysis it is really the latter which influences the cropping decisions. Speaking of profitability, it would perhaps be necessary to calculate the profitability of the entire crop rotation rather than that of any two single crops. Again, profitability cannot be measured by reference to gross returns only. We have to take into account the changing cost structure as well. But, the various problems associated with cost calculations have already been indicated.

Further, the nature of the price expectation model that the farmer would adopt in taking production decisions has also to be known so that the supply response relations could be specified properly. In most such exercises, the previous year's price has been taken to reflect the farmer's expectation. But, it is not certain that the farmer decides his resource allocation pattern on the basis of the average realized price in the year preceding the crop season. Maybe, the pre-sowing or the immediate post-harvest prices also enter in the farmer's expectation model.

The desirability of conducting production response studies at regional levels has been emphasized earlier. But in case the results of the regional studies indicate widely varying regional price structures, the problem of aggregating the regional for deriving the all-India price structure will remain.

Lastly, it is not enough to know the simple fact that production responds to prices. We would need to know the precise coefficient of response if the statistically worked out price structure is to yield the targeted structure of agricultural production.

Empirical evidence relating to the impact of changes in price parities of competing crops on their outputs is very limited. Whatever empirical studies have been done are related to acreage response. Studies on acreage responses to relative price changes have been preferred over the production response alternative on the ground that while acreage allocation together with allocation of other inputs is quite determinate, production levels are not entirely determined by the farmer insofar as he has no control over that part of the variability in yield which is influenced by weather. One of the difficulties in such studies is the non-availability of relevant price data at the regional level over a sufficiently long time. Again, there is the problem as to the price data (wholesale, farm harvest or net prices received by farmers) that should be used in the production response studies.

Notwithstanding these limitations, the Agricultural Prices Commission initiated detailed studies on supply response. So far, only results of the data at the all-India level are available. Though these results are of limited use for deriving the structure of minimum prices, they are indicative of certain broad relations between price relatives and acreage responses. The studies at the all-India level relate to acreage shifts between: (*a*) groundnut and *jowar*, (*b*) groundnut and bajra, (*c*) groundnut and *ragi*, (*d*) groundnut and cotton, (*e*) cotton and jowar, (*f*) jute and rice and (*g*) sugarcane and rice.

The following hypotheses were formulated and tested:

1. Acreage allocation decisions for a crop depend upon the previous year's realized prices for that crop and also for substitutable crop,
2. Acreage allocation decisions for a crop depend upon the ratio of the previous year's realized prices for the crop to that of a substitutable crop, and
3. Acreage allocation decisions for a crop depend upon the ratio of the previous year's gross returns (price x yield) for the crop and that of a substitutable crop.

The results of the exercises broadly indicate that the various model specifications (based on the three hypotheses) yield varying results for various crops. The statistical test of the first hypothesis relating to the acreage response for groundnut to one year lagged prices of groundnut and cotton show that shift in groundnut acreage is satisfactorily explained by the price changes. The price coefficients are significant and 30 per cent of the variance in groundnut acreage is explained by the price movements. Reasonably good results have also been obtained on acreage response for sugarcane taking into consideration the lagged price of sugarcane and rice. The results are very significant and nearly 90 per cent of the sugarcane acreage variance is explained by the one year lagged prices of sugarcane and rice. The statistical test of the second hypothesis shows that the groundnut cotton acreage ratio is significantly related to the one year lagged price ratio for the same crops; 49 per cent of the variance in the acreage ratio is explained by the relevant inter-crop price ratio. The third hypothesis relating acreage ratio to one year lagged gross revenue ratio has yielded overall unsatisfactory results. In the case of other crops which have been studied so far, results are either not statistically significant or they fail to conform to economic logic.

The above results, based as they are on the all-India data and the rather elementary model specifications can, at best, be taken as indicative of certain directional relations. Much more detailed work is called for to determine the precise nature/magnitude of the response coefficients.

In spite of all these difficulties in evolving a balanced and integrated structure of agricultural prices, a distinct outline of a positive price policy has emerged during the past one year.

Firstly, the Government now stands firmly committed to the policy of guaranteeing a minimum support price for a large number of agricultural commodities. At this price the Government will buy all quantities offered for sale and thus prevent a further decline in prices. Though the criteria for deriving the level of minimum prices have not yet been firmly evolved, the levels fixed for minimum prices appear, by any token, fairly liberal. When in 1964 the Jha Committee first fixed the minimum prices for paddy, they were about 10 per cent higher than the average harvest prices which prevailed during 1961–64—which was a period of rising prices. The Agricultural Prices Commission endorsed these with some marginal changes for 1965. I think the categorical acceptance of the principle of minimum support price guaranteed by the Government is a positive advance in the evolution of the price policy. The more acute problem during the last few years, however, has been at the other end of the price range: that of restraining price rise in the interest of the consumer. Here too a positive policy has emerged, particularly in regard to foodgrains and a few other food articles (sugar, edible oils, etc.). The Government has accepted the responsibility of maintaining a system of public distribution of foodgrains through fair price shops, informal or formal rationing and thereby taking care of a certain percentage of consumer demand. In 1965, for example, 8.12 million tonnes of foodgrains (5.76 of wheat and 2.26 of rice) were made available through the system of public distribution. There can be no doubt that this did help to check the rise in prices; at any rate, the recipients of this quantity were able to secure their requirements at reasonable prices. Over and above this, statutory maximum prices are declared for certain crops in several states; but as we know the enforcement of the ceiling limits has not been successful. One economic device by which a public authority can keep the price within the ceiling limits is to release sufficient stocks at the appropriate time. Till a system of public procurement is perfected or there is a possibility of obtaining imports in required quantities, the stocks for such an operation would not be adequate.

Thus, though the range approach has now been accepted, the fixation of the minimum and the maximum points of the range is still made on an ad hoc basis. It should now be our effort to progressively impart a more scientific basis to the determination of the lower and the upper points of the range.

Friends, I have traversed over a wide range of topics and that too haltingly and with much diffidence. I would request you to treat what I have said as a process of thinking aloud, of sharing my thoughts with you. I believe it is the responsibility of our entire profession to make a constructive contribution to agricultural price policy. What has been done hitherto is no more than clearing the decks. Let the whole profession now join the journey.

NOTES

1. Address delivered at the 19th Annual Conference of the Indian Society of Agricultural Statistics at Cuttack, on 30 December 1965. Reprinted from *Journal of Indian Society of Agricultural Statistics*, Vol. 18, No. 1, June 1966.
2. It is assumed that income levels move with output prices.
3. The different cost concepts as used in the Farm Management Studies are given below:
   Cost A1: Hired human labour, farm and hired bullock labour, seed and manure, both farm grown and purchased, irrigation charges if any, depreciation of agricultural implements and farm buildings; interest on farm loans and miscellaneous other charges as may be involved in the production of crops.
   Cost A2: Cost A1 plus rent paid on leased in and owned lands.
   Cost B: Cost A2 plus interest on capital investment in agriculture (including owned and self cultivated land).
   Cost C: Cost B plus the imputed value of human labour provided by the farming family Cost C is really the total cost of cultivation.

CHAPTER 14

Agricultural price policy: Facts and issues[1]

Contrary to the general belief, the prices of agricultural commodities are not 'fixed' or 'controlled' by the Government. The producers are free to sell at any price they can get in the market. All that the Government does is to announce 'minimum support prices' for some commodities. As the words clearly imply, what is fixed is the *minimum* price which the Government binds itself to *support* by buying whatever quantity is offered for sale. If the demand and supply conditions warrant higher prices, there is no ban on the sale of these commodities at higher prices. Obviously, the objective of the minimum support price policy is to prevent what may be called distress selling due to conditions of glut, often a consequence of inadequate or 'ineffective' demand, as in the case of foodgrains. As a matter of fact, the Agricultural Prices Commission (APC) was not reconciled to such a negative view of 'support' price. In one of its earliest reports it viewed it as a price which would not discourage a progressive farmer from augmenting his production through adoption of improved technology and farm practices, out of apprehension of a slump in prices. Whether the support prices announced by the Government are adequate or not for this purpose is an issue which can be independently examined. The limited objective which the support price seeks to serve should not, however, be missed.

Before we discuss the rather controversial issue of what constitutes a fair minimum level of the price which needs to be supported by the Government, let us consider price policies whose objectives are quite different. For example, in the solitary example of monopoly procurement which is operative only in Maharashtra and that too for cotton, the price offered has to be fair in a different sense. Here the farmer has no option but to sell his *kapas*/cotton to the Government and the Government alone, at the 'fixed' price. He cannot sell it to any other party even if that party offers him a higher price. The question about the fair price of a commodity under monopoly procurement (or the basis for determining it) is not easy to answer.

A few years ago, we had a system of compulsory procurement, with or without restrictions on inter-state transport by private parties. Though neither compulsory procurement nor zonal restrictions are in operation at present, a brief discussion of appropriate prices or factors which are relevant for their determination may not be out of place.

The situation under which the Government is constrained to resort to compulsory procurement is exactly the reverse of the one which makes the operation of support prices necessary and desirable. It is a situation of scarcity (in contrast to that of glut) or demand outstripping supply, resulting in excessive price rise which if not checked would cause distress to the consumers (in contrast to the distress to the producers). Even in such a situation, compulsory procurement would be justified mainly for commodities of essential consumption and that too to the extent needed for meeting the requirements of the low-income group.

Keeping in view the purpose of compulsory procurement, it should be obvious that such procurement cannot be made at the prevailing high prices. Much as one may dislike it, compulsory procurement has to be below the prevailing high market prices. The question is how much below the market prices. The answer to this question depends upon some linked policy decisions and even with the best of intention and competent analysis would remain controversial. Briefly, the considerations which could guide the decision regarding the level of procurement prices are

1. the proportion of the production, or strictly that of the marketable surplus, which is sought to be procured through graded levy,
2. the quantum of subsidy which the Government is prepared to bear to bridge the difference between the procurement price of the commodity and the price at which it is issued

to ration/fair price shops, and finally
3. informed judgment as to the price-tolerance level (cost of purchasing the minimum requirement) of the vulnerable section of the community.

The last two factors are obviously related.

Though the limit to the magnitude of subsidy and the price-tolerance limit of the poor are important factors in the determination of the procurement price, their discussion will take us very much beyond the scope of this article. I shall, however, try to explain how the proportion of levy to production/marketable surplus has a bearing on the procurement price. It should be emphasized that except under the condition of monopoly procurement, the Government does not compulsorily procure, through graded levy on the producers or the processors, the entire marketable surplus below the prevailing market price. The principle of graded levy exempts the small farmer from the levy and the proportion of levy rises with the increase in the producer's size of holding or production. Empirical research has established that since the levy removes a portion of the marketable surplus from the market (and release the same to those who would be priced out of the market because of the prevailing high market prices), the price of the non-levy portion of the marketable surplus rules higher than what it would have been, had the entire surplus (levy plus non-levy) been put on the market. In other words, if the proportion of levy to marketable surplus is not too high, the weighted average of levy and non-levy prices would be more than the price which would have prevailed in the absence of levy. In any case, as there is no levy at present all these are academic issues.

Reverting to the question of the appropriate level of minimum support price, the issue revolves on the cost of cultivation. In this connection it is first necessary to get acquainted with different concepts of cost of cultivation. Farm management studies have developed 4 concepts of cost—Cost A1, Cost A2, Cost B and Cost C. It would be tedious to enumerate the content of each of these concepts. For our purpose it would suffice to state that Cost C contains all the components of Cost A1, A2 and B plus the imputed value of human labour provided by the farming family. Naturally, it gives the highest estimate of the cost.

It is generally accepted that Cost C should be taken into consideration while determining the support prices. It should, however, be mentioned that Cost C, besides including the imputed value of family labour, also includes the imputed rental value of owned land and interest on fixed capital. Thus the cost contains several elements of income attributable to the farmer's own land and labour. Thus, the higher the imputed values of land and labour, the higher the cost-based price and the higher the income!

The authenticity of the estimates of the cost of cultivation can be questioned and, in fact, has been questioned. In earlier years the cost data were obtained from the farm management surveys sponsored by the Ministry of Agriculture. For the last several years the data are collected under the comprehensive scheme for studying the cost of cultivation of principal crops— also sponsored by the Ministry. The field work of collecting the data is entrusted mostly to the agricultural universities in different states. The APC relies on these cost data for its recommendations.

There are, however, a few practical difficulties in implementing the decision to accept Cost C as a basis for determining the support price which should be noted. Farm management studies indicate that generally Cost C increases with the decrease in farm size. This happens mainly because of the inclusion of the imputed value of family labour in Cost C. The main concern of the small farmer rightly is to increase his production irrespective of the amount of his and his family labour involved in the process. His Cost C, therefore, includes an element of cost which is strictly attributable to the system which does not provide full employment at the market wage and not to the farm or the process of cultivation.

Secondly, even within a single district the range of variation in the cost of cultivation is very wide. Ignoring the extreme values at both ends, the maximum cost is 2 to 3 times the minimum. When the range is so wide, the average loses much of its meaning. In one of the early exercises made by the APC, it was found in one case that the average cost would not cover the cost of 37 per cent of production, 44 per cent of farms and 38 per cent of area under cultivation. Almost similar results were obtained from the analysis of data of other farm management studies.

To overcome the 'injustice' involved in adopting the average price as a basis for determining support price, adoption of what is known as bulk-line cost was suggested, under which the cost of 85 per cent of production—descending from the least-cost production—is adopted as a 'relevant' cost. It may be noted that even after such 'liberalization', it was found that in West Bengal for Assam paddy in 1955–57 the cost of about 26 per cent of farms and 20 per cent of area would not be covered.

It could be contended that since every quintal of production is needed by the country, the highest cost of production or the production of least efficient farmer (no offence intended) should be covered in determining the support price. As a matter of fact, it has been contended that the cost of production studies consider, for example, only the hours of bullock labour utilized for the purpose of production. But the bullocks have to be maintained round the year, and the cost of maintaining them during the unutilized time should also be included in arriving at the cost of cultivation. The argument can be extended to the cost of unutilized human labour. If we may say so, this is an issue which cannot be accommodated within the discipline of farm economics. Be that as it may, its implications should be clearly grasped. The implication is that what must be supported is not only the cost of production but the cost of 'subsistence' of the farm and the family. From guaranteed employment to guaranteed subsistence is but one step forward.

Even so the problem of technically non-viable or poorly managed farms, which unfortunately are uncomfortably large in numbers, cannot be brushed aside. Except for the growers of cash crops, they yield hardly any surplus for sale. As such higher price does not offer a solution to their problem. Policy measures which are relevant to their problem are strengthening their resource base—mainly land through redistribution of 'surplus' land—establishment of non-exploitative institutional structure for credit and marketing, easy access, at reasonable (subsidized) prices, to modern inputs and extension services providing guidance in the adoption of improved technology and farm practices.

Besides the level of support prices, the question of parity also is raised in connection with the farmers' demand for justice. There is more than one measure of parity. The simplest and perhaps the crudest is provided by commodity terms of trade.

This refers to the relative movements of prices of agricultural and non-agricultural commodities. For want of space we do not explain why this measure is defective. Even so, it may be stated

TABLE 14.1

Ratio of index of prices of manufactured products to the index of agricultural products

(*Index Base 1970–71 = 100*)

1971–72	72–73	73–74	74–75	75–76	76–77	77–78	78–79	79–80
109.1	110.5	100.2	99.4	108.8	110.5	102.5	104.4	114.2

that for more than two decades since Independence—almost till the steep hike in the prices of crude oil and the consequent rise in fertilizer prices—by and large, the terms of trade so measured were not unfavourable to agriculture. For whatever they are worth, the data for the last decade are given in Table 14.1.

A more sophisticated measure is the inter-sectoral terms of trade, i.e., the agricultural sector's terms of trade *vis-à-vis* the non-agricultural sector. Two studies on the subject, one by R. Thamarajakshi (for 1951–52 to 1965–66) and another by L.S. Venkataraman and M. Prahladachar (for 1964–65 to 1973–74) indicate that during the period studied, once again the terms of trade were favourable to the agricultural sector. The following is from the findings of the latter study.

In the period 1964–65 to 1973–74 the annual percentage rate of increase in prices of agricultural products purchased by non-agricultural sector both for intermediate and final consumption, and therefore for all uses, was greater (3.9, 3.3 and 3.5 per cent, respectively) than the corresponding annual percentage rate of increase in prices of non-agricultural products purchased by the agricultural sector for intermediate, final consumption and all uses (3.4, 2.4 and 2.8 per cent, respectively). The growth in net barter terms of trade was 0.5 per cent for intermediate consumption and 0.9 per cent for final consumption. As for the income terms of trade between agriculture and non-agriculture, though they have continued to improve in the period 1964–65 to 1973–74, there has been a fall in the annual per cent growth from 3.4 (1951–52 to 1964–65) to 2.4, because of the fall in the per cent rate of growth in marketed surplus of agriculture from 2.9 to 1.7 (Venkataraman and Prahladachar, 1979).[2]

During the last 3 years, however, the terms of trade may be moving against the agricultural sector, as a result of a sharp escalation in input prices.

A third measure, and perhaps the most appropriate, is the farmers' terms of trade or the ratio of the prices received by the farmer and the prices of inputs purchased by him. To the best of my knowledge—and subject to correction—such ratios have not been systematically and scientifically worked out either at the national or regional level. Compilation of such parity ratios involves a rather elaborate exercise. Assuming that the issue of the Base Year is satisfactorily resolved, we would need 'weighting diagrams' for constructing the index of prices paid. Time-series data of prices received and prices paid do exist in a few states, but some years ago when the data were closely examined, their accuracy and reliability were found to be below acceptability. The Directorate of Economics and Statistics in the Ministry of Agriculture also used to compile what was called an index of input prices. The APC, on its own, compiled an index of input prices and used it while recommending support/procurement prices. Thus the APC report on price policy for kharif cereals for the 1974–75 season, while recommending the procurement price for paddy, did take into consideration the increase in the input prices index in 1973–74 over 1971–72 and 1972–73. It recommended a uniform procurement price of Rs 74 per quintal of paddy for the 1974–75 season. This was higher by Rs 11 or 17 per cent over the price recommended for the previous year, as against the increase of 12 per cent in the index of input prices between 1972–73 and 1973–74 (Government of India, 1975).

While discussing the issue of prices and production it is necessary to understand a little more clearly in what way and to what extent prices would influence production under different economic conditions. If the situation demands that the production of one particular commodity (say rice) needs to be increased, an increase in its price relative to that of a commodity (say jute) which competes with it in the use of land and other inputs will certainly boost the production of the former commodity. But it should be obvious that a relative increase in the price of one commodity (rice) means a relative decrease in the price of the substitutable commodity (jute), whose production will be adversely affected. It would be, perhaps suggested that prices of both (or all) farm commodities should be simultaneously increased. Under such a proposal the production-stimulating effect of higher prices, if any, would be extremely modest. In technical jargon, the aggregate supply response to price is weak. If higher prices could generate higher production, public policy has a very soft option of all-round increase in prices.

Nor can higher agricultural prices bring about a parity between rural and urban producers or consumers. An increase in raw material prices does not necessarily squeeze the profit margin of the industrial producer—unless his prices are pegged through administrative action and no black markets develop. They would instead push up the prices of manufactured articles (sugarcane—sugar, raw cotton—cloth). Higher consumer prices also do not affect the incomes of organized industrial and clerical workers, government servants, bank and insurance employees, inasmuch as they will be compensated through higher dearness allowances. The (surplus) farmers' parity will improve only· *vis-à-vis* the unorganized urban and rural labour, families with fixed (high or low) incomes, pensioners and the like—destitutes not excluded. It would thus appear that an increase in the agricultural price, far from solving the problem of reducing rural-urban disparity, might aggravate the problem of intra-rural disparity and more specifically widen the divide between the (rich) producers and (poor) consumers whether in the rural or urban sector.

This does not mean that agricultural prices should be deliberately kept low. No responsible academician or policy-maker has ever suggested it. One can be even more positive and say that there should be a long-term assurance to the farmers that agricultural prices will not be allowed to fall below a level at which, taking the good and bad years together, good farming on a technically viable unit becomes an uneconomic proposition or hinders adoption of improved technology and farming practices.

Market prices for most of the agricultural commodities are currently above the minimum support prices fixed by the Government. As such, it would appear that the farmers' demand is that the Government should purchase these commodities at higher than the prevailing market prices. Apart from the economic implications of such a proposal, the administrative and organizational problems involved in implementing such a policy will be enormous.

It is indeed significant that the farmers' organizations which demand justice for the farm sector have picked on a single issue of farm prices, an issue within the domain of Government policy. It seems they are not much bothered by other economic factors which depress their income. The outstanding factors are those pertaining to marketing margins and non-institutional credit. It is a notorious fact than in cash crops like jute and onions, the traders' margins are unconscionably high. In regard to jute, the APC report on price policy for jute for the 1979–80 season has the following to say:

> The observed difference in the prices (of jute) between Nowgong (Assam) and Purnea (Bihar) markets and Balokopa (West Bengal) has turned out to be much larger than envisaged. This is a reflection of the imperfections existing in the jute marketing system. Although the legislation for the establishment of regulated markets has been passed in all the jute growing States, regulated markets with all infrastructural facilities are yet to be established. The cooperative structure in these States continues to be weak. The share of the jute grower in the final price paid by mills could be considerably improved by strengthening the cooperative structure and enhancing its involvement in jute marketing (Government of India, 1979).

In regard to commodities like onions, the margin between the retail price and the producer's price is often as high as the cost of cultivation. Yet, strangely during the current agitation hardly anything is said about the exploitative marketing system which saps the incentives of the producers. Obviously, the farmers are keen on presenting a sort of 'united front' and do not wish to raise any awkward questions pertaining to the role of the traders and money-lenders in sucking away a sizeable portion of the consumer's rupee or the producer's price.

Agriculture is such a crucial sector of the national economy that it deserves all the support and encouragement the state policy can give it. Likewise no one would question the need to provide adequate incentives to the farmers to enthuse them to put in their best effort to increase production and productivity. There are in the country 30 million marginal operational holdings in the size group of 0.5 ha and below and 14.5 million small holdings in the size group 0.5 to 1.0 ha. They pose the biggest challenge to agricultural development strategy. The question is how far do higher prices provide a solution to the problems of the farming community, especially the small and marginal farmers, not to speak of the landless agricultural labour and the rural poor. As pointed out earlier, no one is questioning the desirability to providing fair prices for agricultural commodities. Assuming that the currently prevailing prices are less than fair, will a stepping up of their prices through administrative action solve the problem of depressed living standards and if so to what extent? Take the case of foodgrains. Even at current prices millions living below the poverty line are unable to buy their minimum subsistence requirements in spite of a subsidy of Rs 600 crores per year while foodgrains stocks in spite of a bad harvest are 'comfortable'. If foodgrains prices are to be durably sustained at a reasonable level, does it not stand to reason that the major thrust of our policy should be to find ways and means to build up the purchasing power of the poor?

NOTES

1. Reprinted from *The Economic Times*, 7 February 1981.
2. An article by Kahlon and Tyagi in a recent issue of the *Economic and Political Weekly* arrives at contrary conclusions (vide A.S. Kahlon and D.S. Tyagi, 'Inter-Sectoral Terms of Trade', *Economic and Political Weekly*, Vol. XV, No. 52, 27 December 1980: A-173–A-184).

CHAPTER 15

Prices and cropping pattern[1]

The Economic Survey, 1985–86, has rightly expressed its disquiet over the emerging imbalance in the cropping pattern. Elaborating on the subject the Survey states:

> A number of factors influence the changing cropping pattern, including the differential rate of technological change among crops, the spread of irrigation leading to area shrinkage of dry crops, market intervention and support by the government in certain crops but not in other crops, and, *perhaps the most significant of all, the changing relative prices between different crops* [emphasis added] (Government of India, 1986: 10).

Voicing the same concern, it further states: 'Emerging distortions in the cropping pattern can no longer be ignored' and 'a rational price structure has to be evolved for both inputs as well as output in order to bring about a desired change in the cropping pattern' (Government of India, 1986: 18).

The Finance Minister taking cognizance of the emergence of imbalance in the cropping pattern stated in his Budget speech (1986): 'To ensure that our approach is not *ad hoc*, we must work towards a longer term [price] policy, which takes full account of regional differences in yields of different crops.' As a concrete step, he announced that the Minister of Agriculture has already initiated work on a longer-term price policy for important crops in consultation with agricultural experts and scientists.

From the passages quoted above, it seems that the official view considers a change in the relative prices of different crops as the most relevant and effective remedy for removing the imbalance in the cropping · pattern. Our submission is that while a change in relative prices of competing crops can effect a shift in relative production to some extent in specific regions, the effectiveness of this policy measure for bringing about an overall balanced cropping pattern in the country is strictly limited. Besides, policy-induced change in relative prices is likely to result in an overall increase in agricultural prices and may prove to be inflationary.

Changes in relative prices can be brought about in the following ways:

1. increasing the price of the preferred commodity A, whose production is sought to be increased relative to commodity B, whose production needs no increase or a slower increase than in the production commodity A; and
2. lowering the price of commodity B without increasing the price of commodity A.

An intermediate way would be to increase the administered price of commodity A in a larger proportion than that of commodity B.

It is obvious that there is no policy measure in the hands of the Government by which it can lower the market price of any commodity, except when it has a sustainable buffer stock. Lowering the administered price is also not politically feasible. The second alternative mentioned above must therefore be ruled out. As such the Government's effort to bring about a 'rational' price structure will end up in increasing prices of all commodities, with relatively larger increases in the prices of the preferred A commodities.

More importantly, it is not so much the price but the net revenue which the grower obtains from cultivation of a crop which determines his cropping decisions. The quantum of the price increase which the preferred commodity will need to equalize the grower's net revenue with that of the competing crop may be so large that it may be unacceptable to the consumers.

In the absence of improved technology, an increase in the relative price of a commodity may not necessarily result in increase in production. The Economic Survey, 1985–86 itself notes:

During the last two years (1983–85), prices of pulses rose at an annual average rate of 20 per cent. In the absence of a breakthrough in seed technology, the pressure on prices is unlikely to ease in the face of rising demand (Government of India, 1986: 52, para 5.12).

The Index of Wholesale Prices of pulses (1970–71 = 100) increased by four times to 430 in 1984–85, but the annual rate of increase in area and production of pulses was just 0.5 and 0.9 per cent between the quinquennia ending 1953–54 and 1984–85 (i.e., 31 years). The annual rate of increase between the quinquennia ended 1964–65 and 1984–85 in area and production of pulses was –0.2 and 0.1, respectively. As against this, the Index of Wholesale Price of wheat and rice—the two competing crops for gram and *tur*—increased to 213 and 270, respectively in 1984–85, yet their production increased at the annual rate of 6.7 and 2.2 per cent in the corresponding 20 years. The ineffectiveness of changes in relative prices to bring about corresponding change in production becomes evident from Table 15.1.

To be fair to edible oilseeds, it should be stated that in terms of oil content, their production increased by 20.40 per cent between the quinquennia 1975–76 to 1979–80 and 1981–82 to 1984–85 (Government of India, 1986).

Increase in productivity is a better index of progress registered by different crops. In this respect also, gram, *tur* and total pulses reveal poor performance compared to that of the two competing crops, wheat and paddy. The compound rates of growth in yield (kg/ha) for the period 1967–68 and 1983–84 for these five crops were: gram –0.25, *tur* 0.38 and total pulses –0.24, paddy 1.54, wheat 2.90 (Rao and Ray, 1985).

Price and revenue

It has been mentioned earlier that what determines the decision of the farmer on choosing a cropping pattern is his net return and not simply the price of the crop. The foregoing discussion of relative productivity of pulses and that of their competing crops is relevant for this purpose. Rao and Ray (1985) have used the 'cost and return ratio' to derive the net profitability of competing crops. They found that

net return per hectare from paddy and wheat was higher compared to gram and tur in all the states. In states like Haryana and Rajasthan the net profit of gram worked out to Rs. 506 and Rs. 507 per hectare compared with a profit of Rs. 1068 and Rs. 763 per hectare respectively · in the case of wheat (Rao and Ray, 1985: 371).

TABLE 15.1

Prices and production of selected agricultural commodities

Commodity	Index of wholesale prices (1970–71 = 100)		Annual rate of production increase (%) between quinquennia ended 1964–65 and 1984–85
	1971–72	1984–85	
Wheat	103	213	6.7
Rice	105	270	2.2
Pulses	118	430	0.1
Gram	102.8	489.2	–0.8
Tur	103.5	335.4	2.9
Groundnut	83	295	1.0

Sources: CMIE (1986); Chandhok (1978); Government of India (1985a, 1986).

If so, the pulse-wheat ratio of the Index of Wholesale Prices which was 2:1 in 1984–85 will have to be further increased substantially if the area and production of wheat are to shift in favour of gram. The crux of the problem is therefore to increase the · profitability of pulses through as many non-price measures as are available.

Maintenance of remunerative prices for farm products and provision of price support to prevent excessive decline in prices are accepted and unexceptionable principles of price policy. The issue on which we have reservation is that of the potency of price policy to bring about a balanced cropping pattern. The elasticity of production response with respect to price differs greatly between crops. In a well-researched study on growth and instability, S.K. Ray has observed, *inter alia,* 'The elasticity of response ·with respect to price generally turned out significant for all crops except for pulses, tobacco and cereals crop aggregate. Pulses production turned out to be completely insensitive to price changes' (Ray, 1983: 472).

The price and production relationship in regard to oilseeds, another commodity indicating cropping imbalance, is not examined in as many details as have been provided for pulses. We will cite only the findings of one research study. Purkaystha and Subramanian (1986: 353) in a recent study on groundnut state: 'In spite of the increase in the relative price of groundnuts to competing crops, the area under groundnuts as a proportion of net sown area have stagnated.'

The Economic Survey, 1985–86, citing state-level study by the National Council of Applied Economic Research has stated that

> at least in regard to yields per acre, in several states the cropping pattern does not match the states' comparative advantage in yields. Crops for which conditions are most suitable are under-produced and there is over-production of crops which are not suitable (Government of India, 1986: 10).

This is amply illustrated by the eight charts reproduced on page 11 of the Survey. The question to ask is: why does such an irrational cropping pattern emerge in several states? The farmers' behaviour is guided by the comparative revenue obtained from growing different crops, rather than by the technical potential of comparative yields. Changes in relative prices can to some extent reduce the gap, but the increase in price (of the under-produced crop) needed to neutralize the difference in net revenue may be exorbitant. Reduction in the production of over-produced crops will also lead to a rise in their prices (unless the unit cost is simultaneously reduced) and will need a further rise in the price of under-produced crops to equalize the revenue. Therefore, our submission is that while price policy should be fully utilized to correct the imbalance in the cropping pattern, a more appropriate solution to the problem lies in research in the development of unit-cost reducing technology and an intensive extension programme.

Prices vs irrigation

The Economic Survey, 1985–86, states:

> The minimum support prices of the various pulses have been raised by 60 to 70 per cent between 1979–80 and 1984–85. During the same period procurement prices of wheat were raised by only 34 per cent and that of paddy (common variety) by 44 per cent.

However, improvement in the relative prices was obviously inadequate as farmers did not bring additional area under pulses. Since *uncertainty is a major factor against cultivation of pulses*, the coverage of pulses under the scheme of crop insurance introduced since the 1985–86 kharif should help improve conditions for the expansion in the area under the crop . . . [emphasis added] (Government of India, 1986: 16).

The Seventh Five-Year Plan also emphasizes *high risk* and low profitability in the cultivation of pulses and has recommended, *inter alia*, the introduction of pulses in irrigated farming system, as a major element of strategy for expansion of pulse production (Government of India, 1985, Vol. II: 6). Apart from the fact that the farmers' decision (unrestrained by policy intervention) to allocate irrigation water between different crops will be governed by incremental incomes likely to be obtained from such allocation, reduction in risk and uncertainty in pulse cultivation through bringing it under irrigated farming system—or crop insurance— is worth attempting.

Some scholars however prefer to rely more on price incentive than on extension of irrigation. For example, Tyagi (1986: 406) in a rather strident criticism of an earlier article by de Janvry and Subbarao (1984: A-177) (which argues against price subsidy and recommends expansion of irrigation) tries to establish that 'price incentive approach is superior to irrigation approach'.

We hope he has calculated the increase in the price of pulses that would be necessary and the subsidy it would need to bring demand and supply in balance.

Let us for a moment see what price 'disincentive' did to wheat. Tyagi admits:

The administered prices of wheat were not raised by the same proportion as the prices of other commodities. In fact, the wholesale price index of wheat, deflated by the index of agricultural commodities, *declined* from 95.5 in 1976–77 to 84 by 1979–80 and further to 79.7 and 75.3 by 1981–82 and 1983–84 respectively. Yet during this period, the acreage under wheat *increased* from 20.9 to 24.4 million hectares (Tyagi, 1986: 406).

Yet he tries to save his thesis of superiority of the price approach by an elementary observation: 'However, in this context, it needs to be remembered that had the decline in relative prices of wheat been much steeper than warranted by the productivity gains . . . it would have . . . adversely affected the expansion of wheat output . . .' (Tyagi, 1986: 406–407). If the price approach simply means support prices to sustain adoption of improved technology, the proposition can be readily accepted.

Finally, an important issue to which much thought will have to be given is the likely clash between

1. the cropping pattern that may emerge from the strategy of making optimum use of land in different regions based on comparative advantage of growing alternative packages of crops, and
2. the cropping pattern necessary for a better balance between domestic demand and domestic supply, under the assumption of a closed economy.

If such an assumption is relaxed, altogether different sums will have to be made from those being currently made.

We have repeatedly argued that the most critical issue for Indian agriculture is the rising unit cost of production of almost all crops. We are producing wheat and rice at a cost which we are protecting with higher and higher support prices which are beyond the reach of a large section of domestic consumers. Nor are the current prices acceptable in foreign markets. A similar situation has emerged in cotton. For how many commodities are we going to pile up buffer stocks and hopefully wait for crop failures to clear them? Our earlier assertion that the Government will never be able to exercise the choice of lowering the prices of surplus commodities or let the market do it, makes all talk of evolving a rational price structure meaningless. Emphasis on a rational cost-reducing technology (inclusive of irrigation) strategy would be more meaningful.

NOTE

1. Reprinted from *Economic and Political Weekly*, Vol. 31, No. 16, 19 April 1986.

CHAPTER 16

Agricultural policy: Prices and the public distribution system—A review[1]

'Agricultural policy is in crisis,' says a document of the World Bank (*Agriculture: Challenges and Opportunities*, 29 April 1991). The observation reminds one of the title of a report, *India's Food Crisis and Steps to Meet It*, prepared in 1959 by a team of experts sponsored by the Ford Foundation.

Policies do need to be scrutinized and revised from time to time in the light of past performance and changes in the domestic and international situations. Such a revision as may be needed should not however be carried out under the pressure generated by a feeling of crisis.

The World Bank Document (hereafter referred to as WB Document) offers a comprehensive review of the performance of Indian agriculture. The range of the data marshalled and tabulated will be immensely valuable to research scholars. While giving credit where it is due, the WB Document draws attention to the flaws in the current agricultural policy and suggests a strategy framework for an 'Adjustment Programme'. Some of the critical areas identified are input subsidies, prices and procurement, domestic and foreign trade, investment, and technology. This paper is however confined to only three issues: Prices, Procurement, and Public Distribution.

The World Bank's major criticism of India's agricultural policy pertains to 'excessive and pervasive Government involvement in the sector'. There is no difficulty in agreeing with the proposition that the 'Government must sharpen the objectives of its intervention and policy goals . . . and concentrate on those areas where the public sector has a clear and unequivocal role [incentives, infrastructural development, research and food security].' We also agree that 'Marketing is an activity which by its very nature is ill-suited to public sector entities' (World Bank, 1991).

To what extent has the agricultural policy pursued hitherto succeeded in achieving its goals? The World Bank's position on this basic question is somewhat equivocal. In several of its paragraphs, the WB Document recognizes the positive results of the policy. For example, it states:

> At the start of the Green Revolution, policymakers opted for a strategy which concentrated on technology development, expanded input availability and price incentives in a few basic foodcrops . . . and infrastructure development . . . in a few high-potential regions. This strategy paid off: production of wheat and rice accelerated, India became self-sufficient in foodgrains, and food consumption for most [but not all] of the population increased. The strategy was appropriate for its time and the conditions: it targeted the most obvious and pressing needs of feeding the nation, and it opted for concentrating scarce resources where the returns would be highest (World Bank, 1991).

Such concentration, which was the need of the time, had its adverse consequences also. Some regions and crops lagged behind. The question is whether the lag can be attributed directly to the strategy of concentration which determined resource allocation or, at least partially, to the inherent agro-climatic disabilities of the lagging regions.

Much of the analysis and many of the recommendations made in the WB Document, e.g., in regard to input subsidies, are valid and deserve serious consideration. But in two areas, prices and public distribution, we have some reservation which we discuss here.

I. PRICES

At the outset we should like to submit that the Government does not fix market prices of agricultural commodities; it only announces support/procurement prices which, at the most, influence market prices.

The question which deserves serious consideration is: how does one judge whether the incentive framework for agricultural commodities is proper or not? The World Bank's answer, and that of many good economists following its trail, is simple and unequivocal. At the simplest level, comparison of the domestic with international price trends indicates the extent to which commodities are protected or disprotected. The magnitude of protection (disprotection) can be determined by calculating Nominal Protection Coefficient (NPC)—which is the ratio of domestic prices to import/ export parity prices. For greater refinement, one may use Effective Protection Coefficient (EPC) which is the ratio of value added at domestic prices to value added at international prices, and still further ESS, which is EPC adjusted for subsidies/taxes on non-tradables.

Based on calculations made by Gulati and Sharma (1991), it is found that the EPC for wheat, rice, and cotton is less than 1, and hence they are 'disprotected', penalized and taxed. In contrast, sugarcane and oilseeds, whose EPC is more than 1 (sugarcane 1.63 and oilseeds slightly above 1.50), have been 'protected', pampered and unduly subsidized. These are averages for 1980–81 to 1986–87.

Is EPC the only relevant criterion for judging whether the price and the resulting cropping pattern are right? Are not factors like agro-climatic potential of different regions, technological horizon of different crops, domestic demand and supply in the context of balance of payment constraint equally germane? Let us cite an example. Demand projections based on a background paper by Radhakrishna and Ravi (1990) indicate that demand for edible oils will grow at the rate of 3.5 per cent from the base year (1986–87) to the year 2000 compared to 2.37 and 2.65 per cent, respectively for rice and wheat.

From this the World Bank draws the right conclusion that 'rice and wheat cannot be the sole engine of growth in the future' and

> demand will rise most rapidly for non-foodgrains, especially for dairy products, protein foods, fruits and vegetables, sugar and oils. These products tend to have higher value added than staple foodgrains, and thus contribute to raising rural incomes . . . They also tend to be labour intensive not only in production, but also in handling

and processing (World Bank, 1991).

The two tests used to judge the appropriate incentive frame—
the EPC and domestic needs and advantages—seem to indicate
contradictory policies. The first suggests more incentives to the
'disprotected' crops—rice, wheat and cotton—and less to 'protected'
crops—sugarcane and oilseeds. The second test suggests encouragement to edible oils and sugar, and status quo for rice and
wheat.

We do not know enough about the technological dynamism
of different crops and scientific research in the pipeline. But
we do know that in the second decade of the Green Revolution
(1978–79 to 1988–89) trend growth rate of all cereals was 2.8
per cent and that of oilseeds and sugarcane 4.1 per cent and
3.1 per cent, respectively. This pattern of growth, achieved under
the current incentive frame, is also in keeping with the direction
of projected demand and contribution to rural income. It also
deflates the relevance of EPC as a guide to domestic price policy.

Nonetheless, since India is interested in promoting exports
of agricultural commodities, she cannot altogether ignore international
prices. This does not detract from the fact that international
prices are the resultant of highly manipulated domestic prices
and trade policies of exporting countries. If Indian agricultural
policies are flawed by excessive and ill-conceived Government
intervention, the same is true, to a much greater degree, of
domestic agricultural policies of the exporting countries. No country
in the world accepts or applies to its agricultural policy, the
standard of 'market purity'. Here are a few examples of market
intervention by Governments committed to free market.

'American farmers top up every dollar of their earnings from
farming with nearly 50 cents in handouts from American taxpayers
and consumers.'

'Subsidies double the income of their cousins in the EC.'

'In Japan, twice as much of farmers' money comes from
the state as from land.'

'And farmers in Switzerland hardly merit the *name*: 80 per
cent of their income is given to them' (*The Economist*, 12–18
December 1992: 3).

France is stubbornly resisting reduction in subsidy to its
oilseeds production in spite of the US threat to impose 200

per cent duty on French wine imports.

As is well known, Japan and South Korea have banned imports of rice, which is violative of GATT rules. To find a way out 'GATT has offered Japan a formula by which Tokyo could lift the ban and replace it with a 1000 per cent duty on foreign rice' (*The Economist*, 12–18 December 1992).

When such is the state of interventions in international price and trade in agricultural commodities, what is the sanctity of border prices passionately held up as a guide for India's policy-makers?

As to the EPC, 'in Japan rice prices are seven times higher than international prices'; America helps growers of sugarcane get high prices [currently roughly one and a half times those in the world market] by using import quotas to prevent cheaper sugar flooding in. There are ingenuous ways of reducing subsidy. The European Community (EC) has agreed to cut cereal farmers subsidies by 30 per cent—as a gesture to the Uruguay Round negotiations—measured from 1986 when they were at peak. But there is a catch: 'Cereal farmers will henceforth get less money through price support as consumer prices fall by 30 per cent. They will instead be given *direct grants*, provided they agree not to sow some of their land to cereals' (*The Economist*, 12–18 December 1992: 6, 14). When hunger is stalking a large part of the world, it is not considered bad economics to keep productive land out of cultivation. Well, perhaps not, but it certainly is ethically indefensible.

The resentment over the developing countries' policy of keeping farm prices deliberately low springs partially from the 'high price' syndrome deeply rooted in the mindset of the developed countries where farmers constitute a tiny minority. The developing countries in which farm workers constitute two-thirds of the labour force and 40 per cent of its population lives in poverty have a more difficult task of balancing the producers' and consumers' interests.

II. PUBLIC DISTRIBUTION SYSTEM (PDS): PROCUREMENT

It is recognized that 'Poverty considerations will compel India to sustain publicly sponsored foodgrain procurement, storage and distribution efforts. These programs are even more important in a period of economic downturn and adjustment, to ensure an adequate social safety net.' What is needed is 'redirecting the benefits of PDS to the truly poor' and 'improving efficiency, in terms both of cost and nutritional impact' (see World Bank, 1991). These are eminently reasonable propositions.

That there are many deficiencies in the working of the PDS is readily accepted. The high cost of its operations and more importantly, its inability to reach the rural poor, the objective which provides its very rationale, are very serious deficiencies. But some of the criticisms levelled against PDS need a closer look. More importantly, the solutions and the alternative systems suggested are not as sound as they are made out to be.

The PDS has two distinct components: procurement and distribution. *A priori*, it would appear that procurement of essential commodities from producers/processors/traders, involving a degree of compulsion, would be a more difficult and unpopular operation, whereas distribution, at subsidized rates, would be comparatively simple. Procurement has to deal with fluctuating situations—harvest conditions, market prices, etc.—whereas distribution requirements are easily identifiable and relatively stable. Experience however indicates that the procurement operations which involve decisions at the level of support and procurement prices (a distinction removed in later years), state-wise procurement quotas (now abolished), storage and transport have become less bothersome over the years. The procurement system has shown commendable flexibility, criticized as being 'constantly in flux', in adjusting to the changing situations; and much of the adjustment has been in the direction of deregulation. Gradually, as the supply situation improved, the severity of all the components of the procurement regime was relaxed. For example, the war-time practice of graded levy on farmers was quickly given up. Currently, as we shall argue, the use of levy as a method of procurement is limited. Now, there are no quotas of procurement in surplus states for delivery to the Central pool. The centrally imposed strict zonal restrictions on inter-state movement of commodities no longer exist.

The procurement system has been characterized as coercive. We shall argue that 'procurement', as it is practised, is neither pervasive nor coercive, at least not as much as it is made out. Taking the last ten years as a reference period, the bulk of the 'procurement' was at *support prices*, implying that far from being coercive it was protective of the producers. As a matter of fact, it is wrong to term such transactions 'procurement', which suggests some degree of compulsion.

Wheat

Let us examine the procurement system crop-wise. There is not much objection to the manner in which wheat is procured. Wheat is purchased in the open market along with private traders. There is no compulsion, no levy, the FCI and the State agencies have only a right of pre-emption in purchase at the stipulated procurement price. In several years, prices offered have had the effect of arresting the decline in prices below the support level. Zonal restrictions on transport were withdrawn in 1977, though in years of scarcity informal restrictions on movement of wheat outside the state are imposed by surplus states to facilitate procurement.

This leaves rice, cotton and sugarcane. We shall drop sugarcane from our discussion for lack of space.

Cotton

Cotton is purchased by the Cotton Corporation of India (CCI) and procured under the Monopoly Procurement Scheme in Maharashtra. The latter is certainly unwarranted and needs to be discontinued. Even so, it needs to be mentioned that cotton cultivators have vociferously demanded its retention.

Would they do so if the arrangements were coercive? They favour the scheme because they get an assured price. In case the Cooperative Marketing Federation makes a profit through its sales in the open market or exports, the farmers share it in the form of 'bonus', but if it makes a loss, which they often do, it is borne by the State Government, i.e., by the taxpayer. The Maharashtra Government has shown a tendency to keep its procurement prices higher than those fixed by the Central Government. Thus, far from being coercive, the Monopoly Procurement is a device for subsidizing the cotton farmer at the cost of the taxpayer. Be that as it may, it is a needless intervention.

The Cotton Corporation of India, which is the main agency for market intervention, is not bound, as the FCI is, to purchase cotton only at the support/procurement price fixed by the Central Government. There is no obligation, leave aside coercion on anyone, the producer, the processor, or the trader, to sell to the CCI. Yet, the CCI does make substantial purchases at the prevailing market prices, when it feels, rightly or wrongly, that in the absence of its intervention cotton prices will decline to unremunerative levels. Incidentally, the perceived unremunerative levels are higher than the support/procurement prices fixed by the Central Government. Thus the CCI's market intervention is in fact farmer-friendly and not coercive.

Rice

Currently, there is levy on rice mills and traders under which they are required to surrender a certain percentage of their out-turn to the Central or State agencies at procurement prices, which are below the market prices. Hence there is an element of taxation. Besides the levy, the procurement of rice involves movement restrictions imposed by rice-procuring states. Since 30 September 1977, in principle, there have been no restrictions on the movement of levy-free rice and paddy. Nevertheless, several State Governments have imposed certain restrictions. For instance, in Karnataka, the movement of paddy/rice outside the state, as well as within the border area (5 km belt), is regulated by the State Government by issue of permits. In Tamil Nadu, every licensed miller or licensed dealer who intends to transport rice or paddy outside the state, is obliged to deliver to the Government or any other authorized agency, an equal quantity as levy at the procurement price. In Thanjavur district of that state, there is monopoly procurement by the State Government. The State Governments of Andhra Pradesh, Haryana, Uttar Pradesh, and Chandigarh Administration have imposed restrictions on inter-state movement of paddy in order to maximize procurement of rice. Such restrictions are certainly coercive. The Central and State Governments should jointly reassess the need and utility of such restrictions in the light of prevailing market conditions.

Dual pricing

It is argued that procurement at below the market prices amounts to an indirect taxation on farmers. Since procurement prices are also support prices, market prices can never be *below* support prices. They will also not remain 'at par' with support prices. The trader will offer a price higher than the support price knowing that in case the price declines his loss will be limited to the difference between the price paid by him and the support price, but his gain through a price rise will be unlimited because there is no ceiling on market price. Hence support prices will always remain 'below' the market prices.

Wherever there is levy, farmers receive the weighted average of levy price and market price. The extent of 'loss', if any, suffered by the farmers in levy sale would depend on

1. the proportion of the levy to turnout/sale of millers/ traders, and
2. on the difference between the levy price and the (pre-levy) market price. I had argued that under the levy regime, the open market price would be higher than the price that would have prevailed in its absence (Dantwala, 1967).

A study conducted by the Indian Statistical Institute confirms that 'whenever there is procurement . . . the open market price goes up steeply to enable the farmer to receive the weighted average price for his total sales which is not less than what he would have received in the absence of procurement' (ISI, 1985). Radhakrishna and Indrakant (1987), in a study of rice in Andhra Pradesh, found that 'the open market prices of rice in the dual market system have been estimated to be about 20 per cent higher than those in the absence of a dual market system' (quoted in Gulati, 1990: 97). Subsequently, 'Using appropriate parameters for the Indian economy, Hayami, Subbarao and Otuska have shown that this, indeed, is the case' (de Janvry and Subbarao, 1986: 20).

High cost of PDS

PDS has been criticized on two other counts:

1. high cost of its procurement operations, and
2. misdirection in public distribution.

The second criticism pertains to the distribution component of PDS, which we shall discuss later.

Several suggestions have been made for reducing the high cost of PDS and the element of large subsidies involved in it. Alternative mechanisms have also been recommended through which cost and subsidy could presumably be reduced without diluting the objectives which the PDS is meant to serve. Before we examine the alternatives let us note some facts about the high costs and some other aspects of PDS like storage.

It is true that the procurement, storage, and distribution operations of the FCI have become huge and unwieldy. It has been calculated that, in 1987–88, the total cost incurred by the FCI in its procurement, storage, and distribution activities came to Rs 2,200 crores. On a cost per quintal basis (excluding Rs 200 crores for storage), consumer subsidy for wheat and rice comes to Rs 82. Tyagi has estimated that in the 14 years from 1975–76 to 1988–89, the average distribution cost has gone up by about 274 per cent, whereas the procurement incidentals have gone up by 70 per cent (Tyagi, 1990: 124).

For its price support operations, the FCI has to maintain a core establishment and a minimum strength of staff. As it is, there are complaints that the FCI has often failed to provide price support, particularly in backward areas where it is most needed. In 1987–88, the number of purchase centres operated for procurement of paddy (rice) by the FCI along with State Government agencies was 4,417. For wheat procurement, purchase centres were more than 7,800. Since then, the number of purchase centres has increased. How many of these could be dismantled without jeopardizing its function as a price supporter?

Stocks

For two decades since Independence, India suffered from shortages of varying degrees, from marginal to acute, in foodgrains production, and had to depend on imports to feed its people. Almost all committees/commissions between 1943 and 1967 have recommended building up the buffer stock of foodgrains for imparting stability to the food economy of the country. In 1975, a Technical Group was appointed to go into the question of the volume of foodgrains to be handled by the public agencies and the reserve stock that would be required to tide over inter-seasonal variations in production. The Group recommended that a buffer stock of 12 million tonnes (mt) should be maintained in physical terms in the country. In 1981, the Central Government appointed another Technical Group to re-examine the same question. Based on its recommendation, the Government of India decided that

1. the buffer stock to be maintained by public agencies should be 10 mt (net), and
2. in addition, an operational stock varying from 6.5 mt on 1 April to 10.1 mt on 1 January, should be maintained.

Thus the total of buffer plus operational stock would vary from 16.5 mt in April to 20.1 mt in January (Tyagi, 1990: 46). Table 16.1 gives the position of stocks on 1 April and 1 January from 1984 to 1992, compared with desired levels. It will be seen that in only three out of seven years, the stocks exceeded the desired levels.

It would be helpful if the stock position, net of withdrawal or addition, is examined in the context of variations in foodgrains production, along with procurement and public distribution (Table 16.2).

Thus, by and large, the FCI did discharge its function of evening out the effects of fluctuations in the production of foodgrains by higher procurement during years of good harvests and higher distribution during years of sub-normal production. Foodgrains production was very low in two successive years, namely, 1986–87 and 1987–88. The high level of stocks during the preceding

TABLE 16.1

Month-end physical stocks of foodgrains in the central pool and with the state government

(million tonnes)

Month	Desired	1984	1985	1986	1987	1988	1989	1990*	1991*	1992*
31st March	16.5	14.9	21.2	20.9	19.5	9.4	7.3	11.7	17.3	12.1
31st Dec.	20.1	22.5	25.2	23.6	14.1	9.5	12.1	19.1	14.7	13.2

* Provisional.
Sources: Tyagi (1990, Table 2.8: 47); Government of India (1992 a, Table No. 11.5: 84-85); Centre for Monitoring Indian Economy, *Monthly Review of Indian Economy*, Bombay (monthly issues).

TABLE 16.2

Production, procurement and public distribution of foodgrains
(million tonnes)

	1984	1985	1986	1987	1988	1989	1990	1991*
Production	152.37	145.54	150.4	143.4	140.4	169.9	171.0	176.4
Procurement	18.72	20.12	19.7	15.7	14.1	18.9	24.0	17.8
Public distribution	13.33	15.80	17.3	19.7	18.6	15.9	15.3	17.0

Production: Agricultural year July to June. Thus 1984 is July 1983 to June 1984.
Procurement and distribution: Calendar year
Sources: Government of India (1992a, Table No.11); Centre for Monitoring Indian
     Economy, *Monthly Review of Indian Economy*, Bombay (monthly issues).

period, 1985 and 1986, helped the country to tide over a very
critical situation in 1987 and 1988. The monetary cost of holding
(large) buffer stocks should be weighed against the gain of preventing
widespread starvation.

Three major suggestions have been made for reducing the
Government's (FCI's) involvement in the management of the food
economy: better targeting, reduction in buffer stock holding by
greater reliance on imports, and involvement of private trade
in procurement. We shall examine them in that order.

Targeting

As our subsequent discussion reveals, there is considerable leakage
in public distribution in favour of the non-poor. Hence it is
essential to ensure that public distribution and the subsidies involved
in it are better targeted. We are however not sure that quantities
required for targeted distribution would be substantially lower.
Subbarao (1989) has estimated that to ensure the coverage of
the very poor, numbering about 58 million households in 1988,
annual foodgrain requirement would be 11.6 million tonnes, considerably
less than 16 million tonnes distributed in 1988. We view targeting
not so much as a means of reducing the requirement under
PDS or the burden of subsidy but as an obligation to ensure
that the PDS serves the purpose for which it was introduced,
namely, to provide food security to the poor, till poverty is
eliminated through appropriate macro- and micro-economic policies.
We would therefore like to shift the area of debate on the
PDS from a policy issue to one of its proper implementation.

In other words, we are not overly bothered by the *burden* of subsidy but by its misdirection. The PDS should be viewed as an instrument of income transfer in favour of the poor.

No doubt, there are operational problems for effective targeting, such as identification, timely supply and transportation. But in some states like Kerala, Andhra Pradesh, Tamil Nadu, and Gujarat, various types of targeting schemes have been introduced by a process of selective inclusion of school children, old and destitutes, tribals, retrenched workers, etc., and exclusion of income-tax payers, etc. Excellent targeting can be achieved by a massive employment programme assisted by 'food for work'. Some scholars would prefer a massive employment programme to provide money income to the unemployed and let them buy their requirements in the market. The problem, however, is that there is no non-exploitative market for the poor where they can buy.

The Central Government also has initiated steps to revamp the PDS.

> Preference is now being given to population living in the most difficult areas such as drought-prone areas, desert areas, tribal areas, certain designated hilly areas, and the urban slum areas. About 1,700 blocks have been covered in these areas under the revamped PDS (Government of India, 1992b: 53).

However, we notice a slight change in the emphasis from revamping the PDS for the benefit of the poor to a review 'of the management system including procurement, distribution, and pricing of items supplied and the coverage of beneficiaries'. Further, it is proposed to 'review the agricultural policy including buffer stocking so that *it is in tune with the developments in the international trade*' (emphasis added) (Government of India, 1993: 92). The implications of such a review are as yet not clear.

Imports

It has been suggested that instead of holding large stocks, the Government should export a part, block the foreign exchange earned therefrom and use the same to import foodgrains in years of shortages. This presumes that whenever necessary there will be a market for foodgrains export, in terms of prices and quantities,

and availability in foreign markets to meet its emergency needs
through imports at stable prices. One is not so sure of such
a balanced international trading regime in foodgrains. Besides,
the psychological impact of stocks in the country's own warehouses
is much greater than that of foreign exchange 'reserve' searching
to locate foodgrains in world markets.

> In fact, in 1985 when India could have exported a couple of
> million tonnes of wheat, the world market price was substantially
> lower than the economic cost of exports. Thus the Government
> would have been required to heavily subsidise these exports (Tyagi,
> 1990: 135).

In an opposite situation of domestic scarcity, reliance on
foreign trade would also be risky. It seems therefore that

> The world market cannot be relied upon to provide food at stable
> prices. . . . As a course of normal strategy of development and
> for food security, developing countries must take account of the
> extra expenses involved in relying primarily on the world market
> for food in dealing with emergencies short of famine (Parikh,
> 1992: 39).

Parikh refers to the International Monetary Fund (IMF) cereal
facility which provides access to foreign exchange to meet unexpected
import costs. The facility makes it possible to rely more on
trade and relatively less on domestic buffer stock. But, he observes:

> It is often not easy to be an intermittent exporter of small quantities
> of food. If a country is larger and its domestic production fluctuates
> in a way that makes it a major exporter in some years and
> a major importer in others, its exports will depress world prices
> and imports will increase them. It will, therefore, on balance,
> need to export a larger quantity to pay for the import of a given
> quantity. This extra cost will have to be balanced against the
> cost of domestic storage (Parikh, 1992: 39).

Further, 'gains from increased allocative efficiency consequent
on free trade in general and trade liberalisation in agriculture
in particular are marginal' and 'trade policy, like price policy,
and other policies which rely on market mechanism, are not
very effective in bringing food to the poor. They will provide

food to those who have money to buy it but not to those who lack purchasing power' (Parikh, 1992).

Private trade

It has been suggested that commodities needed for public distribution should be obtained through open market purchases. It is not fully realized that once the market knows beforehand that there is a compulsive buyer of a large quantity, say a minimum of 16 million tonnes of foodgrains, it will hold back the stocks till the prices skyrocket and then make a killing by enforcing 'distress' buying on the compulsive buyer. The essence of free market, and particularly of the futures market (suggested by Tyagi and the World Bank) is that the buyers and sellers keep each other constantly guessing about the quantity and the price at which they will buy or sell. It appears that those who are recommending large open market purchases for PDS and buffer stock requirements have not given enough thought to market psychology. A similar misconception about market behaviour can be seen in a recommendation made by some economists and apparently approved by the Government of India for open market sales from PDS stocks to stabilize market prices.

The Cotton Corporation of India (CCI) is able to operate through the open market, precisely because it is under no obligation to purchase any fixed quantities at fixed prices, whereas the FCI has both these obligations.

A suggestion has been made that the FCI should appoint licensed traders/agents to make purchases on its behalf. Once again the same question may be asked: at what prices? Probably within a price range indicated by the FCI. Which licensed trader will make a commitment to deliver the stipulated quantity within the price range knowing that his competitors will soon find out his commitment to the FCI? Briefly, free market can work only under the condition of free purchasers and free sellers. It can be of no use to an unfree purchaser, or unfree seller. The other side of 'distress' sale is 'distress' purchase. In principle, PDS is meant to take care of both distress selling through support prices and distress purchasing through PDS. Is it conceivable that private trade would discharge these functions with a sense of social responsibility?

III. PUBLIC DISTRIBUTION

Besides the high cost and the consequent subsidy burden, the distribution operations of FCI have been criticized for their failure to fulfil its main objective of providing food security to the poor, both in terms of availability and reasonable prices. Better targeting of all social security and poverty alleviation programmes unquestionably has to be one of the most important areas of economic policy reform.

The current public distribution operations are faulted on two grounds: one its 'urban bias' and second, the substantial leakages to the non-poor which would be tantamount to perversion of the PDS. On urban bias, academic opinion is divided. Public intervention in foodgrains distribution commenced during the Second World War under conditions of scarcity. By 1947, about 54 million people in urban areas were covered by statutory rationing and another 19 million by other forms of public distribution. The metropolitan cities in which statutory rationing was introduced were cordoned off and bringing in foodgrains by private trade was prohibited.

The Bengal Famine (1943) had shown that, during periods of scarcity, the big cities with their high purchasing power siphon off disproportionate quantities of foodgrains, depriving the hinterland of its share in the total availability. Shortages and high prices in the rural areas cause severe deprivation often leading to starvation deaths. The Government sought to prevent such a situation by limiting urban consumption through statutory rationing under which there is no free market and other source for purchase. This is how the 'urban bias' crept into the public distribution system.

By 1953, cordoning and statutory rationing were abolished, but the scarcity persisted and the focus shifted to meeting the needs of 'deficit' states. Thus, in the early years after the establishment of the FCI (earlier Food and Warehousing Corporation), Kerala and Maharashtra were the largest recipients of foodgrains from the 'Central pool', built up through compulsory procurement from 'surplus' states for whom quotas were fixed. The success of Kerala's rationing system was largely due to supplies acquired through surplus states like Punjab. This is perhaps the best example of national integration, erroneously perceived by Raj Krishna as partitioning the country through zonal restrictions. So much for the brief history.

Rural-urban bias

The data base for testing the sectoral (rural-urban) and class (rich-poor) bias in PDS is provided by the 42nd Round (July 1986 to June 1987) of the National Sample Survey on 'Utilisation of Public Distribution System' (NSSO, 1990). For assessing rural-urban bias, Dev and Suryanarayana (1991: 2358–59) list seven criteria:

1. visit any village and verify,
2. accessibility as measured by
   a. number of ration shops per thousand of population covered by PDS in rural and urban areas and
   b. number of ration shops per given area,
3. relative proportions of total PDS supplies accruing to the rural and urban sectors,
4. relative dependence on PDS defined as the PDS share in total quantities of an item purchased,
5. per capita PDS quantity purchased,
6. per capita PDS implicit subsidy determined by the gap between the open market price and ration price, and
7. PDS quantity per market dependent (PDSPMD) which takes into account the population that depends on the market for a particular commodity.

Statistical data are provided to facilitate assessment of the bias with different criteria. Each criterion has its limitation. Dev and Suryanarayana prefer the last criterion, namely, PDSPMD. After a careful analysis of all the available data they conclude: 'The nature of the bias varies depending upon the commodity in question and the criterion used' (Dev and Suryanarayana, 1991: 2361). Using the preferred criterion, 'PDS quantity per market dependent' (PDSPMD), they find that 'PDS is rural biased at the all-India level for rice, coarse cereals, sugar and cloth. These items constitute 60 per cent of total PDS purchases. Hence it appears that PDS is not urban biased but pro-rural' (Dev and Suryanarayana, 1991: 2365). The findings at the state level vary. In states like West Bengal the PDS is still urban biased.

Rich-poor bias

The main purpose of public distribution is to provide food security to the poor by supplying foodgrains at reasonable prices through fair price shops, thus reducing their market dependence. Has it succeeded in achieving this objective? Analyzing the relevant data, Dev and Suryanarayana find that

> at the all-India level, the dependence of the poor on the PDS in rural areas for rice, wheat, edible oils, coal, standard cloth is less than 16 per cent. These figures for coarse cereals which are generally consumed by the poor is very low (less than 5 per cent). This would mean that the dependence of the rural poor on the open market is much higher than on the PDS for most of the commodities distributed under the PDS. Similarly, the urban poor also depend, to a substantial extent, on the open market for their consumption requirements (Dev and Suryanarayana, 1991: 2365).

As for the more pertinent question of rich-poor bias, the appropriate criterion for judgement would be the proportion of PDS purchases to total purchases in *different income groups*. Here the data show that 'more or less all the population [income] groups depend uniformly to the same extent on the PDS with respect to all commodities in rural areas, even though there are slight variations' (Dev and Suryanarayana, 1991: 2365).

The authors seem to derive some satisfaction from the even-handedness of PDS in relation to different income groups, but, in fact, their observation demonstrates improper targeting of PDS and leakage towards the non-poor.

Shikha Jha (1991) carries the discussion further. Given that the poor are the target group for public distribution, the effectiveness of targeting can be viewed from two angles: first, the proportion of the poor in the total PDS beneficiaries and second, the proportion of the poor covered under the PDS to the total number of the poor. Ideal targeting would imply that

1. all the beneficiaries of the PDS are poor, and
2. all the poor are covered by the PDS.

Jha conducts two exercises to ascertain the facts. From the

first exercise (TR1), she finds the TR1 ratio, which would be 100 if only the poor were the buyers from PDS, ranges from 40 to 50 for different rationed commodities, except for *jowar* in which it is around 60. To illustrate, while about 40 per cent of the population buys subsidized rice, only half of them are poor. This indicates that a substantial part of the PDS benefit goes to the non-poor purchasers.

The first exercise tells us only about the proportion of the poor within the PDS beneficiaries. It does not tell us about the size of the poor (bottom 40 per cent) left out of the ration scheme as compared to the total poor population. Jha's second exercise (TR2) attempts to find this out. Once again, the ideal situation would be TR2 = 100, i.e., the system covers all the poor. While TR1 indicates a leakage in the system, TR2 indicates coverage of the poor by the PDS. The TR2 exercise shows that the percentage of left-outs among the lowest fractile (0 to 10 per cent) in the rural areas varies from 70 for wheat to 22 for sugar. For rice, the percentage is 57 and for *jowar* a hefty 90. (The PDS for *jowar* is negligible.) The percentage of left-outs in urban area is not significantly different.

The exercises based on numbers of users and non-users—both TR1 and TR2—ignore not only the quantities purchased but also the needs of rural and urban population as also that of different fractile groups within it. It is quite possible that availability from non-PDS sources may be cheaper, besides being convenient. However, if the main concern is with the distribution of subsidies, Jha's finding that a large portion of subsidies accrues to the non-eligible non-poor would be correct.

The amount of subsidy involved in the PDS system is the sum of the per quintal subsidy in different rationed commodities multiplied by the quantities distributed. The first attempt should be to explore the scope for reducing the amount of subsidy without hurting the interest of the poor. Having done so, the second attempt should be to target the distribution in such a manner that the benefit of subsidy accrues, if not exclusively, predominantly to the poor. For this purpose it would be necessary to know the commodity-specific total consumption expenditure and also the share of rationed consumption data for different fractiles, which can be used to calculate commodity-wise rationed and total consumption *quantities* and also the associated subsidies.

This will enable us to find out the extent of leakage in area-wise (rural-urban) distribution of different commodities.

On the basis of this information, the Government can alter the composition of the rationed commodities and their rural and urban distribution such that the maximum benefit from subsidies accrues to the target group. A pre-condition for the success of such a reform would be that the commodity composition of PDS distribution should match the commodity composition of procurement. Under the present system of procurement, the FCI and other procurement agencies are not in a position to ensure such matching. They have no authority to procure the quantities needed for the 'reformed' distribution system. Under the price support system, say for wheat, the FCI is under an obligation to purchase all the quantities offered to it, even though they may not be needed. Besides, the capacity of the procurement agencies depends on the quantum of marketable surplus and its geographical spread. Many scholars have lamented the negligible quantities (2 per cent) of inferior foodgrains, *jowar* and *bajra*, distributed under the PDS, as these are the preferred commodities in the consumption of the poor. The problem is that these inferior goods are generally grown by small farmers for self-consumption. Hence their marketable surplus is not only small but also dispersed. This makes their procurement not only physically difficult but also expensive.

Another criticism of PDS is that 'per capita distribution of foodgrains in different States has not been consistent with the percentage of population below the poverty line in these States' (Tyagi, 1990: 89). For example, in Bihar and Madhya Pradesh where the population below the poverty line is around 50 per cent (1983–84), the per capita distribution (quinquennium ending 1988) was less than 10 kg against the all-India average of 21 kg (Tyagi, 1990: 89). As against this, in Kerala where only 26 per cent of the population is below the poverty line, the per capita per annum distribution of foodgrains has been over 60 kg. The other way of looking at this is that, to some extent, the provision of 60 kg per capita foodgrains to Kerala from the Central pool has helped to reduce the incidence of poverty.

In the mid-sixties, the then Agricultural Prices Commission and FCI used to prepare a rough 'Food Budget' for each state, based on its production and requirement of foodgrains. Procurement/ allocation quotas were determined by the magnitude of the food surplus/food deficit though the states would under-estimate production and over-estimate the requirements. With the improvement in the food situation, the system of procurement and allocation quotas was given up. Still the 'food gap' remains the best tentative guide for the purpose of allocation from the Central pool to the states.

Tyagi does examine the statewise per capita production of foodgrains, their share in the total public distribution and the poverty ratios, and concludes that 'the per capita distribution of foodgrains in different States has not been consistent with the percentage of population below the poverty line'. This is indeed so. But let us examine the same data slightly differently.

The two states, Punjab and Haryana, have the highest per capita production. Their poverty ratios are also the lowest. Their share in public distribution is also the lowest, barely 1 per cent. On the other hand, the four states with the lowest per capita production are Kerala, Gujarat, Maharashtra and Bihar, in that order. They receive 10.4, 5.0, 9.6 and 4.7 per cent share of the public distribution. Poverty ratios are high in Bihar and Maharashtra, but low in Kerala and Gujarat. These data indicate that only Bihar appears to be discriminated against in public distribution. West Bengal and Tamil Nadu in the medium range of per capita production receive a comparatively higher share (12.0 and 9.9 per cent, respectively) in distribution. In both these states poverty ratios are also high. West Bengal is better served by public distribution probably because of its high percentage of urban population. On the basis of per capita distribution also, we find that Punjab and Haryana received about 10 kg as against 62 kg by Kerala (Tyagi, 1990: 90–91).

In a vast country like India in which the food economy is not centrally controlled, intervention through PDS cannot bring about a perfect statewise balance in the availability of food. The relevant question is: would a totally free private trade achieve a better balance?

Government intervention as well as non-intervention in economic management, be it in agriculture or any other sector, are not matters of principle. Their relevance and desirability depend on the purpose they are meant to serve. Non-intervention, say in matters like education, health, food security, research, technological upgradation, and infrastructural development, would be a dereliction.

Likewise, intervention has to be selective. Its need must be clearly established and its effectiveness should be constantly under review. The real problem is not simply to establish the legitimacy of intervention, but that of ensuring its effective and judicious implementation.

NOTE

1. Reprinted from *Indian Journal of Agricultural Economics*, Vol. 48, No. 2, April-June 1993.
   I am grateful to V.M. Dandekar and Nilakantha Rath for many helpful comments.

V
RURAL CREDIT

CHAPTER 17

Agricultural credit in India: The missing link[1]

No plan for Indian agrarian reform can claim to be comprehensive unless it affords due recognition to the importance of providing farmers with adequate credit facilities. While the role of credit in assisting agricultural production is fairly well understood, there is less general appreciation of its contribution in acquiring farm ownership and—what is more to the point in under-developed countries—in preventing its loss. One way to secure an increase in production in under-developed economies is to link it with a social purpose and to assign the primary producer a more significant role in building of the new society. To this end, the relationship of the producer with the factors of production must be made more intimate and stimulating. He cannot reasonably be expected to give off his best in the task of production as long as he thinks that the fruits of his efforts will not accrue either to himself or to the community as a whole, but will be appropriated by a few privileged individuals. Hence the need for social change which will release the genuine producers from their passive role and accord them a status of active partnership.

Credit, without which many farmers cannot attain this higher status and secure a share of the factors of production, can be a powerful instrument for softening the rigid, production-inhibiting stratifications of class structure in the agricultural economy. Under a *laissez-faire* system, credit is extremely class-conscious and plays an important part in perpetuating and even widening inequalities. It is so oriented and organized that it helps only those sections of the community that are economically sound and ignores those that, from its point of view, are not creditworthy. In under-developed economies, in which impoverished farmers constitute the bulk of the agricultural population, this conception of the proper function of credit requires reorientation.

In India the early British administration, attempting to 'improve' the agrarian economy according to the Western concepts of economic and social organization and its own imperial interests, effected a revolutionary change in the system of agricultural credit. In seeking to substitute contract for custom, it gave the customary inequities an institutional cast; the payment of exorbitant interest rates, to which neither borrower nor lender intended to adhere, became a contractual obligation enforceable in the law courts, which issued decrees for the attachment and sale of properties. The consequences were disastrous. Agrarian riots broke out in many parts of the country, assuming grave proportions in the then Bombay Province.

In 1875 the Government of India appointed a Committee on Riots, on whose recommendation one of the earliest legislative measures pertaining to agricultural credit and indebtedness—the Deccan Agriculturalists' Relief Act of 1879—was passed. Though it was intended primarily for Bombay Province, some of its sections were made applicable throughout British India. This and subsequent relief acts, however, accomplished little of a constructive nature. On the contrary, they altered the very basis of moneylending in India. Formerly borrowers had obtained loans without having to execute written documents, or, at most, by placing a signature or thumb-impression in the account book of the moneylender. Now moneylenders insisted upon receiving conditional-sale deeds or usufructuary mortgages before granting credit. The Indian Famine Commission observed in 1901: 'There is positively room for holding that transfers of property both by sale and mortgage have become more frequent in districts to which the Relief Acts apply.' The acts were also responsible for a great increase in the volume of litigation.

On the recommendation of the Indian Famine Commission of 1882, the Central Government instituted two other measures, the Land Improvements Loans Act of 1883 and the Agriculturists Loans Act of 1884, under which the Government assumed responsibility for providing a part of the farmers' credit needs. Both are mainly enabling Acts which empower State Governments to advance loans from state funds and to frame regulations governing their issuance. As its title indicates, the first mentioned is intended to apply to agricultural improvements, while the second is concerned mostly with relief of distress. During the period of British administration, the amount of loans extended under these Acts was insignificant, in no year between the time of their enactment and 1940 did such loans exceed Rs 10 million.

Reporting in 1931, the Central Banking Enquiry Committee estimated rural indebtedness at Rs 9,000 million; a decade later the Reserve Bank placed it at twice that figure. High agricultural prices during and after the Second World War brought some relief, but, as an official enquiry into indebtedness in the Madras Province revealed, their benefits were confined to the big and medium peasants. According to this survey, the total rural debt of the province, which was Rs 2,720 million in 1939, had fallen to Rs 2,180 million in 1945, or by about 20 per cent. If allowance is made for new debts contracted during this period for the purchase of land and for other productive purposes, the gross reduction in debt amounted to Rs 800 million, or about 37.6 per cent. Most of the reduction was due to sales of land, estimated at Rs 469 million; only Rs 247 million was attributed to the effect of higher prices for farm produce. Per capita debt had fallen from Rs 51 in 1939 to Rs 40.8 in 1945; the burden of debt, in real terms, however, had been further reduced to about one-third of the figure for 1939. The enquiry found, on the other hand, that most of the benefit had been confined to the larger and medium landholders (whose debts had decreased by 40 and 25 per cent, respectively), that the position of the small holders had been affected much less (their debts having decreased by only 12 per cent), and that the situation of tenants and labourers had in fact deteriorated (their debts having increased by 4 and 46 per cent, respectively) (Government of Madras, 1946).

Reporting on this matter in 1950, a Central Government committee observed: 'While debts of large and medium landholders have been substantially reduced, those of small holders, tenants and labourers have not been reduced significantly' (Government of India, 1950). Records of the cooperative movement indicate that since 1945 'fresh borrowings and outstandings have tended to increase rapidly' (Government of India, 1950).

That the early legislation undertaken to meet the problem proved largely ineffective may be inferred from the spate of laws which followed the assumption of power by the Congress Ministries, first in 1937 and then in 1945. During this period, almost every state government passed moneylenders' acts, whose main provisions govern licensing and registration of moneylenders, limitations on interest rates, and maintenance of accounts in prescribed form. Some informed observers think that the imposition of restrictions on the activities of moneylenders has had an adverse effect on the availability of rural credit because few other sources of finance exist. The honest moneylender does not consider it worthwhile to conduct business under the new regulations, while the dishonest one has devised devious methods for evading them. On the other hand, the Government and the cooperative movement, even if they possessed the resources—as the latter certainly does not— do not command the administrative machinery necessar⸱ for coping with the problem of dispensing credit in millions of scattered villages. During the first Congress Ministries, attempts were made to reduce the burden of debt through conciliation and scaling-down measures, but the outbreak of the World War and the rise in prices of farm commodities were followed by a marked slackening of such efforts.

Agricultural credit in India is provided by the following agencies: the village moneylender, the cooperative movement, and the Government. If marketing credit is included, the trader, the indigenous banker and a few joint-stock banks may be added to this list. Rough estimates of cultivators' total annual short- and medium-term capital needs are sometimes published. In 1951 the Reserve Bank of India estimated the figure at Rs 5,000 million. In its report published in June 1952, the Grow-More-Food Enquiry Committee appointed by the Government of India placed the figure at Rs 8,000 million, on the basis of Rs 60 per acre of wet land and Rs 20 per acre of dry land. Since no exact statistics are available regarding the shares of these agencies in the supply of credit, it is necessary to accept rough estimates in order to have some perspective for viewing the problem. The moneylender, then, provides, the bulk, perhaps as much as 80 per cent, of agricultural finance; the cooperative movement accounts for 10 to 15 per cent; and the balance is supplied by the other agencies. Complete statistics are not available on the extent of business done by moneylenders. As for the cooperative movement, which in recent years has made good progress, in 1950 there were in the Indian Union 116,534 agricultural societies, with a membership of 4,817,545, a working capital of Rs 352 million, and new loans of Rs 180 million.

This overall picture does not, however, reveal some of the dark spots. For one thing, only landowners can obtain membership of cooperative credit societies; tenants, who cultivate as much as half of the land in India, receive no direct benefit from the cooperative movement. Even amongst the landowners themselves, the small farmers derive little advantage from it. One investigator found that of 674 loans advanced by land mortgage banks in the Bombay Karnatak in 1949–50, only 2.8 per cent had been made to farmers owning five acres or less (Naik, 1951). A survey of the cooperative movement in Kodinar (Bombay State) found that one-third of its members were continuing to borrow from moneylenders despite the relatively high rate of interest involved. It was also discovered that, whereas the larger cultivators had been able to increase their assets by purchasing more land, smaller cultivators had sold some of their land after joining the cooperative societies. The average size of holding cultivated by small and medium farmers, while members of the societies, had declined from 9.3 to 4.3 *bighas* and from 18.5 to 16.5 *bighas*, respectively (ISAE, 1951). (One *bigha* is here equivalent to 0.59 acre.) Thus, in the area surveyed, the cooperative movement had been unable to provide the small farmers with sufficient credit facilities or to arrest the transfer of their land.

The provision of credit is of vital importance in achieving social mobility and a position of greater influence for the depressed sector of the agricultural population. Experience with recent measures of land reform has shown that the purpose of legislation may remain unfulfilled if the latter is not supported by appropriate credit arrangements. Thus, in the absence of financial assistance enabling tenants to purchase land, the abolition of *zamindari* (landlord) tenure, undertaken with a view to transferring the proprietorship to statutory tenants, accomplishes no more than the substitution of the Government for the *zamindar* as landlord. Under the Zamindari Abolition Act in Uttar Pradesh, the Government is to transfer land to certain categories of tenants only after they have paid a sum equivalent to ten times their annual rent. The Uttar Pradesh Government has launched a drive to collect this amount, but only a small percentage of the tenants have been able to produce the necessary funds. In Madhya Pradesh, where tenancy legislation provides for the purchase by tenant-cultivators of land at a reasonable price (absolute occupancy), tenants can acquire proprietary (*Malik Mazbooza*) rights from their landlords by paying an amount equivalent to three times their annual rent; but, although this provision has been in effect for two years, such purchases have been negligible. If the Government is serious in its desire to make land available to the tiller, it will have to provide something more than legal authority. As experience with land reform in many other parts of the world has shown, improvement in tenure status is almost impossible in the absence of credit.

The only source of long-term credit, other than loans extended under the Land Improvements Loans Act, are the land-mortgage banks, most of which constitute part of the cooperative credit organization. Their scale of operation is, however, extremely limited; in 1949–50 there were five central and 283 primary land-mortgage banks in the Indian Union. The primary banks had a membership of 186,330 and a working capital totalling Rs 58.6 million; loans issued by them during the year amounted to Rs 10 million; and loans outstanding at the end of the year stood at Rs 53.4 million. Most land-mortgage loans are extended for the purpose of redeeming agricultural debts. Thus, nearly 90 per cent of the loans advanced by the primary banks in Madras and nearly 54 per cent of those disbursed by primaries in Bombay in 1949–50 were for the redemption of prior debts. Of late, efforts have been made to extend their scope by encouraging grants of loans for land improvements proper, such as sinking, construction and repair of wells, and bunding, and for purchase of costly agricultural implements. The banks are, however, reluctant to undertake this type of business because of a lack of trained personnel capable of assessing the soundness of proposals for land improvement submitted to them. Employment of such personnel would entail costs which might exceed the means of these banks.

The problem to which no serious attention has yet been devoted is that of financing basically uneconomic low-income farmers, who do not represent an isolated phenomenon confined to distressed areas or the result of some emergency but are coextensive with Indian agriculture. If this group is afforded no other source of credit, it must rely on the moneylender, whatever his terms, and even knowingly acquiesce in the infraction of laws that have been enacted for its protection.

Little thought and less action have been directed toward the solution of this problem. Economists and administrators tend to regard cooperation as a panacea. Yet the cooperative movement, not without reason, refuses to shoulder the task of rehabilitation of this vast sector of the agricultural economy which, it maintains, cannot be achieved through the extension of credit, but requires instead an all-out attack upon all of the factors that are responsible for the depressed situation of this group, and which is therefore a task that can be performed only by the Government. The Agricultural Finance Sub-Committee appointed by the Government of India in 1944 recommended the establishment of Government-sponsored agricultural credit corporations, though not specifically for the rehabilitation of the low-income group. Subsequent committees and expert opinion consulted by the Government have found this plan impracticable on the ground that Government machinery is unsuitable for and incapable of maintaining constant direct contact with millions of borrowers in numerous tiny villages. In consequence of this inability of the Government and the unwillingness of the cooperative movement, nothing whatsoever is being done to attack the problem. Yet, although each of these uneconomic farmers individually is an insignificant entity, collectively they are responsible for probably the bulk of agricultural production in India. So long as no planned and determined effort is made to solve one of their greatest difficulties—the unavailability of agricultural credit on reasonable terms—no substantial improvement is to be expected in agricultural production, or, therefore, in the standard of living of the agrarian masses.

An attempt to solve the problem of rehabilitation of low-income farmers and enable them to play an active role in an efficient agricultural economy must seek an answer to two questions: which is the most suitable agency for the provision of credit to farmers in this group, and how can the ancillary rehabilitation measures best be integrated with the provision of such credit? The same agency will presumably be responsible for both credit and rehabilitation functions. With respect to the provision of credit, there are two possible alternative agencies—the cooperative movement or the Government. Neither moneylenders nor private banking institutions are suitable for this purpose, though for different reasons: in view of the large element of risk involved in lending to the low-income group, moneylenders will insist on exacting a rate of interest so high as to be socially unacceptable, while the private banks are likely to regard the business as not worth the trouble involved. The cooperatives too consider the credit risk to be unacceptable and the responsibility for rehabilitation to exceed their proper function. The Government, on its part, cannot divest itself of responsibility for rehabilitation, but it considers the task, particularly that of providing credit at the farmer's end, to be beyond its administrative competence. The result is an impasse.

Since each of these institutions finds the task beyond its particular competence, the solution would appear to lie in the creation of suitable combinations. Thus, in our opinion, there would be much to recommend in a partnership between the Government and the cooperative movement in which the former assumed the risk and the latter the responsibility for administration. In addition, the Government should authorize the cooperative movement to undertake such rehabilitation measures as improvement of tenure relations, consolidation of land fragments, soil-conservation projects and the like, for which an 'independent' cooperative movement lacks authority. This arrangement would have two clear advantages; it would avoid bureaucratization of the administrative machinery, and would make possible a comprehensive attack on the problem. It would, however, involve certain disadvantages as well. For one, it would require a partial surrender of independence by the cooperative movement—to which some psychological opposition exists. Moreover, partnership with the Government might be considered objectionable from the point of view of its possible threat to the proper functioning of the cooperative movement. Yet it is doubtful whether an alternative procedure can be found. If, in the context under discussion, the inadequacy of *laissez-faire* procedures and the dangers for totalitarianism are understood, the creation of suitable machinery for the economic advancement of under-developed countries obviously requires an original approach. In these countries, Government participation in rehabilitation must be vigorous and at the same time the administrative machinery must, as far as possible, be popular and neither bureaucratic nor Government-controlled.

Suitably strengthened by Government support, the cooperative movement should accept the responsibility for supplying credit to low-income farmers and for invigorating their economy. If these tasks are tackled simultaneously, the risk incidental to financing such farmers will be to some extent reduced. The operation of the credit and rehabilitation organization should be modelled somewhat on the lines of that of the Farmers' Home Administration (formerly the Farm Security Administration) in the United States, whose distinctive features include a thorough appraisal of each borrower's home and farm economy, provision of technical guidance for both, and extension of credit accompanied by supervision of its use.

The cooperative movement in India is more or less deficient in all of these respects. Requirements regarding creditworthiness are very strict and often rigid and mechanical, but once credit has been extended, the only responsibility that remains is that of repayment. The cooperative society, for all practical purposes, comes in contact with the borrower only at the time that it sanctions the loan and, later, recovers the dues; in the interim the borrower is left to fend for himself as best he can. This system should be remedied in at least two respects: the creditworthiness of individuals should be assessed more liberally, with credit restrictions being based on their long-term repayment potential rather than on the value of their fixed assets; and stricter, more sustained attention should be given to the affairs of creditors. The task of credit organizations does not end—but in fact begins—with the extension of credit, because the continuing soundness of the borrower's overall economy (including his home), and not merely regular repayments on pain of forfeiture, should be the concern of a credit agency endowed with a social purpose.

In under-developed economies, credit must serve not merely to oil the wheels of a going concern but to build up the economy— a much more difficult enterprise. Its administration, therefore, must be accompanied by interest in improving the overall economy of borrowers. An agreement which assigns credit functions to cooperatives and rehabilitation functions to the Government is both unnecessary and impractical. The two functions should be entrusted to a single agency, the cooperative movement, and wherever it finds the undertaking to be beyond its resources or authority, the Government should come to its assistance.

NOTE

1. Reprinted from *Pacific Affairs*, Vol. 25, No. 4, December 1952.

CHAPTER 18

Credit and its role in poverty alleviation[1]

Though availability is a necessary element of a responsive credit system, it is not sufficient for the purpose of alleviation of poverty. There are other aspects of the supply side of the credit system, to which we shall refer later, but the major obstacles to poverty alleviation are on the demand side. The problem here is that of 'Making the Poor Creditworthy' (the title of Robert Pulley's paper, 1989). The availability of credit has to be converted into entitlement of the poor to credit and this can be done only by strengthening the assets and skills of the poor and enhancing their income-earning capacity. Thrusting more credit on the poor through all manner of subsidies and low interest rates can serve as a mere palliative at best, ultimately resulting in a persistent— and politically irresistible—demand to write off unpaid loans as a component of the poverty alleviation programme.

Several well-intentioned efforts have been made to augment the assets and incomes of the poor through schemes such as IRDP, and employment-providing schemes like NREP, RLEGP, now merged in the Jawahar Rozgar Yojana, but all of them have been hastily conceived and ineptly implemented as the short-term objective of gaining political mileage has acquired primacy over enduring poverty alleviation. The point that needs to be emphasized is that the policy-maker as well as the people, including the poor, must accept the fact that making the poor creditworthy is inevitably a relatively slow process which expedients like loan *melas* cannot accelerate. This caution is sounded because the

new Government in its eagerness to get the better of the previous
Government may tend to be overgenerous in supplying credit
and neglecting the more difficult task of making the poor creditworthy.
Once the primacy of the latter is accepted, other issues pertaining
to the demand and the supply components of the credit system
can be quickly disposed of.

Shortcomings in the operational aspects of institutional credit
supply—cumbersome procedures, delays in sanctioning of loans,
faulty identification of beneficiaries, inadequate scrutiny of project
proposals, neglect of infrastructural facilities and forward and
backward linkages, etc.—are well documented in numerous official
and non-official evaluation reports on poverty alleviation programmes,
and need not be reiterated. Pulley (1989) in his World Bank
Discussion Paper, referred to earlier, has provided a well-researched
and dispassionate account of credit-linked approaches to poverty
alleviation, their success and shortcomings. The findings are based
on a panel survey of 960 beneficiaries of IRDP in 12 districts
of Uttar Pradesh over a four-year period. Pulley's most important
suggestion is to 'replace the objective of crossing the poverty
line [a flawed measure of success] through a single investment
with the aim of ensuring that sustained access to credit contributes
positive income gains that *gradually* shift poor households over
the poverty line'. The emphasis of his approach is on the quality
rather than quantity lent by replacing the system of centrally
determined *targets* based on the number of beneficiaries by a
more *demand driven mechanism* for credit delivery. 'The assessed
limit for any borrower would be based on their *ability to absorb*
and repay loans rather than their distance from the poverty line'
(emphasis added) (Pulley, 1989: 48).

Pulley's suggestions should not be interpreted as de-emphasizing
the poverty alleviation objective of the programme and putting
the accent on financially viable lending. There is no contradiction
between the two approaches. He accepts the fact that poor households
will need subsidy to make them viable for bank credit, though
he recommends replacement of 'the existing front-end capital subsidy
with interest rebate periodically payable to eligible borrowers',
a recommendation about which I have some reservations. His
major plea is to avoid haste imposed by the pressure to reach
targets. The targets need not be lowered, but if the target group
is to maintain sustainability of its improved income status, more

emphasis has to be placed on improving its credit-absorbing capacity, which credit can facilitate but cannot establish firmly on its own. The banking industry, though sore over the increasing magnitude of cross-subsidization, is perhaps over-rating its role in poverty alleviation and unwittingly providing an alibi to the Government for non-performance in the field of poverty alleviation.

Making the poor creditworthy is to make them more productive. This will involve large public expenditure spread over a wide range of programmes for reform and reconstruction of the economic structure. Poor households need credit but they also need access to good soil, good seeds and irrigation water, to make them creditworthy. This aspect of public investment in improving infrastructure is generally neglected by the Government in its eagerness to appease the farmer through liberal credit and write-offs.

Finally, effectiveness of credit would depend on good district development plans. Institutional credit agencies can assist the district planning authority in formulating viable development projects with their feel and knowledge of where the investment potential exists, but district planning per se is not their job.

They should convey a message to the authorities concerned that the efficacy of their credit plans depends in a large measure on the pre-existence of a sound district development plan. The demand for credit has to be viable—with subsidy if need be— if its supply is to contribute to the fulfillment of the objective of poverty alleviation.

NOTE

1. Reprinted from *Indian Journal of Agricultural Economics*, Vol. 44, No. 4, October–December 1989.

CHAPTER 19

Rural credit: Restructuring the credit system and suggested reforms[1]

I. RESTRUCTURING THE SYSTEM

The National Front Government has decided to accord top priority to agriculture and rural development. Not less than 50 per cent of the investible resources will be deployed for this purpose. The 'Right to Work' will be included in the Fundamental Rights guaranteed by the Constitution. As a first step in this direction, a new employment guarantee scheme will be introduced throughout the country. The rural credit institutions will have to gear their operations to match the credit components of the programmes that would be undertaken for the implementation of these policies. The policy decision which will have a direct impact on the rural credit institutions is the declaration that 'loans upto Rs 10,000 of small, marginal and landless cultivators and artisans, as on 2 October 1989, will be written off'. The time, therefore, seems appropriate for taking a fresh look at the functioning of the rural credit system and its structure.

In this context, one of the issues which the monetary authorities should consider is whether past experience and the task ahead warrant a fundamental change in the institutional set-up of the rural credit system. By a happy coincidence, the Report of the Agricultural Credit Review Committee (ACRC) appointed by the Reserve Bank of India (1989), along with the reports of its five consultants, which has exhaustively surveyed all important aspects of the agricultural credit system, has become available.

The main report and the five reports of the consultants contain a wealth of the latest information on the performance, achievements and shortcomings of the credit agencies. The main report has recommended some major changes both in credit policies and the institutional structure.

The implications of the proposed reorientation of public policies need to be clearly spelt out and debated upon to facilitate appropriate decisions in the concerned areas. Let us avail of this opportunity to review the state of the rural credit system as it has emerged after two decades since the nationalization of major commercial banks and, in the light of the past performance of the system and the task ahead, consider whether the situation demands some restricting of the system. There are many other issues regarding functional adjustments needed for the same purpose, which we shall not discuss here, to maintain the compactness of the discussion.

Highlights of performance of rural credit institutions since 1969

The principal aim of institutional credit is to replace the widely prevalent usurious moneylending. From the available statistics it appears that the rural credit institutions have succeeded to a considerable extent in achieving this aim. The Reserve Bank of India has carried out periodic 'All-India Debt and Investment Surveys (AIDIS)', which, among other things, report the indebtedness of rural households and their dependence on different sources for borrowing. Till now four such surveys have been conducted— in 1951, 1961, 1971 and 1981. From this series it becomes evident that over the years, rural households have significantly reduced their dependence on agricultural and professional moneylenders. In 1951, landlords, professional and agricultural moneylenders were providing as much as 75 per cent of the debt owed by rural households. The commercial banks were totally absent from the scene, while the Government and cooperative societies provided just 3.7 and 3.9 per cent of the debt, respectively. The rest was provided by friends and relatives. Even in 1961, the picture was not very different.

By 1981, however, it had changed radically. Fifty-six per cent of the total rural debt was obtained from/provided by cooperative and commercial banks. The share of moneylenders had dropped to 17 per cent. (For a succinct discussion of the subject, see Gothoskar, 1988.)

Since the nationalization of commercial banks, there has been a spectacular expansion in their rural branches. The number of rural branches has increased from just 1,832 in June 1969 to 30,781 in March 1988, constituting 56 per cent of the total branches of commercial banks. Correspondingly, the number of agricultural accounts in public sector banks has increased from 1.65 lakhs in June 1969 to 191 lakhs in June 1988. During this period the amount of outstanding advances to agriculture increased from Rs 162 crores to Rs 12,110 crores.

The progress of primary agricultural credit societies (PACS) is equally impressive in regard to their advances. Short-term loans issued by PACS increased from Rs 305 crores in 1965–66 to Rs 2,746 crores in 1985–86. During the same period term loans issued increased from Rs 37 crores to Rs 394 crores. Their total loans and outstanding advances increased from Rs 1,299 crores in 1975–76 to Rs 4,313 crores in 1985–86.

This order of expansion has been perhaps too rapid and has left in its trail a number of pitfalls. The involvement of commercial banks in the poverty alleviation programme, though necessary and desirable, is neither well planned nor well managed. By June 1986, the overdues of commercial banks amounted to Rs 1,744 crores (43 per cent of the demand), those of regional rural banks (RRBs) were Rs 413 crores (51 per cent of the demand) and those of PACS were Rs 1,807 crores (41 per cent of the demand). More than 53 per cent of the overdues of the commercial banks, 29 per cent of RRBs and 51 per cent of PACS were more than three years old, indicating their sticky nature.

It should be noted that all the three credit institutions make losses on their agricultural/rural business. It is estimated that the rural branches of commercial banks lose Rs 0.48 per Rs 100 of their business. At the 1988 level of business, the losses of the rural branches are likely to reach Rs 103 crores.

The accumulated losses of RRBs were Rs 94 crores in 1986, and they are likely to go up to Rs 133 crores. The RRBs are losing Rs 3.70 per every Rs 100 advanced. The margin of PACS per Rs 100 of agricultural loans was also negative at Rs 3.21. In 1982–83, the latest year for which data are available, only 56.5 per cent of PACS were earning profit.

The task ahead

With the speedier development of agricultural and rural economy with 'jobs for all' promised by the National Front Government, the demand for rural credit is bound to grow and severely strain the resources of rural credit institutions. Some estimates have been made of the demand for short-term and term credit for the entire agricultural system, based on past trends and the dynamics of technological and other changes in agriculture (consultant I of ACRC). The review committee has moderated and scaled down these estimates to bring them closer to its estimates of available resources with the credit institutions. These estimates are very elaborate but to give some idea about the magnitudes involved, we shall refer briefly to the estimates of the short-term credit that would be needed for agricultural production sub-system (APS) and agricultural input distribution sub-system (AIDS) for the years 1989-90, 1994-95 and 1999-2000 given in the report of the ACRC.

Note the marked difference in Table 19.1 between the estimates made by the consultants and the review committee. The latter are substantially lower, particularly for 1995 and the year 2000. We are not committed to either of the two. Besides, as the latter estimates are for stock, they are inclusive of overdues.

The estimates of demand for term credit made by the ACRC are, however, much higher than those made by the consultants. The net result of the estimates of short-term and term credit

TABLE 19.1

*Demand for short-term credit for agricultural production (APS)
and agricultural input distribution sub-systems (AIDS)*

(Rs in crores at 1984-85 prices)

	1989-90		1994-95		1999-2000	
	A	B	A	B	A*	B*
APS						
Crop production	7,959	8,861	19,661	15,733	35,889	23,888
Livestock	2,317	772	2,816	939	3,555	1,185
Fishery	60	60	120	120	200	200
AIDS	660	177	790	315	960	478
Total	10,996	9,870	23,387	17,107	40,604	25,751

* Estimates under A are for flow and those under B are for outstandings or, in other words, stock.

A Estimates made by consultant I.

B Estimates of ACRC.

demand and supply is summarized in Table 19.2.

Table 19.2 indicates that the credit system will come under strain in 1995 and thereafter, if all the assumptions made both for demand and supply hold true. Separate estimates for demand and supply of credit from commercial banks and cooperatives indicate that the cooperatives will have resource deficit even during 1989–90, and will 'continue to depend on NABARD as hitherto' (Reserve Bank of India, 1989).

The point to be emphasized by presenting these estimates of demand and supply of credit extending to the year 2000 is that there are limits to stretching the rural credit system to keep pace with the Government's policy decisions in the field of agricultural and rural development.

The major challenge before the rural credit agencies is 'how to make the poor creditworthy', within a reasonable time-frame (Robert Pulley, 1989). Can this challenge be met merely by improving the organizational efficiency of the system or will it need some restructuring of the system and, more importantly, of the rural economy itself?

Several well-meant measures have been adopted in each of the three constituents of the credit system to improve their performance, but the outcome still leaves much to be desired.

Several innovations have been introduced by commercial banks to improve their operational efficiency, e.g., the lead bank scheme and the service area approach. As for the regional rural banks, the Kelkar Working Group has made several recommendations to improve their viability. Persistent efforts have been made to reorganize and strengthen the cooperative structure as a whole

TABLE 19.2

Demand for credit (stock) for agricultural production sub-system and agricultural input distribution sub-system and supply of resources

(Rs in crores)

	1989–90	1994–95	1999–2000
Demand*	27,551	57,316	1,10,873
Supply	28,694	51,829	89,447
Surplus (+)	+1,143		
Deficit (−)		−5,487	−21,426

* At increased input prices of 5 per cent per annum over 1984–85 prices.

and PACS in particular. Judging by the brief review of the performance of the rural credit system presented earlier, the task of making the poor creditworthy has not been achieved. The same can be said about the big package of poverty alleviation programmes launched by the Government, in which credit institutions have participated.

The Agricultural Credit Review Committee which submitted its report to the RBI has once again comprehensively discussed all these issues and made detailed recommendations for improving the performance of the rural credit system. In regard to structural reorganization, however, its recommendation deserves a closer analysis.

While discussing the issue of the reform and reconstruction of the credit system which can assist the desired type of rural development, it is necessary to consider the distinct and specific credit needs of different categories of rural households—the poor, the non-poor, cultivators, petty traders, artisans, etc. Their credit requirements differ. As development proceeds and social objectives are redefined, the credit system has to be evolved to respond to the demand as it emerges from the changing perspective. While the entire credit system should be available to meet the demand, each of its constituents will have to adopt a more specific role in regard to certain types of demand and categories of household—social or occupational. The credit system as it has evolved, by and large, is in conformity with the perception outlined here. A brief recapitulation of this process of evolution will be helpful for assessing the structural change recommended by the ACRC (Reserve Bank of India, 1989).

The cooperatives

The first noteworthy point is that each and every committee/ working group which has reported on the rural credit system since the Royal Commission on Agriculture (1928) has reaffirmed the primacy of the cooperatives in the rural credit structure. The Rural Credit Survey Committee (Reserve Bank of India, 1954: 372) in its report which is considered as a reference point for all subsequent studies on rural credit, eloquently expressed this view in the oft-quoted statement: 'Cooperation has failed, but cooperation must succeed.' Even the report of the All-India

Rural Credit Review Committee (Reserve Bank of India, 1969), which recommended the entry of commercial banks into the rural credit system, has clearly stated that this was being done to supplement the cooperative structure and not as an alternative. As mentioned earlier, several attempts have been made to reform and reorganize the cooperative system, yet it has not been able to acquire the dynamism needed to discharge the responsibility reposed in it.

In fact, the system has lost to some extent its credibility primarily because it has lost the idealism enshrined in it and instead has become a manipulative tool in the hands of politicians who have usurped its leadership. Let us ponder over the fact that only 27 per cent of the total membership of PACS constitutes borrowing members. In six states—which include Maharashtra—the percentage is even lower. In Bihar, the loan issued per hectare was a paltry Rs 32 and in West Bengal Rs 192.

II. SUGGESTED REFORMS

As a first reform measure, PACS should be geared to meet the bulk of the requirement for crop loans. If this is achieved, much of the stress on the other constituents of the credit structure, commercial banks and RRBs, would be eased, and would permit them to concentrate on other sub-systems of agriculture—input distribution, processing, animal husbandry, forestry—for which they have locational and professional advantage. For crop loans, proximity is of the utmost importance and no other institution is located nearer to the cultivators and has a better perception of their needs than PACS.

Commercial banks

With the advent of HYVs of seeds the process of modernization of agriculture received a fresh stimulus. The new technology needed extensive use of purchased inputs, broadening the net of agriculture's demand for credit. It was felt that the cooperative system, by itself, will not be able to provide the larger quantum and the type of credit needed for the modernization of agriculture and the diversification of the rural economy. This realization led to the adoption of the 'multi-agency' approach, bringing in the commercial banks in the rural credit system. It may, however, be noted that even after the induction of commercial banks no committee or working group reporting on the rural credit system has questioned the primacy of the cooperative as a grassroot credit agency.

Regional rural banks

The Working Group on Rural Banks (Government of India, 1975) recommended the establishment of RRBs as a new experiment in rural banking. The rationale for this was clearly spelt out. The working group rightly sensed that what the rural clientele needed was a low-cost, low-profile credit institution where it could walk in without trepidation. The staff was to be recruited from the neighbouring area and as such would have a better understanding of the local problems and the local people, their needs and their constraints. The commercial banks with their predominantly urban culture are not suited for the purpose, apart from their high overhead cost. The preferred cooperative sector, whose familiarity with local conditions is unquestioned, however lacks the professional competence needed for catering to the steadily growing secondary and tertiary sectors of the rural economy. As it is, the cooperative system has hardly touched the small traders and shopkeepers, repair workshops, artisans and the so-called lower middle class in rural and semi-urban areas. The rural branches of the commercial banks would have found such petty business cumbersome and unrewarding.

The second Working Group on Regional Rural Banks was appointed in 1977 to review the new experiment and suggest whether it deserved to be continued. The working group found that though the performance of the RRBs during the intervening two years was in no way spectacular, in the course of its field visits it saw that the RRBs were in fact serving a class of clientele—petty shopkeepers, *tongawalas*, camel cart-owners, village industry and service sector—which was not and was not likely to be served by the cooperatives or the commercial banks. Hence, it recommended that the RRBs should become an integral part of the rural credit system. Two subsequent committees, the CRAFICARD (Reserve Bank of India, 1981) and the Kelkar Working Group

(Government of India, 1986b), which was appointed to specifically review the working of the RRBs, also recommended the continuation of RRBs as an integral part of the credit system, despite their many deficiencies and loss of viability. The Reserve Bank of India, however, was quite unhappy about the vanishing viability of the RRBs. Finally, the Agricultural Credit Review Committee (1987) which has submitted its report in August 1989 has recommended the effacement of the RRBs through their merger with the commercial banks. The committee has made out a very persuasive case for its recommendation. The issue, however, needs to be discussed more closely.

The unique feature of the RRBs is that they cater exclusively to the weaker sections of the rural community. It is true that the Working Group on RRBs (1977)—under my chairmanship— had recommended that a small percentage of RRBs' advances may be made available to the non-target group. This was done to reduce to some extent the 'non-viability' inherent in the restricted business the RRBs were mandated to undertake, and in no way intended to dilute their image as a poor man's bank, as alleged by the ACRC. In retrospect, however, I would endorse the Government's decision and the Kelkar Group's recommendation that the RRBs should cater exclusively to the weaker sections.

The principal reason for the ACRC's recommendation to merge the RRBs with the commercial banks is what the committee calls their 'built-in non-viability'. The facts about non-viability are not in dispute and must be unhesitatingly accepted. Out of 194 RRBs, 151 were incurring losses in 1987. Their accumulated losses amount to Rs 133 crores. The accumulated losses in the case of 117 RRBs, as on 31 December 1986, have wiped out their entire share capital. In the case of some, the losses have eroded even a part of their deposits. Obviously, there is a strong case for winding up such an insolvent financial agency. The rub is, the proposal to merge it with the commercial banks does not solve the problem of 'non-viability *of the business*' this institution is 'mandated' to undertake. It would have been a different matter if the merger had been recommended on the ground of mismanagement, as is generally done in the case of business or industrial concerns.

The committee does state: 'Poor quality of lending, bad management and large-scale defaults have led to the poor performance of RRBs.' But, in fairness, it immediately adds: '*But these are weaknesses the RRBs share with the rest of the institutions in the credit system*' (Reserve Bank of India, 1989: 143). If so, bad management cannot be the reason for recommending the merger. Even non-viability cannot be accepted as a sufficient reason for their winding up because all rural credit institutions are in the same boat, making losses on their (less onerous) rural/agricultural business and as such, are non-viable. As pointed out earlier, as on March 1988 the commercial banks were losing Re 0.48 per Rs 100 of their rural business, which is not confined to the weaker sections. Their projected losses, at the 1988 level of business, are likely to go up to Rs 128 crores, almost equivalent to the entire accumulated losses of RRBs till 1988. As for the PACs, we have mentioned earlier that only 56 per cent of the PACs were making a profit. According to a sample study conducted by a Consultant of the ACRC and quoted in its report, the average net margin on their agricultural credit was negative at –Rs 3.2 per Rs 100 worth of business. The margin becomes positive (+ 1.22) only as a result of their non-credit business, such as fertilizer distribution. The review committee observes:

> The negative margin [of the PACs] would further increase due to the reduction in the rates of interest on seasonal agricultural operations for over Rs 15,000 up to Rs 25,000 from 12.5–14 per cent per annum to a uniform rate of 12 per cent effective from 1st March 1989.

Ironically, the PACS which depend substantially on their own resources, instead of refinance from the District Central Cooperative Banks, incur higher losses on their credit business.

It may be repeated that non-viability on RRBs is a consequence of the restrictions imposed by public policy on the type of business they are instructed to transact and as such it is in-built in the business entrusted to them and not in their structure. In the committee's own words,

> First, the RRBs are mandated to confine their lendings to weaker sections where the interest earned on loans is the lowest in the banking system. Low interest margins and the high cost of servicing a large number of accounts, coupled with low volume of business on account of their restricted clientele are some other factors

which make for unprofitable working of these banks (Reserve Bank of India, 1989: 140).

Logically it would follow that the only way to remove such non-viability is to dispense with the non-viable business. The committee is at pains to disavow any such intention. The dilemma can be solved by an ingenious device. If you cannot avoid the losses, conceal them. This is precisely what the committee proposes.

> Once the RRBs are merged with the commercial banks with their wide range of lending, the scope for internal cross-subsidisation also widens and the losses on account of having to service the weaker sections can be offset by earnings from the higher interest yielding loan portfolio of the banks (Reserve Bank of India, 1989: 153).

I am certainly not averse to such income transfer from the rich to the poor.

The matter does not rest here. It should be noted that by doing away with the RRBs we shall be abandoning the entire rationale behind the creation of this new credit agency, a rationale which was enunciated by the Narasimham and Dantwala Working Groups and endorsed by the CRAFICARD and the Kelkar Working Group. We believe that this rationale, namely, the 'local feel, low cost, low profile' is highly relevant to rural banking in a poor country and especially for the poor man. Commenting on the local feel, the review committee states that

> there is qualitative difference as between a cooperative and an RRB. First, in a cooperative, membership itself is local and it participates in the management of the institution. In the case of RRB, on the other hand, the local feel is sought to be achieved merely by recruiting middle and lower level staff within the district (Reserve Bank of India, 1989: 147).

We accept the superiority of the cooperatives in the matter of local feel. That is precisely the reason for our recommendation that the cooperatives should assume the major responsibility for providing crop loans, which is a type of business where familiarity with the clientele is of utmost importance. Second, for the weaker section borrower the access hardly goes beyond the middle and lower level of the bank staff. The question, therefore, is not whether the cooperatives are superior to the RRBs in the matter of local feel, but whether the RRBs are superior to the commercial banks to which the committee wants to entrust the business the RRBs are doing.

As regards costs, it is true that 'there has been a steady narrowing down of the difference between the emoluments pattern in RRBs and the commercial banks, as a result of the hike in salary and allowance structures in many state governments.' It is also true that 'the transaction costs are somewhat higher than those of the rural branches of the commercial banks'. For the purpose of relevant comparison, however, the question to be examined is whether the transaction cost of the rural branches of the commercial banks would be lower than that of the RRBs' cost if they were to do the same type of business as the RRBs are doing?

Our hunch is that with their higher establishment costs, the transaction cost of the rural branches would be higher for the type of business undertaken by RRBs. Our biggest apprehension, however, is that in the post-merger scenario, the very concept of poor man's banking will vanish.

Our difference with the ACRC is only in regard to the commercial banks' efficacy in serving the small man. If we view RRBs as a component of the poverty alleviation programme of making the poor creditworthy, some amount of loss in their operations is unavoidable. Such a proposition is implicitly accepted in the case of other poverty alleviation programmes, such as IRDP and SEPDP which involve provision of substantial subsidies. We accept the subsidy element even in development programmes like supply of irrigation and electricity to the poor as well as the non-poor ungrudgingly. If so, it is difficult to understand the lament over non-viability concerning the operations of the regional rural banks which serve the poor exclusively. A strong case has been made for judiciously 'targeting' subsidies. RRB is a unique case of an institution implementing a crucial programme—provision of credit—based on the principle of targeting subsidy, yet the lament over it is the loudest.

NOTE

1. Reprinted from *The Economic Times*, 30 and 31 March 1990.

VI
AGRICULTURAL LABOUR
AND EMPLOYMENT

CHAPTER 20

Notes on some aspects of rural employment[1]

I. CONCEPTS IN RURAL UNEMPLOYMENT

The problem of unemployment is now accepted as a major problem of underdeveloped economies. Of late, much useful thought has been given to the understanding of this vital issue. It is now usual to refer to the situation as one of underemployment rather than that of unemployment. Unemployment as it exists in the West and underemployment as it exists in underdeveloped countries like India, are two basically distinct phenomena and this distinction should be well understood. It is contended that due to the peculiar nature of the underdeveloped economies, the unemployment of the labour force does not express itself as so many people 'out of job', but as lack of enough continuous work for those attached to *some* jobs, who are therefore not on the labour market seeking employment. In a large measure this is due to the preponderance of self-employment in agriculture. Due to the excessive pressure of population, the available employment which is admittedly inadequate is shared, as in the case of land, among too many claimants. Ownership of land thus comes to be regarded not so much as a source of adequate income as a security against total unemployment.

The report of the UN experts on the Measures for the Economic Development of Underdeveloped Countries has observed:

The disguised unemployed are those who work on their own account and who are so numerous relative to the resources with which they work, that if a number of them were withdrawn for work in other sectors of the economy, the total output of the sector from which they are withdrawn would not be diminished even though *no significant reorganization occurred in this sector,* and no significant substitution of capital [emphasis added] (United Nations, 1951: 7).

This however is by no means the best definition of the problem and is probably not accurate in one aspect expressed by underlined words. The main point about disguised unemployment is that the person affected being self-employed is not available for employment in other sectors as and when it occurs and is not as free as the wage-earner to seek alternate employment. And yet, if he—and many like him—decided to withdraw, the output in the sector will diminish unless the withdrawal is accompanied by 'a significant reorganization' in the sector. This relative immobility of the self- but underemployed person has a bearing on the nature of remedial action. To this we turn later; but put briefly, the remedy can be on two lines:

1. an increase in the resources and their employment-providing capacity in the same sector, and
2. a reorganization of the economy of the sector in a manner which will facilitate the withdrawal of some workers without affecting production.

Mr Chiang Hsieh has given an illuminating analysis of the problem in the June and July 1952 issue of the *International Labour Review.* He classifies agricultural underemployment under three headings: visible, disguised and potential. Visible underemployment is defined as the gap between the amount of labour time which the labour force in a region is able to supply and the actual amount of labour time worked. The concept of disguised underemployment is related to a situation arising out of a more rational reorganization of work; and that of potential underemployment to one consequent upon a more fundamental change in the methods of production. These concepts refer to the different stages of development of agriculture. Their use suggests how much idle and under-utilized resources would be realized from agriculture at a particular stage of economic development and the manner in which the resources can be more fully utilized.

The distinction between visible and disguised underemployment does not, however, appear to be worth emphasizing. For anyone interested in the problem of gauging real under-utilization of available resources, it is the total—visible plus disguised—unemployment which has significance. Potential unemployment likely. to follow a major structural change is perhaps common to all enterprises and in all countries and has many indeterminants.

Our analysis of the problem leads us to the hypothesis that there are only two peculiar features of agricultural unemployment. It is also suggested that they owe their importance primarily to the rigidities of an underdeveloped economy, and are likely to diminish in importance as the process of economic development gathers momentum. The two features are:

1. seasonality, and
2. the disguised nature of unemployment.

Both are relevant from the point of devising remedial measures.

The problem of seasonality is by far the problem of 'inelasticities of the time-pattern of primary production'. 'Here nothing is made or manufactured; everything has to grow and become' (Howard, 1935). Among the agricultural operations, there are many which can be successfully performed only within a certain approximate time-span. There are others such as hedging and the general upkeep of farms and buildings, which can be done at any time during the year. There are still others which impose a regular daily routine throughout the year, such as milking and most of the work connected with the livestock. It can be seen that a self-employed person is often not fully employed and yet seldom wholly free. It is therefore clear that the season is never 'off' for one who, for example, has the responsibility of looking after the livestock. It is only in double-cropped area or mixed farming that seasonal unemployment is not a serious problem. Only 16 per cent of cultivated area in India is, however, double-cropped.

Another point regarding seasonality needs to be noted. Seasonality does not necessarily mean that there are well-marked seasons during which there is continuous and full-time employment and seasons in which there is no employment at all. Sporadicity would express the situation better. Even during the so-called active seasons there may be spells of enforced idleness and there is often some work to do even in off seasons. This is so mainly in the case of self-employed small farmers. In a way this imposes a handicap on the smaller farmer inasmuch as he is not totally free to accept outside jobs even when they are available at remunerative wages unless they are complementary in time to and coextensive with his period of idleness. One of the aims of the employment expansion policy should be to encourage measures which would reduce this in-season unemployment. An increase in the size of holdings and diversification of cropping may in some measure meet the situation. There is, therefore, a need to make employment more intensive as well as extensive.

The question in connection with seasonal unemployment is therefore this: is it usually possible for a farmer to find a complementary employment which will exactly fit in with 'no-work' days? If this cannot be done, the situation, though unfortunate, is a part of the game and the alternatives are between scrapping the enterprise or suffering underemployment. It is possible that since periods of idleness arise sporadically, there is no serious effort on the part of the farmer to seek outside work. He takes such periods of enforced idleness as an inevitable feature of his avocation. The unemployment then remains disguised, but leaves its impact on incomes.

II. FIELD RESEARCH IN ESTIMATING
RURAL EMPLOYMENT

In this section we propose to review, in the light of the foregoing observations, data from published results of some field-work on the subject. We shall see whether the empirical evidence confirms, or suggests a change in, our hypothesis.

The Bureau of Economics and Statistics, Government of Bombay, has collected some data on rural employment. The Bureau conducted a detailed survey of Rural Employment, Income and Expenditure in Bombay. Results of the survey have been published in the *Bulletins of the Bureau of Economics and Statistics* (Government of Bombay, 1949, 1950, 1951). The survey was based on stratified random sampling with population groups as strata, a village as the primary unit of sampling and a family as the ultimate unit of sampling.

The published statistical data of the survey cover the period from October 1949 to March 1951. Data for all the districts are, however, not available at present. Till now only six districts have been covered. Out of these six, only two—Ratnagiri and Belgaum—have been covered for the entire period of the survey. For a clear appraisal of the seasonal aspect of the employment situation, factual data for the whole year are necessary. These are available only for Ratnagiri and Belgaum districts. There are, however, some difficulties of interpretation due to changes in the technique and the schedules used by the survey. The methods of collecting and presenting the data have undergone considerable changes as the enquiry progressed, which render quantitative or qualitative comparisons difficult. As a result, the collected data for these two districts are not of much use in providing an idea about the extent of seasonality in employment in agriculture. Employment statistics for the Baroda district for the period from June 1950 to 3 March 1951, however, illustrate some of the relevant facts about seasonality in the case of 'cultivators'.

The survey is primarily directed towards estimating the employment-providing capacity of the agricultural sector and the extent to which it is being supplemented by the non-agricultural sector. The entire problem is thus visualized not from the point of view of the individual cultivator as he faces the unemployment situation, but from the angle of the whole economy. An answer is sought to the question: for how many days and for how many people in a particular week or a month or a year was the economy of a region able to provide employment? The number of days on which and the number of persons for whom some work was available are therefore calculated as providing an indication of the size of employment that an economy could provide. As a next step, these work-days (days on which employment was found) are broken up into sixteen employment categories, showing the employment status of the employed.[2]

A beginning was made with a pilot survey in the Belgaum and Ratnagiri districts by selecting a sample of villages. The results of this survey show a positive correlation between the size as well as the type of the employment and the size of the village as measured in terms of population. A comparative study of the percentage distribution of the work-days of the self-employed persons brings out the fact that the percentage of self-employed work-days is more in the villages with a smaller population and that there is a gradual decrease in this percentage in villages with a larger population.

The pilot survey was initiated to test the questionnaire and assess the efficiency of the sampling procedure. In the light of the experience, the questionnaire and weekly employment schedules were revised and operational efficiency of the enquiry was increased. The sample population was divided into five (age and sex) groups:

1. Children, i.e., persons in the age group 6–15.
2. Adult males in the age group 16–55.
3. Adult females, i.e., females in the age group 16–55.
4. Old males, i.e., males in the age group 56 and above.
5. Old females, i.e., females in the age group 56 and above.

For each of these groups, details regarding the number of days spent by persons in different types of employment are given. This enables us to form an idea of the position of each group separately. This is a welcome improvement.

It has been observed that a large proportion of work-days of 'old men' is devoted to 'own farm'. (The actual percentage varies between districts according to the general employment situation in that district.) A majority in this age group are enumerated as disabled 'from doing work'. The old men very rarely try to look for jobs outside their own farm. A majority of women in the same age group are returned as employed in doing 'household work'.

The adult female group should be studied according to the occupational status of the household, i.e., whether the person belongs to the family of cultivators or that of agricultural labourers. (In the later stage of the survey the data was studied for three different occupational classes, viz., cultivators, agricultural labourers and other non-cultivators.) Important gainful occupation of women in this age group and belonging to the class of 'cultivators' is work 'on own farm', while 'agricultural labour' predominates over other sources of employment for adult females in the class of agricultural labourers. Womenfolk of the cultivators, as a rule, confine themselves to their own farm and do not seek wage-paid employment inside or outside the village. Since there is no other activity for them, they are mostly engaged in household work which is kept at the minimum during the busy season. Household work is a sort of residual work. It is always there when there is nothing else to be employed with. In a way, it does not compete with other sources of gainful activity. In Ratnagiri district, for example, which has a greater proportion of females in the population (and experiences a scarcity of male labour), the proportion of adult females engaged in household work is smaller than that in Belgaum where there is no such disproportion. Adult females of the agricultural labourers' families seek employment outside the village also when necessary. The difference between the activities of the females in these two groups only indicates a relatively better economic condition of the former, and the extreme poverty of the latter. It can also be surmised that employment is sought only when it is absolutely essential for avoiding starvation and that some of the unemployment, in a way, is voluntary.

In the case of children, attendance at school and household duties occupy a major portion of the total work-days. The children of 'cultivators' spend more days in school than do the children of 'labourers'. This also is an index of the better economic position of the former class. Attendance at school affects the employment situation doubly. It not only takes children away from employment and thereby reduces income; it also involves addition to the total expenditure of the family.

Employment for children, when available, is mostly seasonal and in agricultural occupations. Quite a good number of work-days are spent by them in sundry jobs like looking after cattle and doing minor jobs on the farm. It may, however, be noted that not all children of schoolgoing age go to schools. What is more disquieting, a large number of them neither go to school, nor are they employed in any gainful activity. This is a typical picture of an underdeveloped country where children do not attend school because they cannot afford it; education is not free because the State cannot afford it; and there is not enough gainful employment for them because the economy is underdeveloped.

We now come to the most important group, namely, the adult males in the age group 16–55. This group is important both from the point of view of its size as well as its ability to work. All other age groups may be said to be just assistants to this group in its activities. Considering the 'cultivators' in this age group, though an overwhelming majority of work-days are spent on the farm, seasonal fluctuations are important. It may also be noticed that fluctuations in employment opportunities on 'own farm' and in 'agricultural labour' are parallel; when there is less work on one's own farm, the availability of work as agricultural labour also diminishes. The percentage of work-days spent in 'other gainful activity' during the slack season naturally increases. These points have been illustrated in Table 20.1.

It will be seen that gainful employment varies from 71 per cent to 90 per cent of the total available work-days. The highest figure is in September–October and the lowest in July.

Seasonal fluctuations are generally associated with the nature of the crop. The effect of seasons is more marked in Ratnagiri district because it has primarily a one-crop economy. Paddy being the main crop, October is the busiest month. Again, generally speaking, employment both for cultivators and labourers is most scarce in May and most easily available in June, when preparatory operations begin on the farms. In May, due to non-availability of work on the farm, most of the work-days of both the cultivators and the labourers are spent in doing household work.

TABLE 20.1

Percentage of work-days spent by cultivators in specified activities (males, 16–55 years)

Four weeks' period ending	All gainful activity	On own farm	As agri- cultural labour	Other gainful activity
Year 1950				
25th June	81.70	72.80	5.50	3.40
23rd July	71.23	63.00	2.75	5.48
20th August	83.05	74.58	5.28	3.13
16th September	89.91	80.31	7.34	2.26
14th October	90.23	80.85	6.51	2.87
11th November	83.68	73.14	7.22	3.32
9th December	79.71	69.93	4.43	5.35
Year 1951				
6th January	80.64	67.70	5.01	7.93
3rd February	85.20	72.34	3.82	9.04
3rd March	88.13	74.33	6.53	7.27

Source: *Bulletin of the Bureau of Economics and Statistics* (Government of Bombay), Vol. V, No. 1, July 1951: 60.

Commenting on the data for six months (October 1949 to March 1950) for Belgaum district, the Report of the survey contains an important observation on the characteristic of the self-employed cultivators during the busy season. It says:

> It is also clear that a person engaged on his own farm is most always fully engaged throughout the week, since, as will appear from the detailed statement, more than 60 per cent of the persons claim to be employed on their farm for more than six days in a week (Government of Bombay, 1950b, Vol. III, No. 4 April: 6–7).

From this a conclusion was drawn that underemployment or unemployment is not a very serious problem. Later on, it was realized that this was a hasty conclusion based on inadequate data.

During the slack season the problem is less serious for agricultural labourers than for the cultivators (most of them low-income) because whereas the labourers can afford to leave the village and seize every opportunity of employment, the self-employed cultivator is prevented from doing so by the very nature of the enterprise which requires his presence even during the off season. This has been borne out by figures for the Ratnagiri district.

This then is the broad picture of rural employment in the six districts of the Bombay State, as revealed by the Survey conducted by the Bureau.[3] The picture however is not complete and is to some extent unreal, inasmuch as it does not clearly bring out the significant elements of the problem. This is largely due to the lack of exactness in the concepts used. The concepts and terms should have been more sharply defined for a fuller appraisal and understanding of the problem.

Take for example the central concept of 'work-day', which is taken as the unit of measurement of the size of employment. It is not made clear as to how many hours make a 'work-day'. To count a day on which a person does work even for an hour or so as work-day is surely misleading. Not to relate work-day with hours of work is to miss the whole point regarding the disguised nature of unemployment. It has been emphasized by us that self-employment is often deceptive employment. Some idea of the hours of work per day and of the operations on which they were spent is absolutely essential for gauging the extent of employment and unemployment in any meaningful sense of the terms. By using the concept of work-day and not connecting it with hours of work, the survey failed to throw light just where it was most needed, namely, on the question of the disguised nature of unemployment. This omission detracts much from the value of an otherwise comprehensive study. What we want to find out is whether the self-employed person needed the full time-unit—day, week or month—for the type of work he did, or whether the work was spread out either because there was no other available (and equally paying) work during that time; or even if available the farmer did not for a variety of reasons seek it. Employment becomes underemployment when a semblance of work is available, but not enough to keep one fully employed for the given time-unit.

The results of the survey have given us some idea about the capacity of the economy to offer employment in terms of work-days and the percentage distribution of these into sixteen employment categories. It is necessary to know how much of the labour force is employed and how it is employed, but that is not enough. Employment is a phenomenon depending upon many variables. We want to scientifically determine the precise functions of all the variables, and work out a model in which the interrelationship between all the participating factors is clearly brought out.

It is an accepted hypothesis that the volume of employment is in many cases a function of the size—depth and width—of the enterprise. The data on employment should have therefore been presented in a form that would show its correlation with at least the size of holdings if not the capital equipment. Measurement of employment-providing capacity of land in terms of farm size would have been more relevant. This is so because it is not as if the employment that each aspirant gets is equal to the quotient of total available employment and the number of persons in the labour force. This would perhaps be so if all the factors were perfectly mobile or if the entire land of the village were to be operated cooperatively through which the distribution of work could be made equal. But since the total land is not so managed but is divided into several unequal units and because some factors of production are indivisible beyond a point, it is the employment-yielding potential of each unit that is of significance. Undoubtedly transfers and exchange of labour from one unit to another are possible and do take place, but they are contingent on the complementarity of work. In brief, the design of the survey indicates unawareness of the very concept of disguised unemployment.

The survey has tried to furnish a clue to the extent of underemployment. Unemployment has been defined as employment for three or less days in a week, but in the tables compiled from the statistical data, underemployment has been taken to mean unemployment for four days or less in a week. Apart from this inconsistency the basic shortcoming of the concept of underemployment arises from the fact that it is measured in terms of the work-day unit, which itself might have within it concealed underemployment.

Another and more extensive research effort was made by the Ministry of Labour, Government of India during the preliminary agricultural labour enquiry, which took place from June to November 1949. It was meant to be a pilot survey for the main enquiry into the conditions of agricultural workers. The factual material gathered during the preliminary enquiry contains some relevant information. We shall try to appraise the utility and limitations of this factual evidence.

The preliminary enquiry covered 27 villages in 8 states. Data collected in 8 villages have been published as type studies. The reports contain a warning that considering the illiteracy of the villagers and absence of written records, the data should only be regarded as a near approximation. The enquiry was intended to collect data on all aspects of rural economic life and hence the results give an integrated picture. Since the primary purpose of the enquiry was the study of the economic conditions of agricultural workers, it is natural that more attention was focused on the facts relevant to that class. The term 'agricultural worker' includes all those who work in the fields for wages. An agricultural worker's family is defined, for purposes of the enquiry, as one in which the predominant source of income is from farm labour. Thus the description of agricultural worker refers strictly to wage-paid employment. It serves a useful analytical purpose to take the problem in connection with wage-paid employment as a problem of unemployment rather than one of underemployment. Underemployment as we have suggested earlier is peculiar to self-employment.

The reports further deal with the employment patterns of all the classes in the agricultural hierarchy. It may be noted that the Bombay Bureau enquiry referred to the two classes of 'cultivators' and 'agricultural labourers' as if they were mutually exclusive groups. But the Ministry of Labour enquiry relates the data on employment to the following categories:

1. Attached workers with land owned;
2. Attached workers with land free of rent;
3. Casual workers with land owned;
4. Casual workers with land free of rent;
5. Casual workers with land on rent;
6. Attached workers without land;
7. Casual workers without land;
8. Cultivating owners; and
9. Cultivating tenants.

This comprehensiveness enables a fuller analysis and reveals some highly suggestive clues. We give an illustrative table, showing the total and the non-agricultural employment for casual workers

TABLE 20.2

Average number of total work-days and work-days in non-agricultural activities for casual workers with and without land in five study villages

Type of workers	Casual workers with land	Casual workers without land
Khuntuni		
Total days	162.3	300.4
Non-agricultural activities	51.8	163
Khapri		
Total days	240	283.5
Non-agricultural activities	–	45
Mugurpura		
Total days	96	184
Non-agricultural activities	154.9	181.2
Archikarahalli		
Total days	154.9	181.2
Non-agricultural activities	62	80
Brindabanpur		
Total days	310.4	280.5
Non-agricultural activities	83.9	73.3

in five villages.

In Table 20.2, compiled for five villages, data are arranged in a manner that may lead to some definite inferences. It will be noted that the casual workers with land in four out of the five villages for which data are available, suffer larger unemployment than is the case with the casual workers without land. The other suggestive point is that non-agricultural employment is less for casual workers *with land* than that for those *without land*. This evidence is in complete accord with our hypothesis that farm and non-farm employment often conflict; the landowner is not always free when non-farm employment is available and is often free at a time when such employment is not available.

The average size of holding in all the eight villages was below 8 acres—a sure indication of the existence of the low-income group. This is again reflected in all the categories of earners supplementing their income by taking up non-agricultural employment. The reports have brought out the gravity of the extent of unemployment among agricultural labourers. Want of work has been recognized as the main cause of unemployment. It is also shown that these labourers did derive a significant percentage of their income from non-farm employment. We have shown above the occupational groups which can, and which cannot, afford to take up non-farm jobs, as and when they are available.

The seasonality has been brought out more fully because employment on each operation has been recorded in terms of mandays. The only serious drawback that detracts from the utility of the data hinges around the limitations of the concept of mandays noted above. But since the enquiry deals largely with wage-paid labour, whose main problem is unemployment rather than underemployment, the vagueness of the concept was not very material.

III. NATURE AND EXTENT OF NON-FARM EMPLOYMENT AND FACTORS INFLUENCING THEM

Field work on a modest scale was done by W.B. Donde in 16 villages of the Konkan in 1952 with the object of finding out the extent of non-farm employment and the factors which influenced it. Donde (1951) had earlier examined this problem in his doctoral thesis on 'Rural Labour in the Konkan'. We give here some of the inferences which can be drawn from the material gathered during these investigations. The strength of these inferences was further checked by a brief investigation this year by N.H. Shah in some regions of Gujarat and Saurashtra; in the latter with the help of the Community Development Project and Evaluation Staff at Manavadar.

We found that the avenues for non-farm employment in the villages were numerous, although several of them had a very low employment potential. The following were some of the activities which provided employment: *bidi*-making, work on salt-pans, forest work and charcoal burning, bamboo work, i.e., preparing of corn bins, baskets, cart roofs, bamboo trays, mats, etc., coir making, making brooms from coconut leaves, preparing lime by burning some kinds of sea-shell, and so on. Except the first few, the potentiality of these sources of employment is limited by purely local demand. Those with a wider demand depend upon the availability of special resources.

In taking up the field work in the Konkan villages, we started with a working hypothesis that opportunities of employment—both farm and non-farm—depended on certain clearly definable set of economic conditions. Accordingly, we classified the villages into the following six categories with the assumption that the peculiar features of each would have a bearing on the nature and extent of non-farm employment. The six groups are as follows:

1. villages with a single (rice) crop cultivation,
2. villages with Bagayat (garden) and double crop cultivation,
3. villages in the interior with difficult access,
4. villages with good transport and communication links with centres of organized industries,
5. villages with regular seasonal industries nearby, and
6. villages inhabited largely by aborigines.

The results provided ample justification for the classification; because the socio-economic factors represented by the various groups distinctly influenced both farm and non-farm employment. The data were collected separately for the following categories of occupations: uneconomic farmers—cultivating between 1 to 3 acres of land—landless labourers, artisans with land and without land. It may be noted that the composition of these groups in the various types of villages selected by us itself varied, being a function of the socio-economic milieu they represent. The total volume of employment available would also be affected by these factors. No estimates were made of this; hence our data are meaningful only in indicating the relative importance of farm and non-farm employment in these groups of villages. It may be noted that the enquiry was in regard to wage-paid employment only—thus excluding from its purview self-employment which is quite significant in rural areas.

For all groups—uneconomic farmers, landless labourers, artisans with and without land—taken together, the relative importance of non-farm to farm work was the greatest in the villages near seasonal industries (category 5) and least in villages with garden or double cropping (category 2). The order in terms of relative importance was: villages with seasonal industries (80.9 per cent);[4] villages with links to industrial centres (65 per cent); villages inhabited by aborigines (56.4 per cent); villages with single crop cultivation (39.5 per cent); villages with difficult access (29.5 per cent); and villages with garden or double crop cultivation (15.8 per cent).

Villages with seasonal industries

Some of these correlations are obvious; others need some explanation. The two main seasonal industries which gave such a high percentage of non-farm employment in the total wage-paid employment in these villages were salt works and *bidi* (indigenous cigarettes) making. Both these pursuits are complementary—in time—to agricultural seasons, and therefore all categories of occupational groups took advantage of opportunities of employment they offer. The uneconomic cultivators in these villages, unlike their counterparts in other groups of villages, hardly took up any wage-paid farm work outside their own farms. All their wage-paid work was in these seasonal industries. Even the landless workers got 61 per cent of their wage-paid employment—more than what they got from farm work—from these industries. The artisans in their turn did not care very much for supplementary farm work as they appeared to do in other types of villages.

Villages with transport link with perennial factories

In this group of villages the employment-generating factors were the perennial factories; those engaged in farm work could not take advantage of the employment offered by factories, as they could when the subsidiary employment was seasonal and complementary to the agricultural season. Yet the non-farm employment in these villages is quite high because the transport system and works auxiliary to perennial factories offered many opportunities of casual employment as coolies or gangmen. The higher percentage of commercial crops in the crop pattern also created opportunities of tertiary employment.

Villages with a large aboriginal population

The aborigines usually live in villages surrounded by forests. They, therefore, derive a large part of their employment and income from forest work such as tree-felling and woodcutting. Carting is also an important occupation in these villages. All this results in a high proportion of non-farm employment.

In the mono-culture villages, employment opportunities are very few and those for wage-paid employment fewer. The villages in the interior are the poorest in this respect, most of the labour being self-employed. Capital investment in farm as well as non-farm enterprises is very limited. In garden and double crop villages, on the other hand, the volume of employment is larger, but most of it is on the farm itself; non-farm employment is, therefore, negligible.

Further research

A crucial limitation of this investigation was that it did not go into the question of the influence of these socio-economic factors on the absolute volume of available employment opportunities, within and outside the village. The enquiry was restricted only to the relative importance of non-farm employment in the varying socio-economic complex. Even with this limitation, it has provided clues for development policies.

There are more avenues of productive employment than the

central planners usually think of. True, they are scattered and by themselves small; yet cumulatively they constitute a significant sector of employment. They also do not need much capital investment, their main weakness is probably faulty and inefficient organization. This results not only in low returns to the enterprise but also in the exploitation of labourers. If cooperative organizations could be promoted, not as monopolists but as effective competitors to private enterprise in these fields, employment in them might improve the social status and economic conditions of the participants. Once some organizational set-up is built, it may be possible to promote new small-scale enterprises in rural areas. At present when the city-dweller thinks of non-farm employment, his mind works in a very limited orbit. A better acquaintance with rural life alone can widen the possibilities of utilizing more fully idle hours and idle resources of the countryside. The Community Development Projects Administration would be a proper agency for exploring these possibilities.

NOTES

1. Reprinted from *Indian Journal of Agricultural Economics*, Vol. 8, No. 2, August 1953.
   These three notes, though somewhat unconnected, are pieces on a single theme. The only justification for placing them together is that they are all related to the problem of Rural Employment. The notes were prepared with valuable assistance from Dr W.B. Donde and Shri N.H. Shah.
2. Some of the categories were: work on own farm; work as exchange labour; agricultural labour; non-agricultural labour; household work; school; rest; etc. (Government of Bombay, 1950b), Vol. III, No. 4.
3. The Bureau itself made hardly any analytical comments.
4. Figures in parentheses indicate the percentage days occupied in non-farm work—as per cent of the total number of days of farm and non-farm work.

CHAPTER 21

Rural employment: Facts and issues[1]

The eradication of poverty and unemployment has been a major goal of development planning since its inception in our country. The success achieved in the realization of this goal has been patently disappointing. Judging by the economic policy statements of the Janata Government and the Draft Five-Year Plan, 1978–83, it appears that more earnest efforts will now be made to tackle the problem. Some decisive policy shifts have been introduced to make a more visible impact on the problem during the Plan period. As a result, it is expected that by 1982–83, the 'employment gap' will be reduced from 40.7 million 'standard years' to 15.5 million 'standard years' in 1982–83.

The employment strategy for reducing unemployment has three basic ingredients:

1. a policy to maintain the highest feasible rate of growth,
2. a policy to make the pattern of production more labour-intensive, and
3. a policy to regulate the technological change so that the rate of growth of employment is maintained at a satisfactory level.

No one can demur against a policy statement at this level of abstraction. At a somewhat more concrete level, it is stated that 'the employment-content of the structure of production is sought to be increased by redirecting private demand through redistribution of purchasing power and public demand through greater expansion of public services'. Redistribution of purchasing power is sought to be achieved through 'accelerated implementation of land reform, differential input supply policy favouring small farmers, the minimum needs programme and the public distribution system' (Government of India, 1978a). All this is expected to increase the demand for labour-intensive goods.

Our major grievance against the estimates of employment and unemployment made by the Planning Commission is that they are too aggregative and therefore fail to reveal the highly heterogeneous character of the unemployment situation. If the problem of unemployment is to be effectively tackled, this heterogeneity should be thoroughly understood. The macro policies like a massive shift in public outlay in favour of rural areas and encouragement of labour-intensive technology may not decisively redistribute purchasing power in favour of the lower income group, unless such policies are backed by appropriate organizational mobilization and institutional changes.

Economists now understand that unemployment cannot be eliminated merely by pumping in purchasing power in the economy, but they may still find it difficult to accept that a policy of generating a certain aggregate number of jobs or even person-days of employment may not necessarily bring about a corresponding reduction in unemployment. Unemployment or the demand for jobs is highly dispersed, not only regionally (which everyone knows), but also by age, sex and class of the worker. Besides being widely dispersed, it is fragmented in terms of timing and duration for a large number of the unemployed, except those who are chronically unemployed. It is therefore essential for employment planning to match employment generation with the demand for work, if not for each individual, at least for each major category of the unemployed. We have, I presume, by now understood the distinction between additional jobs and additional person-days of employment. The distinction between the number of unemployed persons and the number of person-weeks or person-days of unemployment was driven home, against much academic resistance. A large majority of persons in the 'labour market' may not want new jobs, they want more stable—and more remunerative—employment in their existing or allied occupations. Of course, if driven to the wall, as during a famine or severe drought, they would accept whatever is offered and would be 'willing' to move wherever the planner would move them. During normal times, their behaviour is found to be quite different. Thus, in the current year (1978–79) the gap between the number of persons who have *registered* themselves under Maharashtra's Employment Guarantee Scheme (EGS) and those amongst them who actually *reported* for work has been quite substantial. The number of persons registered in the current year was about 28 lakhs. The average attendance in various works under the EGS was about 5.2 lakhs, the maximum being about 7.69 lakhs. It would be interesting to know how many of these 28 lakh registered work-seekers had reported for work and the distribution of such persons according to the number of days for which they were employed under the EGS or elsewhere. A systematic districtwise and projectwise record of variations in the attendance of registered (and unregistered) job-seekers and its seasonal pattern would provide rich material for employment planning.

In sum, the employment strategy to be effective has to be based on the understanding of the characteristics of various types of unemployment (the choice of the plural is deliberate), tracing them to their root causes, particularly the iniquitous social and economic structure and iniquitous institutional set-up.

It is necessary to remember a very elementary fact that all the millions of days of additional employment sought to be created under the Sixth Plan have to be provided to the unemployed and underemployed in the five and a half lakh villages of India. Therefore, the most critical issues in employment planning are not only the magnitude of the aggregate employment generation and its sectoral distribution but also its spatial and occupational spread. It should be admitted that there are many constraints on such matching of employment generation with the variegated needs and limitations of the unemployed and the underemployed. The important limiting factors would be the inadequacy of natural endowments of the area and the capabilities and aptitudes of those in need of work. It may be possible to overcome the latter constraint to some extent through an appropriate programme of training and skill formation. Beyond that some migration of population in a planned and purposeful manner may be inevitable. However, an important desideratum of this strategy of tailoring employment generation to the needs and aptitudes of the people within the limits of the development potential of the area is a genuine commitment to the establishment of a competent planning authority and implementing machinery at the district or block level. Consonant macro policies are no doubt equally important. Vyas and Mathai (1978) have advanced another cogent argument for decentralized planning. Planning at the micro level, they argue, enables planning of various activities 'in a mutually supportive manner' (Vyas and Mathai, 1978: 345) and thereby enhances the productivity of each individual activity. The obvious example is that of power and irrigation or irrigation and land-levelling.

The Planning Commission certainly knows this and has therefore attached a great deal of importance to block-level planning, thus acknowledging its own limitations as a remote central planning agency. The Planning Commission can, at best, analyze the problem, allocate resources for its solution, devise a policy frame, and provide technical guidance. But the rest, particularly actual implementation, has to be at a much disaggregated level.

Obviously, we cannot rest content with the general statement that unemployment is a heterogeneous phenomenon. We should, to the best of our ability, put together as much information as is available on the different facets of the unemployment situation, analyze it and spell out its policy implications. Thanks to the 25th, 27th and 32nd Rounds of the NSS and quite a few Farm Management Surveys, plentiful information is now available. Several research workers have made commendable attempts to analyze it in a manner which not only enhances our understanding of the phenomenon of unemployment but also unravels various economic inter-relationships. All these data and analyses should be extremely useful in devising appropriate policy instruments. Obviously, an individual (and a retired teacher at that) cannot aspire to make a total or even a cursory survey of research germane to the understanding of the problem of poverty and unemployment. The best he can do is to pick at random some pieces to which he has a chance access and utilize the same to emphasize a few points which he considers important for designing a strategy for the reduction of unemployment.

In what follows we shall note and comment upon only two or three salient features of the unemployment situation, and certain relationships between the incidence of unemployment and some of the characteristics of the labour force.

I. HIGHER INCIDENCE OF UNEMPLOYMENT
AMONG FEMALES

First, we find that unemployment' rates for 1973 as estimated by the Planning Commission for the country as a whole and measured in terms of weekly status and daily status (but not usual status) are higher for females than for males:

1. 5.90 per cent for females and 3.62 per cent for males, and
2. 11.42 per cent for females and 7.08 per cent for males, respectively (Government of India, 1978a, Table 4.15).

These estimates are based on the 27th Round of the NSS which reports the figures separately for the urban and rural areas. In terms of the daily status or person-days, the 27th Round rate of unemployment among urban females (12.58 per cent) was 57 per cent higher than that among urban males (7.99 per cent); in the rural areas also, the rate for females (9.92 per cent) was about 47 per cent higher than among males (6.75 per cent). If one looks to the weekly status data showing the incidence of 'week-long unemployment', the differential appears even larger, with the female rates both in the urban and rural areas (9.78 and 5.51 per cent, respectively) exceeding those for males (5.97 and 3.03 per cent, respectively) by 64 and 82 per cent.

However, the higher rate (or incidence) of unemployment among females does not necessarily mean a higher number of unemployed women, because the rate of unemployment shows the days or person-weeks of unemployment as per cent of the days or person-weeks in the labour force. To illustrate, the 27th Round data show the percentage of unemployed among all women (aged five and over) to be 1.44 and 1.90 per cent in the urban and rural areas, respectively, lower than the corresponding figures for men—3.55 and 1.94 per cent, respectively. The sex differential in the percentage of unemployed persons in the rural areas is quite small; it could even arise because of the possible random or sampling error.

The NSS data for the first sub-round of the 32nd Round (July–September 1977) provide more recent information on the

TABLE 21.1

Percentage of unemployed persons in the labour force according to alternative concepts, by rural-urban residence and sex, July–September 1977, NSS, 32nd Round (first sub-round)

(age group: 15–59)

Concept	Rural		Urban	
	Male	Female	Male	Female
Daily activity (person-days)	7.32	8.89	9.85	16.41
Weekly activity (person-weeks)	3.68	3.41	7.41	13.05

subject (Government of India, 1978b). The results, summarized in Table 21.1, pertain to persons aged 15–59 only and some adjustment may be necessary before they can be compared with the 27th Round data.

Some scholars consider the NSS rates of unemployment as under-estimates. In their view, withdrawals from the labour force of those who are usually/currently in the labour force during the daily or weekly count are involuntary—due to lack of perception of employment opportunity. They, therefore, suggest that such days of withdrawals should be counted as unemployment. This phenomenon of seasonal or sporadic withdrawals is more common for those who report 'domestic work' as their usual activity, i.e., housewives (Bardhan, 1979).

The policy implications of data on female unemployment are well spelt out by the Plan document: 'The primary need of a majority of women is part-time employment or employment in certain parts of the year' (Government of India, 1978a: 89). In other words, they would prefer employment in household enterprises so that they can combine them with their domestic work. Further, with a little bit of training, the employment of women can be augmented significantly in fields like expanded Minimum Needs Programme, particularly health, family planning, sanitation, nutrition and education.

Unemployment among 'employee' class

Another salient feature of rural unemployment is that the incidence of unemployment is markedly higher among the 'employee' class, and particularly casual labourers as compared to the self-employed.

An elaborate analysis of the NSS data by Visaria for Gujarat and Maharashtra also confirms the relationship (Visaria, 1981a). He finds that as a class (by usual status) rural employees in Gujarat suffered from almost three times as high an incidence of unemployment (in terms of person-weeks) as all the other classes of workers employed in the rural areas, and the casual labourers fared even worse. This analysis in terms of person-days, which is a more comprehensive measure of incidence of unemployment, also confirms the finding. The casual labour class accounted for 56 and 89 per cent of the total unemployed mandays in the rural areas of Gujarat and Maharashtra, respectively.

Relationship between state-level unemployment and proportion of casual labour in labour force

This analysis provides the explanation for the observed correlation between state-level unemployment rates and the proportion of agricultural labour in the labour force. Parthasarathy finds that 'all States with high proportion of agricultural labour fall into cells with higher rates of unemployment, and *vice versa*, the only exception being Karnataka' (Parthasarathy, 1978: 1). Visaria finds that

> in the rural areas of the major 17 states of India, the correlation coefficients between the percentage of casual labourers in the labour force and the incidence of unemployment in terms of person-days are high and positive, being 0.82 and 0.90 for males and females respectively, all statistically significant at the one per cent level (Visaria, 1981a).

His regression coefficients suggest that 'a one percentage point increase in the percentage of casual labourers in the rural labour force in a state can be expected to result in the increase of about 0.4 percentage points in the reported incidence of unemployment (in terms of person-days)' (Visaria, 1981a: 286–89).

This finding about the high positive association between the percentage of casual labour in labour force and the incidence of unemployment ties up neatly with the postulated association between poverty and unemployment when we find that the casual labourers as a class are over-represented among the bottom Monthly Per Capita Expenditure (MPCE) deciles of rural households. The bottom 40 per cent of the households (ranked according to MPCE) include, *inter alia*, over 62 per cent of the casual labourers in rural Gujarat and almost 53 per cent of those in rural Maharashtra (Visaria, 1981a).

This is perhaps the most disturbing feature of the unemployment situation. It is evident that in years to come the percentage of agricultural labourers in the total labour force is bound to grow, because of

1. demographic pressure on available land, and
2. proletarianization of small farmers and artisans as a result of eviction and/or technological displacement.

After making due adjustments to ensure comparability, we find that between 1961 and 1971 the number of landless agricultural workers has increased by about 19 million and their share in the total unorganized labour force has increased from 18 to 24 per cent. Between 1978 and 1983, the working force in agriculture is likely to increase by 21.4 million persons (Government of India, 1978a, Table 4.11: 98). Assuming that the ratio of agricultural labour to total workforce in agriculture remains the same (namely 30 per cent), there will be an addition of about 7 million persons to the ranks of agricultural labourers.

According to the Fourth Rural Labour Enquiry, 1974–75, while 'the estimated number of total rural households increased from 70.4 million in 1964–65 to 82.1 million in 1974–75, i.e., by 16.6 per cent that of agricultural labour households shot up from 15.34 million to 20.74 million, or by over 35 per cent'. The enquiry also reveals that

> the estimated number of full days worked by men of agricultural households for wage employment in different agricultural operations *declined* from 208 in 1964–65 to 185 in 1974–75, that by women from 138 to 129. This decline in wage employment has not been made by more self-employment [emphasis added] (*Economic and Political Weekly*, 1978: 1726).

These trends were observed despite the fact that the percentage of households with land among the agricultural labour households has gone up from 43.9 to 49.2.

Size of farm and unemployment

The high incidence of unemployment among agricultural labourers/ casual labour may be confirmed by looking at the relationship between the size of farm and the incidence of unemployment. Visaria's analysis of the 27th Round State sample data for Gujarat and Maharashtra indicates 'an inverse relationship between the incidence of week-long unemployment (weekly status) and the size of land holdings, particularly in Gujarat' (Visaria, 1981b: 53). In Maharashtra, the relationship seems weak with respect to the incidence of male unemployment. In rural Gujarat, almost 50 per cent of men and 65 per cent of women reporting week-long unemployment were from households with less than one acre of land. The corresponding figures for rural Maharashtra were 40 and 50 per cent, respectively. Unemployment measured in person-days not only gives a higher estimate of unemployment, but 'the inverse relationship between land and unemployment becomes more strongly evident' (Visaria, 1981b: 55). In the rural areas of the country as a whole also, the incidence of unemployment in person-days varies inversely with the size of landholding, although the highest incidence of unemployment is reported amongst households with less than one acre of land rather than among the landless, who include some non-cultivating white-collar workers.

We now turn our attention to some other aspects of unemployment and examine the relationship between

1. unemployment and poverty, and
2. unemployment and agricultural growth.

Poverty and unemployment

On the basis of the data on consumption levels from the 25th Round of the NSS and data on rates of unemployment from the 27th Round, Lakdawala observes that 'in many poor regions of the country unemployment rates are comparatively low' and further 'in many parts of the country low standards of living of landless labourers are associated with fairly low unemployment rates' (Lakdawala, 1977: 5, 6). As this is a rather unexpected phenomenon, let us examine the data presented by Lakdawala a little more closely. The data are for 56 NSS regions, the

TABLE 21.2
Association between poverty and unemployment at the regional level

Unemployment rates	No. of regions	Per capita consumption of wage earners	No. of regions
Below national average	33	Below national average	11
		Above national average	22
Above national average	23	Below national average	15
		Above national average	8

cut-off points for the level of consumption and the level of unemployment are national averages—Rs 26.82 and 7.83 per cent. Rearranging his Table IV, we get the picture presented in Table 21.2. Thus from amongst the (33) regions with low (lower than national average) rates of unemployment, in a majority of regions (22) the level of consumption of landless labourers was higher than the national average. On the other hand, among the (23) regions in which the rate of unemployment was high, in a majority (15) of such regions, the level of consumption of landless labourers was below the national average.

Sau has subjected Lakdawala's data and inferences to a more rigorous test and has found justification for almost a contrary view, namely, 'a low level of standard of agricultural labourers goes with a high rate of unemployment' (Sau, 1978: 1280).

Parthasarathy adopts 'expenditure level at which the minimum diet of 2250 calories is reached' for drawing the poverty line based on Dandekar and Rath's study (Dandekar and Rath, 1971) and examines the relationship between poverty and rates of unemployment and finds it positive, i.e., states with a higher percentage of population below the poverty line are generally states with higher rates of unemployment—with only three exceptions, Bihar and Karnataka with higher (than average) rates of unemployment but lower level percentage of persons below the poverty line and vice versa for Assam (Parthasarathy, 1978).

Visaria has also attempted to ascertain the relationship between poverty as indicated by monthly per capita expenditure (MPCE) and incidence of unemployment according to the three measures of unemployment mentioned earlier. He finds that

While the incidence of unemployment in terms of usual or current activity does not show any consistent relationship with MPCE

decile of household, *a more or less steady inverse relationship
is evident between MPCE decile and the incidence* of unemployment
in terms of person-days [emphasis added] (Visaria, 1981a: 282).

In other words, the labour force in poorer households suffers
from a significantly higher incidence of unemployment and/or
underemployment. This analysis, in terms of MPCE deciles, is
confined to the State sample data for Gujarat and Maharashtra
only, for which some special tabulation was done by Visaria.
The NSS tabulation of data on employment and unemployment
is available only for 6 discrete classes of MPCE, but even from
them Visaria finds that the poor households did report higher
levels of unemployment (in person-days) than the better-off households.

In the light of these findings, Lakdawala's observation regarding
the absence of a clear association between poverty and unemployment
needs closer scrutiny. Perhaps when household data get aggregated
at the level of a NSS region, the relationship between poverty
and unemployment gets blurred. It is also necessary to examine
the correspondence between the MPCE of non-cultivating wage
earners (25th Round) and the MPCE of the total sample population
(27th Round) in different regions. (It may be noted that Lakdawala
uses the consumption data of the 25th Round and the unemployment
data of the 27th Round of the NSS.) Even so, it must be admitted
that there *are* quite a few regions in which low standards of
living are associated with low levels of employment. In such
regions, the problem of poverty cannot be solved merely by
the generation of more employment as measured in terms of
time (mandays). A more appropriate approach for the removal
of poverty would be to direct investment to increasing the productivity
of labour and ensure that it gets reflected in higher wage rates.
Perhaps, this was the limited point which Lakdawala rightly wanted
to emphasize.

II. AGRICULTURAL GROWTH AND UNEMPLOYMENT

The industrial development of the past 30 years has failed to
reduce the heavy dependence of our labour force on agriculture.
In 1971, out of a total labour force of 230.48 million, 167.33
million or 73.8 per cent of the total was engaged in agriculture.

The Planning Commission has estimated that by 1978, the total labour force (workforce plus unemployed) would have gone up to 265.3 million and this agriculture would be employing 192.4 million of them. By 1983, the working force in agriculture is likely to go up to 213.8 million, indicating an addition of 21.4 million persons in just 5 years (Government of India, 1978a, Table 4.11). The Planning Commission envisages that

> if the planned pattern of investment and production materialises, it is likely to create 49.3 million additional (adjusted standard) person-years of employment. Of this 22.8 million will be in agriculture and allied sectors as a result of planned growth in irrigation capacity and in animal husbandry, fishery and forestry sectors (Government of India, 1978a: 87).

Incidentally, as many as 16.2 million or 71 per cent of the projected increase of labour absorption in 'agriculture' is expected to take place in plantations (0.75 million), other crops (3.16 million) and other agricultural sectors (12.23 million), i.e., in activities in which only a small percentage of labour force is presently absorbed.

How realistic are these projections? What does past experience suggest? In discussing this issue the following types of questions would be of interest. What is the impact of the level of agricultural output on employment? What is the relationship between the level of agricultural production and the incidence of unemployment?

There cannot be any unique relationship between the level of agricultural output or its growth rate on the one hand and employment on the other. Apart from the variations in the basic agronomic (soil-climate) conditions, the type of techniques and technology of agricultural production and its class bias would be important determinants of the employment effect. In simple language, what would matter is where (apart from agronomic conditions), how and for whom the growth takes place. Besides, in the discussion on labour input in agriculture, it is important to bear in mind the distinction between

1. labour input per unit of cropped area,
2. labour input per unit of cultivated area, and
3. labour input per unit of output (Bartsch, 1977).

In what follows, we cite the findings of a few studies which relate the impact of agricultural development (on employment) in India since the early fifties. The studies, though painstaking, should be read with a great deal of caution. The findings of some of the studies (Alagh et al., 1978; Bardhan, 1978; Vaidyanathan, 1978) have been questioned by many scholars on grounds of conceptual infirmity, doubtful data base and methodological flaws.[2] Yet, it is worthwhile to get acquainted with them.

Level of Output and Employment

Lakdawala has stated that the elasticity of person-day employment per hectare with respect to output (kg per ha) is negative at −0.94 to 0.97 for all regions and −1.86 for developed regions. It may be noted however that though the per hectare output-employment relationship is negative, 'with a quantum jump in output levels, employment generated may still be quite high'.

Parthasarathy examines the same sets of data as are examined by Lakdawala. Aggregating the region/district data for the relevant states, he finds that in 7 out of 16 states, the relationship between the rates of unemployment and the output per hectare is positive; it is negative in 4 states; and no firm relationship is found for the remaining 5 states. Aggregation of region/district data of relevant states however is likely to vitiate comparisons and therefore the finding.

Vyas and Mathai confirm that though on an aggregate basis they did not find a statistically significant relationship between the increase in agricultural production and agricultural employment (Vyas and Mathai, 1978), the results based on more localized studies, with a firmer data base, show output employment elasticities in the range of 0.3 to 0.7.

> The study of output-employment relationship, conducted in connection with the Second Asian Agricultural Survey, suggests a figure in the range of 0.4 to 0.6 per cent in the more labour intensive countries of Southeast Asia. For a country like India a figure of 0.5 may be more realistic (Vyas and Mathai, 1978: 339).

It may be noted that the Draft Plan has assumed an almost 1 to 1 relationship between growth in agricultural output (4 per cent per annum) and growth in employment in agriculture and allied sectors (4.22 per cent per annum).

Mehra (1976) and Vaidyanathan (1978) find that over a period of time, labour input per hectare for *individual crops* has declined. Mehra's study reveals that 'the decline in labour input per hectare in the 1960s over that of the 1950s is about 24 per cent for *deshi* wheat, 21 per cent for American cotton and 15 per cent for *deshi* cotton'. Vaidyanathan also finds that in the three districts for which the Farm Management Survey can be compared over time, namely, Muzaffarnagar, Ferozepur and Coimbatore, human labour days per gross cropped hectare had fallen for individual crops—wheat, paddy, sugarcane, cotton and groundnuts—between Period I (1954–55 to 1956–57) and Period II (1966–68 for Muzaffarnagar, 1967–70 for Ferozepur and 1970–73 for Coimbatore).

Mehra however finds that for all crops taken together, labour input per cultivated hectare has increased over time. For example, she reports that the overall labour input per cultivated hectare in Ferozepur increased by about 40 per cent (by 22.94 mandays) between 1966–67 and 1969–70 and the mid 1950s. Out of the increase of 22.94 mandays per cultivated hectare, 7.87 mandays are attributed to the increase in the cropping intensity and the rest, i.e., 15.07 mandays, to the increased application of labour to individual crops resulting from

1. expansion of irrigation,
2. new technology, and
3. associated changes in the cropping pattern.

Mehra attributes 46 per cent (10.56 mandays) of the overall increase (22.94 mandays) in labour input to irrigation: 4.72 mandays *via* increase in cropping intensity and 5.84 mandays *via* increased input on individual crops. The remaining 54 per cent (or 12.38 mandays) of the increase is attributed to new technology and change in the cropping pattern induced by it: 3.15 mandays to the former and 9.23 mandays to the latter. She concludes: 'The hand of new technology in increasing the employment of human labour on farms does not in the main appear to be operating directly but indirectly *via* changes in the cropping pattern.'

Using Farm Management Survey data for 17 districts, Vaidyanathan (1978) has tested the following hypotheses: the level of human labour input is determined by:

1. the level of productivity per unit area, taken as a proxy
   for the more fundamental determinants (namely the quality
   of land, agro-climatic conditions and other physical inputs)
   of total energy input needed for crop husbandry;
2. the use of energy resources other than human labour; and
3. the relative costs and efficiencies of different energy sources.

Vaidyanathan tests his hypothesis through a variety of data
sets and methodology. His *inter-district* cross-section analysis shows
that the correlation coefficient between human labour days per
hectare (HLD/ha) and yield per hectare has a positive sign (+0.37),
but the coefficient is not statistically significant. The multiple
regression analysis however shows that the yield per hectare has
a significantly positive relation with human labour input. But
Vaidyanathan's explanatory variables—output/ha, bullock labour
days (BLD)/ha, cost of human labour relative to animal labour,
and horsepower/ha—explain no more than 40 per cent of the
variations in human labour input. The introduction of another
variable—proportion of area under paddy and sugarcane as a
proxy for variations in cropping pattern—does not improve the
significance of relationships.

Changing over to the analysis of *intra-district* variations in
labour input, Vaidyanathan finds that human labour input and
production per hectare are positively associated in most (11 out
of 14) districts for which data are available. The correlation
is statistically significant in five cases, and not significant in
the other six. Of the other three districts where the correlation
is negative, the coefficient is significant only in one district.

The picture is much the same when the data for different
districts or zones (combining districts) are pooled by size class.
The intensity of human labour is positively associated with productivity
in 5 out of 6 cases, and significantly so in 4 of them. Multiple
regression analysis also shows that production per hectare has
a significant positive influence on labour absorption in half the
groups.

Vaidyanathan sums up his findings by observing that

> the analysis corroborates Ishikawa's hypothesis that in general the
> intensity of human labour input tends to rise as yield per acre
> increases. But the relation does not hold in all cases, nor is

it as strong as one might expect. The relation seems to hold better when inter-district variations rather than intra-district variations are considered (Vaidyanathan, 1978: 48).

Bardhan (1978) however finds that in the Hoogly district of West Bengal, between 1956–57 and 1970–71, the input of human labour per year per acre of cultivated area had nearly doubled, and it had more than trebled on small farms not exceeding three-quarters of an acre. This phenomenal increase in the intensity of labour input per hectare over a period of less than 15 years was a consequence of extension of irrigation in surveyed farms from 15 per cent of the sown area to 55 per cent, diversification of the cropping pattern in favour of potato, wheat and summer paddy, and an increase in the cropping intensity index from 1.23 to 1.53.

A significant finding of Vaidyanathan's study pertains to the differential impact of increased production on the use of family labour and hired labour.

> There is some indication that between Period I and II, the intensity of family labour participation in cultivation may have declined both in terms of Labour Force Participation Rate (LFPR) in cultivating households and of the average number of days per annum for which farm family labour is employed.

Correspondingly, 'in general', the proportion of hired labour in the total labour used in crop production has increased sharply in three (out of four) districts. In Coimbatore, the increase was from 26.2 per cent to 84.9 per cent. In Muzaffarnagar, however, 'the labour force participation rate in farm families has risen sharply [from 31 to 49 per cent], while the average annual employment per adult male has fallen [from 287 to 190 days]' (Vaidyanathan, 1978: 75). The phenomenal rise in the hired labour component of the total labour input is associated with a general tendency in all districts for an increase in the size of the operational holdings and a sharp reduction—especially in Ferozepur and Coimbatore—in land cultivated under tenancy arrangement. How far these phenomena, particularly the former, are the result of the sampling design in the second series of FMS is a point which would need further investigation (see Saini, 1976).

Vaidyanathan interprets 'the significant rise in the ratio of hired to total labour input as an indication of growing proletarianisation of agricultural labour force' (Vaidyanathan, 1978: 73). It seems to us that the latter, even if it is a fact, does not necessarily follow from the first. It is possible that if employment opportunities in non-farm employment become attractive, a part of family labour may be hired out for such work (see Ishikawa, 1978: 81) and replaced by cheaper hired labour. Alternatively, the observed change may be an indication of higher leisure preference among farmers with larger landholdings. A more exacting regimen of farming operations under the HYV technology may favour hired labour *vis-à-vis* family labour, especially female labour. Proletarianization would be reflected more in the incidence of unemployment rather than in the increasing proportion of hired labour to total labour input in agriculture. It must, however, be noted that in all the three districts, the average farm business income from crop production per manday of work contributed by the family members of cultivators has risen much faster than the average daily wage rate per manday of hired labour. In Muzaffarnagar, the former rose nearly ten times as much as the latter and in Ferozepur and Coimbatore by 2 and 2½ times. The moral is clear enough. The emphasis on agricultural development is not enough; as much, if not more, attention needs to be given to the distribution of gains from development not merely in terms of employment but also income.

Level of output and incidence of unemployment

Let us now attempt to identify the relationship between the level of output per hectare and the incidence of unemployment. Normally one would expect that a relatively prosperous agriculture would help to reduce both poverty and unemployment. Empirical evidence however does not lend support to this expectation. Table VI in Lakdawala's Presidential Address (1977) provides data for 65 NSS regions in respect of

1. agricultural output per hectare—from the JNU-PPD Study, and
2. unemployment rate (in person-days) as per 27th Round of the NSS.

The correlation coefficient between the two turns out to be positive at 0.30 (significant at 5 per cent level), which implies that higher agricultural productivity is associated with higher unemployment.

Parthasarathy examined the relationship between the state-level growth rates of agricultural production per annum (from Yechuri's paper, 1976) and rates of unemployment, and found that

> States with very high rates of growth of agriculture (exceeding 5 per cent) such as Punjab and Haryana do show very low rates of unemployment. But the scatter of the states with the same rates of growth among varying rates of unemployment does suggest that there is no firm inverse relationship between rate of growth of agriculture and level of rural unemployment (Parthasarathy, 1978: 6).

Bartsch also observes that 'Any innovation, whether biological, chemical or mechanical reduces labour-hours of labour input per unit of output' (Bartsch, 1977: 61).

There may be a variety of factors responsible for the positive association between agricultural productivity (or growth) and unemployment. We have referred earlier to the inverse relationship between productivity and labour input. The inverse relationship would be accentuated if growth in input is achieved through labour-displacing technology and practices. But one would except that the positive effect of growth of production and its forward and backward linkages on the rest of the economy would outpace the negative effect of rising productivity (output per area of cropped area) on labour input. Or maybe, agricultural prosperity acts as a pull factor to attract labour from neighbouring areas and the enhanced employment potential due to growth is more than offset by a large number of claimants for work.

A paper by Alagh et al. (1978) throws some light on this phenomenon. In 100 districts—out of 281 districts for which data are presented—where the average rate of increase of output between 1962–65 and 1970–73 was 5.21 per cent per annum and where increase in the yield was the main contributing factor, the rate of increase in the male labour force engaged in agriculture[3] was 2.71 per cent per annum along with an increase in their productivity of 2.44 per cent per annum. At the other end, in 64 districts in which the initial (1962–65) yields per hectare were only slightly below the yields in the above 100 districts,

growth rates were negative (−2.30 per cent). Yet, since the rate
of increase of the number of male workers 'engaged in agriculture'
remained fairly high (2.29 per cent), there was a sharp decline
(−4.49 per cent) in their productivity.

From the evidence presented in the paper, the authors argue
that in the high-growth districts, a sort of 'suction process'—
from the non-farm sector rather than inward migration—operates
which leads to a high rate of absorption of labour in agriculture
along with a marked increase in its productivity. At the other
end of the spectrum with low and negative growth rate, 'the
suction-mechanism seems almost inoperative'. The fact however
is that even the latter districts did 'absorb' labour (male workers)
at only a slightly lower rate (2.29 per cent per annum) than
the high-growth districts (2.71 per cent), but at a heavy price
of a severe decline in their productivity. The more appropriate
way of describing this phenomenon would be to say that agricultural
labour in such regions is caught in a sort of an 'environmental
trap' from which it finds it difficult to escape. The authors
suggest that the capital cost involved in raising output and employment
in areas with relatively low yields (strictly low-growth potential
as judged by the experience of the decade) would probably be
very high, if not prohibitive. In view of this, 'faster generation
of employment outside agriculture cannot be considered a closed
issue in the Indian context' (Alagh et al., 1978: 122, 162).

Prospects of growth in employment in agriculture

Alagh (1978) with a more elaborate exercise, estimates the likely
growth in agricultural employment on three different assumptions:

1. continuation of past trends,
2. attainment of the objectives of the Draft Plan with respect
   to production, inputs and land reforms, and
3. a faster growth rate in the rate of spread of the development
   of high productivity commercialized agriculture.

The exercise indicates that 'a continuation of past trends
spells disaster on the employment front'. 'Effective employment'[4]
growth declines by 2.61 per cent compound per annum implying
increasing unemployment, immiserization of the workforce or both.

The Draft Plan's production and input programme targets for the agricultural sector imply a nominal growth rate of 0.85 per cent compound per annum in effective employment, which will not be able to take care of the growth in labour force. If, in addition, the land reform objectives of the Draft Plan are successfully achieved, the growth rate in effective employment will be 1.51 per cent compound per annum (because of the inverse relationship between employment per hectare and size of holdings).[5] It is only if, in addition, the effectiveness of regional development strategies of accelerated commercialization and development of agriculture is raised considerably from past levels of performance that a growth rate in employment of 3.74 per cent compound per annum is achieved (Alagh, 1978: 206, 209).

After this rather discursive sojourn into the pathways of researchers, we should know where we have arrived. First, we find that not only the findings but also their interpretations are conflicting and so are, to some extent, their policy implications. The consensus however seems to be that labour input in agriculture is likely to increase with the increase in agricultural output and, whatever be the reasons, the proportion of hired labour in the total labour input will tend to increase. Irrigation and, even more importantly, a shift in the cropping pattern towards a more labour-intensive crop cycle are major contributors to an increase in labour input. Small farmers devote more labour per hectare to individual crops, hence redistribution of land and production on small farms should be encouraged, but left to themselves, their capacity to take to 'high productivity commercialized agriculture' is limited. Thus, if land reforms have to serve their social and economic purpose, they must be accompanied by 'supportive systems geared to their requirements' (Vyas, 1979). While we should do all that is conceivably possible to augment the labour-absorptive capacity of agriculture, the sheer magnitude of the projected increase in the labour force will compel us to explore intensively the avenues for non-farm employment. But how much scope does it hold?

We do not have adequate knowledge about the absorptive capacity of the other or allied agricultural sectors which according to the Draft Plan are expected to provide additional 12.2 million person-years of employment during the Plan period, i.e., slightly higher than that budgeted to the main (crop and plantation) agricultural sector. We are told that the cooperative dairy programme will undergo a ten-fold expansion.

> Today a million households are within such a programme earning Rs 100 crores a year. The new programme Operation Flood II seeks to reach 10 million rural households with a view to generating additional income of Rs 500 to Rs 1000 crores—quite a range!—over the next five years (Mehta, 1979).

It is difficult to judge the strength of this forecast, but whatever may be the employment potential of this and similar programmes in the allied agricultural sector, animal husbandry, forestry, poultry or fisheries, there should be a deliberate policy to ensure that benefits from its development go to the maximum feasible extent to the marginal farmers and landless labourers and are not pre-empted by the large farmers. We may go a little further and say that all rural development programmes undertaken through public investment, especially those involving subsidies, should have the sole aim of generating employment and income for the weaker sections.

Next to agriculture and the allied sector, the hope of a big step-up in employment is pinned on the village and small-scale industries for which the Plan allocation is being increased by nearly three times. This sector is expected to generate 6.8 million person-years of additional full-time employment (3 million in small-scale industries, 0.3 million in powerlooms and 3.5 million in handlooms) by 1983. In addition, it is expected that part-time employment for 6.27 million persons will be generated including 4.89 million in *Khadi* and Village industries, 0.58 million in handicrafts and 0.8 million in sericulture (Government of India, 1978a).

It is devoutly to be wished that these expectations are fulfilled. But for a variety of reasons, which have been admirably elucidated by Sandesara (1978) there are serious doubts about their feasibility. First, the step-up in the allocation for this sector in the Draft Plan is not as spectacular as it is made out. The public sector outlay on village and the small-scale sector envisaged in the Draft Plan forms barely 2 per cent of the total outlay, which, though higher than in the Fifth Plan (1.3 per cent), is actually smaller in proportion than in the Second and Third Plan and only marginally higher than that in the Annual Plan period (1.9

per cent).

Secondly, the production increases envisaged for the various sub-sectors are far too ambitious to be taken seriously. Thus, the value of production in Khadi and Village industries is slated to increase from Rs 270 crores in 1977–78 (estimated) to Rs 2561 crores in 1982–83, or at an annual compound rate of 56.8 per cent. The realism of this projection should be assessed in the light of the increase of only 14.6 per cent per annum during the period from 1974–75 to 1977–78 and that too in money terms. In physical terms the increases are much more modest. As the projected increases in employment are based on the projected increase in production, the doubts regarding the latter apply *pro tanto* to the former also.[6]

It must be noted that apart from the larger allocation to the village and small-scale sector, many supportive policy measures are to be adopted for stimulating production and employment in the small scale sector. The list of industries reserved for this sector is expanded to cover 504 items from 180 earlier. On the organizational side, an innovative step has been taken to establish a District Industries Centre in all districts. There is also a proposal to 'phase out' the organized sector from the production of commodities like soap and matches. This is not the place to assess the effectiveness of this package of policies in generating a substantially large income and employment in this sector. We should like to utter a word of caution only on two counts. One is the demand for the products of the sector, especially that of the tiny sector; and the other is the question of price. The question of price becomes very pertinent if the goods produced are for mass consumption. If they cost more or last less than those produced by the organized sector, what is given by one hand will be taken away by the other. As for the demand, this is probably the most frustrating aspect of the problem of revival of cottage industries, as has been revealed by several experiments and field studies, particularly those conducted by Ravi Matthai in Jawaja (Matthai, 1979). Ironically, they thrive better when they produce 'luxury' goods in demand by the higher income groups. Finally, we hope that the policy-makers are alive to the social and political implications of the elimination of the middlemen in the supply of credit, inputs and marketing, without which all the other policy measures for augmenting income and unemployment will come to naught.

III. SUMMING UP

Usually, the main exercise in employment planning is confined to the estimation of the magnitude of likely unemployment, say, five years hence and providing investments, within a (new) policy frame, which would generate the maximum possible person-years of employment so as to reduce the gap between the need and availability of employment. Such an aggregative estimation is necessary and useful up to a point, but may not serve the purpose of reducing unemployment as per the expectations of the Plan. The crux of employment planning is its ability to generate employment where, when and for whom it is needed.

Take the case of agriculture. We have some idea of the distribution of unemployment in the rural areas or the agricultural sector. We have already referred to Visaria's study which reports that

> the casual labour class accounted for 56 and 89 per cent of the total unemployed person-days in the rural areas of Gujarat and Maharashtra respectively. The self-employed, on the other hand, accounted for only 14 and 9 per cent of the unemployed person-days in the two areas, even though in 9 out of the 12 months of the survey covered by the 27th Round, Gujarat and Maharashtra were affected by severe scarcity.

Again, the rural employee class in Gujarat suffered from almost three times as high an incidence of unemployment as all the employed in the rural areas and casual labourers fared even worse (Visaria, 1981a: 283, 286).

Has anyone any idea as to how the 22.7 million additional (adjusted standard) person-years of employment to be generated in agriculture and allied sectors between 1977–78 and 1982–83 will be distributed—if not in the first round, in the second—between the different classes of unemployed/underemployed workers?

The main thrust of agricultural development in the Draft Plan is on planned growth of irrigation capacity—by 17 million hectares, about half of which, namely, 9 million hectares, would be from minor irrigation. With the prevalent distribution of land, other resources and access to credit, it is not very difficult to guess who will benefit the most and who the least from this expansion of irrigation facilities, especially from unregulated groundwater exploitation. Apart from its adverse income distribution effect, the share of the agricultural labourers (who suffer most from unemployment) in the additional employment generated is not likely to be proportionate to their numbers. Increase in fertilizer consumption and extension of HYVs, the other important planks in the strategy of agricultural developments, will also have a similarly differential impact on the different sections of the labour force. The Draft Plan does emphasize institutional reforms—land reforms, provision of credit, etc.—to ensure a better distribution of gains of development, but the limitations of land redistribution programme are by now well recognized by even its most ardent advocates.

If so, what can be the employment strategy for those whom agricultural development *per se* is not likely to benefit significantly? Most observers of the situation would straightaway suggest a public works programme. We shall refer to it a little later. Apart from the chronically unemployed, for whom some sort of public works programme would be needed, those who are unemployed for varying durations at some time or the other (i.e., those who are underemployed) do have some occupation, which provides them livelihood, albeit much below the desired level. In such cases, the objective of employment policy should be to augment, to the extent possible, the duration of their employment in their existing occupations. This, we believe, would be psychologically more satisfying to the underemployed than the offer of employment on public works.

No doubt, there are social, economic and structural factors which inhibit full employment of the weaker sections in their existing occupations. The planning exercise should try to identify these factors and eliminate them to the extent possible. The exercise may reveal that the root cause of the low level of employment is either an inadequate resource base or lack of skill. Maybe, the demand for the goods produced or services rendered by them is inadequate. This in turn may be due to the given pattern of income distribution, fair or unfair competition from the organized sector, inferior technology and the consequent low quality and/or high price of their products, inadequacy of infrastructure and institutional support needed for fair competition, and the last but not the least, exploitative character of the input and output markets, which either raises the price of the product or depresses the earnings of the producers.

Though the nature of the malady affecting the different sectors of the economy or categories of income earners can be identified at a general and somewhat abstract level through distant observation and macro studies, very often a much closer and personal contact is necessary to grasp the complex socio-economic and political constellations which depress unemployment and the income of the disadvantaged groups. In any case, effective remedial action can be taken only by authoritative intervention at the local (district/block) level. This leads us to the conclusion that while an appropriate policy frame at the macro level is essential for the eradication of poverty and unemployment, a meaningful planning exercise and an effective action programme have to be undertaken at a fairly decentralized level with the requisite devolution of authority and active participation of the disadvantaged groups.

The emphasis on the rehabilitation of the underemployed persons in their existing occupations should not be interpreted as denial of upward mobility, wherever the possibility exists and much less as a plea for the *status quo*. In fact, a sincere pursuit of the policy outlined earlier would involve quite a few revolutionary changes in the structure and functioning of the rural economy. The break-up of the exploitative landowner-tenant and landowner-labourer relationship and the credit and marketing institutions alone will have far-reaching consequences. The effective implementation of such structural and institutional reforms, perhaps, has a greater employment generation potential than the so-called 'special' programme for the weaker sections.

It must be admitted that such a transformation of rural society will take time—5 to 10 years depending on the will of the political leadership. In the meanwhile, some immediate action must be taken to relieve the acuteness of the unemployment problem. A substantial portion of the rural labour force consists of landless labourers or has practically no asset base, either of land or skill. For such persons, the proposition to rehabilitate them in their 'existing occupation' does not make much sense. Diversification of the agricultural economy through the development of animal husbandry, fisheries, poultry, forestry, and horticulture would help to absorb some of them in gainful work provided they are assisted through exclusive credit, marketing and training support. Some may be diverted towards cottage industries and handicrafts—though there is already a lot of concealed unemployment amongst rural craftsmen and artisans.

There need be no illusion that these programmes will close the unemployment gap. There is however another avenue for productive employment which, for good many years to come, can absorb a large number of the chronically unemployed. It is well known that productivity of agriculture can be greatly improved through land reclamation, land levelling, drainage, consolidation of holdings, proper distribution of irrigation waters, improvement of village roads and the rural sanitation system. All these schemes can form the core of the public works programmes or special employment schemes—with or without guarantee—for the landless.

While recognizing the importance of the public works programmes and special employment schemes, a few cautionary remarks may be made. First, they must not become the main plank of the employment programme and thus divert the attention of the planners from the major task of rural development, namely, removal of all hurdles which impede the efforts of the poor and the unemployed to be self-reliant and earn their livelihood through their own work and merit. The planner's aim should be to integrate them within the mainstream of economic activity and not to segregate them into a footloose class of camp followers or retinues perpetually dependent on the benevolence of a Government-sponsored employment programme.

Second, all 'special' schemes and projects—EGS, SFDA, DIC, tiny sector, whoever their sponsors may be—must emerge as an outcome of an integral area plan, and they must shed their departmental/sectoral heritage. There is a world of difference between a minor irrigation project—even though duly tested for economic and technical feasibility—taken up under the compulsion of an employment guarantee scheme and the one which emerges as a result of a thorough review of resource inventory and development potential of the area, made by the District Planning Team. Even after several years of experience of EGS in Maharashtra, as late as in November 1978, it was noticed that 'most of the works taken up under the EGS have been done in a haphazard manner without ensuring proper integration between them' and 'though considerable number of percolation tanks are being taken up under EGS now, determined efforts to utilise the water impounded in these tanks have not been made'. Hopefully, such deficiencies can be reduced, if not eliminated, through integrated area planning.

Third, the success of the special employment schemes should be judged by the progressive reduction in reliance on them. In other words, the aim should be to ensure that in due course the development of the area would be such, in quality and scale, that it would be able to provide income and employment to all its labour force, and fewer and fewer persons would find it necessary to register themselves as candidates for employment guarantee.

I must confess that there is a strong (and sound) body of academic opinion which favours giving pride of place to the public works programme—or guaranteed employment—in the employment policy. Partly, this is an outcome of disappointment with the post-Independence experience of the feeble impact of the varied development programmes including those specially meant for the benefit of the weaker sections on the magnitude and intensity of poverty and unemployment. But more importantly, in some regions the resource base and potential are so meagre that even with the best of planning intentions and skills, it may not be possible to provide gainful employment to the swelling labour force within the mainstream of development. In such cases, a purposeful—and preferably permanent—shifting of population may be unavoidable, and this can be best achieved through a well-planned public works programme aimed at capital formation. While we concede the force of this argument, we would once again submit that the public works programme should not become a soft option and an alibi for basic structural and institutional reforms which constitute a basic condition for employment-oriented development.

NOTES

1. Reprinted from *Economic and Political Weekly*, Vol. 14, No. 25, 23 June 1979.

   This is a revised version of the author's Presidential Address delivered at the All-India Labour Economics Conference held at Ahmedabad in December 1978. The author is grateful to Pravin Visaria, T.R. Sundaram and other friends for their valuable comments on the earlier draft.

2. See, for example, Proceedings of the Technical Seminar: Labour Absorption in Indian Agriculture, sponsored by the Asian Employment Programme of ILO (ARTEP) and Institute of Economic Growth, Delhi, 22–23 January 1979 (mimeo) and Preface by K.N. Raj to ARTEP publication cited in Bardhan, 1978.

3. Actually, the number of male agricultural workers as given in the population Census 1961 and 1971, unadjusted for definitional changes.

4. Alagh's 'effective employment' concept is different from the Draft Plan's adjusted standard person-years of employment due to the introduction of an income criterion.

5. A one per cent increase in the percentage of farms with up to 2 hectares of land would lead to a 0.31 to 0.49 per cent increase in employment in person-days per hectare (see Lakdawala, 1977).

6. It is worth noting that between 1960–61 and 1976–77, the value of production of *khadi* increased from Rs 14.2 crores to Rs 55 crores but during the same period full-time and part-time employment in its production declined respectively from 2.06 lakh to 1.40 lakh persons and from 15.08 to 8.83 lakh persons. During the same period, while production in village industries increased from Rs 33.2 crores to Rs 181 crores, part-time employment increased from 4.46 to 9.87 lakh persons and full-time employment only by 0.76 lakh persons (from 1.18 to 1.94 lakh persons). (Source: Commerce, 15 October 1977).

CHAPTER 22

Some neglected issues in employment planning[1]

Planning for employment can be conceived with two somewhat different perspectives. Under the first, a plan is evolved to provide (and/or even guarantee) immediate employment to as many persons as are currently unemployed or underemployed and who express their desire and availability for work. This is sought to be achieved through a massive programme of public works. The case for such a .plan rests on the principle of the right to work. It is estimated that some 60 million persons are affected by various degrees of unemployment at one time or another and ways and means must be found to provide work for them whenever they need it. This should be done in a more systematic way than is done under the pressure and urgency of a scarcity or drought. For this purpose, the state and the district authorities should prepare a package of projects which would result in the creation of productive assets and avoid the wastefulness of hurriedly conceived and poorly implemented relief works.

Under the other perspective, the emphasis is on progressively augmenting the employment potential of the economy as a whole, through a restructuring of the economy and its institutions. The policy-frame needed for the purpose would encompass a wide spectrum of measures, such as pricing of capital and labour, encouragement of labour-intensive technology, an appropriate package of taxation and subsidies, land reform and re-orientation of the institutional network of which the major aim would be augmenting the employment and income of the poor.

It will be argued that the two approaches are not mutually exclusive and can be simultaneously pursued. It is the contention of this paper that the pursuit of the first approach may detract attention from the hard technical exercise and the equally hard political decisions needed under the second approach. The second approach is liable to the criticism that it ignores the immediacy of the unemployment problem and shirks the responsibility of accepting and implementing without any excuses the principle of the right to work. The second approach need not, therefore, rule out action under the first approach—provided it is understood that it does not provide a solution to the *problem* of unemployment.

The public works approach to unemployment would make sense if it is so organized that there will be progressively less and less reliance on it, so that ultimately it becomes redundant. Its role should be accepted as transitional, and deliberate efforts should be made to rehabilitate those engaged on public works within the mainstream of the economic system. Unless this perspective is strongly emphasized, there is every possibility that a pernicious type of dualistic economy would be perpetuated. Under this economy, given the magnitude of existing unemployment and underemployment and the expected additions to the labour force, we will end up with two segments of the economy, one providing 'regular' employment to those who are lucky enough to have some productive assets (property or skill) and the other a hapless contingent of employment-seekers wholly dependent on those in charge of public works, as and when and where these are organized. In certain ominous political conditions, there is a danger of the workers on public works becoming inmates of labour camps, if not worse, though some of us may dream of their becoming a revolutionary army.

The Employment Guarantee Scheme (EGS) in Maharashtra lays down that 'only productive works which create durable community assets should be taken up under the scheme' and 'when productive works are taken up under the scheme, the technical and financial norms should be strictly adhered to and there should be no deviation from the normal pattern'. If so, what is the point in including them under an employment scheme rather than making them an integral part of the district development plan? The question may be asked: Does it make a difference whether they are included under an 'employment' plan or a 'development' plan? Surely it does. A minor irrigation scheme, undertaken as a part of the total irrigation plan of a district, will have much better technical and economic discipline than an irrigation work undertaken under pressure of having to provide employment to the needy. If the employment objective is paramount, one should frankly accept that it may be necessary to relax at least the financial norms in order to fulfil the social objective. Blurring of the issues involved is of no help.

There is also the major problem of matching supply and demand under a public works programme. Much emphasis is now placed on the preparation of a manpower budget to ascertain the availability for additional employment. The past experience of 'registration' of persons who said they were available for work, and the record of their actual reporting, regular attendance, etc. is very discouraging. Quite often, a substantial proportion of persons who had earlier 'registered' themselves as available, either did not report for work, or did so fitfully. On the other hand, a large number of persons on the muster rolls had not been registered (Government of India, 1977b). Anyway, there is certainly room for improvement in the methodology of preparing manpower budgets, and it would not be fair to prejudge their outcome. But on one point some public discussion would be useful. Should a guarantee of employment carry with it the obligation to work, if work is offered to those who 'register' their names under the scheme? Under the Maharashtra Employment Guarantee Scheme—as embodied in Bill No. XXVIII of 1977—the registered person cannot be compelled to report for work, when work is offered. This is perhaps as it ought to be. But, even when he chooses to exercise his right to work through a letter addressed to a local authority, he has only to indicate 'the period for which employment is required and the period for which he will be willing to work continuously, which shall not be less than one month'. If, however, when work is offered and he does not accept it or does not report for work within seven days of being asked to do so, or continuously remains absent from work, the only consequence he suffers is loss of entitlement to 'unemployment allowance' of Rs one per day. 'He shall stand debarred from claiming unemployment allowance for a period of three months, but during this period of three months shall not be debarred from getting employment on any work.' With so much uncertainty regarding the regular supply of labour, the district authorities may find it difficult to execute the works programme on schedule and without infringing technical and financial norms. It is for this reason that we suggest that the public works programme should have a more modest objective of providing work mainly to the chronically unemployed. In any case, being the worst sufferers, they deserve priority in the public works programme. Besides, since their local attachments are minimal because of the absence of occupation and assets, their availability and regular attendance can be depended upon.

Under our preferred perspective, the main objective of employment planning will thus be to build up the employment potential of the economy through an appropriate process of development. The appropriateness pertains not only to technology but also to the structure of the economy, institutions, and above all a value system under which work will be valued according to *social* utility. Here, the emphasis would be on the understanding of the anatomy of employment (and poverty) rather than that of unemployment, though the distinction need not be over-stretched. What is meant is that we should try to find out who is employed where, when, and for how long, and whether what he earns is commensurate with the social utility of his work. If what he earns is excessive by social norms, what is it that makes this possible—his command over property, the pricing of occupations/ skills, or the social and economic institutional framework? More rewarding would be an exercise to ascertain the reason for the low incomes of various categories of persons which may or may not be because of inadequate employment, though the latter may appear to be the proximate cause. Behind this proximate cause there are most probably deeper causes, such as inadequacy or total absence of an asset base (property or skill), an exploitative institutional set-up, or a perverted value system. Employment planning should try to remedy this, instead of rushing into guaranteeing employment on public works.

The contention that structural and institutional changes are more efficacious as a cure to the problem of unemployment than the symptomatic treatment of providing relief to the unemployed through the public works programme, needs supportive evidence.

Expansion of irrigation is recognized as a critical factor in the development of agriculture. But its income distribution

effect, and by implication its employment effect, will depend
on which class of cultivators benefits from the expanded irrigation
and the resulting cropping pattern. Take the case of Maharashtra.
Between 1960–61 and 1971–72, about Rs 530 crores were spent
on creating additional irrigation facilities. Yet, in this state, agricultural
production during the period remained almost stagnant[2] (see Bhalla,
1977). Rs 290 crores were spent on canal irrigation, but the
additional canal irrigated area was no more than 69,000 hectares.
In some districts, the canal irrigated area actually declined, because
the bulk of the irrigation water went to sugarcane cultivation,
which requires 18 times as much water as any cereal crop.
Sugarcane, and fruits and vegetables consume 58 per cent and
28 per cent, respectively, of the total quality of irrigation water
available in the state. Giving the above information. Nilkantha
Rath observes: 'Thus nearly three-fourths of the total investment
in irrigation in the state went to the benefit of farmers, who
were growing sugarcane, fruits and vegetables.' He concludes:
'Irrigation is very expensive and is being used in a concentrated
way to benefit only one or two per cent of land and as many
farmers' (Rath, 1977).

In another study it was found

> in the Kosi region of Bihar, the number of tubewells (masonry
> and bamboo) increased from a mere 300 in 1965–66 to 23,000
> in 1972–73, but more than half the investment in this expansion
> was made by farmers with holdings of 20 acres and above. The
> share of farmers holding less than 5 acres was negligible (Clay,
> 1975: 77, 78).

The two illustrations underscore the need to ensure that investment
in irrigation should help to optimize not only production but
also employment.

The recent industrial policy statement lays great stress not
only on the small-scale and cottage industries, but also on the
tiny sector. A policy of 'reservations' too has been thought of
to protect the interests of the small-scale sector. Is it possible
to think of reservation, in the utilization of irrigation water (especially
underground water) and of other inputs, for the small and marginal
farmers to help them raise their cropping intensity and take to
animal husbandry and hence reduce the duration of their unemployment? There is reason to believe that the employment

potential of irrigation can be considerably enhanced if institutional measures are adopted for a more even and purposeful distribution/ utilization of the irrigation water.

It may come as a surprise to many that, for the country as a whole, in the agricultural sector 'employment elasticities with respect to output per hectare are negative'. Similarly, 'surrogate variables for the new technology like fertilizer inputs per hectare, tractor per hectare, and gross value of assets per hectare, also show negative elasticities'. Thus, growth in agricultural production by itself may not be of much help in augmenting employment. But the same growth, if it is accomplished through a large contribution from small farms, will make a significant contribution to augment employment. It has been found that 'employment per hectare or employment per rupee of output was strongly associated with and showed significantly positive elasticities with respect to percentage of land operated in farms of 5 acres and less' (Government of India, 1977a). If so, employment planning must be closely associated with land reform which makes available more land to the small farmers, either through proprietory rights or through tenurial security.

A word about employment in the small-scale, cottage, and tiny sectors. Expansion of markets for their products is obviously the most important desideratum. The advisability of the policy of reservations for encouraging their production needs very careful consideration. A premature imposition of curbs on investment or production in the organized sector may give rise to scarcities which may actually benefit the established units in the organized sector and adversely affect the masses through price rise, particularly if the commodities concerned are necessities of life. Measures leading to cost reduction and quality improvement would be the most apposite for stimulating demand, production, and employment in this sector. Here again, while the importance of upgrading the technology is recognized, scant attention is paid to the exploitative institutional steel-frame which, like a double-edged weapon, harms both the consumers and the producers by pushing up the prices of the products (and profits of the middlemen) and pushing down the wages of the craftsmen and artisans. Photographic delineation of the process can be witnessed through the unique experiments of the group of volunteers under the leadership of Ravi Matthai in Jawaja in Rajasthan. A few extracts from the newsletters sent out by Matthai will illustrate the point.

At Kotra new tanning pits were needed and capital loans for this were given. When, however, Kotra Raigars attempted to start construction, the *Sarpanch* and other higher caste villagers raised objections as to the location of the pits and even intervened physically.

Subsequently, Hajari of Sargoan went to Kanpur on behalf of his group to buy skins. It appears, however, that poor Hajari was hoodwinked by the Kanpur merchants who wet and salted some old hides and sold them as new.

Learning from his direct involvement in the problems of cottage workers, Matthai writes:

> The level of entrepreneurship that is most capable of exploitation and most difficult to regulate is the one of the village-level entrepreneur who converts self-employed people into starvation wage labourers. This type of exploitative entrepreneurship abounds throughout the villages of India and many of the well-intentioned national policies are subverted by this type of entrepreneur to serve his own purpose by diverting the benefits intended for the most deprived to himself.

Unemployment and severe underemployment are overt symptoms of deep-rooted maladies of the present economic system. Symptomatic treatment through the public works programme is legitimate for relieving the severity of the condition, but a lasting cure would need elimination of the root cause.

This article has aimed to draw attention to some of the neglected issues in employment planning. To keep the focus sharp, many other pertinent issues have been kept out.

NOTES

1. Reprinted from *Economic and Political Weekly*, Vol. 13, Nos. 6 and 7, Annual Number, February 1978.
2. The annual compound growth rate of output of all crops in Maharashtra between 1962–65 and 1970–73 was 3.77 per cent.

References

Acharya, B.T. 1990. *Rural Industrialization: A Catalyst in Action*, Himalaya Publishing House, Bombay.

Adelman, Irma and Sherman Robinson. 1978. *Income Distribution Policy in Developing Countries: A Case Study of Korea*, Published for World Bank, Oxford University Press, New York.

Agricultural Rural Development Corporation (ARDC). 1982. *Ground Water Irrigation in Kota District, Rajasthan* (An Ex-Post Evaluation Study), Evaluation Study Series, No. 11. Bombay.

Agro-Economic Research Centre, University of Delhi. 1967. 'An Enquiry Into an IADP District of Aligarh (U.P.)', cited in *The Economic Times*, 12 April.

Alagh, Y.K. 1978. *Indian Planning in the Eighties*, Presidential Address delivered at the Tenth Gujarat Economic Conference, November.

Alagh, Y.K., G.S. Bhalla and A. Bhaduri, 1978. *Agricultural Growth and Manpower Absorption in Indian Agriculture: Some Exploratory Investigations*, Asian Regional Programme for Employment Promotion, ILO, Bangkok.

Ambannavar, J.P. 1975. *Second India Studies: Population*, The Macmillan Company of India Ltd., Bombay.

Bardhan, K. 1970. 'Price and Output Response of Marketed Surplus of Foodgrains: A Cross-Sectional Study of Some North Indian Villages', *American Journal of Agricultural Economics*, Vol. 52, No. 1, February.

Bardhan, K. in ICSSR Discussion Paper on Problems Related to Public Distribution of Foodgrains, New Delhi (mimeo).

Bardhan, Pranab K. 1978. 'On Labour Absorption in South Asian Rice Cultivation, with Particular Reference to India', in *Labour Absorption in Indian Agriculture: Some Exploratory Investigations*, Asian Regional Programme for Employment Production, ILO, Bangkok.

Bardhan, Pranab K. 1979. 'Wages and Unemployment in a Poor Agrarian Economy: A Theoretical and Empirical Analysis', *Journal of Political Economy*, Vol. 87, No. 3, June: 479–500.

Bardhan, Pranab K. 1986. 'Poverty and "Trickle-Down" in Rural India: A Quantitative Analysis' in John W. Mellor and Gunvant M. Desai, eds. (1986). *Agricultural Change and Rural Poverty: Variations on a Theme by Dharm Narain*, Oxford University Press, Delhi.

Barker, R. and M. Mangahas. 1970. *Environmental and Other Factors Influencing the Performance of HYV of Wheat and Rice*, Paper submitted to the XIV

International Conference of Agricultural Economics, Minsk, USSR, August.

Bartsch, William H. 1977. *Employment and Technology Choice in Asian Agriculture*, International Labour Organization, Geneva, Praeger Publishers, Inc., New York, USA.

Bhalla, G.S. 1977. 'Spatial Pattern of Levels and Growth of Agricultural Output in India', in Seminar on Regional Disparities of Growth and Productivity in Indian Agriculture, Indian Society of Agricultural Economics and Gokhale Institute of Politics and Economics, Pune.

Bhalla, G.S. and Y.K. Alagh. 1979. *Performance of Indian Agriculture: A District-wise Study*, Sterling Publishers, New Delhi.

Bhalla, G.S. and G.K. Chandha. 1981. *Structural Changes in Income Distribution: A Study of the Impact of the Green Revolution*, Jawaharlal Nehru University (mimeo), New Delhi.

Bhalla, Sheila. 1981. 'The New Structure of Field Crop Labour in Haryana and Its Impact on the Poverty of Landless Agricultural Households', *Anvesak* 2 (June–December).

Bhartan, R.K. (Edited). 1979. *Trusteeship: The Indian Contribution to a New Social Order*, Shriniketan, Madras.

Birla Institute of Scientific Research (BISR). 1981. *Agricultural Growth and Employment Shifts in Punjab*. New Delhi.

Blyn, George. 1966. *Agricultural Trends in India, 1891–1947: Output Availability and Productivity*, Philadelphia, University of Pennsylvania Press: 96 and 337.

Bombay, Government of. 1949. A Note on the Survey of Rural Employment, Income and Expenditure in the State of Bombay, *Bulletin of the Bureau of Economics and Statistics*, Vol. III, No. 1, July.

Bombay, Government of. 1950a. Notes on Income of Bombay Province, *Bulletin of the Bureau of Economics and Statistics*, Vol. III, No. 3, January.

Bombay, Government of. 1950b. A Note on Survey of Employment, Income and Expenditure of the People of Bombay State, *Bulletin of the Bureau of Economics and Statistics*, Vol. III, No. 4, April; Vol. IV, No. 1, July; Vol. IV, No. 2 October.

Bombay, Government of. 1951. A Note on Survey of Employment, Income and Expenditure of the People of Bombay State, *Bulletin of the Bureau of Economics and Statistics*, Vol. V, No. 1 July.

Brown, Lester, R. 1965. 'Increasing World Food Output: Problems and Prospects', *Foreign Agriculture Economic Report No. 25*, U.S. Department of Agriculture: vi.

Brown, Lester. 1970. *Seeds of Change: The Green Revolution in the 1970s*, Praeger Publishers, Praeger, New York: 41.

Centre for Development Studies. 1977. *Poverty, Unemployment and Development Policy*, Trivandrum.

Centre for Science and Environment (CSE). 1985. *The State of India's Environment 1984-85: The Second Citizens' Report*, New Delhi.

Centre for Monitoring Indian Economy (CMIE). 1986. *Agricultural Production in India, 1949–50 to 1984–85*, Bombay, February.

Centre for Monitoring Indian Economy (CMIE). 1986. *Basic Statistics Relating to Indian Economy*, Vol. I, All India, Bombay, August.

Centre for Development Studies (CDS). 1986. *Development of Cardamom Plantation in the High Ranges of Kerala*, K. Narayanan Nair et al. Trivandrum (mimeo).

Chandhok, H.L. 1978. *Wholesale Price Statistics—India, 1947–1978*, Vols I and II, Economic and Scientific Research Foundation, New Delhi.

Chowdhury, B.K. 1970. 'Disparity in Income in the Context of HYV', *Economic and Political Weekly*, Vol. V, No. 39, 26 September: A91.

Clay, Edward J. 1975. 'Equity and Productivity Effects of a Package of Technical Innovations and Changes in Social Institutions: Tubewells, Tractors and High-Yielding Varieties', *Indian Journal of Agricultural Economics*, Vol. XXX, No. 4, October–December.

Commerce Research Bureau. 1976. 'Land Ceilings—Laws and Achievement', January.

Dandekar, V.M. 1967. *Food and Freedom*, Karnataka University, Dharwar.

Dandekar, V.M. 1970. 'Agricultural Growth with Social Justice in Overpopulated Countries', *Economic and Political Weekly*, Vol. V, Nos. 29, 30 and 31 (Special Number), July: 1233.

Dandekar, V.M. and Nilakanth Rath, 1971. *Poverty in India*, Indian School of Political Economy, Pune.

Dandekar, V.M. 1986. 'Agriculture, Employment and Poverty', *Economic and Political Weekly*, Vol. XXI, Nos. 38 and 39, 20–27 September.

Dantwala, M.L. 1937. *Marketing of Raw Cotton in India*. Longmans, Green and Co. Ltd. Bombay.

Dantwala, M.L. 1945. *Gandhism Reconsidered*, Padma Publications Ltd., Bombay, Revised and Enlarged Edition, July.

Dantwala, M.L. 1961. 'Agrarian Structure in Twelve Districts', *The Economic Weekly*, Vol. XIII, Nos. 27, 28, and 29 (Special Number), July.

Dantwala, M.L. 1963. *International Planning to Combat the Scourge of Hunger Throughout the World*, Annals of Collective Economy, Vol. 34, No. 1, January–March.

Dantwala, M.L. 1966. 'Institutional Credit in Subsistence Agriculture', *International Journal of Agrarian Affairs*, Vol. 5, No. 1, December.

Dantwala, M.L. 1968. 'Rejuvenating Sick Agriculture: Indian Experience', *Netherlands Journal of Agricultural Science*, Vol. 16 No. 4.

Dantwala, M.L. 1979. 'The Challenge of Turning Needs into Effective Demand', paper presented at a workshop organized by the Ford Foundation, New Delhi, December, at Trivandrum.

Dantwala, M.L. 1983. 'Two-Way Planning: Logic and Limitations—A Critical Review of Indian Experience', Paper prepared for the FAO Regional Office for Asia and the Pacific, Bangkok, Thailand and subsequently reproduced in *Indian Journal of Agricultural Economics*, Vol. XXXVIII, No. 1, April–June.

de Janvry, Alain and K. Subbarao. 1986, 1984. *Agricultural Price Policy and Income Distribution in India*, Oxford University Press, New Delhi; and *Economic and Political Weekly*, Vol. XIX, Nos. 51 and 52, 22–29 December.

Dev, S. Mahendra and M.H. Suryanarayana. 1991. 'Is PDS Urban Biased and Pro-Rich: An Evaluation', *Economic and Political Weekly*, Vol. 26, No. 41, 12 October: 2357–66.

Dev, Mahendra, Kirit Parikh and M.H. Suryanarayana. 1991. 'Rural Poverty in India: Incidence, Issues and Policies', Discussion Paper No. 55, Indira Gandhi Institute of Development Research, Bombay.

Dholakia, R.H. 1985. *Regional Disparity in Economic Growth in India*, Himalaya

Publishing House, Bombay.

Donde, W.B. 1951. 'Rural Labour in the Konkan', Unpublished Doctoral Dissertation, University of Bombay, Bombay.

Economic and Political Weekly. 1978. 'Agricultural Labour: Getting Poorer', Vol. XIII, No. 41, 14 October.

Economic and Scientific Research Foundation. 1967. 'Fourth Plan, Inflation Without Growth', Occasional Paper Two, New Delhi.

Economic Advisory Council. 1990. 'Towards Evolving an Employment Oriented Strategy for Development in 1990s' (Chairman: Sukhamoy Chakravarty), Planning Commission, Government of India, New Delhi.

Falcon, Walter P. 1970. 'The Green Revolution', *American Journal of Agricultural Economics*, Vol. 52, No. 5, December.

Fisher, Franklin M. 1963. 'A Theoretical Analysis of the Impact of Food Surplus Disposal on Agricultural Production in Recipient Countries', *Journal of Farm Economics*, Vol. 45, No. 4, November: 868.

Food and Agriculture Organization (FAO) of the United Nations. 1982a. *1981 Production Year Book*, Vol. 35, Rome.

Food and Agriculture Organization (FAO) of the United Nations. 1982b. *Potential Population Supporting Capacities of Lands in the Developing World*, FAO/ IIASA/UNEPA, Rome, Italy.

Gandhi, M.K. 1948. Constructive Programme: Its Meaning and Place, Navajivan Publishing House, Ahmedabad: 31.

Gandhi, Ved P. 1966. *Tax Burden on Indian Agriculture*, The Law School of Harvard University, Cambridge, USA.

Gothashar, S.P. 1988. 'Some Estimates of Rural Indebtedness', *Reserve Bank of India Occasional Papers*, Vol. 9, No. 4, December.

Gotsch, Carl H. 1973. 'Economics, Institutions and Employment Generation in Rural Areas', Paper prepared for Ford Foundation Seminar in Rural Development and Employment, Ibadan, 9–12 April (mimeo).

Griffin, Keith. 1974. *The Political Economy of Agrarian Change*, The Macmillan Press Ltd.: 210.

Gulati, Ashok and P.K. Sharma. 1991. 'Government Intervention in Agricultural Markets: Nature, Impact and Implications', *Journal of Indian School of Political Economy*, Vol. 3, No. 2, April–June.

Gupta, Anand. 1980. *Who Benefits from Government Expenditure in India*, Centre for Monitoring Indian Economy, Bombay, July.

Gupta, Ranjit. 1988. 'Sustained Development through People: Insights from an Experiment', *Vikalpa*, Vol. 13, No. 1, January–March (Indian Institute of Management, Ahmedabad).

Gupta, Ranjit (mimeo). *From Dependency to Self-Reliance: The Jawaja Experiment in Learning and Development,* Indian Institute of Management, Ahmedabad.

Gupta, S.C. and A. Majid. 1962. *Producers' Response to Changes in Prices and Marketing Policies*, Asia Publishing House, Bombay.

Hayami, Yujiro, K. Subbarao and K. Otsuka. 1982. 'Efficiency and Equity in Producer Levy in India', *American Journal of Agricultural Economics*, Vol. 64, No. 4, November.

Hazell, Peter B.R. 1982. *Instability in Indian Foodgrain Production*. Research Report 30. International Food Policy Research Institute, Washington. D.C.

Hingorani, Anand T. Compiled. 1970. *My Theory of Trusteeship*: *M.K. Gandhi*, Bharatiya Vidya Bhavan, Bombay.

Hopper, W. David. 1976. 'Sixth Coromandal Lecture: A Perspective on India's Food Production, January 5', reproduced in *Eastern Economist*, 30 January.

Howard, Louise E. 1935. *Labour in Agriculture: An International Survey*, Oxford University Press, London.

India, Government of. 1928. *Report of the Royal Commission on Agriculture in India 1920*, Delhi.

India, Government of. 1950. *Report of the Rural Banking Enquiry Committee*, Delhi.

India, Government of. 1953. *First Five-Year Plan*, Planning Commission: 173.12–18.

India, Government of. 1956. *Second Five-Year Plan, Planning Commission*, New Delhi.

India, Government of. 1957. *Report of the Foodgrains Enquiry Committee*, Ministry of Food and Agriculture.

India, Government of. 1959. *Report on India's Food Crisis and Steps to Meet It*, The Agricultural Production Team sponsored by the Ford Foundation, Ministry of Agriculture, New Delhi.

India, Government of. 1961. *Third Five-Year Plan*, Planning Commission: 130.

India, Government of. 1965. *Report of the Committee on Fertilizers*, Ministry of Food and Agriculture: 30.

India, Government of. 1965. *Report of the Agricultural Prices Commission on Price Policy for Kharif Cereals for 1965-66 Season* (Chairman: M.L. Dantwala), Department of Agriculture, Ministry of Agriculture and Irrigation, New Delhi.

India, Government of. 1966. *Report of the Foodgrains Policy Committee*, Ministry of Food and Agriculture.

India, Government of. 1966. *Growth Rates in Agriculture 1949–50 to 1964–65*, Ministry of Food and Agriculture, New Delhi, March (mimeo).

India, Government of. 1969. 'Modernising Indian Agriculture', *Report on the Intensive Agricultural District, Planning (1960-68)*, Vol. I, Expert Committee on Assessment and Evaluation, Ministry of Food, Agriculture, Community Development and Co-operation (Department of Agriculture), New Delhi.

India, Government of. 1974. *Report of the Agricultural Prices Commission on Price Policy for Kharif Cereals for the 1974–75 Season*, Ministry of Agriculture and Irrigation (Department of Agriculture), New Delhi.

India, Government of. 1975. *Report of the Agricultural Prices Commission on the Policy for Kharif Cereals: 1974–75 Season*, Department of Agriculture, Ministry of Agriculture and Irrigation, New Delhi.

India, Government of. 1976a. *Economic Survey, 1975–76*, Ministry of Finance, New Delhi.

India, Government of. 1976b. *Report 1975-76*, Ministry of Agriculture and Irrigation (Department of Agriculture), New Delhi.

India, Government of. 1976c. *Report on Price Policy for Wheat for 1975-76 Season*, Agricultural Prices Commission, original source.

India, Government of. 1977a. *Employment Structure and Planning Policy*, Perspective Planning Division, Planning Commission. May.

India, Government of. 1977b. *Report of the Review Committee on Pilot Intensive*

Rural Employment Project (PIREP), Ministry of Agriculture.

India, Government of. 1977c. National Sample Survey Organization. 'Employment and Unemployment Situation at A Glance', *Sarvekshana* (Journal of the NSSO), Vol. 1, No. 2, New Delhi, October 1977: 81–102.

India, Government of. 1978a. *Draft Five-Year Plan, 1978–83*, Planning Commission, New Delhi.

India, Government of. 1978b. National Sample Survey. *Some Key Results from the Survey of Employment, and Unemployment*, 32nd Round, Department of Statistics, New Delhi, July.

India, Government of. 1978c. *Report of the Working Group on Block Level Planning* (Chairman: M.L. Dantwala), Planning Commission, New Delhi.

India, Government of. 1979. *Report of the Agricultural Prices Commission on Price Policy for Jute for the 1979-80 Season*, Ministry of Agriculture and Irrigation, (Department of Agriculture), New Delhi.

India, Government of. 1980. *Accessibility of the Poor to Rural Water Supply*. Programme Evaluation Organization, Planning Commission.

India, Government of. 1981. *All India Agricultural Census, 1976–77*. Ministry of Agriculture and Rural Reconstruction. Manager of Publications, New Delhi.

India, Government of. 1982a. *Report of the Technical Group on Buffer Stocking Policy of Foodgrains*, Department of Food, Ministry of Agriculture, New Delhi.

India, Government of. 1982b. *The Economic Survey 1981–82*, Ministry of Finance, New Delhi.

India, Government of. 1985a. *Revised Index Numbers of Wholesale Prices in India, 1984–85*, issued by Economic Adviser, Ministry of Industry, New Delhi, May.

India, Government of. 1985b. *Seventh Five-Year Plan 1985-90*, Vol. I & II, Planning Commission, New Delhi.

India, Government of. 1986a. *The Economic Survey 1985-86*, Ministry of Finance, Government of India, New Delhi.

India, Government of. 1986b. *Report of the Working Group on Regional Rural Banks* (Chairman: S.M. Kelkar), Ministry of Finance, New Delhi.

India, Government of. 1992a. *Bulletin on Food Statistics 1990*, Directorate of Economics and Statistics, Ministry of Agriculture, New Delhi.

India, Government of. 1992b. *Economic Survey 1991–92*, Part II: Sectoral Developments, Ministry of Finance, New Delhi.

India, Government of. 1993. *Economic Survey 1992-93*, Ministry of Finance, New Delhi.

Indian Council of Social Science Research (ICSSR). 1980. *Alternatives in Agricultural Development*. Allied Publishers, New Delhi.

Indian Society of Agricultural Economics (IASE). 1951. *Cooperation in Kodinar*, Bombay.

Indian Statistical Institute (ISI). 1985. *Report of Project on Price and Distribution Controls in India*, Delhi Centre, New Delhi.

International Rice Research Institute. 1968. *Annual Report*, Manila, Philippines: 336.

International Rice Research Institute. 1969. *Annual Report*, Manila, Philippines: 2, 4.

Ishikawa, Shigeru (ed). 1978. *Labour Absorption in Asian Agriculture*, Asian Regional Programme for Employment Promotion, ILO, Bangkok.

Ishikawa, S. 1981. *Essays on Technology, Employment and Institutions in Economic Development: Comparative Asian Experience*. Kinokuniya Co., Tokyo.

Jha, Shikha. 1991. 'Consumer Subsidies in India: Is Targetting Effective', Discussion Paper No. 64, Indira Gandhi Institute of Development Research, Bombay, September.

Jodha, N.S. 1983. 'Market Forces and Erosion of Common Property Resources', paper presented at the International Workshop on Agricultural Markets in the Semi-Arid Tropics, ICRISAT Centre, Pattancheru (A.P.).

Joshi, C. 1982. 'The Dilemma of Growth and Inequality', in a *Survey of Agriculture*, Supplement to *New Delhi Patriot*, 19 May.

Kalbag, S.S. 1985. *Science, Technology and Rural Development*, Economic Research and Training Foundation, Indian Merchants' Chamber, Bombay.

Krishna, Jai and Radhakrishna.. 'Factors Affecting Agricultural Prices in India: 1957–1965' (unpublished).

Kurien, C.T. 1986. 'Reconciling Growth and Social Justice: Strategies Versus Structure', in M.L. Dantwala et al. (eds.), *Asian Seminar on Rural Development—The Indian Experience*, Oxford & IBH Publishing Co. Pvt. Ltd., New Delhi.

Ladejinsky, Wolf. 1969. 'Green Revolution in Bihar-Kosi Area: A Field Trip', *Economic and Political Weekly*, Vol. IV, No. 39, 27 September.

Lakdawala, D.T. 1977. *Growth, Employment and Poverty*, Presidential Address delivered at the All India Labour Economics Conference, Tirupati, December.

Lakdawala, D.T. 1979. *Plan Finances in a Federal Economy*, Dr V.S. Krishna Endowment Lectures, Andhra University, Waltair.

Lipton, Michael. 1969. 'Agriculture: Urban Bias and Rural Planning', in P. Streeten and Michael Lipton (eds.), *Crisis of Indian Planning*, Oxford University Press, London: 102.

Lipton, Michael. 1975. 'Urban Bias and Food Policy in Poor Countries', *Food Policy*, Vol. I, November.

Madras, Government of. 1946. *Report of Enquiry into Rural Indebtedness*, Madras.

Madras Institute of Development Studies. 1980. 'Structure and Intervention, An Evaluation of DPAP, IRDP and Related Programmes in Ramanathapuram and Dharmapuri Districts of Tamil Nadu, Madras', August (unpublished).

Maharashtra, Government of. 1974. *Report of the Committee Appointed by the Government of Maharashtra for Evaluation of Land Reforms*, Bombay.

Mandel, Ernest. 1971. *The Foundation of the Economic Thought of Karl Marx*, translated by Brian Pearce, Monthly Review Press.

Manektalas. 1965. *Proceedings of the International Seminar on Social Responsibility of Business*.

Mangahas, Mahar, Aida E. Recto and V.W. Ruttan. 1966. 'Price and Market Relationship for Rice and Corn in the Philippines', *Journal of Farm Economics*, Vol. 48, No. 3, Part I, August.

Martin, Abel. 1970. 'Agriculture in India in the 1970s', *Economic and Political Weekly*, Vol. V, No. 13, 28 March.

Mason, Edward. 1966. *Economic Development of India and Pakistan*, Harvard University Press, Cambridge.

Matthai, Ravi J. 1979. *Experiments in Educational Innovation of Rural University,*

Jawaja Project, Indian Institute of Management, Ahmedabad (mimeo).

Mehra, Shakuntla. 1976. *Some Aspects of Labour Use in Indian Agriculture*, Occasional Paper No. 88, Cornell University, Ithaca, New York.

Mehra, Shakuntla. 1981. *Instability in Indian Agriculture in the Context of the New Technology*. Research Report 25. Washington D.C.: International Food Policy Research Institute.

Mehta, Asoka. 1979. 'Economy—Strengths and Weaknesses', *Janata*, 11 February.

Mellor, J.W. and A. Dhar. 1967. 'Changes in the Relative Prices of Agricultural Commodities in India, 1952–53 to 1964–65', *Agricultural Situation in India*, Vol. XXII, No. 7, October.

Mellor, John. 1968. 'The Functions of Agricultural Prices in Economic Development', *Indian Journal of Agricultural Economics*, Vol. XXIII, No. 1, January–March.

Mellor, John W. 1974. *Agricultural Price Policy and Income Distribution*, Department of Agricultural Economics, Cornell University, Ithaca, New York, 24 June (mimeo).

Mellon, John W. 1976. *The New Economics of Growth*, Cornell University Press, Ithaca, New York: 48–49.

Mellor, John W. and Gunvant M. Desai (eds.). 1986. *Agricultural Change and Rural Poverty: Variations on a Theme by Dharm Narain*, Oxford University Press, Delhi.

Michael, Frolic B. 1971. 'A Visit to Peking University: What the Cultural Revolution Was All About', *The New York Times Magazine*, 24 October.

Minhas, B.S. 1970. 'Rural Poverty, Land Redistribution and Development Strategy', *Indian Economic Review*, Vol. 5, No. 1, April: 97–126.

Minhas, B.S. 1976. 'Towards National Food Security', Presidential Address delivered at the 36th Annual Conference of the Indian Society of Agricultural Economics, *Indian Journal of Agricultural Economics*, Vol. XXXI, No. 4, October–December.

Minhas, B.S. and Grace Majumdar. 1987. 'Unemployment and Casual Labour: An Analysis of Recent NSS Data', *Indian Journal of Industrial Relations*, Vol. 22, No. 3.

Morse, David. 1970. 'Unemployment in Developing Countries', *Political Science Quarterly*, Vol. 85, March.

Mukherjee: K. 1979. 'The HYV Programme: Variables that Matter', *Economic and Political Weekly*, Vol. V, No. 13, 28 March.

Mukhopadhyay, S.K. 1976. *Sources of Variation in Agricultural Productivity: A Cross-Section Times-Series Study in India*, The Macmillan Company of India Ltd. New Delhi.

NABARD. 1982a. 'River Lift Irrigation Schemes in Pune District, Maharashtra' (An Ex-Post Evaluation Study), Evaluation Study Series, No. 14, Bombay.

NABARD. 1982b. 'River Lift Irrigation Schemes in Kolhapur District, Maharashtra' (An Ex-Post Evaluation Study), Evaluation Study Series, No. 16, Bombay.

Naidu, I.J. 1975. 'All India Report on Agricultural Census, 1970-71', Ministry of Agriculture and Irrigation (Department of Agriculture), Government of India, New Delhi.

Naik, K.N. 1951. 'Cooperative Movement in Bombay Province', unpublished Doctoral Dissertation, University of Bombay, Bombay.

Narain, Dharm. 1965. *The Impact of Price Movements on Areas Under Selected Crops in India, 1990–39*, Cambridge University Press, Cambridge.

Narain, Dharm, and Roy, Shyamal. 1980. *Impact of Irrigation and Labour Availability on Multiple Cropping: A Case Study of India.* Research Report 20, International Food Policy Research Institute, Washington, D.C.

Natesan, G.A. 1917. *Speeches and Writings by M.K. Gandhi*, 4th edition, G.A. Natesan and Co., Madras.

National Commission on Agriculture. 1971. *Interim Report on Milk Production through Small and Marginal Farmers and Landless Labourers*, New Delhi, December.

National Sample Survey Organization (NSSO). 1990. 'Utilization of Public Distribution System: NSS 42nd Round (July 1986–June 1987)', *Sarvekshana*, Vol. 13, No. 4, April–June.

National Council of Applied Economic Research (NCAER). 1966. *Cropping Pattern in Punjab*, New Delhi.

Paddock, William and Paul. 1968. *Famine 1975!* Wiedenfeld and Nicolson, London.

Parikh, Kirit. 1992. 'Food Security: Issues and Options', in Papers of the Plenary and Invited Paper Sessions, XXIst International Conference of Agricultural Economists, 22–29 August, Tokyo, Japan.

Parthasarathy, G. 1978. 'Inter-State Variations in Rural Unemployment and Growth of Agriculture', Occasional Paper 6, Agro-Economic Research Centre, Andhra University, Waltair, March.

Patel, S.M., D.S. Thakur and M.K. Pandey. 1975. *Impact of the Milk Co-operatives*, Institute of Co-operative Management, Ahmedabad (unpublished).

Patel, H.F. 1974. *A Study of Integrated Dryland Agricultural Development*, Agro-Economic Research Centre, Sardar Patel University, Vallabh Vidyanagar.

Pearson, Lester B. 1969. *Partners in Development: Report of the Commission on International Development*, Praeger Publishers, Inc., Pall Mall Press, London.

Peters, G.H. and B.F. Stanton (eds.). 1992. *Sustainable Agricultural Development: The Role of International Cooperation*, Proceedings of the Twenty-first International Conference of Agricultural Economists, held at Tokyo, Japan, 22-29 August 1991, Dartmouth Publishing Company Ltd., Aldershot, Hanto, England.

Pulley, Robert V. 1989. Making the Poor Creditworthy—A Case Study of Integrated Development Program in India, World Bank Discussion Paper, 58, The World Bank, Washington, D.C.

Punjab Agricultural University. 1966. *Dynamics of Punjab Agriculture*, Ludhiana.

Purkayastha, Dipankar and Alka Subramanian. 1986. 'Price and Income Stabilization Issues in the Indian Groundnut Market', *Economic and Political Weekly*, Vol. XXI, No. 8, 22 February.

Pyarelal. 1957. *Towards New Horizons*, Navjivan Trust, Ahmedabad.

Pyarelal. 1958. *Mahatma Gandhi, The Last Phase*, Vol. II, Navjivan Publishing House, Ahmedabad: 90–93.

Radhakrishna, R. and C. Ravi. 1990. *Food Demand Projection for India*, Centre for Economic and Social Studies, Hyderabad (AP), May.

Radhakrishna, R. and S. Indrakant. 1987. *Effect on Rice Market Intervention Policies in India—The Case of Andhra Pradesh*, Centre for Economic and Social Studies, Hyderabad (AP)

Raghavendra Rao, K. 1985. 'The Moral Economy of Trusteeship', *Gandhi Marg*, November–December.

Raj, K.N. 1969. 'Some Questions Concerning Growth, Transformation and Planning of Agriculture in Developing Countries', *Journal of Development Planning*, No. 1, United Nations.

Rao, C.H. Hanumantha. 1975. *Technological Change and Distribution of Gains in Indian Agriculture*, Institute of Economic Growth, The Macmillan Company of India Ltd., Delhi.

Rao, C.H. Hanumantha. 1976. 'Summaries of Group Discussion: Subject I—Changes in the Structural Distribution of Land Ownership and Use (Since Independence)', *Indian Journal of Agricultural Economics*, Vol. XXXI, No. 4, October to December: 21–22.

Rao, I.V. Ranga and A.K. Ray. 1985. 'Stagnation in Production of Pulses: A Quantitative Analysis', *Agricultural Situation in India*, Vol. XL, No. 5, August.

Rao, V.K.R.V. 1974. 'Some Fundamental Aspects of Socialistic Change in India', Inaugural Address to 56th Session of Indian Economic Conference, 1973, published in *Indian Economic Journal*, Vol. 21, No. 3, January–March.

Rao, V.M. 1975. *Second India Studies: Food*, The Macmillan Company of India Ltd., Bombay.

Rao, V.M. 1987. 'Changing Village Structure: Impact of Rural Development Programmes', *Economic and Political Weekly*, Vol. 22, No. 13, 28 March.

Rath, Nilkantha. 1977. 'Performance of Agriculture in Maharashtra, 1960–1972', in Seminar on Regional Disparities in Rates of Growth and Productivity in Indian Agriculture; Indian Society of Agricultural Economics and Gokhale Institute of Politics and Economics. Pune.

Ray, S.K.L. 1983. 'An Empirical Investigation of the Nature and Causes for Growth and Instability in Indian Agriculture: 1950–80', *Indian Journal of Agricultural Economics*, Vol. XXXVIII, No. 4, October–December.

Reserve Bank of India. 1954. *All India Rural Credit Survey: Report of the Committee of Direction*, Vol. II: The General Report, Bombay.

Reserve Bank of India. 1969. *Report of the All-India Rural Credit Review Committee* (Chairman: B. Venkatappiah), Bombay.

Reserve Bank of India. 1974. *Report on Currency and Finance for the Year 1973–74*, Bombay, Table III.48: 70.

Reserve Bank of India. 1975. *Report on Currency and Finance*, Vol. I: Economic Review, 1974–75 Bombay, Table III. 50: 65.

Reserve Bank of India. 1976. 'Statistical Statements relating to the Co-operative Movement in India, 1974–75', Part I: Credit Societies, Agricultural Credit Department, Bombay.

Reserve Bank of India. 1978. *Report of the Review Committee on Regional Rural Banks* (Chairman: M.L. Dantwala), Bombay.

Reserve Bank of India. 1981. *Report of the Committee to Review Arrangements for Institutional Credit for Agriculture and Rural Development (CRAFICARD)* (Chairman: B. Sivaraman), Bombay.

Reserve Bank of India. 1983. *Report of the Working Group on the Role of Banks in Implementation of New 20–Point Programme*, Bombay.

Reserve Bank of India. 1989. *A Review of the Agricultural Credit System in India*, Report of the Agricultural Credit Review Committee (Chairman: A.M. Khusro), Bombay.

Robinson, Joan. 1969. *The Cultural Revolution in China*, a Pelican original, England: 90 and 11.

Sahasrabudhe, A.W. 1966. *Report on Koraput Gramdan, 1956–59*, Akhil Bharatiya Sarva Seva Sangh, Sevagram, Wardha: 9.

Saini, G.R. 1976. 'Green Revolution and Disparities in Farm Incomes: A Comment', *Economic and Political Weekly*, Vol. XI, No. 46, 13 November: 1804–6.

Sandesara, J.C. 1978. 'Small Industries Production: A Quick Comment', *Economic and Political Weekly*, Vol. XIII, No. 17, 29 April.

Saran, Ram. 1975. *Growth in Indian Agriculture—An Analysis*, New Delhi, December.

Sarma, J.S., Shyamal Roy and P. S. George. 1979. *Two Analyses of Indian Foodgrain production and Consumption Data*, Research Report 12, Washington, D.C.: International Food Policy Research Institute.

Sau, Ranjit. 1978. 'Growth, Employment and Removal of Poverty', *Economic and Political Weekly*, Vol. XIII, Nos 31, 32 and 33, Special Number, August.

Sawhny, Leslie. 1980. 'Programme of Training for Democracy and Trusteeship: Foundation', *in Trusteeship: A Possible Solution to Problems of Power, Exploitation Conflict and Alienation*, Distributors: India Book House, Bombay.

Schultz, T.W. 1964. *Economic Crises in World Agriculture*, The University of Michigan Press, Ann Arbor, U.S.A.

Schultz, Theodore W. 1966. *U.S. Malinvestment in Food for the World*, paper presented at the Ames Conference on Balancing Future World Food Production and Needs, Iowa State University, November.

Schultz, T.W. 1968. 'Production Opportunities in Asian Agriculture: An Economist's Agenda', Agricultural Economics Paper No. 68: 12, Department of Economics, University of Chicago (revised July 12), and published in *Development and Change in Tradifond Agriculture: Focus on South Asia*, Asian Studies Centre, Michigan State University, East Lamsing, Michigan, 1968.

Sen, B. 1970. 'Opportunities in the Green Revolution', *Economic and Political Weekly*, Vol. V, No. 13, 28 March.

Sen, S.R. 1967. 'Growth and Instability in Indian Agriculture', *Agricultural Situation in India*, Vol. XXI, No. 10, January, Directorate of Economics and Statistics, Ministry of Food and Agriculture, Government of India.

Sethi, J.D. 1978. *Gandhi Today*, Vikas Publishing House Pvt. Ltd., New Delhi.

Shrivastava. R.K. 1970. *Impact of Cattle Development on Rural Economy of the Kaira District*, Institute of Agricultural Research Statistics, New Delhi.

Singh, Chhatrapati. 1986. *Common Property and Common Poverty: India's Forest Dwellers and the Law* (OUP, 1986), review in *The Times of India*, Sunday Review, 13 July ('The Tree of Judgement' by Anna Khanna).

Sinha, R. et al. 1979. *Income Distribution, Growth and Basic Needs in India*, Croom Helm, London.

Streeter, Paul P. 1983. 'Development Ideas in Historical Perspective', reprinted in *Impact*, No. 40, from *Development Perspectives*, Macmillan Publishers.

Streeter, Carroll P. 1969. *A Partnership to Improve Food Production in India*, a special report from the Rockefeller Foundation Rockefeller Foundation: 132.

Subbarao, K. 1973. 'Market Structure in Indian Agriculture', unpublished Ph.D. Dissertation, University of Delhi, Delhi.

Subbarao, K. 1989. 'Improving Nutrition in India: Policies and Programmes and Their Impact', *World Bank Discussion Papers No. 49*, The World Bank, Washington, D.C., USA.

Sundaram, K. 1984. 'Registrar General's Population Projection, 1981-2001: An Appraisal and an Alternative Scenario', *Economic and Political Weekly*, Vol. XIX, No. 34, 25 August.

Swenson, Clyde Geoffrey. 1976. 'The Effect of Increases in Rice Production on Employment and Income Distribution in Thanjavur District, South India', unpublished Ph.D. Dissertation, Michigan State University, 1973. A summary of results of this research is published under the title 'The Distribution of Benefits from Increased Rice Production in Thanjavur District, South India', *Indian Journal of Agricultural Economics*, Vol. XXXI, No. 1, January–March.

Swindale, L.D. 1981. *A Time for Rainfed Agriculture*. Coromandel Lecture, 10 December, New Delhi.

Taori, Kamal and Singh, S.N. 1991. 'Marketing Rural Industry Products: Experiments and Experiences in Uttar Pradesh', *Economic and Political Weekly*, Vol.. 26, No. 8, 23 February.

Tendulkar, D.G. 1954. *Mahatma, Life of Mohandas Karamchand Gandhi*, Vol. IV, Distributors, Publication Department, The Times of India Press, Bombay.-

Thamarajakshi, R. 1968. 'Intersectoral Terms of Trade and Marketed Surplus of Agricultural Produce, 1951–52 to 1965–66', *Economic and Political Weekly*, Vol. IV, No. 26, 28 June (Review of Agriculture): A-91–A-102.

Thamarajakshi, R. 1971. 'Prices, Production and Marketable Surplus of Foodgrains in Indian Economy, 1951–52—1965–66', *Agricultural Situation in India*, Vol. XXV, No. 10, January.

Thamarajakshi, R. 1977. 'Role of Price Incentives in Stimulating Agricultural Production in a Developing Economy', in Ensimnger, Douglas (ed.), *Food Enough or Starvation for Millions*, Tata McGraw-Hill, New Delhi.

The Times of India. 18 March 1976.

The Times of India. 20 May 1976.

The Times of India. 1981. 'Coal Nightmare for Dream Canal', New Delhi, 21 January (UNI).

The Times of India. 1982a. Bombay, 25 September.

The Times of India. 1982b. Bombay, 16 October.

The Economist. 1992. 'A Survey of Agriculture', 12–18 December.

Tyagi, D.S. 1986. 'Discussion: On the Relevance of Farm Prices', *Economic and Political Weekly*, Vol. XXI, No. 9, 1 March.

Tyagi, D.S. 1990. *Managing India's Food Economy: Problems and Alternatives*, Sage Publications, New Delhi.

United Nations. 1951. *Measures for the Economic Development of Under-developed Countries*, Department of Economic Affairs, New York.

United Nations. 1953. *Measures for the Economic Development of Underdeveloped Countries*. p. 7, reprinted from *Indian Journal of Agricultural Economics*, Vol. 8, No. 2, August.

Vaidyanathan, A. 1978. 'Labour Use in Indian Agriculture', Working Paper No. 72, Centre for Development Studies, Trivandrum, August.

Vaidyanathan, A. 1990. 'Cottage and Small Industries in India: Policy and Performance', Sir Purshottamdas Thakurdas Memorial Lecture, The Indian Institute of Bankers, Bombay (also in *Fortune India*, 15 June 1991).

Vaikunth Mehta Smarak Trust. 1982. Centre for Studies in Decentralized Industries. 'A Study of Nature and Causes of Poverty among Rural Artisans—Maharashtra

State: Cane-Bamboo Workers, Ratnagiri District', Bombay.

Venkataramanan, L.S. and M. Prahladchar. 1979. 'Inter-Sectoral Terms of Trade and Marketed Surplus of Agriculture: 1964–65 to 1973–74', paper presented to the Indo-Hungarian Economists Seminar, held at the Indian School of Political Economy, Lonavla, 26–28 February (mimeo).

Visaria, Pravin. 1981a. 'Poverty and Unemployment in India: An Analysis of Recent Evidence' (mimeo), later published in *World Development*, Vol. 9, No. 3, March 1981.

Visaria, Pravin. 1981b. 'Size of Land Holding, Living Standards and Employment in Rural Western India, 1972–73', World Bank Staff Working Paper No. 459, Washington D.C.

Visaria, 1984. 'The Growth of Population and Labour Force in India: 1961–2000', paper presented at the Workshop on Population Growth and Labour Absorption in the Developing World, 1960–2000, 1–6 July, Bellagio, Italy.

Visaria, Pravin and B.S. Minhas. 1991. 'Evolving an Employment Policy for the 1990s: What do the Data Tell Us?' *Economic and Political Weekly*, Vol. 26, No. 15, 13 April.

Vyas, V.S., D.S. Tyagi and V.N. Mishra. 1969. *Significance of New Strategy of Agricultural Development for Small Farmers*, Agro–Economic Research Centre, Sardar Patel University, Vallabh Vidyanagar.

Vyas, V.S. 1979. 'Some Aspects of Structural Change in Indian Agriculture', Presidential Address delivered at 38th All-India Agricultural Economics Conference, Jorhat, January.

Vyas, V.S., and George Mathai. 1978. 'Farm and Non-Farm Employment in Rural Areas', *Economic and Political Weekly*, Vol. XIII, Nos. 6 and 7, Annual Number, February.

Vyas, V.S. 1982. 'Division of Gains: Organizational Challenge', in a *Survey of Agriculture* See Joshi, 1982.

World Bank. 1991. 'India, 1991 Country Economic Memorandum', Vol. II: *Agriculture: Challenges and Opportunities,* Agriculture Operations Division, India Department, Asia Region, Washington, D.C., USA.

Yechuri, Sitaram. 1976. 'Inter-State Variations in Agricultural Growth Rate, 1962 to 1974', *Economic and Political Weekly*, Vol. XI, No. 52, 25 December: A-151–A-155.

Select bibliography*

A. BOOKS/MONOGRAPHS/LECTURES

1. *Marketing and Trade in Raw Cotton in India.* Longmans Green and Co. Ltd. Bombay, 1937.
2. *Gandhism Reconsidered.* Revised & Enlarged Edition. Padma Publications Ltd., Bombay, 1945.
3. *Food Crops of Gujarat, 1939-46,* Vora & Co., Bombay, 1946.
4. *A Hundred Years of Indian Cotton.* East India Cotton Association, Orient Longman Ltd., Bombay, 1947.
5. *Indian Agriculture.* National Information & Publications Ltd., 1949. Economic Handbook No. 5.
6. *India's Food Problem.* Asia Publishing House, Bombay, 1960.
7. *Agriculture in a Developing Economy: The Indian Experience.* R.R. Kale Memorial Lecture delivered in 1964 at Gokhale Institute of Politics and Economics, Pune. Asia Publishing House, Bombay, 1966.
8. 'The Green Revolution: Before and After', Lal Bahadur Shastri Memorial Lecture, University of Pune, March 1970.
9. *Evaluation of Land Reforms: With Special Reference to the Western Region of India.* (Jointly with C.H. Shah), Department of Economics, University of Bombay, Bombay, 1971.
10. *Poverty in India: Then and Now 1870–1970.* Dadabhai Naoroji Memorial Fellowship Lectures. Macmillan India, Delhi, 1973.
11. *Asian Seminar on Rural Development: The Indian Experience.* Edited jointly with Ranjit Gupta and Keith C. D'Souza, Oxford & IBH Publishing Co. Ltd., New Delhi, 1986.
12. 'Agriculture and Rural Poverty', Yusuf Meherally Memorial Lecture delivered on 23rd September 1987, Bombay (also distributed by Centre for Monitoring Indian Economy, September 1987).
13. *Indian Agricultural Development Since Independence: A Collection of Essays.* (Edited) 2nd Revised Edition, Oxford & IBH Publishers Co. Pvt. Ltd., New Delhi, 1991.

* This bibliography does not carry articles included in this volume.

B. ARTICLES, PAPERS AND UNPUBLISHED ADDRESSES

I: Reflections on economic planning

1. 'The Role of Agriculture in the Third Five Year Plan', *Indian Journal of Agricultural Economics*, Vol. XV, No. 1, January–March, 1960: 268–71.
2. 'International Planning to Combat the Scourge of Hunger Throughout the World', *Annals of Collective Economy*, Vol. XXXIV, No. 1, January–March 1963: 71–75.
3. 'Third Five Year Plan: Is it Over-Ambitious?' A speech delivered at a Symposium on the 'Draft Third Five Year Plan', organized by the Maharashtra Chamber of Commerce.
4. 'Not Over-Ambitious—4th Plan—Symposium on the Plan Draft', *Yojana*, Vol. X, No. 18, 18 September 1966: 3–47.
5. 'Generous Outlay for Agriculture', *Yojana*, Vol. X, No. 19, 2 October 1966: 33–36.
6. 'Agricultural Sector and the Implementation of Plans', Proceedings of a Series of Talks held at Ahmedabad under the auspices of the Ahmedabad Management Association, January–February 1967.
7. 'Block Level Planning Revisited', *Economic and Political Weekly*, Vol. XV, No. 30, 26 July 1980: 1279–81.
8. 'The Eluding Panacea', *The Basic Needs Approach to Indian Planning*, International Labour Organization/Asian Employment Programme, Bangkok, 1980: 43–54.
9. 'Reflections on Indian Planning', Inaugural Address at the Annual Conference of the Gujarat Economic Association, Vallabh Vidyanagar, 3 February 1985.
10. 'Indian Economy: The New Phase', *Economic Times Silver Jubilee Feature*, 1961–86, 19 December 1986.
11. 'Decentralisation for Rural Development', a paper prepared for the Commemorative Volume to celebrate the Silver Jubilee of the Panchayati Raj Institutions in the State of Maharashtra, 30 September 1988.
12. 'Relevance of Social Action Under the New Economic Policy', *IASSI Quarterly*, Vol. 11, No. 1, July–September 1992: 113–118.
13. 'Dialogue on New Economic Policy', *Janata*, Vol. 47, No. 26, 1 November 1992: 5–6, 12.
14. 'Vision and the Reality: Comments on the Report of the Economic Programme Committee, 1948', *IASSI Quarterly*, Vol. 12, Nos. 1&2, July–December 1993: 2–14.

II: Agricultural development

15. 'The Uneconomic Cultivator' (jointly with W.B. Donde), *Indian Journal of Agricultural Economics*, Vol. IV, No. 2, August 1949: 9–48.
16. 'Population and Agricultural Productivity in India', *Indian Economic Journal*, Vol. 1, No. 3, January 1954: 296–301.
17. 'Regional Variations in Agricultural Employment and Wages', in Seminar on *Rationale of Regional Variations in Agrarian Structure in India*, Indian

Society of Agricultural Economics, Bombay, 1957.

18. 'Agriculture and Economic Development in India', *The Chinese Journal*, October 1957.
19. 'Accent on Functional Efficiency', *AICC Economic Review*, Vol. 11, No. 16–18, 16 January 1960: 59–60.
20. 'Diagnosis and Pathology of Peasant Farming', Proceedings of the International Conference of Agricultural Economists, Oxford University Press, Bombay, 1960.
21. 'Trends in Yield Per Acre of Crops', in *Changing India*, Essays in Honour of Professor D.R. Gadgil, edited by V.M. Dandekar and N.V. Sovani, Asia Publishing House, 1961: 21–40.
22. 'The Two Worlds of Food and Agriculture', *The Economic Weekly*, Vol. XIV, No. 4, October–December 1962.
23. 'Agricultural Employment in a Developing Economy', a paper presented to the Conference on Comprehensive Planning of Agriculture, Rehovoth, Israel, August 1963.
24. 'Role of Agriculture in Indian Economic Development', a paper submitted to ECAFE for its Annual Report, 1964.
25. 'Agriculture in the Five Year Plans', *The Hindu Survey of Indian Industry*, December 1966, Madras.
26. 'Intensive Agricultural Development', *Economic and Political Weekly*, Vol. II, No. 24, 17 June 1967: 1079–81.
27. 'Rejuvenating Sick Agriculture: Indian Experience', *Netherlands Journal of Agricultural Science*, Vol. 16, No. 4, 1968: 235–242.
28. 'On the Economic Transformation of Family Farming', *Netherlands Journal of Agricultural Science*, Vol. 16, 1968.
29. 'Is Economics in Farming Dead?' A review article on the Lonely Furrow: Farming in United States, Japan and India by Kusum Nair, University of Michigan Press, Ann Arbor, 1969, *Economic and Political Weekly*, Vol. IV, No. 39, 27 September 1969: A 130–31.
30. Preface to 'Agricultural Development in Developing Countries: Comparative Experience', Indian Society of Agricultural Economics, Bombay, 1972: 1–55.
31. 'The Poor Should Become Producers', *Commerce*, Annual Number, 1979.
32. 'Agriculture in the Eighties: Unanswered Questions', *Financial Express*, 5 November 1981.
33. 'Growth and Equity in Agriculture', *Janata*, Vol. XXXVII, No. 27, Independence Day 1982: 7–10.
34. 'Lessons from Uneven Growth in Agriculture', *The Hindu Survey of Indian Industry*, 1984, Madras.
35. 'Performance and Prospects of Indian Agriculture', *The Economic Times*, 19 December 1984.
36. 'Indian Agriculture: Performance and Prospects', *The Hindu Survey of Indian Industry*, 1985, Madras.
37. 'Agricultural Development: Performance and Prospects', *The Economic Times*, Silver Jubilee issue, December 1986.
38. 'Growth vs Equity in Agricultural Development Strategy', a paper presented to the Eighth World Economic Congress, Indian Economic Association, December 1986 (also in *The Development Process of Indian Economy*, edited by P.R.

Brahmananda and V.R. Panchamukhi, Himalaya Publishing House, Bombay, 1987: 147–160).

39. Foreword to *Institutional Aspects of Agricultural Development*, by P.C. Joshi, Allied Publishers, Ahmedabad, 1987: vii–x.

40. 'Agricultural Growth Strategy in Retrospect and Prospect', *Janata*, Vol. 43, No. 18, Independence Day Number, 1988: 13–15.

41. 'Strategy of Agricultural Development Since Independence', in *Indian Agricultural Development Since Independence* (edited), 2nd revised edition, Oxford & IBH Publishing Co., 1991: 1–15.

42. 'Emerging Challenges in Indian Agriculture', a paper presented at the National Seminar on 'India: The Emerging Challenges' organized to felicitate Professor V.K.R.V. Rao, Institute for Social and Economic Change, Bangalore, 5–7 October 1988 (also in *India: The Emerging Challenges*, Essays in Honour of Professor V.K.R.V. Rao, edited by M.V. Nadkarni, A.S. Seetharamu and Abdul Aziz, Sage Publications India Pvt. Ltd., New Delhi, 1991: 121–28).

III: Rural development: Approaches and issues

43. 'Composition of Rural Population', *Indian Journal of Agricultural Economics*, Vol. XI, No. 1, January–March 1956: 70–72.

44. 'Role of Voluntary Agencies in Rural Development', *Janata*, Vol. XXXII, No. 35, 9 October 1977: 41–43.

45. 'And What We Need Doing', *Kurukshetra*, Vol. 38, No. 1, 1 October 1979: 12–13.

46. 'Electrification—I: Promise and Performance in Rural Areas', and 'Rural Electrification—II: Integration Lacking', *The Economic Times*, 3 and 4 November 1980.

47. 'Challenge of Turning Needs into Effective Demand', a paper presented at a workshop organized by the Ford Foundation (New Delhi), at Trivandrum, December 1980.

48. 'Understanding Rural India', *Artha-Jijnasa*, Vol. 2, No. 2, April–June 1982.

49. 'Poverty Alleviation Through Rural Development', National Workshop on Administrative Arrangement for Rural Development, NIRD, Hyderabad, July 1985.

50. 'IRDP and Village Structure', *Economic and Political Weekly*, Vol. 22, No. 22, 30 May 1987: 858–59.

51. 'New Credit Strategy for Rural Development', Inaugural Address. Seminar on 'Rural Credit', Reserve Bank of India, 1988.

52. 'Rural Development: Approaches and Issues' (jointly with J.N. Barmeda), in *Indian Agricultural Development Since Independence* (edited), 2nd revised edition, Oxford & IBH Publishing Co., Bombay, 1991: 425–49.

IV. Poverty and unemployment in rural India

53. 'Concepts in Employment-Unemployment Surveys', *Indian Journal of Agricultural Economics*, Vol. XI, No, 3, July–September 1956: 65–67.

54. 'Development of Warehousing', *Indian Journal of Agricultural Economics*,

Vol. XI, No. 4, October–December 1956: 50–51.

55. 'Second Agricultural Labour Enquiry', *Indian Journal of Agricultural Economics,* Vol. XVI, No. 2, April–June 1961: 47–50.

56. 'Minimum Price for Farm Produce', *Agricultural Situation in India,* Vol. XX, No. 5, August 1965: 301–303.

57. 'Definition of Unemployment in a Developing Economy and Problems of Measurement', a paper presented at a seminar organized by the Organization for Economic Cooperation and Development, Paris, 13–17 July 1970.

58. 'Approaches to Growth and Employment', *Economic and Political Weekly,* Vol. VII, No. 51, 16 December 1972: 2457–64.

59. 'Report of the Committee of Experts on Unemployment Estimates—A Clarification', *Indian Journal of Agricultural Economics,* Vol. XXVIII, No. 1.

60. 'Planning Strategy and Rural Unemployment: Some Notes', in *Seminar on Rural Development for Weaker Sections,* Indian Society of Agricultural Economics, Bombay, Seminar Series XII, May 1974: 788–92.

61. 'Not by Statistics Alone'. A review article on *Poverty and Income Distribution in India,* edited by T.N. Srinivasan and P.K. Bardhan, Statistical Publishing Society, Calcutta, 1974 (*Economic and Political Weekly,* Vol. X, No. 16, 19 April 1975: 661–63).

62. 'A Profile of Poverty and Unemployment in 12 Villages', *Indian Journal of Agricultural Economics,* Vol. XXX, No. 2, April–June 1975: 1–75.

63. 'Rural Labour Force and Employment Policy' (jointly with Pravin Visaria) in *Economic Theory and Planning Essays,* in Honour of A.K. Dasgupta, edited by Ashok Mitra, Oxford University Press, Bombay, 1976: 236–54.

64. 'Understanding Poverty and Unemployment', Brochure 2, Indian Merchants Chamber, Economic Research and Training Foundation, Bombay 1980 (also in *Artha-Jijnasa,* Vol. 1, No. 2, April–June 1981).

65. 'Poverty and Unemployment in India', a report submitted to International Development Research Centre, Ottawa, Canada, 1974.

66. 'Prospects for the Poor' *Vyapar,* Vol. 35, No. 97, Diwali Special Number 1984: 25–26.

67. 'Garibi Hatao: Strategy Options', *Economic and Political Weekly,* Vol. XX, No. 11, 16 March 1985: 475–76.

68. 'I.R.D.P. and Village Structure', *Economic and Political Weekly,* Vol. XII, No. 22, 30 May 1987: 858–59.

69. 'Poverty Alleviation Programmes Require Reorientation', a paper presented at the Seminar on 'Poverty Alleviation Programmes' organized by the Ministry of Agriculture, Government of India. 2 February 1988, *Kurukshetra,* Vol. XXXVI, No. 7, April 1988: 26–27.

70. 'Estimates of Demand for Credit and Its Role in Poverty Alleviation', *Indian Journal of Agricultural Economics,* Vol. XLIV, No. 4, October–December 1989: 416–422.

71. 'Search for an Employment-Oriented Growth Strategy: A Discussion-I', *Economic and Political Weekly,* Vol. 25, No. 21, 26 May 1990: 1147–49.

72. 'Growth Through Full Employment: A Vision', *Kurukshetra,* Vol. 38, No. 11, August 1990: 9–11.

73. 'Problems in Critique of IRDP: Discussion', *Economic and Political Weekly,* Vol. 25, No. 51, 22 December 1990: 2806.

V: Food problem

74. 'Obstacles to Grow More Food', *Indian Journal of Agricultural Economics,* Vol. V, No. 2, August 1950: 50–57.
75. 'Obstacles to Grow More Food Campaign' (Dhulia Taluka) (jointly with R.G. Gupta), *Indian Journal of Agricultural Economics,* Vol. V, No. 2, August 1950: 87–105.
76. 'Geography of Food Production' (jointly with C.H. Shah), *Indian Journal of Agricultural Economics,* Vol. XII, No. 3, July–September 1957: 51–54.
77. 'Foodgrains Enquiry Committee Report', *Indian Journal of Agricultural Economics,* Vol. XII, No. 4, October–December 1957: 62–65.
78. 'India's Food Problem in a Perspective', India Merchants' Chamber Diamond Jubilee Commemoration Volume, 1967.
79. 'India's Food Problem', *Bhavan's Journal,* Vol. XVI, No. 1, 10 August 1969: 291–98.
80. 'The Green Revolution or A Palace Revolt', Indian Merchants' Chamber Presentation of Awards Souvenir: 34–36.
81. 'Public Distribution of Foodgrains', *The Radical Humanist,* Vol. 41, No. 5, August 1977.
82. 'A Note on Food Surplus', a paper presented at the *Seminar on Poverty Alleviation—Policy Options,* Ministry of Rural Development, Government of India, New Delhi, 26 August 1985.
83. 'Some Issues in Public Distribution of Foodgrains', paper submitted to the Meeting of Economists convened by the Government of West Bengal, Calcutta, 14–16 September 1985.

VI: Agricultural marketing and price policy

84. 'Agricultural Price Goals and Policy for a Backward Country', *Indian Journal of Agricultural Economics,* Vol. VI, No. 1, March 1951: 144–47.
85. 'Price and Production in Agriculture, *Indian Journal of Agricultural Economics,* Vol. IX, No. 1, March 1954: 14–19.
86. 'Problems Before the New Marketing Agencies', *Indian Journal of Agricultural Economics,* Vol. XII, No. 2, April–June 1957: 182–86.
87. 'State Trading in Foodgrains', *Indian Journal of Agricultural Economics,* Vol. XIV, No. 2, April–June 1959: 38–40.
88. 'Farm Cost Studies as Aid to Economic Analysis and Policies', *Seminar on Cost Studies in Agriculture,* Seminar Series-III, Indian Society of Agricultural Economics, Bombay, 1961.
89. 'Price Policy for Agricultural Development', *Indian Journal of Agricultural Economics,* Vol. XVII, No. 1, January–March 1962: 107–13.
90. 'International Trade in Primary Commodities: A Factual Note', *Indian Economic Journal,* Vol. X, No. 2, October 1962: 158–63.
91. 'Government Operations in Foodgrains: Comment-I', *Economic and Political Weekly,* Vol. II, No. 41, 14 October 1967.
92. 'Growing Irrelevance of Economics in Planning: Case of Procurement Prices', *Economic and Political Weekly,* Vol. II, No. 43, 28 October 1967: 1945–47.

93. 'Agricultural Price Policy: Reply', *Economic and Political Weekly*, Vol. III, No. 11, 16 March 1968.
94. 'Problems of Buffer Stock', *Economic and Political Weekly*, Vol. IV, No. 13, 29 March 1969: A64–A67.
95. 'Summary of Discussions at the Seminar on Foodgrain Buffer Stock', in *Seminar on Foodgrain Buffer Stock in India*, Indian Society of Agricultural Economics, Seminar Series VIII, Bombay, 1969: 1–11.
96. 'Politics of Prices', *Commerce*, Vol. 128, No. 3280, 23 March 1974.
97. 'The New Agricultural Price Policy', *Janata*, 24 April 1977: 5–6, 1 May 1977.
98. 'Policy on Production and Distribution of Essential Commodities', presented at the Round Table on Public Distribution of Essential Commodities, 9 June 1979, Indian Merchants Chamber, Bombay: 13.
99. 'Agricultural Prices, Production and "Surplus" Stock', a paper presented at the *Seminar on the Role of Foodgrain Agencies in Food Security in Asia and the Pacific* (AFMA) and Food Corporation of India, New Delhi, 23–25 April 1985.
100. 'Price Policy for Oilseeds', in *Self Sufficiency in Oilseeds Production in India*, Maharashtra Hybrid Seeds Company Ltd., Bombay, 1988.
101. 'Agricultural Prices Under Political Pressure', *Economic and Political Weekly*, Vol. XXV, No. 38, 22 September 1990: 2136–37.

VII: Agricultural credit

102. 'Rural Credit: Follow-up Survey', *Indian Journal of Agricultural Economics*, Vol. XV, No. 3, July–September 1960: 46–50.
103. 'Rural Credit Policy: Business vs. Co-operation?' *AICC Economic Review*, Vol. 12, No. 3, 22 August 1960: 41–42.
104. 'Institutional Credit in Subsistence Agriculture', *International Journal of Agrarian Affairs*, Vol. V, No. 1, December 1966.
105. 'Regional Rural Banks: A Clarification', *Economic and Political Weekly*, Vol. 13, No. 42, 21 October 1978: 1776–77.
106. 'Restructuring Rural Credit System' *The Economic Times*, 30 and 31 March 1990.

VIII: Agrarian problem

107. 'Problems of the Low Income or Sub-marginal Farmers', *Indian Journal of Agricultural Economics*, Vol. V, No. 1, January–March 1950: 38–42.
108. 'Land Tenure Problems in Countries with Heavy Pressure of Population in Land', paper submitted to the Conference on World Tenure Problems, University of Wisconsin, 1951.
109. 'Land Reforms in India', *International Labour Review*, Vol. 66, Nos. 5 and 6, November–December 1951.
110. 'Land Reforms in India', *International Labour Review*, Vol. LXVI, No. 1, July 1952.
111. 'The Basic Approach to Land Reforms', *Indian Journal of Agricultural Economics*, Vol. VIII, No. 1, January–March 1953: 95–99.

112. 'Progress of Agrarian Reforms in India', *Land Economics*, 1953.
113. 'The Basic Approach to Land Reforms', *Indian Journal of Agricultural Economics*, Vol. VIII, No. 1, March 1953.
114. 'Objective and Criteria of Land Reform', a paper submitted to Land Reform Centre, Bangkok, 1954.
115. 'Land Policies in Asia and the Far East', *India Quarterly*, Vol. XI, No. 2, April–June 1955: 158–67.
116. 'Ceiling on Land Holdings—Revision of the Formula', *Economic Weekly*, Vol. VIII, No. 22, 2 June 1956.
117. 'Land Reforms Proposals in the Second Five Year Plan', *Economic Weekly*, 23 June 1956.
118. 'Land Reforms in the Second Plan', *Indian Affairs Record*, Vol. II, No. 8, 'September 1956.
119. 'Tenancy Reforms in Bombay State', *Indian Journal of Agricultural Economics*, Vol. XI, No. 3, July–September 1956.
120. 'Agricultural Productivity, Land Reforms and Community Development', a paper presented at the Conference on Problems of Economic Growth, Tokyo, 1957.
121. 'Prospects and Problems of Land Reforms in India', *Economic Development and Cultural Change*, Vol. VI, No. 1, October 1957: 3–15.
122. 'Reorganisation of Agrarian Structure', a paper submitted to the Planning Commission, 1959.
123. 'Impact of Re-distribution and Pooling of Land on Agrarian Structure and Efficiency of Resource Use', *Indian Journal of Agricultural Economics*, Vol. XIV, No. 4, October–December 1959: 80–86.
124. 'Land Reforms in India'. In *Problems of Economic Growth*, edited by M.K. Haldar and Robin Ghosh, Office for Asian Affairs, Congress for Cultural Freedom, New Delhi, 1960.
125. 'Land Reforms and Policy in India', Rapporteur's Report, *Indian Economic Journal*, Vol. VII, No. 4, April 1960: 461–63.
126. 'Agrarian Structure and Economic Development', Presidential Address, *Indian Journal of Agricultural Economics*, Vol. XVI, No. 1, January–March 1961: 10–25.
127. 'Ten Years of Land Reforms in India', a paper presented at the Land Reform Panel, Third Five-Year Plan, 1961.
128. 'Development with Welfare Premise', a paper submitted to the Seminar on Tensions of Economic Development in South-East Asia, 1961.
129. 'Financial and Fiscal Aspects of Land Reforms in India', a paper prepared for the Economic Commission for Asia and the Far East, 1961.
130. 'Inter-Relationship Between Land Reforms and Community Development', a paper prepared for ECAFE, March 1961.
131. 'Impact of Land Reforms on Fiscal Resources of State Governments', a paper prepared for ECAFE, June 1961.
132. 'Agrarian Structure in Twelve Districts', *Economic Weekly*, Vol. 13, Special No., July 1961: 1159–60.
133. 'Review of Next Step in Village India, A Study of Land Reforms and Group Dynamics', *Indian Journal of Agricultural Economics*, Vol. XVI, No. 4, October–December 1961.

134. 'Failure in Land Reforms', *Janata*, Vol. XVII, No. 1, 26 January 1962.
135. 'Financial Implications of Land Reform Zamindari Abolition', *Indian Journal of Agricultural Economics*, Vol. XVII, No. 4, October–December 1962: 1–11.
136. 'Land Reforms in India', *Indian and Foreign Review*, Vol. I, No. 21, 15 August 1964.
137. 'Problems of Methodology in Land Reforms Research', *Seminar on Land Reforms, Proceedings and Papers*, Socio-Economic Research Division, Planning Commission, New Delhi, February 1966.
138. 'Agricultural Taxation and Land Reform in India', University of Hartford, Connecticut, USA, October 1966.
139. 'Problem of Subsistence Farm Economy: The Indian Case', in *Seminar on Problems of Small Farmers*. Indian Society of Agricultural Economics, Seminar Series VII, Bombay 1968: 1–8.
140. 'An Efficient and Just Land System', *Yojana*, Vol. XIII, No. 23, November 1969: 3–5.
141. 'Pre-Reform and Post-Reform Agrarian Structure' (jointly with C.H. Shah), *Indian Journal of Agricultural Economics*, Vol. XXVI, No. 3, July–September, 1971: 183–200.
142. 'Inequality of Farm Incomes: A Comment' (jointly with V.M. Rao), *Economic and Political Weekly*, Vol. IX, No. 20, 18 May 1974: 801–806.
143. 'Future of Institutional Reform and Technological Change in Indian Agricultural Development', *Economic and Political Weekly*, Vol. XIII, Nos. 31, 32, 33, August 1978: 1299–1306.
144. 'Agrarian Structure: Relevance to India's Food and Poverty Situation', *The Economic Times*, 23 July 1984.
145. 'Agrarian Structure and Poverty', a paper submitted to the seminar held at Madras Institute of Development Studies, August 1985.
146. 'Rural Assets Distribution and Composition of Labour Force', *Indian Journal of Agricultural Economics*, Vol. 42, No. 3, July–September 1987: 275–85.
147. 'Changing Structure of Ownership of Land and Associated Assets and Rural Labour Force Absorption in Different Regions', *Indian Journal of Agricultural Economics*, Vol. XLII, No. 3, July–September 1987: 275–85.
148. Agrarian Structure and Agrarian Relations in India', in *Indian Agricultural Development Since Independence* (edited), 2nd revised edition, Oxford & IBH Publishers Co. Pvt. Ltd., New Delhi, 1991: 51–73.

IX: General: Agriculture

149. 'Wage-paid Employment and Other Concepts in Agriculture', *Indian Journal of Agricultural Economics*, Vol. XI, No. 4, October–December 1956: 48–49.
150. 'Dawn at Koraput', *Economic Weekly*, January, 1957: 133–135.
151. 'Definition of Personal Cultivation', *Indian Journal of Agricultural Economics*, Vol. XII, No. 1, January–March, 1957: 67–68.
152. 'Progress in Research in Agricultural Economics in India', in *Studies in Indian Agricultural Economics*, edited by J.P. Bhattacharjee, Indian Society of Agricultural Economics, Bombay, 1958: 310–26.
153. 'Small Farmers Not Small Farms', *Indian Journal of Agricultural Economics*, Vol. XIV, No. 3, July–September 1959: 57–58.

154. 'Cost Studies & Farm Policies: A Macro Approach', in *Seminar on Cost Studies in Agriculture*, Indian Society of Agricultural Economics, Seminar III, May 1961: 9–24.
155. 'Commodity Terms of Trade', a paper presented at the 2nd Congress of International Economics Association held in Vienna, 30 August–6 September 1962.
156. 'Agriculture and Allied Industries' (jointly with C.H. Shah and P.C. Bansil) *The Gazetteer of India* (Ministry of Education and Social Welfare, Government of India), Vol. III, *Economic Structure and Activities*, New Delhi, 1975: 197–404.
157. 'Agricultural Taxation: Travails of Tax Designers', *Economic and Political Weekly*, Vol. VII, No. 53, 30 December 1972: A 154–56.
158. 'Comments on the World Bank Report on Agriculture: Challenges and Opportunities', presented at a seminar held at Indira Gandhi Institute of Development Research, Bombay, 12 July 1991.

X: Cooperative movement

159. 'Cooperative Farming: Views and Reviews', *Indian Economic Journal*, Vol. V, No. 1 July 1957: 29–37.
160. 'Co-operative Farming: Will it Augment Marketable Surplus?' *The Economic Weekly*, Vol. XI, No. 9, 28 February 1959.
161. 'Report of Working Group on Co-operative Farming', *Indian Journal of Agricultural Economics*, Vol. XV, No. 3, July–September 1960: 44–46.
162. 'State and the Co-operative Movement', *Kurukshetra*, December 1960: 5–6.
163. 'Problem of Co-operative Farming in India', *Indian Journal of Agricultural Economics*, Vol. XVI, No. 4, October–December 1961: 48–51.
164. 'Agricultural Cooperation in Gujarat', Souvenir of AICC, 1961.

XI: Small-scale industries

165. 'The case for village and Small Scale Industries', *Indian Economic Journal*, Vol. III, No. 3, January 1956: 269–277.
166. 'Problems of Decentralised Sector', *Khadigramodyog*, Vol. XIV, No. 11, August 1968: 751–52.

XII: General

167. 'Notes on Government Publications', *Indian Journal of Agricultural Economics*, Vol. II, No. 1, April 1947: 66–73.
168. 'Institutional Base for Moral Ideas', *Gandhi Marg*, Vol. II, No. 1, January 1958.
169. 'The Organizational Approach and Socialism's Institutional Patterns', *AICC Economic Review*, Vol. 11, Nos. 6–7, 22 July 1959: 25–29.
170. 'Socialism in Hot Climates', *Socialist Commentary*, January 1960.
171. 'Development with Welfare Premise', a paper presented at the Seminar on

Tensions of Economic Development in South-East Asia, 1961.

172. 'Economic Ideology of Jawaharlal Nehru', *Economic Weekly*, Special number, July 1964. Reprinted in *Indian Economic Thought and Development,* Vol. I, edited by Ashok V. Bhuleshkar, Popular Prakashan, Bombay, 1969.

173. 'Socialism at the Grassroots', *Economic and Political Weekly*, Vol. VII, No. 21, 20 May 1972: 1017–18.

174. 'The Intellectual Legacy of Professor Anjaria', *Commerce*, Vol. 125, No. 3005, 7 October 1972.

175. 'The Policy Frame', *Janata*, Vol. 23, 30 July 1978.

176. 'Promise and Performance' (Editorial), *Janata*, Vol. XXXIII, No. 23, 30 July 1978.

177. Foreword to '*Indian Socialism: Past and Present*', edited by F.A. Mechery and Maneesha Tikekar, Bombay, 1985.

178. 'Equality: The Forgotten Ideal', *The Other Side*, May 1987: 7–13. Distributed also by the Centre for Monitoring Indian Economy, Bombay, March 1987.

179. 'Making Administration Responsive', *Kurukshetra*, Vol. XL, No. 1, October 1991: 13–16.

180. 'East Asian Miracle and the Role of the State', *Janata*, Vol. 48, No. 32 28 November 1993: 5–6, 15.

181. 'Redefining Democratic Socialism', *Janata*, Vol. 47, No. 2, February 1992: 7–8.

182. 'How the Landlords Escape Land Laws—Tenants are Still Deceived and Bullied', *Yojana*, 1 October 1957: 7.

183. 'Agricultural Policies', *Yojana*, 1 October 1961.

184. 'What Leading Economists Say of the Budget—More Economics', Comment, *Yojana*, 31 March 1963: 5.

185. 'Progress that Eludes Agriculture', *Yojana*, 13 October 1963: 24.

186. 'We Can Live With the Food We Grow', *Yojana*, 10 October 1965: 13.

187. 'Generous Outlay for Agriculture', *Yojana*, 2 October 1966: 33.

188. 'Comments on the Approach to the IV Plan' (with others), *Yojana*, 9 June 1968.

189. 'An Efficient and Just Land System', *Yojana*, 30 November 1969: 3.

190. 'Poverty Alleviation Programmes Require Reorientation', *Kurukshetra*, April 1988: 26–27, 30.

Index